four european plays

edited by
ARMAND ZIMMERMANN
Chairman, Department of English
Branford High School
Branford, Connecticut

THE MACMILLAN COMPANY, NEW YORK

© Copyright The Macmillan Company 1965

All rights reserved. No part of this book may be reproduced or utilized in any form or by any means, electronic or mechanical, including photocopying, recording or by any information storage and retrieval system, without permission in writing from the Publisher.

Acknowledgments

For permission to use the plays in this book, grateful acknowledgment is made to the following:

Holt, Rinehart and Winston, Inc.: For Brian Hooker's translation of *Cyrano de Bergerac* by Edmond Rostand. Copyright 1923 by Holt, Rinehart and Winston, Inc. Copyright 1951 by Doris C. Hooker. Reprinted by permission of Holt, Rinehart and Winston, Inc.

Dr. Jan van Loewen, Ltd.: For *Thieves' Carnival* by Jean Anouilh, translated by Lucienne Hill. This play is protected by copyright in all countries of the world. All applications for professional performances must be made to the Authors' agents, Dr. Jan van Loewen, Ltd., 81-83 Shaftesbury Avenue, London, W.1., and for amateur performances to Messrs. Samuel French Inc., 25 West 45th Street, New York 36. No performance may take place unless a license has been obtained first.

Harold Ober Associates, Inc.: For *An Enemy of the People* by Henrik Ibsen, translated by Michael Meyer. Reprinted by permission of Harold Ober Associates, Inc. This translation of *An Enemy of the People* is the sole property of the translator and is fully protected by copyright. It may not be acted by professionals or amateurs without formal permission and the payment of a royalty. All rights, including professional, amateur, stock, radio and television broadcasting, motion picture, recitation, lecturing, public reading, and the right of translation in foreign languages are reserved. All inquiries with respect to such rights should be addressed to Harold Freeman, Brandt & Brandt Dramatic Department, Inc., 101 Park Avenue, New York 17, New York.

Leah Salisbury, Inc.: For *The Cherry Orchard* by Anton Chekhov. Copyright © 1956 by Stark Young. Reprinted from *Best Plays by Chekhov*, translated by Stark Young. Reprinted by permission of Random House and Leah Salisbury, Inc.

The Macmillan Company, New York
Collier-Macmillan Canada, Ltd., Toronto, Ontario
Printed in the United States of America

four european plays

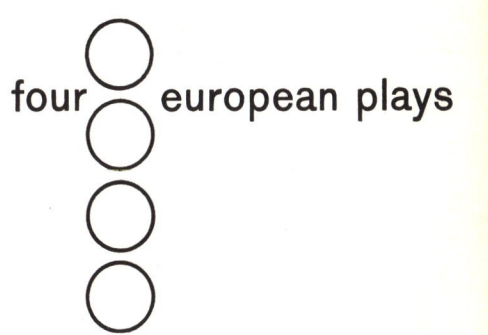

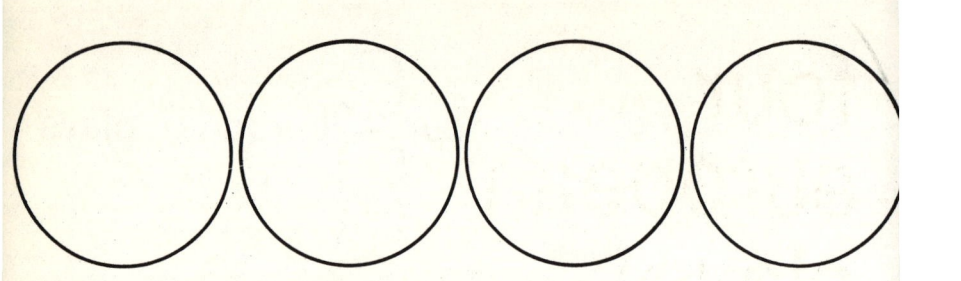

LITERARY HERITAGE
Unabridged School Edition

ADVISORY EDITORIAL BOARD

Dora V. Smith
Joseph Mersand
James Squire

contents

Introduction
vii

An Enemy of the People
Henrik Ibsen
1

Cyrano de Bergerac
Edmond Rostand
139

The Cherry Orchard
Anton Chekhov
369

Thieves' Carnival
Jean Anouilh
449

About the Playwrights
539

Glossary of Terms
543

introduction

Toward the end of the nineteenth century in Europe, new and exciting things began to happen in the theater. For the first time in over two hundred years, plays began to reflect the ideas and ideals of the times, to challenge existing values, to provoke people to think. The theater ceased to be a place of idle entertainment and became what it had been during the classical age in Greece and the Elizabethan period in England—a stirring life experience, and a source of deep insight into human questions.

For the greater part of the nineteenth century, the theater had been particularly sterile. Romances and melodramas were the most popular forms of drama. The romances dealt with the exploits of high-born persons of long ago, the melodramas with innocent heroines threatened by mustachioed villains and saved, in the nick of time, by upstanding heroes. Both types of plays were characterized by contrived or sensational plots, superficial characterizations, bombastic speeches, and trite morals "tacked on" to the endings. Many of the plays were written simply to give the "stars" of the day a chance to exhibit their histrionic skills. Overelaborate settings and sumptuous costuming further diverted the spectator's attention from the play itself.

For most of the nineteenth century, there existed a tremendous gap between what happened on stage in the theater and what was happening off stage in the real world of which the spectators were a part. One would never know, from seeing these plays, that an industrial revolution was creating both tremendous opportunities and tremendous problems for the people of the age; that political upheavals had erupted in the major capitals of Europe in 1848, the reverberations of which were being felt long after they had been quelled; that in 1859 Charles Darwin had published a work with vast social and philosophic, as well as scientific, implications. To discover how the leading minds of the nineteenth century were reacting to contemporary questions, one would have to read Matthew Arnold's "Dover Beach," Dickens' *Hard Times*, or Carlyle's *Sartor Resartus*. Poets, novelists, and essayists responded to the problems of their age, but not the dramatists. They wrote plays to entertain, not to edify; to enable theatergoers to escape, not to understand, reality.

The person most responsible for changing this situation in the theater was the Norwegian-born dramatist, Henrik Ibsen. The "father of the modern drama," Ibsen was the first playwright to treat the significant social issues of the day in a realistic manner. Ibsen began his dramatic career (which extended almost fifty years) by writing plays in the tradition of his time: long poetic romances about ancient heroes from classical or from Norwegian history. Then, midway in his career, Ibsen's plays changed. Written in prose, they portrayed "average" people living in Ibsen's own age, and dealt squarely with contemporary themes. *A Doll's House* (1879) took up the question of women's rights. *Ghosts* (1881) showed how old ideas can dominate and ruin people's lives. *An Enemy of the People* (1882) illustrated a crucial problem which democratic societies face. In these plays, and others, Ibsen exposed hypocrisy in public office, in the business community, in the church, and in the home. He attacked public complacency, apathy, and ignorance.

Besides their pertinent themes, Ibsen's plays were written with a new *realism* that was common to the novels of the time, but rare in the theater. The plots of Ibsen's plays are plausible, not fantastic. The characters are neither all black nor all white but complex human beings, with whom the members of the audience can readily identify or, at least, recognize from their own experience. The dialogue is natural, colloquial, and "strong" by Victorian standards. In short, what happens on stage in these plays is a replica of what happens in real life and not a distortion of it, as is the case in the romances and melodramas of the period.

Soon after they were first produced, Ibsen's plays were translated into most major languages. Performed in the new, experimental theaters which were opening throughout Europe, they inspired the younger dramatists to write in the same serious, realistic, and uncompromising spirit as Ibsen.

One type of writing which arose from the new realism, whose effects were first felt in the theater in the late '80's and '90's, was *naturalism*. This was best illustrated in the early plays of August

Strindberg (*The Father* and *Miss Julia*) and Gerhart Hauptmann (*Before Dawn* and *The Weavers*). Naturalism emphasized the uglier aspects of life—depravity, grinding poverty, intense suffering. If a realistic play was usually set in the living room of a typical middle class home, a naturalistic play frequently took place in a cheap tavern or a slum tenement. The naturalistic writer exposed the "lower depths" of society for a reason. Basing the central thesis of his plays on the implications of the most recent scientific discoveries, he attempted to show that people's "fates" were determined solely by their heredity and their environment. These plays strongly implied that society should eradicate social evils and seek to understand, rather than to condemn, those who had failed in life.

As the nineteenth century was drawing to a close, however, a number of dramatists began to react against the tide of realistic and naturalistic plays which was engulfing the stage. Realistic and naturalistic playwrights could treat adequately problems of a social nature. However, they grossly simplified, or simply ignored, the complex interior life of the individual with his conscious and unconscious hopes and fears, and his often highly subjective, contradictory views of reality and of himself. These writers neglected, too, those mysterious aspects of human experience, for which science has no satisfactory explanations.

Consequently, many playwrights began to make use of symbols in an effort to get "behind life" to the truth of the human heart and of the human experience. In the *symbolic dramas* which they wrote, the plot, characters, and many of the details have a figurative meaning as well as a literal one. They represent, or "stand for," ideas which cannot be translated into other terms for, if they are, they lose most of their force and persuasiveness. One of the first and most popular symbolic dramas was Maurice Maeterlinck's *Pelléas and Mélisande* (1892) whose truth, the author claimed, must be "felt along the heart." Ibsen himself, in his last plays, made use of symbols, most successfully in *The Master Builder* (1892) and *When We Dead Awaken* (1899). Strindberg turned to symbolism, creating in *To Damascus* (1898), *The Dream Play* (1902), and *The Ghost Sonata* (1907) a dreamlike atmosphere which suggests some of life's mystery and complexity.

The four plays in this anthology represent the major types of plays which have dominated the theater for the past one hundred years: the realistic play, the romantic play, and the symbolic play. *An Enemy of the People* is an excellent example of the first type. Ibsen's play deals with a doctor in a small Norwegian resort town who discovers that the Baths, upon which the town's economy depends, are polluted. When Dr. Stockmann attempts to make his discovery public, he finds himself caught in the midst of violent crosscurrents which force him to make decisions affecting his whole life. Through the realistic plot, the sharp characterizations, and the pungent dialogue, Ibsen examines one of the cherished assumptions of modern society—that the majority is always right—and also exposes the hypocrisy that exists among many of the "pillars of society." Written over eighty years ago, *An Enemy of the People* was recently adapted to the modern stage by one of the foremost American playwrights, Arthur Miller. The questions it poses remain pertinent, and its answers are still provocative.

Cyrano de Bergerac was written fifteen years after *An Enemy of the People* by a young French poet, Edmond Rostand. Rostand rejected the new creed of realism and sought to revive in his plays the color, grandeur, and poetry of the romance. In *Cyrano de Bergerac*, he succeeded beyond his greatest expectations. The play took five hours to perform on its opening night, December 28, 1897, thunderous ovations breaking out after each of Cyrano's great speeches and at the end of each act. Described by one critic as "the most intoxicating play of modern times," *Cyrano* has never lost its popularity. It has been translated into scores of languages and successfully revived on numerous occasions. French students still memorize passages from it, much as English-speaking students learn by heart the most famous soliloquies from the plays of Shakespeare.

Rostand based his play upon the life of the seventeenth-century swordsman and poet, Savinien Cyrano de Bergerac (1619-1655), who reputedly engaged in hundreds of duels over insults to his enormous nose. As portrayed in Rostand's play, Cyrano is brave, generous, proud, and intensely individualistic. He is also extremely sensitive about the size of his nose, a fact which keeps him from proposing to the woman he loves, the beautiful Roxane. When Cyrano learns that Roxane is in love with Christian de

Neuvillette, he befriends the young man and helps him to woo her. *Cyrano de Bergerac* possesses all the elements of a great romance: an unforgettable hero, a moving love story, exciting swordplay and battle scenes, a colorful setting, and poetry of lasting beauty.

Despite the phenomenal success of *Cyrano*, however, realism and naturalism continued to be the prevalent forces in the theater. But playwrights of these schools were beginning to make use of symbols to deepen and universalize their subjects. The Russian writer, Anton Chekhov, was the first dramatist to fuse successfully realism and symbolism. This synthesis is best seen in his play, *The Cherry Orchard*, first produced by the Moscow Art Theater in 1904.

At first reading, *The Cherry Orchard* appears to be a straightforward example of realism. The plot is a simple, "untheatrical" one, about the sale of an estate on which an aristocratic family has lived for many generations. The main action of the play is often interrupted by trivial, seemingly irrelevant, actions, created intentionally by Chekhov who felt that, in the theater, the inconsequential and the important should be mingled as they are in life. The characters, too, are realistic. Subject to abrupt changes of mood, they are alternately hopeful and despairing, ecstatic and bored. Their dialogue—prosaic, disjointed, repetitive—closely follows the patterns of everyday speech.

Examining *The Cherry Orchard* more carefully, one sees that symbolism is at the very core of it. The orchard itself symbolizes a way of life, and the fact that it is being sold reveals the theme of Chekhov's play. The two sounds heard in the distance—the axes felling trees and "string breaking"—and the last scene, in which Fiers finds himself locked in the abandoned house, have implications and overtones which further illuminate the play's theme.

The characters in *The Cherry Orchard* are symbolic, too. For example, Lyuboff Andreevna is a woman of striking beauty and grace. A widow with two daughters (and the haunting memory of a drowned son), she is a goodhearted, highly emotional, and thoroughly impractical person. She is, first and foremost, a *particular* individual whom you remember long after you have finished the play. At the same time, she is a *symbol* of all the

Russian gentry who found themselves unable to cope with the great social changes occurring within Russia at the turn of the century. Further still, she symbolizes all people, of any country or time, who can neither comprehend, nor adjust to, a new way of life. Lopahin, Fiers, Yasha, and Trofimoff are types, too, as well as individuals.

Written almost fifty years after *The Cherry Orchard*, Jean Anouilh's *Thieves' Carnival* is a light fantasy with serious themes. Anouilh's play fuses the fanciful and the realistic, the wildly improbable and the ordinary. The twists and turns of its plot make it almost impossible to summarize. However, its bizarre and hilarious qualities are suggested by the unusual cast of characters which includes three charming but thoroughly inept thieves, whose preposterous disguises confuse themselves as much as everyone else; a bored dowager looking for excitement; her absentminded friend, and two beautiful nieces, each heir to a huge fortune; a scheming father and son who are frantically endeavoring to hold on to their collapsing financial empire; and an impish clarinetist who musically comments upon what is happening on stage. An immensely entertaining play, *Thieves' Carnival* takes up two of the most pervasive themes in modern literature: the problem of human identity, and the problem of distinguishing between what is real and what is illusion.

The four plays represented in the book illustrate the diversity of theme, technique, and style of the contemporary theater. They also suggest the important role the theater has played in helping modern man to understand himself and the complex age in which he is living. For the foremost modern plays, besides giving great pleasure, have fulfilled the traditional role of the drama, which is to interpret and to clarify life. They have been able, in the words of Hamlet, "to hold, as 'twere, the mirror up to nature; to show virtue her own feature, scorn her own image, and the very age and body of the time his form and pressure."

an enemy of the people

HENRIK IBSEN
Translated by Michael Meyer

an enemy of the people

CHARACTERS

DR. THOMAS STOCKMANN, *medical officer at the Baths*
MRS. STOCKMANN, *his wife*
PETRA, *their daughter, a schoolteacher*
EILIF
MORTEN } *their sons, aged 13 and 10*
PETER STOCKMANN, *the* DOCTOR'S *elder brother,*
  Mayor and Chief Constable,
  Chairman of the Baths Committee, etc.
MORTEN KIIL, *master tanner, foster father to* MRS. STOCKMANN
HOVSTAD, *editor of the* People's Tribune
BILLING, *an employee on the newspaper*
HORSTER, *a sea captain*
ASLAKSEN, *a printer*

People at a public meeting—men of all classes, a few women and a bunch of schoolboys.

The action takes place in a coastal town in southern Norway.

ACT 1

Evening in DR. STOCKMANN'S *living room. It is humbly but neatly furnished and decorated. In the wall to the right are two doors, of which the further leads out to the hall and the nearer to the* DOCTOR'S *study. In the opposite wall, facing the hall door, is a door that leads to the other rooms occupied by the family. In the middle of this wall stands a tiled stove; further downstage is a sofa with a mirror above it. In front of the sofa is an oval table with a cloth on it. Upon this table stands a lighted lamp with a shade. Upstage, an open door to the dining room, in which can be seen a table laid for the evening meal, with a lamp on it.*

At this table BILLING *is seated, a napkin tucked beneath his chin.* MRS. STOCKMANN *is standing by the table, offering him a plate with a large joint of beef on it. The other places around the table are empty, and the table is in the disorder of a meal that has been finished.*

MRS. STOCKMANN
 There, Mr. Billing! But if you will come an hour late, you'll have to put up with cold.

BILLING
 (eating)
 Oh, but this is capital. Absolutely capital!

MRS. STOCKMANN
 Well you know how punctually my husband always likes to eat—

BILLING
 It doesn't bother me. I enjoy eating alone, without having to talk to anyone.

MRS. STOCKMANN
 Oh. Well, as long as you're enjoying it, that's—*(Listens towards the hall.)* Ah, this must be Mr. Hovstad.

BILLING
>Very likely.

(Mayor PETER STOCKMANN *enters wearing an overcoat and his official hat, and carrying a stick.)*

MAYOR
>Good evening to you, my dear sister-in-law.

MRS. STOCKMANN
>*(goes into the living room)*
>Why, good evening! Fancy seeing you here! How nice of you to come and call on us!

MAYOR
>I just happened to be passing, so—*(Glances towards the dining room.)* But I hear you have company.

MRS. STOCKMANN
>*(a little embarrassed)*
>Oh, no, no, that's no one. *(Quickly)* Won't you have something too?

MAYOR
>I? No, thank you! A cooked meal at night! My digestion would never stand that!

MRS. STOCKMANN
>Oh, but surely just for once—

MAYOR
>No, no! It's very kind of you, but I'll stick to my tea and sandwiches. It's healthier in the long run; and a little less expensive.

MRS. STOCKMANN
>*(smiles)*
>You speak as though Thomas and I were spendthrifts!

MAYOR
>Not you, my dear sister-in-law. Such a thought was far from my mind. *(Points towards the* DOCTOR's *study.)* Isn't he at home?

MRS. STOCKMANN
>No, he's gone for a little walk with the boys.

MAYOR

I wonder if that's wise so soon after a meal? *(Listens.)* Ah, this must be he.

MRS. STOCKMANN

No, I don't think it can be, yet. *(A knock on the door)* Come in!

(HOVSTAD, *the editor of the local newspaper, enters from the hall.*)

MRS. STOCKMANN

Oh—Mr. Hovstad—?

HOVSTAD

Yes, please excuse me, I was detained down at the printer's. Good evening, Your Worship.

MAYOR

(greets him somewhat stiffly)

Good evening. I suppose you are here on business?

HOVSTAD

Partly. About an article for my newspaper—

MAYOR

I guessed as much. I hear my brother is a regular contributor to the *People's Tribune*.

HOVSTAD

Yes, he usually drops us a line when he thinks the truth needs to be told about something.

MRS. STOCKMANN

(to HOVSTAD, pointing towards the dining room)

Er—won't you—?

MAYOR

Great heavens, you mustn't think I blame him for writing for the kind of public he's most likely to find sympathetic to his ideas. Besides, I have no reason to bear your newspaper any ill will, Mr. Hovstad—

HOVSTAD

I should hope not.

MAYOR

On the whole I think I may say that an admirable spirit of tolerance reigns in our town. A fine communal spirit! And the reason for this is that we have this great common interest that binds us together—an interest which is the close concern of every right-minded citizen—

HOVSTAD

You mean the Baths?

MAYOR

Exactly! Our magnificent new Baths! Mark my words, sir! These Baths will prove the very heart and essence of our life! There can be no doubt about it.

MRS. STOCKMANN

Yes, that's just what Thomas says.

MAYOR

It's really astounding the strides this place has made during the past two or three years! The town is becoming prosperous. People are waking up and beginning to live. Buildings and ground rents are increasing in value every day.

HOVSTAD

And unemployment is going down.

MAYOR

Yes, there's that too. The burden upon the propertied classes of poor relief has been most gratifyingly reduced—and will be still more if only we have a really good summer this year, with plenty of visitors. What we want most is invalids. They'll give the Baths a good name.

HOVSTAD

And I hear the indications are promising.

MAYOR

They are indeed. Enquiries about accommodation are pouring in every day.

HOVSTAD

Well then, the Doctor's article will be most opportune.

MAYOR

Oh, has he written something new?

HOVSTAD

No, it's something he wrote last winter; a eulogy of the Baths and the excellent health facilities of the town. But I decided to hold it over.

MAYOR

Ah, there was a snag somewhere?

HOVSTAD

No, it wasn't that. I just thought it would be better to wait till the spring. Now people are thinking about where to spend their summer holidays—

MAYOR

Quite right! Quite right, Mr. Hovstad!

MRS. STOCKMANN

Thomas never stops thinking about those Baths.

MAYOR

Well, he *is* employed there.

HOVSTAD

Yes, and he was the one who really created it all, wasn't he?

MAYOR

Was he? Really? Yes, I have heard that certain people do hold that opinion. I must say I was laboring under the delusion that I had had some modest share in promoting the enterprise.

MRS. STOCKMANN

That's what Thomas is always telling people.

HOVSTAD

No one denies that, Your Worship. You got it going and saw to all the practical details—we all know that. I only meant that the idea originated with the Doctor.

MAYOR

Yes, my brother's always been full of ideas—unfortunately. But when things have to be done, another kind of man is needed, Mr. Hovstad. And I should have thought that least of all in this house would—

MRS. STOCKMANN

But my dear brother-in-law—!

HOVSTAD

Surely Your Worship doesn't—?

MRS. STOCKMANN

Do go inside and get yourself something to eat, Mr. Hovstad. My husband will be here any moment.

HOVSTAD

Thank you—just a bite, perhaps. *(Goes into the dining room.)*

MAYOR

(lowers his voice slightly)

It's extraordinary about people of peasant stock. They never learn the meaning of tact.

MRS. STOCKMANN

But is it really anything to bother about? Can't you and Thomas share the honor as brothers?

MAYOR

Well, I should have thought so. But it seems not everyone is content to share.

MRS. STOCKMANN

Oh, nonsense! You and Thomas always get on so well together. Ah, this sounds like him.

(Goes over and opens the door leading to the hall.)

DR. STOCKMANN

(laughing and boisterous)
Hullo, Catherine! I've another guest for you here! The more the merrier, what? Come in, Captain Horster! Hang your overcoat up there on the hook. No, of course, you don't wear an overcoat, do you? Fancy, Catherine, I bumped into him in the street! Had the devil of a job persuading him to come back with me!

(CAPTAIN HORSTER enters and shakes hands with MRS. STOCKMANN.)

DR. STOCKMANN

(in the doorway)
Run along in now, lads. *(To MRS. STOCKMANN)* They're hungry again already! This way, Captain Horster, you're going to have the finest roast beef you ever—!

(Drives HORSTER into the dining room. EILIF and MORTEN go in too.)

MRS. STOCKMANN

Thomas! Don't you see who's—?

DR. STOCKMANN

(turns in the doorway)
Oh, hullo, Peter! *(Goes over and shakes his hand.)* Well, it's good to see you!

MAYOR

I'm afraid I can only spare a few minutes—

DR. STOCKMANN

Rubbish! We'll be having some hot toddy soon. You haven't forgotten the toddy, Catherine?

MRS. STOCKMANN

No, of course not. I've got the kettle on— *(Goes into the dining room.)*

MAYOR

Hot toddy too—!

DR. STOCKMANN

Yes. Now sit down, and we'll have a good time.

MAYOR

Thank you. I never partake in drinking parties.

DR. STOCKMANN

But this isn't a party.

MAYOR

Well, but—! *(Glances towards the dining room.)* It's really extraordinary the amount they eat!

DR. STOCKMANN

(rubs his hands)

Yes, there's nothing better than to see young people tuck in, is there? Always hungry! That's the way it should be! They've got to have food! Gives them strength! They're the ones who've got to ginger up the future, Peter.

MAYOR

May one ask what it is that needs to be "gingered up," as you put it?

DR. STOCKMANN

You must ask the young ones that—when the time comes. We can't see it, of course. Obviously—a couple of old fogeys like you and me—

MAYOR

Well, really! That's a most extraordinary way to describe us.

DR. STOCKMANN

Oh, you mustn't take me too seriously, Peter. I feel so happy and exhilarated, you see! It's so wonderful to be alive at a time like this, with everything germinating and bursting all around us! Oh, it's a glorious age we live in! It's as though a whole new world were coming to birth before our eyes!

MAYOR

Do you really feel that?

DR. STOCKMANN

Yes. Of course, you can't see it as clearly as I do. You've spent your life in this background, so it doesn't make the same impression on you as it does on me. But I've had to spend all these years sitting up there in that damned northern backwater, hardly ever seeing a new face that had a stimulating word to say to me. To me it's as though I had moved into the heart of some pulsing metropolis—

MAYOR

Hm; metropolis—!

DR. STOCKMANN

Oh, I know it must seem small in comparison with lots of other cities. But there's life here—promise—so many things to work and fight for! And that's what matters. *(Shouts.)* Catherine, hasn't the post come yet?

MRS. STOCKMANN

(from the dining room)

No, not yet.

DR. STOCKMANN

And to be making a decent living, Peter! That's something one learns to appreciate when one's been living on the edge of starvation, as we have—

MAYOR

Oh, surely!

DR. STOCKMANN

Oh, yes, I can tell you we were often pretty hard pressed up there. But now, we can live like lords! Today, for instance, we had roast beef for dinner! *And* there was enough left over for supper! Won't you have a bit? Let me show it to you anyway. Come on, have a look—

MAYOR

No, really—

DR. STOCKMANN

Well, look at this, then! Do you see? We've got a tablecloth!

MAYOR

Yes, I've noticed it.

DR. STOCKMANN

And a lampshade too! See? All from what Catherine's managed

to save! It makes the room so cosy, don't you think? Come and stand here—no, no, no, not there! There, now! Look! See how the light sort of concentrates downwards? I really think it looks very elegant, don't you?

MAYOR
Well, if one can indulge in that kind of luxury—

DR. STOCKMANN
Oh, I think I can permit myself that now. Catherine says I earn almost as much as we spend.

MAYOR
Almost!

DR. STOCKMANN
Well, a man of science ought to live in a little style. I'm sure any magistrate spends far more in a year than I do.

MAYOR
Yes, I should think so! After all, a magistrate is an important public official—

DR. STOCKMANN
Well, a wholesale merchant, then. A man like that spends much more—

MAYOR
His circumstances are different.

DR. STOCKMANN
Oh, it isn't that I'm wasteful, Peter. I just can't deny myself the pleasure of having people around me! I need that, you know. I've been living outside the world for so long, and for me it's a necessity to be with people who are young, bold, and cheerful, and have lively, liberal minds—and that's what they are, all the men who are sitting in there enjoying a good meal! I wish you knew Hovstad a little better—

MAYOR
That reminds me, Hovstad told me he's going to print another article by you.

DR. STOCKMANN
An article by me?

MAYOR
Yes, about the Baths. Something you wrote last winter.

DR. STOCKMANN
Oh, that. No, I don't want them to print that now.

MAYOR

Not? But I should have thought now would be the most suitable time.

DR. STOCKMANN

I dare say it would under ordinary circumstances. *(Walks across the room.)*

MAYOR

(watches him)

And what is extraordinary about the circumstances now?

DR. STOCKMANN

(stops)

I'm sorry, Peter, I can't tell you that yet. Not this evening, anyway. There may be a great deal that's extraordinary; or there may be nothing at all. It may be my imagination—

MAYOR

I must say you're making it all sound very mysterious. Is there something the matter? Something I mustn't be told about? I should have thought that I, as Chairman of the Baths Committee—

DR. STOCKMANN

And I should have thought that I, as—well, let's not start flying off the handle.

MAYOR

Heaven forbid. I'm not in the habit of "flying off the handle," as you phrase it. But I must absolutely insist that all arrangements be made and executed through the proper channels and through the authorities legally appointed for that purpose. I cannot permit any underhand or backdoor methods.

DR. STOCKMANN

Have I ever used underhand or backdoor methods?

MAYOR

You will always insist on going your own way. And that's almost equally inadmissible in a well-ordered community. The individual must learn to fall in line with the general will—or, to be more accurate, with that of the authorities whose business it is to watch over the common good.

DR. STOCKMANN

I dare say. But what the devil has that to do with me?

MAYOR

Because that, my dear Thomas, is what you seem never to be willing to learn. But take care. You'll pay for it some time. Well, I've warned you. Goodbye.

DR. STOCKMANN

Are you raving mad? You're barking completely up the wrong tree—

MAYOR

I'm not in the habit of doing that. Well, if you'll excuse me— *(Bows towards the dining room.)* Goodbye, sister-in-law. Good day, gentlemen. *(Goes.)*

MRS. STOCKMANN

(comes back into the living room)
Has he gone?

DR. STOCKMANN

Yes, Catherine, and in a damned bad temper.

MRS. STOCKMANN

Oh, Thomas, what have you done to him now?

DR. STOCKMANN

Absolutely nothing. He can't expect me to account to him until the times comes.

DR. STOCKMANN

Account to him? For what?

DR. STOCKMANN

Hm; never mind, Catherine. Why the devil doesn't the post come?

(HOVSTAD, BILLING, *and* HORSTER *have got up from the dining table and come into the living room.* EILIF *and* MORTEN *follow a few moments later.*)

BILLING

(stretches his arms)
Ah, a meal like that makes one feel like a new man! By Jingo, yes!

HOVSTAD

His Worship wasn't in a very cheerful mood tonight.

DR. STOCKMANN

Oh, that's his stomach. He's got a bad digestion.

HOVSTAD

I expect we radical journalists stuck in his gullet.

MRS. STOCKMANN

I thought you were getting on rather well with him.

HOVSTAD

Oh, it's only an armistice.

BILLING

That's it! The word epitomizes the situation in a nutshell.

DR. STOCKMANN

Peter's a lonely man, poor fellow. We must remember that. He has no home where he can relax; only business, business. And all that damned tea he pours into himself! Well, lads, pull up your chairs! Catherine, where's that toddy?

MRS. STOCKMANN

(goes into the dining room)
It's just coming.

DR. STOCKMANN

You sit down here on the sofa with me, Captain Horster. You're too rare a guest in this house! Sit, sit, gentlemen!

(The GENTLEMEN sit at the table. MRS. STOCKMANN brings a tray with a kettle, decanters, glasses, etc.)

MRS. STOCKMANN

Here you are. This is arrack, and this is rum; and there's the brandy. Now everyone must help himself.

DR. STOCKMANN

(takes a glass)
Don't you worry about that! *(As the toddy is mixed)* But where are the cigars? Eilif, you know where the box is. Morten, you can bring me my pipe. *(The BOYS go into the room on the right.)* I've a suspicion Eilif pinches a cigar once in a while, but I pretend I don't know! *(Shouts.)* And my smoking cap, Morten! Catherine, can't you tell him where I've put it? Oh, good, he's found it. *(The BOYS return with the things he asked for.)* Help yourselves, my friends! I stick to my pipe, you know; this old friend's been my companion on many a stormy round up there in the north. *(Clinks his glass with theirs.)*

Skoal! Ah, I must say it's better to be sitting here, warm and relaxed!

MRS. STOCKMANN

(who is sitting, knitting)
Will you be sailing soon, Captain Horster?

HORSTER

I expect to be off next week.

MRS. STOCKMANN

It's America this time, isn't it?

HORSTER

That's the idea.

BILLING

But then you won't be able to vote in the next council elections!

HORSTER

Is there going to be a new election?

BILLING

Didn't you know?

HORSTER

No, such things don't interest me.

BILLING

But you must care about public affairs?

HORSTER

No, I don't understand these matters.

BILLING

All the same, one ought at least to vote.

HORSTER

Even if one doesn't understand what it's about?

BILLING

Understand? What's that got to do with it? Society's like a ship: Everyone's got to lend a hand at the rudder.

HORSTER

Not in my ship!

HOVSTAD

It's curious how little sailors bother about what goes on in their own country.

BILLING

Most abnormal.

DR. STOCKMANN

Sailors are like birds of passage; wherever they happen to be, they regard that as home. Which means the rest of us must be all the more active, Mr. Hovstad. Have you anything salutary to offer us in the *People's Tribune* tomorrow?

HOVSTAD

Nothing of local interest. But the day after, I thought of printing your article—

DR. STOCKMANN

Oh God, yes, that article! No, look, you'll have to sit on that.

HOVSTAD

Oh? We've plenty of space just now; and I thought this would be the most suitable time—

DR. STOCKMANN

Yes, yes, I dare say you're right, but you'll have to wait all the same. I'll explain later—

(PETRA, *in hat and cloak, with a pile of exercise books under her arm, enters from the hall.*)

PETRA

Good evening.

DR. STOCKMANN

Hullo, Petra, is that you?

(*The others greet her, and she them. She puts down her cloak, hat, and books on a chair by the door.*)

PETRA

And you're all sitting here having a party while I've been out working!

DR. STOCKMANN

Well, come and have a party too.

BILLING

May I mix you a tiny glass?

PETRA

(*comes over to the table*)

Thanks, I'll do it myself; you always make it too strong. Oh, by the way, Father, I've a letter for you.

(*Goes over to the chair on which her things are lying.*)

DR. STOCKMANN
A letter? Who from?

PETRA
(looks in her coat pocket)
The postman gave it to me just as I was going out—

DR. STOCKMANN
(gets up and goes over to her)
Why on earth didn't you let me have it before?

PETRA
I really didn't have time to run up again. Here it is.

DR. STOCKMANN
(seizes the letter)
Let me see it, child, let me see it! *(Looks at the envelope.)* Yes, this is it!

MRS. STOCKMANN
Is this what you've been waiting for so anxiously, Thomas?

DR. STOCKMANN
It is indeed. I must go and read it at once. Where can I find a light, Catherine? Is there no lamp in my room again?

MRS. STOCKMANN
Yes, there's one burning on your desk.

DR. STOCKMANN
Good, good. Excuse me a moment—

(Goes into the room on the right.)

PETRA
What on earth can that be, Mother?

MRS. STOCKMANN
I don't know. These last few days he's done nothing but ask about the post.

BILLING
Probably some patient out of town—

PETRA
Poor father! He'll soon find he's bitten off more than he can chew. *(Mixes herself a glass.)* Ah, that tastes good!

HOVSTAD
Have you been at evening classes tonight, too?

PETRA
(sips her drink)
Two hours.

BILLING
And four hours this morning at the technical college—

PETRA
(sits at the table)
Five hours.

MRS. STOCKMANN
And you've got exercises to correct tonight, I see.

PETRA
Yes, lots.

HORSTER
You seem to have bitten off more than you can chew too, by the sound of it.

PETRA
Yes, but I like it. It makes you feel so wonderfully tired afterwards.

BILLING
Wonderfully?

PETRA
Yes. One sleeps so soundly afterwards.

MORTEN
You must be very wicked, Petra.

PETRA
Wicked?

MORTEN
Yes, if you work so much. Dr. Roerlund says work is a punishment for our sins.

EILIF
(sniffs)
Silly! Fancy believing stuff like that!

MRS. STOCKMANN
Now, now, Eilif!

BILLING
(laughs)
Ha! Very good!

HOVSTAD
Don't you want to work hard too, Morten?

MORTEN

No! Not me!

HOVSTAD

But surely you want to become something?

MORTEN

I want to be a Viking!

EILIF

But then you'll have to be a heathen.

MORTEN

All right, I'll be a heathen!

BILLING

I'm with you there, Morten! That's just the way I feel!

MRS. STOCKMANN

(makes a sign)
I'm sure you don't really, Mr. Billing.

BILLING

By Jingo, I do! I *am* a heathen, and I'm proud of it! Before long we'll all be heathens. Just you wait and see.

MORTEN

Shall we be able to do anything we like then?

BILLING

Yes, Morten! You see—

MRS. STOCKMANN

Hurry off now, boys. I'm sure you've some homework to do.

EILIF

I can stay a few minutes longer—

MRS. STOCKMANN

No, you can't. Be off, the pair of you!

(The BOYS *say good night and go into the room on the left.)*

HOVSTAD

Do you really think it can do the boys any harm to hear this kind of thing?

MRS. STOCKMANN

Well, I don't know. I just don't like it.

PETRA

Oh, really, mother! I think you're being very stupid.

MRS. STOCKMANN
Perhaps I am; but I don't like it. Not here in the home.
PETRA
Oh, there's so much fear of the truth everywhere! At home and at school. Here we've got to keep our mouths shut, and at school we have to stand up and tell lies to the children.
HORSTER
Lie to them?
PETRA
Yes, surely you realize we have to teach them all kinds of things we don't believe in ourselves.
BILLING
I fear that is all too true!
PETRA
If only I had the money, I'd start a school of my own. And there things would be different.
BILLING
Ah! Money!
HORSTER
If you mean that seriously, Miss Stockmann, I could gladly let you have a room at my place. My father's old house is almost empty; there's a great big dining room downstairs—
PETRA
(laughs)
Thank you! But I don't suppose it'll ever come to anything.
HOVSTAD
No, I think Miss Petra will probably turn to journalism. By the way, have you found time to look at that English novel you promised to translate for us?
PETRA
Not yet. But I'll see you get it in time.

(DR. STOCKMANN *enters from his room with the letter open in his hand.*)

DR. STOCKMANN
(waves the letter)
Here's news that's going to set this town by the ears, believe you me!

BILLING
> News?

MRS. STOCKMANN
> Why, what's happened?

DR. STOCKMANN
> A great discovery has been made, Catherine!

HOVSTAD
> Really?

MRS. STOCKMANN
> By you?

DR. STOCKMANN
> Precisely! By me! *(Walks up and down.)* Now let them come as usual and say it's all madman's talk and I'm imagining things! But they'll have to watch their step this time! *(Laughs.)* Yes, I fancy they'll have to watch their step!

PETRA
> Father, for heaven's sake tell us what it is!

DR. STOCKMANN
> Yes, yes, just give me time and you'll hear everything. Oh, if only I had Peter here now! Well, it only goes to show how blindly we mortals can form our judgments—

HOVSTAD
> What do you mean by that, Doctor?

DR. STOCKMANN
> *(stops by the table)*
> Is it not popularly supposed that our town is a healthy place?

HOVSTAD
> Yes, of course.

DR. STOCKMANN
> A quite unusually healthy place? A place which deserves to be recommended in the warmest possible terms both for the sick and for their more fortunate brethren?

MRS. STOCKMANN
> Yes, but my dear Thomas—!

DR. STOCKMANN
> And we ourselves have praised and recommended it, have we not? I have written thousands of words of eulogy both in the *People's Tribune,* and in pamphlets—

HOVSTAD

Yes, well, what of it?

DR. STOCKMANN

These Baths, which have been called the artery of the town, and its central nerve and—and God knows what else—

BILLING

"The pulsing heart of our city" is a phrase I once, in a festive moment, ventured to—

DR. STOCKMANN

No doubt. But do you know what they really are, these beloved Baths of ours which have been so puffed up and which have cost so much money? Do you know what they are?

HOVSTAD

No, what are they?

DR. STOCKMANN

Nothing but a damned cesspit!

PETRA

The Baths, father?

MRS. STOCKMANN

(simultaneously)
Our Baths!

HOVSTAD

(simultaneously)
But, Doctor—!

BILLING

Absolutely incredible!

DR. STOCKMANN

These Baths are a whited sepulchre—and a poisoned one at that. Dangerous to health in the highest degree! All that filth up at Moellerdal—you know, that stinking refuse from the tanneries—has infected the water in the pipes that feed the Pump Room. And that's not all. This damnable muck has even seeped out on to the beach—

HORSTER

Where the sea baths are?

DR. STOCKMANN

Exactly!

HOVSTAD

But how can you be so sure about all this, Doctor?

DR. STOCKMANN
I've investigated the whole thing most thoroughly. Oh, I've long suspected something of this kind. Last year there were a lot of curious complaints among visitors who'd come for the bathing—typhoid, and gastric troubles—

MRS. STOCKMANN
Yes, so there were.

DR. STOCKMANN
At the time we thought these people had brought the disease with them. But later, during the winter, I began to have other thoughts. So I set to work to analyze the water as closely as I was able.

MRS. STOCKMANN
So that's what you've been toiling so hard at!

DR. STOCKMANN
Yes, you may well say I have toiled, Catherine. But of course I lacked the proper scientific facilities. So I sent specimens of both the drinking water and the sea water to the University to have them analyzed by a chemist.

HOVSTAD
And now you have that analysis?

DR. STOCKMANN
(shows the letter)
Here it is! It establishes conclusively that the water here contains putrid organic matter—millions of bacteria! It is definitely noxious to the health even for external use.

MRS. STOCKMANN
What a miracle you found this out in time!

DR. STOCKMANN
You may well say that, Catherine.

HOVSTAD
And what do you intend to do now, Doctor?

DR. STOCKMANN
Put the matter right, of course.

HOVSTAD
Can that be done?

DR. STOCKMANN
It must be done! Otherwise the Baths are unusable—and all our

work has been wasted. But don't worry. I'm pretty sure I know what needs to be done.

MRS. STOCKMANN

But, my dear Thomas, why have you kept all this so secret?

DR. STOCKMANN

Did you expect me to go round the town talking about it before I was certain? No, thank you, I'm not that mad.

PETRA

You might have told us—

DR. STOCKMANN

I wasn't going to tell anyone. But tomorrow you can run along to the Badger and—

MRS. STOCKMANN

Thomas, really!

DR. STOCKMANN

Sorry, I mean your grandfather. It'll shock the old boy out of his skin. He thinks I'm a bit gone in the head anyway—oh, and there are plenty of others who think the same! I know! But now these good people shall see! Now they shall see! *(Walks around and rubs his hands.)* There's going to be such a to-do in this town, Catherine! You've no idea! The whole water system will have to be relaid.

HOVSTAD

(gets up)

The whole of the water system—?

DR. STOCKMANN

Of course. The intake is too low. It'll have to be raised much higher up.

PETRA

Then you were right after all!

DR. STOCKMANN

Yes, Petra, do you remember? I wrote protesting against the plans when they were about to start laying it. But no one would listen to me then. Well, now I'll give them a real broadside. Of course, I've written a full report to the Baths Committee; it's been ready for a whole week, I've only been waiting to receive this. *(Shows the letter.)* But now I shall send it to them at once! *(Goes into his room and returns with a sheaf of papers.*) Look at this! Ten foolscap pages—closely written! I'm sending the analysis with it. A newspaper, Catherine! Get me something to wrap these up in. Good! There, now! Give it to—to—! *(Stamps his foot.)* What the devil's her name? You know, the maid! Tell her to take it straight down to the Mayor.

(MRS. STOCKMANN *goes out through the dining room with the parcel.*)

PETRA
What do you think Uncle Peter will say, Father?

DR. STOCKMANN
What can he say? He must be grateful that so important a fact has been brought to light.

HOVSTAD
May I have your permission to print a short piece about your discovery in the *People's Tribune?*

DR. STOCKMANN
I'd be very grateful if you would.

HOVSTAD
I think it's desirable that the community should be informed as quickly as possible.

DR. STOCKMANN
Yes, yes, of course.

MRS. STOCKMANN
(comes back)
She's gone with it now.

BILLING
You'll be the first citizen in the town, Doctor, by Jingo, you will!

DR. STOCKMANN
(walks around contentedly)
Oh, nonsense. I've really done nothing except my duty. I dug for treasure and struck lucky, that's all. All the same—!

BILLING
Hovstad, don't you think the town ought to organize a torchlight procession in honor of Dr. Stockmann?

HOVSTAD
I'll suggest it, certainly.

BILLING

And I'll have a word with Aslaksen.

DR. STOCKMANN

No, my dear friends, please don't bother with that nonsense. I don't want any fuss made. And if the Baths Committee should decide to raise my salary, I won't accept it! It's no good, Catherine, I won't accept it!

MRS. STOCKMANN

Quite right, Thomas.

PETRA

(raises her glass)
Skoal, Father!

HOVSTAD
BILLING } Skoal, skoal, Doctor!

HORSTER

(clinks his glass with the DOCTOR's)
Here's hoping your discovery will bring you nothing but joy!

DR. STOCKMANN

Thank you, my dear friends, thank you! I'm so deeply happy! Oh, it's good to know that one has the respect of one's fellow-citizens! Hurrah, Catherine!

(Seizes her round the neck with both hands and whirls round with her. MRS. STOCKMANN screams and struggles. Laughter, applause, and cheers for the DOCTOR. The BOYS stick their heads in through the door.)

(Curtain)

ACT 2

The DOCTOR's living room. The door to the dining room is shut. Morning.

MRS. STOCKMANN
(enters from the dining room with a sealed letter in her hand, goes over to the door downstage right and peeps in)
Are you at home, Thomas?

DR. STOCKMANN
(offstage)
Yes, I've just come in. *(Enters.)* What is it?

MRS. STOCKMANN
A letter from your brother. *(Hands it to him.)*

DR. STOCKMANN
Aha, let's see what he says. *(Opens the envelope and reads.)* "I return herewith the manuscript you sent me—" *(Reads on, mumbling.)* Hm—!

MRS. STOCKMANN
Well, what does he say?

DR. STOCKMANN
(puts the papers in his pocket)
No, he just writes that he'll be coming up here to see me towards noon.

MRS. STOCKMANN
You must remember to stay at home, then.

DR. STOCKMANN
Oh, that'll be all right. I've finished my round for today.

MRS. STOCKMANN
I'm very curious to know how he's taken it.

DR. STOCKMANN
You'll see. He won't like the fact that I made this discovery and not he.

MRS. STOCKMANN

Doesn't it worry you? It does me.

DR. STOCKMANN

Well, he'll be happy at heart, of course. The trouble is, Peter gets so damned angry at the idea of anyone but himself doing anything for the good of the town.

MRS. STOCKMANN

You know, Thomas, I really think you ought to share the honor with him. Couldn't you say it was he who started you thinking along these lines—?

DR. STOCKMANN

Gladly, as far as I'm concerned. As long as I get the matter put right, I—

MORTEN KIIL

(puts his head in through the door leading from the hall, looks around inquiringly, chuckles to himself and asks slyly)

Is it—is it true?

MRS. STOCKMANN

Why, Father!

DR. STOCKMANN

Hullo, father-in-law! Good morning, good morning!

MRS. STOCKMANN

Well, aren't you going to come in?

MORTEN KIIL

I will if it's true. If not, I'll be off—

DR. STOCKMANN

If what's true?

MORTEN KIIL

This nonsense about the water system. Is it true, eh?

DR. STOCKMANN

Of course it's true. But how did you hear about it?

MORTEN KIIL

(comes in)

Petra looked in on her way to school—

DR. STOCKMANN

Oh, did she?

MORTEN KIIL

Mm. And she told me. I thought she was just pulling my leg. But that's not like Petra.

DR. STOCKMANN
    How could you think she'd do a thing like that?
MORTEN KIIL
    Never trust anyone. That's my motto. You get made a fool of before you know where you are. So it is true, then?
DR. STOCKMANN
    Absolutely true. Sit down now, father. *(Coaxes him down onto the sofa.)* Isn't it a stroke of luck for the town?
MORTEN KIIL
    (stifles a laugh)
    Stroke of luck for the town?
DR. STOCKMANN
    That I made this discovery in time—
MORTEN KIIL
    (as before)
    Oh, yes, yes! But I never thought you'd start playing monkey tricks with your own flesh and blood!
DR. STOCKMANN
    Monkey tricks?
MRS. STOCKMANN
    Father dear—?
MORTEN KIIL
    (rests his hands and chin on the handle of his stick and winks slyly at the DOCTOR*)*
    What was it, now? Didn't you say some animals had got into the water pipes?
DR. STOCKMANN
    Yes, bacteria.
MORTEN KIIL
    Quite a number of them, so Petra told me. Regular army!
DR. STOCKMANN
    Millions, probably.
MORTEN KIIL
    But no one can see them. Isn't that right?
DR. STOCKMANN
    Of course one can't *see* them.
MORTEN KIIL
    (chuckles silently)
    Devil take me if this isn't the best I've heard from you yet!

DR. STOCKMANN
What do you mean?
MORTEN KIIL
But you'll never get the Mayor to believe a tale like that.
DR. STOCKMANN
We'll see.
MORTEN KIIL
Do you think he's that daft?
DR. STOCKMANN
I hope the whole town will be that daft.
MORTEN KIIL
The whole town? That's perfectly possible! Serve them right, it'll teach them a lesson! They hounded me out of the Council —yes, that's what I call it, for they drove me out like a dog, they did! But now they're going to pay for it! You make fools of them, Stockmann!
DR. STOCKMANN
But, father—
MORTEN KIIL
You make fools of them, my boy! *(Gets up.)* If you can put the Mayor and his friends out of countenance, I'll give a hundred crowns to the poor—immediately!
DR. STOCKMANN
That's very generous of you.
MORTEN KIIL
I'm not a rich man, mind! But if you do that, I'll remember the poor to the tune of fifty crowns at Christmas.

(HOVSTAD *enters from the hall.*)

HOVSTAD
Good morning! *(Stops.)* Oh, am I intruding?
DR. STOCKMANN
No, come in, come in!
MORTEN KIIL
(chuckles again)
Him! Is he in with you on this?
HOVSTAD
What do you mean?

DR. STOCKMANN

Indeed he is.

MORTEN KIIL

I might have guessed it! So it's to be in the papers! Yes, you're a card all right, Stockmann! Well, you two put your heads together. I'm off.

DR. STOCKMANN

Oh, father, stay a little longer.

MORTEN KIIL

No, I'm off. Pull out all the tricks you know! By God, I'll see you don't lose by it! *(Goes.* MRS. STOCKMANN *accompanies him out.)*

DR. STOCKMANN

(laughs)

Imagine, Hovstad, the old man doesn't believe a word I say about the water system!

HOVSTAD

Oh, so *that* was—?

DR. STOCKMANN

Yes, that's what we were talking about. I suppose that's why you've come too?

HOVSTAD

Yes. Can you spare me a moment or two, Doctor?

DR. STOCKMANN

As long as you want, my dear fellow.

HOVSTAD

Have you heard anything from the Mayor?

DR. STOCKMANN

Not yet. He'll be along shortly.

HOVSTAD

I've been thinking a lot about this since last night.

DR. STOCKMANN

Yes?

HOVSTAD

You're a doctor and a man of science, and to you this business of the water is something to be considered in isolation. I think you don't perhaps realize how it's tied up with a lot of other things.

DR. STOCKMANN

I don't quite understand you. Let's sit down, my dear chap. No, over there on the sofa.

(HOVSTAD *sits on the sofa*, DR. STOCKMANN *in an armchair on the other side of the table.*)

DR. STOCKMANN

Well?

HOVSTAD

You said yesterday that the pollution of the water was the result of impurities in the soil.

DR. STOCKMANN

Yes, we're pretty certain that filthy swamp up at Moellerdal is the cause of the evil.

HOVSTAD

Forgive me, Doctor, but I believe the real cause of all the evil is to be found in quite a different swamp.

DR. STOCKMANN

Which one?

HOVSTAD

The swamp in which our whole communal life is slowly rotting.

DR. STOCKMANN

Damn it, Mr. Hovstad, what kind of talk is this?

HOVSTAD

Little by little all the affairs of this town have fallen into the hands of a small clique of bureaucrats.

DR. STOCKMANN

Oh, come, you can't group them all under that description.

HOVSTAD

No, but the ones who don't belong to it are the friends and hangers-on of the ones who do. It's the rich men, the ones with names—they're the people who rule our life.

DR. STOCKMANN

They're shrewd and intelligent men.

HOVSTAD

Did they show shrewdness or intelligence when they laid the water pipes where they are now?

DR. STOCKMANN
No, that was very stupid, of course. But it's going to be put right now.

HOVSTAD
You think they'll enjoy doing that?

DR. STOCKMANN
Enjoy it or not, they'll be forced to do it.

HOVSTAD
If the press is allowed to use its influence.

DR. STOCKMANN
That won't be necessary, my dear fellow. I'm sure my brother will—

HOVSTAD
I'm sorry, Doctor, but I intend to take this matter up myself.

DR. STOCKMANN
In the newspaper?

HOVSTAD
When I took over the *People's Tribune* I did so with the fixed purpose of breaking up this ring of obstinate bigots who hold all the power in their hands.

DR. STOCKMANN
But you told me yourself what happened as a result. The paper almost had to close down.

HOVSTAD
We had to play it easy then, that's true. There was a risk that if these men fell, the Baths might not be built. But now we have them and these fine gentlemen have become dispensable.

DR. STOCKMANN
Dispensable, perhaps. But we owe them a debt all the same.

HOVSTAD
Oh, that'll be handsomely acknowledged. But a radical writer like me can't let an opportunity like this pass unused. We must destroy the myth of these men's infallibility. It must be rooted out like any other kind of superstition.

DR. STOCKMANN
Ah, I'm with you there. If it is a superstition, then away with it!

HOVSTAD
I'd prefer not to attack the Mayor, since he's your brother. But

I know you feel as strongly as I do that truth must precede all other considerations.

DR. STOCKMANN

Of course. *(Bursts out.)* But—! But—!

HOVSTAD

You mustn't think ill of me. I'm not more ambitious or self-seeking than most men.

DR. STOCKMANN

But my dear fellow, who suggests you are?

HOVSTAD

I'm the son of poor people, as you know, and I've had the chance to see what's needed most in the lower strata of society. It's to have a share in the control of public affairs. That's what develops ability, and knowledge, and human dignity.

DR. STOCKMANN

I appreciate that.

HOVSTAD

And then I think a journalist has a lot to answer for if he neglects an opportunity to achieve emancipation for the masses —the small and the oppressed. Oh, I know—the big boys will call me a demagogue and all that—but I don't care. As long as my conscience is clear, I—

DR. STOCKMANN

That's the point, yes! That's exactly it, Mr. Hovstad! All the same—damn it—*(A knock at the door)* Come in!

(ASLAKSEN, *the printer, appears in the doorway leading from the hall. He is humbly but decently dressed in black, with a white and somewhat crumpled cravat, gloves, and a silk hat in his hand.)*

ASLAKSEN

(bows)

I trust you'll forgive me for being so bold, Doctor—

DR. STOCKMANN

(gets up)

Why, hullo! Aren't you Aslaksen the printer?

ASLAKSEN

I am indeed, Doctor.

HOVSTAD

(gets up)

Are you looking for me, Aslaksen?

ASLAKSEN

No, I'd no idea I'd see you here. It was the Doctor himself I—

DR. STOCKMANN

Well, what can I do for you?

ASLAKSEN

Is it true what Mr. Billing tells me, that you're thinking of getting us a better water system?

DR. STOCKMANN

Yes, for the Baths.

ASLAKSEN

Ah, yes; I see. Well, I just came to say that I'm right behind you

HOVSTAD

(to DR. STOCKMANN*)*

You see!

DR. STOCKMANN

I'm most grateful; but—

ASLAKSEN

You might find it useful to have us tradespeople behind you. We form a pretty solid majority in this town—when we choose to, mind! And it's always good to have the majority behind you, Doctor.

DR. STOCKMANN

True enough. But I don't see that any special effort is necessary here. Surely it's a perfectly straightforward matter—

ASLAKSEN

Yes, but you might be glad of us all the same. I know these local authorities. The boys in power don't like accepting suggestions from outside. So I thought it might not be out of place if we organized a little demonstration.

HOVSTAD

That's just what I feel.

DR. STOCKMANN

Demonstration? In what way will you demonstrate?

ASLAKSEN

Oh, with restraint, Doctor. I always insist on restraint. Restraint is the primary virtue of every citizen. That's my opinion, anyway.

DR. STOCKMANN

Yes, yes, Mr. Aslaksen. Your views are well known—

ASLAKSEN

Yes, I fancy they are. Now this business of the water system is very important to us tradespeople. It looks as though the Baths are going to prove, as you might say, a little goldmine for the town. We'll all be depending on the Baths for our livelihood, especially us property owners. That's why we want to give the project every support we can. And seeing as I'm chairman of the Property Owners' Association—

DR. STOCKMANN

Yes?

ASLAKSEN

And seeing as I'm also on the Council of the Temperance Society—you do know I'm a temperance worker—

DR. STOCKMANN

Yes, yes.

ASLAKSEN

Well, so it stands to reason I come into contact with a lot of people. And seeing as I'm known to be a level-headed and law-abiding citizen, as you said yourself, it means I have a certain influence in the town—I wield a little power—though I say it myself.

DR. STOCKMANN

I'm well aware of that, Mr. Aslaksen.

ASLAKSEN

Yes, well—so it'd be an easy matter for me to arrange an address, if the occasion should arise.

DR. STOCKMANN

An address?

ASLAKSEN

Yes, a kind of vote of thanks from the citizens of this town to you for having carried this important matter to a successful conclusion. Of course, it stands to reason the wording's got to be restrained, so it won't offend the authorities and the other people as has the power. And so long as we're careful about that, I don't think anyone can take offense, can they?

HOVSTAD

Well, even if they don't particularly like it, they—

ASLAKSEN

No, no, no! We mustn't offend authority, Mr. Hovstad! We can't afford to defy the people on whom our lives depend. I've seen plenty of that in my time, and no good ever came out of it. But the sober expression of liberal sentiments can cause no affront.

DR. STOCKMANN

(shakes his hand)

My dear Mr. Aslaksen, I can't tell you how deeply happy I am to find all this support among my fellow citizens. I am most moved, most moved. Well, now! What about a small glass of sherry?

ASLAKSEN

No, thank you! I never touch spirits.

DR. STOCKMANN

A glass of beer, then? What do you say to that?

ASLAKSEN

No, thank you, not that either, Doctor. I never touch anything so early in the day. And now I must be getting back to town to talk to some of the other property owners and prepare the atmosphere.

DR. STOCKMANN

It's really most kind of you, Mr. Aslaksen. But I simply cannot get it into my head that all this fuss is really necessary. I should have thought the matter would solve itself.

ASLAKSEN

The authorities move somewhat ponderously, Doctor. Heaven knows I don't intend any reflection on them—!

HOVSTAD

We'll give them a drubbing in print tomorrow, Mr. Aslaksen.

ASLAKSEN

But no violence, Mr. Hovstad! Proceed with restraint! Otherwise you'll get nowhere with them. You can rely on my judgment, for I have culled my knowledge in the school of life. Yes, well, I must say goodbye. You know now that we tradespeople stand behind you like a wall, Doctor. You have the solid majority on your side, whatever else may happen.

DR. STOCKMANN
Thank you, my dear Mr. Aslaksen. *(Shakes his hand.)* Goodbye, goodbye!
ASLAKSEN
Are you coming down to the press too, Mr. Hovstad?
HOVSTAD
I'll follow later. I've a few things to arrange first.
ASLAKSEN
Yes, yes.

(Bows and goes out. DR. STOCKMANN *accompanies him out into the hall.)*

HOVSTAD
(as the DOCTOR *returns)*
Well, what do you say to that, Doctor? Don't you think it's time this town was shaken out of its torpidity and its weak-kneed half-heartedness?
DR. STOCKMANN
You mean Aslaksen?
HOVSTAD
Yes, I do. Oh, he's honest enough in some respects, but he's stuck in the swamp. And most of the others are the same. They swing this way and that, and spend so much time looking at every side of the question that they never make a move in any direction.
DR. STOCKMANN
But Aslaksen seemed very well-meaning, I thought.
HOVSTAD
There's something I regard as more important than that. To know your own mind and have the courage of your convictions.
DR. STOCKMANN
Yes, you're right there.
HOVSTAD
That's why I'm so keen to seize this opportunity and see if I can't get these well-meaning idiots to act like men for once. All this grovelling to authority has got to be stopped. This blunder they've made about the water system is quite indefensible, and that fact's got to be drummed into the ears of every citizen who's got the right to vote.

DR. STOCKMANN

Very well. If you think it's for the communal good, go ahead. But not till I've talked with my brother.

HOVSTAD

I'll get my editorial written anyway. And if the Mayor refuses to take action, then—

DR. STOCKMANN

Oh, but that's unthinkable.

HOVSTAD

It's a possibility. And if it should happen—?

DR. STOCKMANN

If it does, I promise you that—yes, you can print my report. Print the whole damned thing.

HOVSTAD

Is that a promise?

DR. STOCKMANN

(hands him the manuscript)
Here it is. Take it with you. It won't do any harm for you to read through it; and you can give it back to me afterwards.

HOVSTAD

Right, I'll do that. Well, goodbye, Doctor.

DR. STOCKMANN

Goodbye, goodbye! Don't you worry, Mr. Hovstad—everything's going to go quite smoothly. Quite smoothly!

HOVSTAD

Hm. We shall see. *(Nods and goes out through the hall.)*

DR. STOCKMANN

(goes over to the dining room and looks in)
Catherine—! Oh, hullo, Petra, are you here?

PETRA

(enters)
Yes, I've just got back from school.

MRS. STOCKMANN

(enters)
Hasn't he come yet?

DR. STOCKMANN

Peter? No. But I've been having a long talk with Hovstad. He's quite excited about this discovery of mine. It seems it has a much wider significance than I'd supposed. So he's placed his newspaper at my disposal, if I should need it.

MRS. STOCKMANN
But do you think you will?
DR. STOCKMANN
Oh no, I'm sure I won't. But it's good to know that one has the free press on one's side—the mouthpiece of liberal opinion. And what do you think? I've had a visit from the Chairman of the Property Owners' Association!
MRS. STOCKMANN
Oh? And what did he want?
DR. STOCKMANN
He's going to support me too. They're all going to support me, if there's any trouble. Catherine, do you know what I have behind me?
MRS. STOCKMANN
Behind you? No, what have you behind you?
DR. STOCKMANN
The solid majority.
MRS. STOCKMANN
I see. And that's a good thing, is it?
DR. STOCKMANN
Of course, it's a good thing! *(Rubs his hands and walks up and down.)* How splendid to feel that one stands shoulder to shoulder with one's fellow citizens in brotherly concord!
PETRA
And that one's doing so much that's good and useful, Father.
DR. STOCKMANN
Yes, and for one's home town too!
MRS. STOCKMANN
There's the doorbell.
DR. STOCKMANN
Ah, this must be him! *(A knock on the inner door)* Come in!
MAYOR
(enters from the hall)
Good morning.
DR. STOCKMANN
(warmly)
Hullo, Peter!
MRS. STOCKMANN
Good morning, brother-in-law. How are you?

MAYOR

Oh, thank you; so-so. *(To the* DOCTOR*)* Last night, after office hours, I received a thesis from you regarding the state of the water at the Baths.

DR. STOCKMANN

Yes. Have you read it?

MAYOR

I have.

DR. STOCKMANN

Well! What do you think?

MAYOR

(glances at the others)
Hm—

MRS. STOCKMANN

Come, Petra.

(She and PETRA *go into the room on the left.)*

MAYOR

(after a pause)
Was it necessary to conduct all these investigations behind my back?

DR. STOCKMANN

Well, until I was absolutely certain, I—

MAYOR

And now you are?

DR. STOCKMANN

Yes. Surely you must be convinced—?

MAYOR

Is it your intention to place this document before the Baths Committee as an official statement?

DR. STOCKMANN

Of course! Something must be done. And quickly.

MAYOR

I find your phraseology in this document, as usual, somewhat extravagant. Among other things, you say that all we have to offer our visitors at present is a permanent state of ill health.

DR. STOCKMANN

Peter, how else can you describe it? Just think! That water's poisonous even if you bathe in it, let alone drink it! And we're offering this to unfortunate people who are ill and who have turned to us in good faith, and are paying us good money, in order to get their health back!

MAYOR

And your conclusion is that we must build a sewer to drain away these aforesaid impurities from the swamp at Moellerdal, and that the whole water system must be relaid.

DR. STOCKMANN

Can you think of any other solution? I can't.

MAYOR

This morning I called upon the town engineer. In the course of our discussion, I half jokingly mentioned these proposals as a thing we might possibly undertake some time in the future.

DR. STOCKMANN

Some time in the future?

MAYOR

He smiled at what he obviously regarded as my extravagance—as I knew he would. Have you ever troubled to consider what these alterations you suggest would cost? According to the information I received, the expense would probably run into several hundred thousand crowns.

DR. STOCKMANN

Would it be that much?

MAYOR

Yes. But that's not the worst. The work would take at least two years.

DR. STOCKMANN

Two years, did you say? Two whole years?

MAYOR

At least. And what do we do with the Baths in the meanwhile? Close them? Yes, we'd be forced to. You don't imagine anyone would come here once the rumor got around that the water was impure?

DR. STOCKMANN

But, Peter, it is!

MAYOR

And for this to happen just now, when the whole enterprise is coming to fruition! There are other towns around with qualifications to be regarded as health resorts. Do you think they won't start trying to attract the market? Of course they will! And there we shall be! We'll probably have to abandon the whole expensive scheme, and you will have ruined the town that gave you birth.

DR. STOCKMANN

I—ruined—!

MAYOR

It's only as a health resort—a spa—that this town has any future worth speaking of. Surely you realize that as well as I do.

DR. STOCKMANN

But what do you propose we do?

MAYOR

Your report has not completely convinced me that the situation is as dangerous as you imply.

DR. STOCKMANN

Oh, Peter, if anything it's worse! Or at least it will be in the summer, once the hot weather starts.

MAYOR

As I said, I believe that you are exaggerating the danger. A capable medical officer must be able to take measures. He must know how to forestall such unpleasantnesses, and how to remedy them if they should become obvious.

DR. STOCKMANN

Go on.

MAYOR

The existing water system at the Baths is a fact, and must be accepted as such. However, in due course, I dare say, the Committee might not be inflexibly opposed to considering whether, without unreasonable pecuniary sacrifice, it might not be possible to introduce certain improvements.

DR. STOCKMANN

And you think I'd lend my name to such chicanery?

MAYOR

Chicanery!

DR. STOCKMANN

That's what it would be! A fraud, a lie, a crime against the community, against the whole of society!

MAYOR

As I have already pointed out, I have not succeeded in convincing myself that any immediate or critical danger exists.

DR. STOCKMANN

Oh, yes you have! You must have! My arguments are irrefutable—I know they are! And you know that as well as I do, Peter! But you won't admit it, because it was you who forced through the proposal that the Baths and the water pipes should be sited where they are, and you refuse to admit that you made a gross blunder. Don't be such a fool, do you think I don't see through you?

MAYOR

And suppose you were right? If I do guard my reputation with a certain anxiety, it is because I have the welfare of our town at heart. Without moral authority I cannot guide and direct affairs as I deem most fit for the general good. For this, and diverse other reasons, it is vital to me that your reports should not be placed before the Baths Committee. It must be suppressed for the general good. At a later date I shall bring the matter up for discussion, and we shall discreetly do the best we can. But nothing, not a single word, about this unfortunate matter must come to the public ear.

DR. STOCKMANN

Well, it can't be stopped now, my dear Peter.

MAYOR

It must and shall be stopped.

DR. STOCKMANN

It can't, I tell you. Too many people know.

MAYOR

Know? Who knows? You don't mean those fellows from the *People's Tribune*—?

DR. STOCKMANN

Oh, yes, they too. The free press of our country will see to it that you do your duty.

MAYOR

(after a short pause)
You're an exceedingly foolish man, Thomas. Haven't you considered what the consequences of this action may be for you?

DR. STOCKMANN
Consequences? Consequences for me?
MAYOR
Yes. For you and for your family.
DR. STOCKMANN
What the devil do you mean by that?
MAYOR
I think I have always shown myself a good brother to you, whenever you've needed help.
DR. STOCKMANN
You have, and I thank you for it.
MAYOR
I'm not asking for thanks. To a certain extent I've been forced to do it—for my own sake. I always hoped I might be able to curb you a little if I could help to improve your economic position.
DR. STOCKMANN
What! So it was only for your own sake that you—
MAYOR
Partly, I said. It's painful for a public servant to see his next of kin spend his entire time compromising himself.
DR. STOCKMANN
And you think I do that?
MAYOR
Unfortunately you do, without knowing it. You have a restless, combative, rebellious nature. And then you've this unfortunate passion for rushing into print upon every possible—and impossible—subject. The moment you get an idea you have to sit down and write a newspaper article or a whole pamphlet about it.
DR. STOCKMANN
Surely if a man gets hold of a new idea it's his duty as a citizen to tell it to the public?
MAYOR
People don't want new ideas. They're best served by the good old accepted ideas they have already.
DR. STOCKMANN
And you can say that to my face!

MAYOR

Yes, Thomas. I'm going to speak bluntly to you for once. Up to now I've tried to avoid it, because I know how hasty you are; but now I've got to tell you the truth. You've no idea how much harm you do yourself by this impulsiveness of yours. You abuse the authorities, and even the government—you throw mud at them, you claim you've been cold-shouldered and persecuted. But what else can you expect, when you're such a difficult person?

DR. STOCKMANN

Oh, so I'm difficult too, am I?

MAYOR

Oh, Thomas, you're impossible to work with. I've discovered that for myself. You never consider anyone else's feelings. You even seem to forget it's me you have to thank for getting you your job at the Baths—

DR. STOCKMANN

It was mine by right! I was the first person to see that this town could become a flourishing watering place! And I was the only person who did see it at that time! For years I fought alone for this idea! I wrote, and wrote—

MAYOR

No one denies that. But the time wasn't ripe then. Of course you weren't to know that, tucked away in your northern backwater. But as soon as the right moment arrived, I—and others—took the matter up—

DR. STOCKMANN

Yes, and made a mess of my wonderful plan! Oh yes, it's becoming very clear now what brilliant fellows you were!

MAYOR

As far as I can see, all you're looking for now is just another excuse for a fight. You've always got to pick a quarrel with your superiors—it's your old failing. You can't bear to have anyone in authority over you. You look askance at anyone who occupies a position higher than yours. You regard him as a personal enemy—and then, as far as you're concerned, one weapon of attack is as good as another. But now I've shown you what's at stake, for the whole town, and for myself too. And I'm not prepared to compromise.

DR. STOCKMANN

What do you mean?

MAYOR

Since you have been so indiscreet as to discuss this delicate matter, which you ought to have kept a professional secret, the affair obviously cannot be hushed up. All kinds of rumors will spread around, and the malicious elements among us will feed these rumors with details of their own invention. It is therefore necessary that you publicly deny these rumors.

DR. STOCKMANN

I don't understand you.

MAYOR

I feel sure that on further investigation you will convince yourself that the situation is not nearly as critical as you had at first supposed.

DR. STOCKMANN

Aha; you feel sure, do you?

MAYOR

I also feel sure you will publicly express your confidence that the Committee will painstakingly and conscientiously take all necessary measures to remedy any possible defects which may exist.

DR. STOCKMANN

But you can't remedy the defect by just patching things up! I'm telling you, Peter, unless you start again from scratch, it's my absolute conviction that—

MAYOR

As an employee you have no right to any independent conviction.

DR. STOCKMANN

(starts)
No right!

MAYOR

As an employee. As a private person—well, heaven knows that's another matter. But as a subordinate official at the Baths you have no right to express any opinion which conflicts with that of your superiors.

DR. STOCKMANN

This is going too far! I, a doctor, a man of science, have no right—!

MAYOR

The question is not merely one of science. The problem is complex. The issues involved are both technical and economical.

DR. STOCKMANN

I don't care how you define the bloody thing! I must be free to say what I think about anything!

MAYOR

Go ahead. As long as it isn't anything connected with the Baths. That we forbid you.

DR. STOCKMANN

(shouts)
You forbid—! You—! Why, you're just a—

MAYOR

I forbid you—I, your chief! And when I forbid you to do something, you must obey!

DR. STOCKMANN

(controls himself)
Peter—if you weren't my brother—!

PETRA

(throws open the door)
Father, don't put up with this!

MRS. STOCKMANN

(follows her)
Petra, Petra!

MAYOR

Ha! Eavesdroppers!

MRS. STOCKMANN

You were talking so loud—we couldn't help hearing—

PETRA

I was listening.

MAYOR

Well, I'm not altogether sorry—

DR. STOCKMANN

(goes closer to him)
You spoke to me of forbidding and obeying?

MAYOR

You forced me to use that tone.

DR. STOCKMANN

And you expect me to publicly swallow my own words?

MAYOR

We regard it as an unavoidable necessity that you issue a statement on the lines I have indicated.

DR. STOCKMANN

And if I don't—obey?

MAYOR

Then we shall be forced to issue an explanation, to calm the public.

DR. STOCKMANN

All right! But I shall write and refute you. I stick to my view. I shall prove that I am right and you are wrong. And what will you do then?

MAYOR

Then I shall be unable to prevent your dismissal.

DR. STOCKMANN

What—!

PETRA

Father! Dismissal!

MRS. STOCKMANN

Dismissal!

MAYOR

Dismissal from your post as public medical officer. I shall feel compelled to apply for immediate notice to be served on you, barring you from any further connection with the Baths.

DR. STOCKMANN

You'd have the impudence to do that?

MAYOR

You're the one who's being impudent.

PETRA

Uncle, this is a disgraceful way to treat a man like Father!

MRS. STOCKMANN

Be quiet, Petra.

MAYOR

(looks at PETRA*)*
So we've opinions of our own already, have we? But of course! *(To* MRS. STOCKMANN*)* Sister-in-law, you seem to be the most sensible person in this house. Use what influence you have over your husband. Make him realize the consequences this will have both for his family and—

DR. STOCKMANN

My family concerns no one but myself.

MAYOR

—both for his family, and for the town he lives in.

DR. STOCKMANN

I'm the one who has the town's real interest at heart! I want to expose the evils that sooner or later must come to light. I'm going to prove to people that I love this town where I was born.

MAYOR

Oh, you're blind! All you're trying to do is to stop up the source of the town's prosperity.

DR. STOCKMANN

That source is poisoned, man! Are you mad? We live by hawking filth and disease! And all this communal life you boast so much about is based upon a lie!

MAYOR

That's pure imagination—if nothing worse. The man who casts such foul aspersions against the town he lives in is an enemy of society.

DR. STOCKMANN

(goes towards him)

You dare to—!

MRS. STOCKMANN

(throws herself between them)

Thomas!

PETRA

(grasps her father by the arm)

Keep calm, Father!

MAYOR

I shall not expose myself to violence. You've been warned. Consider what is your duty to yourself and your family. Goodbye. *(Goes.)*

DR. STOCKMANN

(walks up and down)

And in my own house too, Catherine!

MRS. STOCKMANN

Yes, Thomas. It's a shame and a scandal—

PETRA

I'd like to get my hands on him—!

DR. STOCKMANN
> It's my own fault. I ought to have exposed them long ago; I should have bared my teeth; and used them! Calling me an enemy of society! By God, I'm not going to take that lying down!

MRS. STOCKMANN
> But, Thomas dear, might is right—

DR. STOCKMANN
> I'm the one who's right!

MRS. STOCKMANN
> What's the good of being right if you don't have the might?

PETRA
> Mother, how can you speak like that?

DR. STOCKMANN
> So it's no use in a free society to have right on one's side? Don't be absurd, Catherine. Besides—don't I have the free press in front of me—and the solid majority behind me? That's might enough, I should have thought!

MRS. STOCKMANN
> For heaven's sake, Thomas, surely you're not thinking of setting yourself up against your brother?

DR. STOCKMANN
> What the devil else do you expect me to do? Don't you want me to stand up for what I believe to be right?

PETRA
> Yes, Father, you must!

MRS. STOCKMANN
> It'll do you no good. If they won't, they won't.

DR. STOCKMANN
> *(laughs)*
> Oh, Catherine, just give me time. You'll see! I'm going to fight this war to the end.

MRS. STOCKMANN
> Yes, and the end will be that you'll lose your job. You'll see.

DR. STOCKMANN
> At least I shall have done my duty to the community; my duty to society. And they call me an enemy of society—!

MRS. STOCKMANN
> What about your family, Thomas? And your home? Do you

think you'll be doing your duty to the ones who depend on you?

PETRA

Oh, mother, don't always think only of us.

MRS. STOCKMANN

It's easy for you to talk. You can stand on your own feet, if need be. But think of the boys, Thomas! And think of yourself too—and me—

DR. STOCKMANN

You must be mad, Catherine! If I give in like a coward to Peter and his wretched gang, do you think I'd ever have another moment of happiness in my life?

MRS. STOCKMANN

I don't know about that. But God preserve us from the happiness we're likely to enjoy if you go on digging your heels in. You'll have no means of livelihood, no regular income. Didn't we have enough of that in the old days? Remember that, Thomas. Think what it'll mean.

DR. STOCKMANN

(writhes, fighting with himself, and clenches his fists)

And these office lackeys can do this to a free and honorable man! Isn't it monstrous, Catherine?

MRS. STOCKMANN

Yes, they've behaved very wickedly to you, that's true. But heaven knows, there's so much injustice one has to put up with in this world. There are the boys, Thomas. Look at them. What's to become of them? No, no, you can't have the heart. (EILIF *and* MORTEN *have meanwhile entered, carrying their schoolbooks.*)

DR. STOCKMANN

My sons! *(Suddenly stands erect, his mind made up.)* Even if my whole world crashes about me, I shall never bow my head. *(Goes towards his room.)*

MRS. STOCKMANN

Thomas, what are you going to do?

DR. STOCKMANN

(in the doorway)

I want to have the right to look my sons in the eyes when they grow up into free men! *(Goes into his room.)*

MRS. STOCKMANN

Oh, God help us!

PETRA

Father's right, mother! He'll never give in.

(Curtain)

ACT 3

The editorial office of the People's Tribune. *On the left in the background is the entrance door; to the right in the same wall is another door with glass panes through which the composing room is visible. Another door is in the wall on the right. In the middle of the room is a big table covered with papers, newspapers and books. Downstage left is a window; by it is a writing desk with a high stool. Two armchairs stand by the table, and there are other chairs along the walls. The room is gloomy and uncomfortable; the furniture is old, the armchairs dirty and torn. In the composing room one or two compositors are at work. Beyond them, a handpress is being operated.*

HOVSTAD *sits writing at the desk. After a few moments* BILLING *enters right, with the* DOCTOR'S *manuscript in his hand.*

BILLING

I say, I say, I say!

HOVSTAD

(writing)

Have you read it?

BILLING

(puts the manuscript on the desk)

I should say I have!

HOVSTAD

Pretty forceful, isn't it?

BILLING

Forceful? He'll butcher them, by Jingo! Every paragraph's a knockout!

HOVSTAD

Those fellows won't give in at the first blow, though.

BILLING

That's true. But we'll go on bashing them, punch after punch, till their whole damned oligarchy falls to the ground! As I sat in there reading this, it was as though I saw the revolution dawning from afar!

HOVSTAD

(turns)

Hush, don't let Aslaksen hear.

BILLING

(lowers his voice)

Aslaksen's a coward, a jellyfish! He hasn't the guts of a man! But you'll have your way? You will publish the Doctor's article?

HOVSTAD

Yes, unless the Mayor backs down—

BILLING

That'd be a damned nuisance!

HOVSTAD

Whichever way it turns out, we can exploit the situation. If the Mayor doesn't agree to the Doctor's proposal, he'll have all the tradespeople down on him—the Property Owners' Association, and the rest. And if he does agree to it, he'll antagonize all the big shareholders in the Baths who up to now have been his chief supporters—

BILLING

Of course! They'll have to fork out a pile of money—

HOVSTAD

You bet they will. And then the clique will be broken, and day after day we'll drum it into the public that the Mayor's incompetent in more respects than one, and that all the responsible offices in the town, the whole municipal authority, ought to be handed over to the people of liberal opinions.

BILLING

By Jingo, that's the truth! I see it! I see it! We stand on the threshold of a revolution!

(A knock on the door)

HOVSTAD
Quiet! *(Shouts.)* Come in.

(DR. STOCKMANN enters through the door upstage left.)

HOVSTAD
(goes to greet him)
Ah, here is the Doctor! Well?
DR. STOCKMANN
Print away, Mr. Hovstad!
HOVSTAD
So it's come to that?
BILLING
Hurrah!
DR. STOCKMANN
Print away, I say! Yes, it's come to that, all right! Well, now they shall have it the way they want it. It's war now, Mr. Billing!
BILLING
War to the death, I hope! Give it to them, Doctor!
DR. STOCKMANN
This report is only the beginning. My head's already teeming with ideas for four or five other articles. Where's Aslaksen?
BILLING
(calls into the composing room)
Aslaksen, come here a moment!
HOVSTAD
Four or five other articles, did you say? On the same theme?
DR. STOCKMANN
No—oh, good heavens no, my dear fellow! No, they'll be about quite different things. But it all stems from this business of the water system and the sewer. One thing leads to another, you know. It's like when you start to pull down an old building. Exactly like that.
BILLING
By Jingo, that's true! You suddenly realize you'll never be finished till you've pulled down the whole rotten structure!
ASLAKSEN
(from the composing room)

Pulled down! You're surely not thinking of pulling the Baths down, Doctor?

HOVSTAD

No, no, don't get frightened.

DR. STOCKMANN

No, we were talking about something else. Well, Mr. Hovstad, what do you think of my report?

HOVSTAD

I think it's an absolute masterpiece—

DR. STOCKMANN

Do you think so? That makes me very happy—very happy.

HOVSTAD

It's so clear and to the point; you don't have to be a specialist to follow the argument. I'm sure you'll have every enlightened person on your side.

ASLAKSEN

Every discriminating one too, I trust?

BILLING

Discriminating or not—you'll have the whole town behind you.

ASLAKSEN

Well then, I don't think we need be afraid to print it.

DR. STOCKMANN

I should damn well hope not.

HOVSTAD

It'll be in tomorrow morning.

DR. STOCKMANN

Good God, yes, we can't afford to waste a single day. Oh, Mr. Aslaksen, there was one thing I wanted to ask you. You must take charge of this manuscript yourself.

ASLAKSEN

If you wish.

DR. STOCKMANN

Treat it as though it was gold. No misprints! Every word is important. I'll drop back later; perhaps you'd let me look at a proof. I can't tell you how eager I am to see this thing in print —launched—!

BILLING

Launched, yes! Like a thunderbolt!

DR. STOCKMANN
—and submitted to the judgment of every intelligent citizen. Oh, you'd never guess what I've had to put up with today! I've been threatened with God knows what. They want to rob me of my elementary rights as a human being—

BILLING
Your rights as a human being!

DR. STOCKMANN
They want to degrade me, reduce me to the level of a beggar. They demand that I put my private interests above my most sacred and innermost convictions—

BILLING
By Jingo, that's going too far!

HOVSTAD
You can expect anything from that lot.

DR. STOCKMANN
But they won't get far with me! I'll give it to them in black and white! I'll grapple with them every day in the *People's Tribune!* I'll sweep them with one broadside after another—!

ASLAKSEN
Yes, but remember—

BILLING
Hurrah! It's war, it's war!

DR. STOCKMANN
I'll beat them to the ground, I'll crush them, I'll flatten their defenses for every honest man to see! By God I will!

ASLAKSEN
But do it soberly, Doctor. Act with restraint—

BILLING
No, no! Don't spare your powder!

DR. STOCKMANN
(continues imperturbably)
You see, it isn't just a question of the water system and the sewer. This whole community's got to be cleansed and decontaminated—

BILLING
That's the very word!

DR. STOCKMANN
All these skimpers and compromisers have got to be thrown

out! There's got to be a clean sweep! Oh, such endless vistas have been opened up before my eyes today! I don't see my way quite clearly yet. But I will! We need fresh standard-bearers, my friends! Young men! Our advance posts must be manned by new captains!

BILLING

Hear, hear!

DR. STOCKMANN

As long as we stick together, it'll all happen so easily—so easily! The whole revolution will glide into existence like a ship from the stocks! Don't you agree?

HOVSTAD

I think we've every prospect now of getting the helm into the right hands.

ASLAKSEN

As long as we proceed with restraint, I don't think there can be any danger.

DR. STOCKMANN

Who cares about danger! I'm doing this in the name of truth and of my conscience!

HOVSTAD

You're a man who deserves support, Doctor.

ASLAKSEN

Yes, the Doctor's a true friend of the town, that's certain. I'll go further; he's a friend of society!

BILLING

By Jingo, Mr. Aslaksen, Dr. Stockmann is a friend of the people!

ASLAKSEN

I think the Property Owners' Association might be able to use that phrase.

DR. STOCKMANN

(moved, presses their hands)

Thank you, my dear, good friends—thank you! It's so refreshing for me to hear this. My brother described me in vastly different terms. By God, I'll give it back to him with interest! Now I must go and see a poor devil of a patient. But I'll be back! Take good care of that manuscript, Mr. Aslaksen. And for heaven's sake don't cut out any of the exclamation marks!

If anything, put in a few more. Good, good. Well, goodbye! Goodbye, goodbye!

(He shakes hands with them as they accompany him to the door and he goes out.)

HOVSTAD

He's going to be bloody useful to us.

ASLAKSEN

As long as he sticks to the Baths. But if he tries to go further, we'd be unwise to stay with him.

HOVSTAD

Hm; that all depends—

BILLING

You're such a damned coward, Aslaksen!

ASLAKSEN

Coward? Yes, when it's a question of fighting local authorities, I am a coward, Mr. Billing. That's a lesson I have learned in the school of life. But elevate me into the field of high politics, confront me with the government, and then see if I am a coward!

BILLING

No, no, I'm sure you're not. But that's just where you're so inconsistent.

ASLAKSEN

Because I know my responsibilities as a citizen! Throwing stones at the government can't harm society. It doesn't bother those fellows—they stay put. But local authorities can be overthrown, and then you may get inexperience at the helm. With disastrous results for property owners and the like.

HOVSTAD

But what about the education of people through self-government?

ASLAKSEN

When a man has interests to protect he can't think of everything, Mr. Hovstad.

HOVSTAD

Then I hope to God I never have any interests to protect.

BILLING

Hear, hear!

HOVSTAD

I'm not a trimmer, and I never will be.

ASLAKSEN

A politician should never commit himself, Mr. Hovstad. And you, Mr. Billing, you ought to put a reef or two in your sails if you want that job of clerk to the council.

BILLING

I—!

HOVSTAD

You, Billing?

BILLING

Of course I only applied for it to put their backs up, you understand.

ASLAKSEN

Well, it's no business of mine. But since I'm being accused of cowardice and inconsistency, I'd like to make this clear. My political record is open for anyone to investigate. I've never changed my standpoint—apart from having learned more restraint. My heart still belongs with the people; but I don't deny that my head keeps one ear cocked towards the authorities. The local ones, anyway. *(Goes into the composing room.)*

BILLING

Couldn't we change to some other printer, Hovstad?

HOVSTAD

Do you know anyone else who'd give us credit for printing and paper?

BILLING

It's a damned nuisance not having any capital!

HOVSTAD

(sits at the desk)
Yes, if we only had *that*—

BILLING

Ever thought of trying Dr. Stockmann?

HOVSTAD

(glancing through his papers)
What'd be the use of that? He hasn't a bean.

BILLING

No; but he's got a good man behind him. Old Morten Kiil—the fellow they call the Badger—

HOVSTAD

(writing)

Do you really think he's got much?

BILLING

By Jingo, of course he has! And part of it must go to the Stockmanns. He's bound to provide for—well, the children, anyway.

HOVSTAD

(half turns)

Are you banking on that?

BILLING

Banking? I never bank on anything.

HOVSTAD

You'd better not. And don't bank on becoming clerk to the council either, because I can promise you you won't.

BILLING

Do you think I don't know? *Not* to get it is just what I want! A snub like that puts you on your mettle. It gives you a fresh supply of gall, and you need that in a backwater like this, where hardly anything really infuriating ever happens.

HOVSTAD

(writing)

Yes, yes.

BILLING

Well, they'll soon hear from me! I'll go and write that appeal for funds to the Property Owners' Association. *(Goes into the room on the right.)*

HOVSTAD

(sitting at the desk, chews his pen and says slowly)

Hm! So that's the way the wind blows! *(There is a knock on the door.)* Come in!

(PETRA enters through the door upstage left.)

HOVSTAD

(gets up)

Why, hullo! Fancy seeing you here!

PETRA

Please forgive me—

HOVSTAD

(pushes forward an armchair)

Won't you sit down?

PETRA

No, thank you. I'm only staying a moment.

HOVSTAD

Is it something from your father—?

PETRA

No, something from me. *(Takes a book from her coat pocket.)* Here's that English novel.

HOVSTAD

Why are you giving it back to me?

PETRA

I don't want to translate it.

HOVSTAD

But you promised—

PETRA

I hadn't read it then. You can't have, either!

HOVSTAD

No—you know I don't understand English. But—

PETRA

Exactly. That's why I wanted to tell you—you'll have to find something else to serialize. *(Puts the book on the table.)* You can't possibly print this in the *People's Tribune*.

HOVSTAD

Why not?

PETRA

Because it's diametrically opposed to what you believe.

HOVSTAD

Oh, that's the reason?

PETRA

I don't think you understand. Its theme is that there's a supernatural power which takes care of all the so-called good people in this world, and works things so that in the end everything turns out well for them and all the so-called bad people get punished.

HOVSTAD

Yes, well, that's all right. That's just what people want to read.

PETRA
But do you want to be the one who provides it for them? You don't believe a word of that! You know quite well it doesn't happen like that in real life.

HOVSTAD
Of course not. But an editor can't always do as he wishes. One often has to bow to people's feelings in minor matters. After all, politics are the most important things in life—for a newspaper, anyway. And if I want to win people over to my views about freedom and progress, I mustn't frighten them away. If they find a moral story like this in the back pages of the newspaper they're more likely to go along with what we print on the front page. It reassures them.

PETRA
Oh, really! You're not as crafty as that. I don't see you as a spider spinning webs to catch your readers!

HOVSTAD
(smiles)
Thank you for holding such a high opinion of me. No, actually this was Billing's idea, not mine.

PETRA
Billing's!

HOVSTAD
Yes. He was talking on those lines here the other day. He's the one who's so keen that we should publish this novel. I'd never heard of the book.

PETRA
But Billing holds such progressive views—

HOVSTAD
Oh, there's more in Billing than meets the eye. I've just heard he's applied for the post of clerk to the council.

PETRA
I don't believe that, Mr. Hovstad. How could he reconcile himself to doing a thing like that?

HOVSTAD
You'd better ask him.

PETRA
I'd never have thought that of Billing.

HOVSTAD
Wouldn't you? Does it so surprise you?

PETRA

Yes. Perhaps not, though. I don't really know—

HOVSTAD

We journalists aren't worth much, Miss Stockmann.

PETRA

How can you say that?

HOVSTAD

I sometimes think it.

PETRA

In the ordinary run of events, perhaps not—that I can understand. But now, when you've taken up such an important cause—now surely you must feel you're worth more than most men.

HOVSTAD

Yes, today I do feel a bit like that.

PETRA

It's true, isn't it! You do! Oh, it's a wonderful vocation you've chosen! To be able to pioneer neglected truths and brave new doctrines—the mere fact of standing fearlessly forth to defend a man who's been wronged—

HOVSTAD

Especially when this man who's been wronged is—hm—

PETRA

When he is a man of such honor and integrity?

HOVSTAD

(more quietly)

I was about to say: especially when he is your father.

PETRA

(astounded)

Mr. Hovstad!

HOVSTAD

Yes, Petra—Miss Petra—

PETRA

Is that what seems important to you? Not the issue itself. Not the truth—or the fact that this means everything to Father—

HOVSTAD

Yes—yes, of course—those things too—

PETRA

No, thank you. You let the cat out of the bag there, Mr. Hovstad. Now I shall never believe you again. About anything.

HOVSTAD

Does it make you so angry that I've done this for your sake?

PETRA

I'm angry because you haven't been honest with Father. You've been talking to him as though truth and the good of the people were what mattered most to you. You've been fooling both of us. You're not the man you've been pretending you are. And that I'll never forgive you—never!

HOVSTAD

You shouldn't speak so sharply to me, Miss Petra. Least of all just now.

PETRA

Why not now?

HOVSTAD

Because your father needs my help.

PETRA

So that's the sort of man you are!

HOVSTAD

No, no, I didn't mean that—Please believe me—!

PETRA

I know what to believe. Goodbye.

ASLAKSEN

(hurries in furtively from the composing room)

For God's sake, Mr. Hovstad—! *(Sees* PETRA.*)* Oh, dear, that's unlucky—!

HOVSTAD

(goes after her)

But, Miss Petra—!

PETRA

Goodbye. *(Goes.)*

ASLAKSEN

Mr. Hovstad, listen, please!

HOVSTAD

Yes, yes, what is it?

ASLAKSEN

The Mayor's standing outside there in the composing room!

HOVSTAD

The Mayor?

ASLAKSEN

Yes. He wants to talk to you. He came in the back way—didn't want to be seen, I suppose.

HOVSTAD

What can he want? No, wait, I'd better—*(Goes to the door of the composing room, opens it, bows, and invites the* MAYOR *to enter.)*

HOVSTAD

Keep a look out, Aslaksen, and make sure no one—

ASLAKSEN

Of course. *(Goes into the composing room.)*

MAYOR

You weren't expecting to see me here.

HOVSTAD

No, frankly, I wasn't.

MAYOR

(looks round)

You've done this up quite nicely. Very pleasant.

HOVSTAD

Oh—

MAYOR

And here I am coming along and making demands on your time.

HOVSTAD

Not at all, sir. What can I do for you? Please allow me—*(Takes the* MAYOR'S *hat and stick, and puts them on a chair.)* Won't you sit down?

MAYOR

(sits at the table)

Thank you.

*(*HOVSTAD *also sits at the table.)*

MAYOR

Something—something extremely irritating has happened to me today, Mr. Hovstad.

HOVSTAD

Really? Of course, Your Worship has so many responsibilities—

MAYOR

This particular matter concerns the medical officer at the Baths.

HOVSTAD
Oh—the Doctor—?
MAYOR
He's written a sort of—report to the Baths Committee regarding some supposed defects in the Baths.
HOVSTAD
You amaze me.
MAYOR
Hasn't he told you? I thought he said—
HOVSTAD
Oh yes, that's true, he did say something—
ASLAKSEN
(from the composing room)
I'd better have that manuscript—
HOVSTAD
(irritated)
Hm—it's there on the desk—
ASLAKSEN
(finds it)
Good.
MAYOR
Why, surely that's it!
ASLAKSEN
Yes, this is the Doctor's article, Your Worship.
HOVSTAD
Oh, is this what you were talking about?
MAYOR
The very thing. What do you think of it?
HOVSTAD
Of course I'm not a specialist, and I've only glanced through it—
MAYOR
But you're going to print it?
HOVSTAD
I can't very well refuse a signed contribution—
ASLAKSEN
I have no say in the contents of the paper, Your Worship—
MAYOR
Of course not.

ASLAKSEN

I only print what's put into my hands.

MAYOR

Absolutely.

ASLAKSEN

So if you'll excuse me—(*Goes towards the composing room.*)

MAYOR

No, wait a moment, Mr. Aslaksen. With your permission, Mr. Hovstad—

HOVSTAD

Of course, Your Worship.

MAYOR

You're an intelligent and discriminating man, Mr. Aslaksen.

ASLAKSEN

I'm glad Your Worship thinks so.

MAYOR

And a man of wide influence in more circles than one.

ASLAKSEN

Oh—mostly among humble people—

MAYOR

The small taxpayers are the most numerous, here as elsewhere.

ASLAKSEN

Yes, that's true.

MAYOR

And I've no doubt you know how most of them feel. Don't you?

ASLAKSEN

Yes, I think I may say I do, Your Worship.

MAYOR

Well then, since the less affluent of the citizens of this town are so laudably disposed to make this sacrifice, I—

ASLAKSEN

What!

HOVSTAD

Sacrifice?

MAYOR

It's a fine token of public spirit. A remarkably fine token. I was about to confess I hadn't expected it. But you know the mood of the people better than I do.

ASLAKSEN
But, Your Worship—

MAYOR
And it will probably be no mean sacrifice that the ratepayers will be called upon to make.

HOVSTAD
The ratepayers?

ASLAKSEN
But I don't understand—surely the shareholders—?

MAYOR
According to a provisional estimate the alterations that the medical officer at the Baths regards as desirable will cost some two to three hundred thousand crowns.

ASLAKSEN
That's a lot of money; but—

MAYOR
We shall of course be forced to raise a municipal loan.

HOVSTAD
(gets up)
You surely don't mean that the ordinary citizens—?

ASLAKSEN
You mean you'd charge it on the rates! Empty the pockets of the tradespeople—?

MAYOR
Well, my dear Mr. Aslaksen, where else is the money to come from?

ASLAKSEN
That's the business of the gentlemen who own the Baths.

MAYOR
The Committee cannot see their way towards authorizing any further expenditure.

ASLAKSEN
Is that quite definite, Your Worship?

MAYOR
I have gone into the matter very thoroughly. If the people want all these comprehensive alterations, then the people themselves will have to pay for them.

ASLAKSEN
But good God Almighty—oh, I beg Your Worship's pardon!—

but this puts a completely different face on the situation, Mr. Hovstad.

HOVSTAD

It certainly does.

MAYOR

The worst of the matter is that we shall be compelled to close the Baths for two or three years.

HOVSTAD

Close them? You mean—close them completely?

ASLAKSEN

For two years?

MAYOR

That's how long the work will take, at the lowest calculation.

ASLAKSEN

But, good heavens, we'll never be able to stand that, Your Worship! How are we property owners to live in the meantime?

MAYOR

I'm afraid that's a very difficult question to answer, Mr. Aslaksen. But what do you expect us to do? Do you imagine we shall get a single visitor here if we start spreading the idea that the water is contaminated, that we are living over a cesspit, that the whole town—?

ASLAKSEN

And all this is just pure speculation?

MAYOR

With the best will in the world I have been unable to convince myself that it is anything else.

ASLAKSEN

But if that's the case it's monstrous of Dr. Stockmann to have—I beg Your Worship's pardon, but—

MAYOR

I deplore your observation, Mr. Aslaksen, but I'm afraid it represents the truth. My brother has unfortunately always been an impulsive man.

ASLAKSEN

And you still want to support him in this action, Mr. Hovstad?

HOVSTAD

But who could have possibly guessed that—?

MAYOR
I have written a brief résumé of the situation as it appears to an impartial observer; and in it I have suggested how any possible flaws in the existing arrangements could safely be remedied by measures within the financial resources at present possessed by the Baths.

HOVSTAD
Have you that document with you, Your Worship?

MAYOR
(feels in his pocket)
Yes, I brought it with me just in case you—

ASLAKSEN
(quickly)
Oh, my goodness, there he is!

MAYOR
Who? My brother?

HOVSTAD
Where—where?

ASLAKSEN
He's just coming through the composing room.

MAYOR
Most unfortunate! I don't want to meet him here, and I've something else I wanted to speak to you about.

HOVSTAD
(points towards the door, right)
Go in there till he's gone.

MAYOR
But—?

HOVSTAD
There's only Billing there.

ASLAKSEN
Quick, quick, Your Worship! He's coming now!

MAYOR
Very well. But get rid of him as soon as you can.

(Goes out through the door on the right, which ASLAKSEN *opens and closes for him.)*

HOVSTAD

Find something to do, Aslaksen.

(He sits down and writes. ASLAKSEN *starts looking through a pile of newspapers on a chair to the right.)*

DR. STOCKMANN

(enters from the composing room)

Well, here I am again! *(Puts down his hat and stick.)*

HOVSTAD

(writing)

Already, Doctor? Aslaksen, hurry up with that thing we were talking about. We're badly behindhand today.

DR. STOCKMANN

(to ASLAKSEN*)*

No proofs yet, by the sound of it?

ASLAKSEN

(without turning)

No, surely you didn't think they'd be ready yet.

DR. STOCKMANN

That's all right. I'm just impatient, as I know you'll appreciate. I can't rest till I've seen that thing in print.

HOVSTAD

Hm—it'll be a good time yet. Won't it, Aslaksen?

ASLAKSEN

I'm afraid so.

DR. STOCKMANN

Very well, my dear friends. I'll be back later. I don't mind making the journey twice if need be! In such a vital matter, with the welfare of the whole town at stake, one mustn't grudge a little extra effort! *(Is about to go, but stops and comes back.)* Oh, by the way, there's one more thing I must speak to you about.

HOVSTAD

I'm sorry, but couldn't it wait till another time—?

DR. STOCKMANN

I can tell you in two words. It's just this. When people read my article in the paper tomorrow and discover I've been racking my brains all winter working silently for the welfare of the town—

HOVSTAD
But, Doctor—

DR. STOCKMANN
I know what you're going to say! You think it was no more than my damned duty—my job as a citizen. Yes, of course—I know that as well as you do. But my fellow-citizens, you see—oh dear, those good people, they're so fond of me—

ASLAKSEN
Yes, the people of this town have been very fond of you, Doctor, up to today.

DR. STOCKMANN
Yes, and that's exactly why I'm frightened that—what I mean is—when they read this—especially the poorer people—as a clarion call bidding them take the government of their town into their own hands—

HOVSTAD
(gets up)
Look, Doctor, I don't want to hide anything from you—

DR. STOCKMANN
Ah, something's already afoot! I might have guessed! But I don't want it! If anything like that's being organized, I—

HOVSTAD
Like what?

DR. STOCKMANN
Well, if anything like a torchlight procession or a banquet or—a subscription for some little token of thanks is being organized, you must promise me solemnly you'll squash the idea. And you too, Mr. Aslaksen! You hear?

HOVSTAD
I'm sorry, Doctor, but we might as well tell you the truth now as later—

(MRS. STOCKMANN, *in hat and cloak, enters through the door upstage left.*)

MRS. STOCKMANN
(*sees the* DOCTOR)
I knew it!

An Enemy of the People 75

HOVSTAD

(goes towards her)
You here too, Mrs. Stockmann?

DR. STOCKMANN

What the devil do you want here, Catherine?

MRS. STOCKMANN

Surely you can guess.

HOVSTAD

Won't you sit down? Or perhaps—?

MRS. STOCKMANN

Thank you, you needn't bother. And you mustn't take offense at my coming here to fetch my husband, for I'm the mother of three children, I'd have you realize.

DR. STOCKMANN

Oh really, Catherine, we know all this.

MRS. STOCKMANN

Well, it doesn't seem you've much thought for your wife and children today, or you wouldn't have come here to cause all of us misery.

DR. STOCKMANN

Are you quite mad, Catherine? Simply because a man has a wife and children, is he to be forbidden to proclaim the truth—to be a useful and active citizen—to serve the town he lives in?

MRS. STOCKMANN

Oh, Thomas, if only you'd use some restraint.

ASLAKSEN

That's exactly what I say. Restraint in all things.

MRS. STOCKMANN

And as for you, Mr. Hovstad, it's not right for you to persuade my husband to leave his house and home and trick him into involving himself in all this—

HOVSTAD

I haven't tricked anyone—

DR. STOCKMANN

Tricked! You think *I* allow myself to be tricked?

MRS. STOCKMANN

Yes, you do. Oh, I know you're the cleverest man in the town, but you're so dreadfully easy to fool, Thomas. *(To* HOVSTAD*)* And don't forget, he'll lose his job at the Baths if you print that thing he's written—

ASLAKSEN
   What!

HOVSTAD
   But Doctor, I—

DR. STOCKMANN
   (laughs)
   Just let them try! Oh no, Catherine—they'll watch their step! You see, I have the majority behind me!

MRS. STOCKMANN
   Yes, that's just the trouble. They're an ugly thing to have behind you.

DR. STOCKMANN
   Rubbish Catherine! You go home now and take care of the house, and let me take care of society. How can you be frightened when I feel so calm and happy? *(Rubs his hands and walks up and down.)* Truth and the people will win this battle, never you fear! Oh, I can see every liberal-minded citizen in this town marching forward in an unconquerable army—! *(Stops by a chair.)* What—the devil is *this?*

ASLAKSEN
   (looks at it)
   Oh dear!

DR. STOCKMANN
   The crown of authority! *(Takes the MAYOR's hat carefully in his fingers and holds it in the air.)*

MRS. STOCKMANN
   The Mayor's hat!

DR. STOCKMANN
   And his marshal's baton too. How in the name of—?

HOVSTAD
   Well—

DR. STOCKMANN
   Ah, I see! He's been here to talk you over! *(Laughs.)* He came to the wrong men! And then he saw me in the composing room—*(Roars with laughter.)* Did he run away, Mr. Aslaksen?

ASLAKSEN
   (quickly)
   Oh yes, Doctor, he ran away.

DR. STOCKMANN

Ran away leaving his stick and—? Rubbish! Peter never left anything behind in his life! But where the devil have you put him? Ah, yes, of course—in there! Now, Catherine, you watch!

MRS. STOCKMANN

Thomas, I beg you—!

ASLAKSEN

Don't do anything rash, Doctor!

(DR. STOCKMANN has put the MAYOR's hat on his head and taken his stick. Then he goes across, throws the door open, and brings his hand up to the hat in salute. The MAYOR enters, red with anger. BILLING follows him.)

MAYOR

What is the meaning of this disorderly scene?

DR. STOCKMANN

A little more respect if you please my dear Peter. I am the supreme authority in this town now. *(He walks up and down.)*

MRS. STOCKMANN

(almost in tears)

Thomas, please!

MAYOR

(follows him)

Give me my hat and stick!

DR. STOCKMANN

(as before)

You may be Chief of Police, but I'm the Mayor! I'm master of this whole town, I am!

MAYOR

Take off that hat, I tell you! Remember that that hat is an official emblem—

DR. STOCKMANN

Rubbish! Do you think the awakening lion of public opinion is going to let itself be frightened by a hat? We're starting a revolution tomorrow, I'd have you know! You threatened to sack me, but now I'm going to sack you—sack you from all your positions of responsibility! You think I can't? You're wrong, Peter! I have as my allies the conquering forces of social revolution! Hovstad and Billing will thunder in the *People's Tribune*, and Mr. Aslaksen will march forth at the head of the entire Property Owners' Association—

ASLAKSEN

No, Doctor, I won't.

DR. STOCKMANN

Indeed you will—!

MAYOR

Aha. But perhaps Mr. Hovstad will support this uprising?

HOVSTAD

No, Your Worship.

ASLAKSEN

Mr. Hovstad isn't so mad as to ruin himself and his newspaper for the sake of an hallucination.

DR. STOCKMANN

(looks around)

What the devil—?

HOVSTAD

You have presented your case in a false light, Doctor; and therefore I cannot support you.

BILLING

No, after what His Worship has had the grace to tell me in there, I shouldn't—

DR. STOCKMANN

Lies! I'll answer for the truth of my report! You just print it. I shan't be frightened to defend it.

HOVSTAD

I'm not printing it. I can't and I won't and I dare not print it.

DR. STOCKMANN

Dare not? What nonsense is this? You're the editor, and it's the editors who rule the press.

ASLAKSEN

No, Doctor. It's the subscribers.

MAYOR

Fortunately.

ASLAKSEN

It's public opinion, the educated reader, the property owners, and so forth—they're the ones who rule the press.

DR. STOCKMANN
(calmly)
And all these forces are ranged against me?

ASLAKSEN
They are. If your report got printed, it would mean ruin for the entire community.

DR. STOCKMANN
I see.

MAYOR
My hat and stick!

(DR. STOCKMANN *takes off the hat and puts it on the table together with the stick.*)

MAYOR
(takes them both)
Your little reign didn't last long.

DR. STOCKMANN
It isn't over yet. *(To* HOVSTAD*)* You refuse absolutely, then, to print my report in the *People's Tribune?*

HOVSTAD
Absolutely. Out of consideration for your family, if for no other reason.

MRS. STOCKMANN
Never you mind his family, Mr. Hovstad.

MAYOR
(takes a paper from his pocket)
This will give the public full possession of the facts. It's an official statement Mr. Hovstad.

HOVSTAD
(takes the paper)
Right. I'll see it's set up at once.

DR. STOCKMANN
But not mine! You think you can gag me and stifle the truth! But it won't be as easy as you think. Mr. Aslaksen, take this manuscript of mine and print it immediately as a pamphlet—at my own expense! I'll publish it myself! I want four hundred copies—five—no, make it six hundred copies!

ASLAKSEN

I wouldn't give you the use of my press if you offered me gold, Doctor. I daren't. Public opinion wouldn't allow me. You won't find a printer to take it anywhere in this town.

DR. STOCKMANN

Give it back to me then.

(HOVSTAD *hands him the manuscript.*)

DR. STOCKMANN

(takes his hat and stick)

I'll see the contents are made known all the same. I'll summon a public meeting and read it! All my fellow citizens shall know the truth!

MAYOR

You won't find anyone in this town who'll lease you a hall for such a purpose.

ASLAKSEN

Not one. I'm sure of that.

BILLING

By Jingo, you won't.

MRS. STOCKMANN

This is too disgraceful! Why are they all against you?

DR. STOCKMANN

(hotly)

I'll tell you why! It's because in this town all the men are old women! Like you, they just think of their families and not of the community.

MRS. STOCKMANN

(grasps his arm)

Then I'll show them that an—an old woman can be a man—for once. I'm sticking with you, Thomas.

DR. STOCKMANN

Well said, Catherine! The truth shall be told—by God it will! If I can't lease a hall, I'll hire a drummer to march through the town with me, and I'll read it out at every street corner!

MAYOR

You can't be so crazy as to do that!

DR. STOCKMANN

I am!

ASLAKSEN

You won't find a single man in the whole town who'll go with you.

BILLING

No, by Jingo!

MRS. STOCKMANN

Don't you give in, Thomas! I'll ask the boys to go with you.

DR. STOCKMANN

That's a splendid idea!

MRS. STOCKMANN

Morten will love to do it. And so will Eilif, I'm sure.

DR. STOCKMANN

Yes, and Petra, too! And you, Catherine!

MRS. STOCKMANN

No, no, not me. But I'll stand at the window and watch you. I'll do that.

DR. STOCKMANN

(throws his arms around her and kisses her)

Thank you! Well, my fine gentlemen, let the trumpets sound! Let's see whether meanness and mediocrity have the power to gag a man who wants to clean up society!

(DR. *and* MRS. STOCKMANN *go out through the door upstage left.*)

MAYOR

(shakes his head thoughtfully)
Now he's driven her mad, too!

(Curtain)

ACT 4

A big, old-fashioned room in CAPTAIN HORSTER'S *house. In the background an open double-leaved door leads to a lobby. In the left-hand wall are three windows. Against the middle of the opposite wall has been placed a dais, on which stands a small table with two candles, a water carafe, a glass, and a bell. The room is further illuminated by bracket lamps between the windows. Downstage left stands a table with a candle on it, and a chair. Downstage right is a door with a few chairs by it.*

A large gathering of CITIZENS, *of all classes. Here and there women can be seen among the crowd, and there are a few schoolboys. More and more people gradually stream in from the back, filling the room.*

A CITIZEN
(to another, as he bumps against him)
Hullo, Lamstad! You here too this evening?

2ND CITIZEN
I never miss a public meeting.

3RD CITIZEN
(standing near them)
Brought your whistle, I hope?

2ND CITIZEN
Course I have. Haven't you?

3RD CITIZEN
You bet! And Skipper Evensen said he'd bring a bloody great horn!

2ND CITIZEN
He's a card, old Evensen!

(Laughter among the crowd)

4TH CITIZEN
(joins them)
I say, what's this meeting about?

2ND CITIZEN

Dr. Stockmann's going to deliver a lecture attacking the Mayor.

4TH CITIZEN

But the Mayor's his brother.

1ST CITIZEN

That don't matter. Dr. Stockmann ain't afraid of no one.

3RD CITIZEN

But he's in the wrong. It said so in the *People's Tribune*.

2ND CITIZEN

Yes, he must be in the wrong this time. The Property Owners wouldn't let him use their hall, nor the People's Club neither.

1ST CITIZEN

He couldn't even get the hall at the Baths.

2ND CITIZEN

Well, what do you expect?

1ST CITIZEN

Which one do you think we ought to support?

4TH CITIZEN

Just keep your eye on old Aslaksen, and do as he does.

BILLING

(with a portfolio under his arm, pushes his way through the crowd)

Excuse me please, gentlemen! Can I get through please? I'm reporting the meeting for the *People's Tribune*. Thank you! *(Sits down at the table, left.)*

(CAPTAIN HORSTER *escorts* MRS. STOCKMANN *and* PETRA *in through the door downstage right.* EILIF *and* MORTEN *are with them.)*

HORSTER

I thought you might sit here. You can slip out easily if anything should happen.

MRS. STOCKMANN

Do you think there'll be trouble?

HORSTER

One never knows, with a crowd like this. But sit down, and don't worry.

MRS. STOCKMANN
(sits)
It was very kind of you to offer my husband this room.
HORSTER
Well, no one else would, so I—
PETRA
(who had sat down too)
It was brave of you, too, Captain Horster.
HORSTER
Oh, that didn't call for much courage.

(HOVSTAD and ASLAKSEN come through the crowd, at the same time but separately.)

ASLAKSEN
(goes over to HORSTER)
Hasn't the Doctor come yet?
HORSTER
He's waiting in there.

(There is a stir among the crowd near the door backstage.)

HOVSTAD
(to BILLING)
There's the Mayor! See?
BILLING
Yes, by Jingo! So he's come after all!

(The MAYOR gently pushes his way through the crowd, greeting people politely, and stations himself against the wall on the left. A few moments later DR. STOCKMANN enters through the door downstage right. He is dressed in black, with a frock coat and a white cravat. A few people clap uncertainly, but are countered by subdued hissing. Silence falls.)

DR. STOCKMANN
(in a low voice)
How do you feel, Catherine?

MRS. STOCKMANN

I'm all right. *(More quietly)* Now don't lose your temper, Thomas!

DR. STOCKMANN

Oh, I'll control myself, don't you worry. *(Looks at his watch, steps up on to the dais and bows.)* It's a quarter past, so I'll begin—*(Takes out his manuscript.)*

ASLAKSEN

Surely a Chairman ought to be elected first?

DR. STOCKMANN

No, no, there's no need for that.

SEVERAL MEN

(shout)

Yes, yes!

MAYOR

I really think we should have someone in the chair.

DR. STOCKMANN

But Peter, I've called this meeting to deliver a lecture!

MAYOR

The Doctor's lecture may possibly give rise to divergent expressions of opinion.

SEVERAL VOICES FROM THE CROWD

A Chairman! A Chairman!

HOVSTAD

Public opinion seems to demand a Chairman.

DR. STOCKMANN

(controlling himself)

Very well. Let public opinion have its way.

ASLAKSEN

Would His Worship the Mayor be willing to undertake that function?

THREE MEN

(clap)

Bravo! Hear, hear!

MAYOR

For reasons which I'm sure you will appreciate, I must decline that honor. But fortunately we have among us a man whom I think we can all accept. I refer to the Chairman of the Property Owners' Association, Mr. Aslaksen.

MANY VOICES
Yes, yes! Good old Aslaksen! Hurrah for Aslaksen!

(DR. STOCKMANN *picks up his manuscript and descends from the dais.*)

ASLAKSEN
If my fellow citizens want to express their trust in me, I won't refuse their call.

(*Applause and cheers.* ASLAKSEN *steps up onto the dais.*)

BILLING
(*writes*)
Mr. Aslaksen was chosen amid acclamation . . ."

ASLAKSEN
Now that I stand here may I crave permission to say a few brief words? I'm a mild and peace-loving man who believes in sensible discretion, and in—and in discreet good sense. Everyone who knows me knows that.

MANY VOICES
Yes! That's right, Aslaksen!

ASLAKSEN
Experience in the school of life has taught me that the most valuable virtue for any citizen is restraint—

MAYOR
Hear, hear!

ASLAKSEN
And that discretion and restraint are the best servants of society. I would therefore suggest to our respected fellow-citizen who has summoned this meeting that he endeavor to keep himself within the bounds of temperance.

DRUNKEN MAN
(*by the entrance door*)
Three cheers for the Temperance Society! Jolly good health!

A VOICE
Shut your bloody trap.

MANY VOICES
Hush, hush!

ASLAKSEN

No interruptions, gentlemen, please! Does anyone wish to say anything before I—?

MAYOR

Mr. Chairman!

ASLAKSEN

Your Worship!

MAYOR

As everyone here is doubtless aware, I have close ties of relationship with the present medical officer at the Baths, and would consequently have preferred not to speak this evening. But my official position on the Committee of that organization, and my anxiety for the best interests of the town, force me to table a resolution. I hope I may assume that no citizens here present would regard it as desirable that dubious and exaggerated allegations concerning the sanitary conditions at the Baths should circulate outside this town.

MANY VOICES

No, no, no! Certainly not! We protest!

MAYOR

I therefore move that this meeting refuse the aforesaid medical officer permission to read or dilate upon his theories concerning the matter in question.

DR. STOCKMANN

(explosively)

Refuse permission? What the devil—?

(MRS. STOCKMANN *coughs.*)

DR. STOCKMANN

(composes himself)

Very well. You refuse permission.

MAYOR

In my statement to the *People's Tribune* I have acquainted the public with the essential facts so that every intelligent citizen can form his own judgment. Among other things I pointed out that the medical officer's proposals—quite apart from the fact that they amount to a vote of no confidence in the leading citizens of this town—will burden the ratepayers with the unnecessary expenditure of at least a hundred thousand crowns.

(Groans and a few whistles)

ASLAKSEN
(rings his bell)
Order please, gentlemen! I beg leave to second His Worship's motion. I would add that in my view the Doctor has had an ulterior motive, no doubt unconscious, in stirring up this agitation; he talks about the Baths, but what he's really aiming at is a revolution. He wants to transfer authority into other hands. No one doubts the honesty of the Doctor's intentions. Heaven knows, there can be no two opinions about that! I too believe in popular self-government, so long as it doesn't impose too heavy an expense upon the taxpayer. But that's just what would happen here; so I'm blowed, if you'll excuse the expression, if I can support Dr. Stockmann in this matter. One can pay too high a price for gold; that's my opinion.

(Lively expressions of assent from all sides)

HOVSTAD
I too feel impelled to explain my position. Dr. Stockmann's agitation won considerable sympathy at first, and I myself supported it as impartially as I was able. But then we found we had allowed ourselves to be misled by a false picture of the facts—

DR. STOCKMANN
That's a lie!

HOVSTAD
A not completely reliable picture, then. His Worship's statement has proved that. I hope no one here doubts the liberality of my views. The *People's Tribune* attitude on major political questions is well known to you all. But I have learned from men of discretion and experience that in local matters it is the duty of a newspaper to observe a certain caution.

ASLAKSEN
Exactly my feelings.

HOVSTAD

Now in the matter under discussion it's quite clear that Dr. Stockmann has popular opinion against him. Well, I ask you, gentlemen, what is the primary duty of an editor? Is it not to reflect the opinions of his readers? Has he not been entrusted with what might be described as an unspoken mandate to advance the cause of those who hold the same views as himself, with all the eloquence of which he is capable? Or am I mistaken?

MANY VOICES

No, no, no! Mr. Hovstad is right!

HOVSTAD

It has caused me much heart-searching to break with a man under whose roof I have lately been a not infrequent guest—a man who has until this day rejoiced in the undivided affection of his fellow-citizens—a man whose only, or anyway principal, fault is that he follows his heart rather than his head.

SCATTERED VOICES

That's true. Hurrah for Dr. Stockmann!

HOVSTAD

But my duty towards society left me no alternative. And there's one further consideration which forces me to oppose him, in the hope of halting him on the inauspicious road he has now begun to tread—consideration for his family—

DR. STOCKMANN

Stick to the water system and the sewer!

HOVSTAD

—consideration for his wife and the children he has abandoned.

MORTEN

Does he mean us, Mother?

MRS. STOCKMANN

Hush!

ASLAKSEN

I shall now put His Worship's resolution to the vote.

DR. STOCKMANN

Don't bother! I won't say a word about those damned Baths. No. I've something else to tell you tonight.

MAYOR

(in a low voice)
What the devil's this?

A DRUNKEN MAN
(near the entrance door)
I pay my taxes! So I'm entitled to express my opinion! And it's my absolute 'n unintelligible opinion that—
SEVERAL VOICES
Keep quiet there!
OTHERS
He's drunk! Throw him out!

(The DRUNK MAN *is removed.)*

DR. STOCKMANN
Have I the floor?
ASLAKSEN
(rings his bell)
Dr. Stockmann has the floor.
DR. STOCKMANN
A few days ago, if anyone had tried to gag me like this I'd have fought like a lion for my sacred human rights! But now that doesn't matter. Now I have more important things to talk about.

(The CROWD *moves closer around him.* MORTEN KIIL *can be seen among them.)*

DR. STOCKMANN
(continues)
I've been thinking a great deal these past few days. I've brooded so deeply that in the end my head began to spin—
MAYOR
(coughs)
Hm—!
DR. STOCKMANN
But then everything began to fall into place. I saw the whole picture of things quite clearly. And that's why I'm standing here this evening. I'm going to make a mighty revelation to you, my friends! I'm going to tell you about a discovery that is infinitely more important than the fiddling little fact that our water system is poisoned and our health baths sited above a cesspit!

MANY VOICES
(shout)
Leave the Baths alone! Don't talk about them! We won't listen!
DR. STOCKMANN
This great discovery that I have made during these last few days is that all our spiritual sources are poisoned, and that the whole of our vaunted social system is founded upon a cesspit of lies!
ASTONISHED VOICES
(mutter in low tones)
What's that? What did he say?
MAYOR
These are ridiculous insinuations—
ASLAKSEN
(his hand on the bell)
I must request the speaker to moderate his language.
DR. STOCKMANN
I was young when I left home, and distance, hunger, and memory threw, as it were, a brighter luster over this place and the people who dwelt here.

(Some applause and cheers are heard.)

DR. STOCKMANN
For years I lived far up in the north. As I wandered among those people who lived scattered over the mountains, I often thought it would have been better for those poor degraded creatures if they'd had a vet instead of a man like me!

(Murmurs)

BILLING
(puts down his pen)
By Jingo, I've never heard the like of that—!
HOVSTAD
That's a filthy slander against a worthy community!
DR. STOCKMANN
Wait a moment! I sat there brooding like a duck on an egg; and the chick I hatched was—the plan for these Baths. *(Clap-*

ping, and murmurs of approval) And then, my fellow-citizens, then I thought I had nothing left to wish for in this world. Then at long last fate smiled upon me and allowed me to return. No—I had one ambition left—a burning desire to work with all my heart and soul for the welfare of my home and my community.

MAYOR
(gazing into space)
You've a strange way of showing it!

DR. STOCKMANN
I went around here reveling blindly in my new-found happiness. But yesterday morning—no, it was the previous night, actually—my eyes were opened, and the first thing that greeted them was the stupendous imbecility of the authorities—

(Noise, shouting, and laughter. MRS. STOCKMANN *coughs loudly.)*

MAYOR
Mr. Chairman!

ASLAKSEN
(rings his bell)
As Chairman of this meeting, I—

DR. STOCKMANN
Oh, let's not start quibbling about words, Mr. Aslaksen. I only mean that I suddenly realized how really revolting our politicians had behaved down there at the Baths. I can't stand politicians! They're like goats in a plantation of young trees! They destroy everything! They block the way for a free man, however much he may twist and turn—and I'd like to see them rooted out and exterminated, like other vermin—

(Commotion in the hall)

MAYOR
Mr. Chairman, are such calumnies to be permitted?

ASLAKSEN
(his hand on the bell)
Dr. Stockmann—!

DR. STOCKMANN

I can't understand why I'd never had a proper look at these gentlemen before. I'd had a prime example right in front of my eyes all the time—my brother Peter—procrastinating and purblind—!

(Laughter, confusion, and whistling. MRS. STOCKMANN *sits and coughs.* ASLAKSEN *rings his bell loudly.)*

THE DRUNK MAN
(who has come back)
Are you referring to me? My name's Peterson, but don't you bloody well—

ANGRY VOICES
Throw that drunk out! Get rid of him!

(The DRUNK *is thrown out again.)*

MAYOR

Who was that person?

A BYSTANDER

I don't know, Your Worship.

ASLAKSEN

The man was obviously intoxicated with German beer. Continue, Doctor; but please try to use restraint!

DR. STOCKMANN

Well, my fellow-citizens, I won't say anything more about our politicians. If anyone imagines from what I've just said that I've come here this evening to immolate these gentlemen, he's wrong—quite wrong. For I cherish the comforting belief that these laggards, these survivors from a dying world, are studiously cutting their own throats. They need no doctor's help to hasten their demise. And anyway, it isn't they who are the chief danger to society! They aren't the ones who are most active in poisoning the sources of our spiritual life and contaminating the ground on which we tread! It isn't they who are the most dangerous enemies of truth and freedom in our society!

SHOUTS FROM ALL SIDES
Who, then? Who is? Name them!
DR. STOCKMANN
Don't worry, I'll name them! Because this is the great discovery I've made today! *(Raises his voice)* The most dangerous enemies of truth and freedom are the majority! Yes, the solid, liberal, bloody majority—they're the ones we have to fear! Now you know!

(Complete uproar. Nearly everyone is shouting, stamping, and whistling. Some of the older men exchange covert glances and seem to be enjoying the situation. MRS. STOCKMANN *gets up anxiously.* EILIF *and* MORTEN *go threateningly over to the schoolboys, who are making a commotion.* ASLAKSEN *rings his bell and calls for silence.* HOVSTAD *and* BILLING *are both talking, but neither can be heard. At last silence is restored.)*

ASLAKSEN
As Chairman I call upon the speaker to withdraw those mischievous observations.
DR. STOCKMANN
Never, Mr. Aslaksen! It's the majority in this community that is depriving me of my freedom and trying to forbid me to proclaim the truth.
HOVSTAD
The majority is always right.
BILLING
And speaks the truth, by Jingo!
DR. STOCKMANN
The majority is never right! Never, I tell you! That's one of those community lies that free, thinking men have got to rebel against! Who form the majority—in any country? The wise, or the fools? I think we'd all have to agree that the fools are in a terrifying, overwhelming majority all over the world! But in the name of God it can't be right that the fools should rule the wise! *(Uproar and shouting)* Yes, yes, you can shout me down! But you can't say I'm wrong! The majority has the power—unfortunately—but the majority is not right! The ones who are

right are a few isolated individuals like me! The minority is always right!

(Uproar again)

HOVSTAD

So Dr. Stockmann's turned aristocrat since the day before yesterday!

DR. STOCKMANN

I've already said I don't want to waste words on the little flock of short-winded sheep puffing along in the rear! Life has nothing exciting left to offer them. But I'm thinking of the few, the individuals among us, who have adopted the new, fresh, burgeoning truths as their watchword!

HOVSTAD

I see, so you've become a revolutionary!

DR. STOCKMANN

Yes, Mr. Hovstad, by God I have! I intend to start a revolution against the lie that truth is a monopoly of the majority! What are these truths to which the majority clings? They're the truths which are so old that they're on the way to becoming decrepit! But when a truth's as old as that, gentlemen, it's also well on the way to becoming a lie!

(Laughter and jeers)

DR. STOCKMANN

All these majority truths are like last year's salt pork; they're hams that have gone sour and green and tainted. And they're the cause of all the moral scurvy that's rotting our society!

ASLAKSEN

It seems to me that the honorable speaker has strayed somewhat from his text.

MAYOR

I warmly endorse the Chairman's observation.

DR. STOCKMANN

Oh, really, Peter, I think you must be quite mad! I'm sticking as close to my text as any man could! My whole point is precisely this, that it's the masses, the mob, this damned majority—they're the thing that's poisoning the sources of our spiritual life and contaminating the ground we walk on!

HOVSTAD

And the great progressive majority does this simply by being sensible enough to believe in these truths which are indisputable and generally acknowledged?

DR. STOCKMANN

Oh, my good Mr. Hovstad, don't talk to me about undisputed truths! There's only one indisputable truth. It is that no society can live a healthy life if it feeds on truths that are old and marrowless.

HOVSTAD

Instead of all this generalizing why don't you give us a few examples of these old and marrowless truths on which we're living?

(Murmurs of agreement from several quarters)

DR. STOCKMANN

Oh, I could reel you off a whole list of the beastly things; but to start with I'll limit myself to one "acknowledged" truth which is really a damned lie, but which Mr. Hovstad and the *People's Tribune* and all the hangers-on of the *People's Tribune* feed on all the same.

HOVSTAD

And that is—?

DR. STOCKMANN

That is the doctrine which you have inherited from your forefathers and which you continue thoughtlessly to proclaim far and wide—the doctrine that the plebs, the masses, the mob, are the living heart of the people—that they *are* the people—and that the common man, all those ignorant and incompetent millions, have the same right to sanction and condemn, to advise and to govern, as the few individuals who are intellectually aristocrats.

BILLING

Now, really, by Jingo—!

HOVSTAD

(simultaneously, shouts)

Mark that, fellow-citizens!

FURIOUS VOICES

Oh-ho, so we're not the people, aren't we? So it's only the aristocrats who have the right to rule?

A WORKER

Throw him out if he talks like that!

OTHERS

Chuck him through the door!

A CITIZEN

(shouts)

Blow that horn, Evensen!

(Loud horn-blasts are heard. Whistles and furious uproar in the hall)

DR. STOCKMANN

(when the noise has abated somewhat)

Can't you be reasonable? Can't you bear to hear the truth just for once? I'm not asking you all to agree with me immediately! But I did expect Mr. Hovstad would admit I was right once he'd given the matter a little thought. After all, Mr. Hovstad claims to be a freethinker—

SURPRISED VOICES

(murmur)

Freethinker, did he say! What? Is Mr. Hovstad a freethinker?

HOVSTAD

(shouts)

Prove that, Dr. Stockmann! When have I said so in print?

DR. STOCKMANN

(thinks)

No, by Jove, you're right! You've never had the guts to admit it publicly. Well, I won't corner you, Mr. Hovstad. Let me be the freethinker, then. I shall now prove to you that the masses are nothing but raw material which may, some day, be refined into individuals!

(Growls, laughter, and disturbances in the hall)

DR. STOCKMANN
Well, isn't that the way life works with the rest of creation? Look at the enormous difference there is between a breed of animal that's cultivated and one that is uncultivated! Consider dogs, with which we human beings have so much in common! Think first of a simple mongrel—one of those filthy, ragged, common curs that lope along the streets and defile the walls of our houses. And then put that mongrel next to a greyhound with a distinguished pedigree whose ancestors have been fed delicate meals for generations and have had the opportunity to listen to harmonious voices and music. Don't you think the brain of that greyhound is differently developed from that of the mongrel? You bet your life it is! It's the pups of these cultivated animals that trainers teach to perform the most amazing tricks. A common mongrel couldn't learn to do such things if you stood it on its head!

(Noise and laughter)

A CITIZEN
(shouts)
So we're dogs too now, are we?

ANOTHER
We're not animals, Doctor!

DR. STOCKMANN
Yes, my friend, we are animals! But there aren't many aristocratic animals among us. There's a terrifying difference between men who are greyhounds and men who are mongrels. And that's what's so absurd, that Mr. Hovstad is quite at one with me as long as we're talking about four-legged animals—

HOVSTAD
Well, they're only beasts.

DR. STOCKMANN

All right! But as soon as I start to apply the law to the ones who are two-legged, Mr. Hovstad balks at the consequences; he turns his whole philosophy upside down, and proclaims in the *People's Tribune* that the street mongrel is the champion of the menagerie. But that's how it always is, as long as a man remains possessed by this blind worship of the mob and hasn't worked his way out of spiritual bondage into aristocracy.

HOVSTAD

I don't want any kind of aristocracy. I come of simple peasant stock; and I'm proud that I have my roots deep down in the mob whom you deride.

MANY WORKERS

Hurrah for Hovstad! Hurrah, hurrah!

DR. STOCKMANN

The kind of mob I'm talking about isn't only to be found at the bottom of the barrel. It swarms and mills all around us, even among the high peaks of society. Just look at your own smug, sleek Mayor! My brother Peter's as good a mobster as ever walked in two shoes!

(Laughter and hisses)

MAYOR

I protest against these personal insinuations.

DR. STOCKMANN

(unperturbed)

And that isn't because he stems like me from a villainous old pirate from Pomerania or somewhere down there—for we do—!

MAYOR

It's absurd, it's a myth! I deny it!

DR. STOCKMANN

Because he thinks what his superiors think, and his opinions are the opinions he's heard them express. The men who do that are spiritually of the mob; and that's why my noble brother Peter is so frighteningly unaristocratic in all essentials—and consequently so terrified of all things liberal.

MAYOR

Mr. Chairman—!

HOVSTAD

So it's the aristocrats who are the liberals in this country? That really is a new discovery!

(Laughter among the crowd)

DR. STOCKMANN

Yes, that's part of my discovery too. And the reason is that liberality is almost exactly the same as morality. And I say it's quite indefensible of the *Tribune* day after day to proclaim the false gospel that the masses, the mob, the solid majority, have a monopoly on liberality and morality, and that vice and corruption and every kind of spiritual filth are a kind of pus that oozes out of culture just as all that beastly stuff in the Baths oozes down from the tanneries at Moellerdal!

(Confusion and interruptions)

DR. STOCKMANN

(unperturbed, laughs in his excitement)
And yet this same *People's Tribune* can preach that the masses and the mob must be elevated to a higher standard of living! Good God Almighty, if what the *People's Tribune* teaches were true, then to elevate the masses would simply be to start them on the road to ruin! But luckily the idea that culture demoralizes is an old inherited fairy tale. No, it's stupidity, poverty and foul living conditions that do the devil's work! In a house where the rooms aren't aired and the floors swept every day—my wife Catherine says they ought to be scrubbed too, but there can be two opinions on that—in such a house, I say, within two or three years people lose the capacity for moral thought and moral action. Lack of oxygen debilitates the conscience. And there's a shortage of oxygen in many, many houses in this town, from the sound of things, if the whole of this damned majority can be so devoid of conscience as to want to build the prosperity of their town on a quagmire of deceit and lies.

ASLAKSEN

You can't cast an accusation like that against a whole community!

A MAN

I appeal to the Chairman to order the speaker to stand down.

EXCITED VOICES

Yes, yes! That's right! Make him stand down!

DR. STOCKMANN

(explodes)

Then I'll shout the truth at every street corner! I'll write in the newspapers of other towns! The whole country shall be told what is happening here!

HOVSTAD

It sounds almost as though the Doctor wishes to destroy this town.

DR. STOCKMANN

Yes, I love this town where I was born so dearly that I would rather destroy it than see it flourish because of a lie!

ASLAKSEN

Those are strong words.

(Shouts and whistling. MRS. STOCKMANN *coughs in vain; the* DOCTOR *no longer hears her.)*

HOVSTAD

(shouts through the uproar)

The man who can want to destroy a whole community must be a public enemy!

DR. STOCKMANN

(with increasing excitement)

A community that lives on lies deserves to be destroyed! I say that the town that houses such a community should be leveled to the ground! All those who live by lies ought to be exterminated like vermin! You will end by contaminating the entire country! You will bring it to the pass where the whole land will deserve to be laid waste! And if things go that far, then I say with all my heart: "Let the whole land be laid waste! Let the whole people be exterminated!"

A MAN

That's talking like an enemy of the people!

BILLING

There speaks the voice of the people, by Jingo!

THE WHOLE CROWD
(screams)
Yes, yes, yes! He's an enemy of the people! He hates his country! He hates the people!

ASLAKSEN
Both as a citizen and as a human being I am deeply shocked by what I have had to hear. Dr. Stockmann has shown himself in his true colors—in a manner of which I should never have dreamed him capable. I fear I must support the view expressed a moment ago by respected citizens; and I move that we embody this opinion in a resolution. I suggest the following: "This meeting declares that it regards the medical officer at the Baths, Dr. Thomas Stockmann, an enemy of the people."

(Deafening cheers and applause. Many of the CROWD *form a circle around* DR. STOCKMANN *and whistle at him.* MRS. STOCKMANN *and* PETRA *have got to their feet.* MORTEN *and* EILIF *are fighting with the other* SCHOOLBOYS, *who have been whistling too. Some* ADULTS *part them.)*

DR. STOCKMANN
(to the people who have been whistling)
You fools! I tell you—!

ASLAKSEN
(rings his bell)
The Doctor no longer has the floor. A formal ballot will take place; but to protect personal feelings the voting should be done in writing and anonymously. Have you any clean paper, Mr. Billing?

BILLING
I've both blue and white here—

ASLAKSEN
(descends from the dais)
Good, that'll save time. Tear it into squares; like that, yes. *(To the* CROWD*)* Blue means no; white means yes. I'll collect the votes myself.

(The MAYOR *leaves the hall.* ASLAKSEN *and a couple of other citizens go around the crowd with the pieces of paper in hats.)*

1ST CITIZEN

(*to* HOVSTAD)

What's come over the Doctor? What's one to think?

HOVSTAD

You know how impulsive he is.

2ND CITIZEN

(*to* BILLING)

I say, you're a regular visitor in that house. Have you ever noticed—does the fellow drink?

BILLING

I don't know what to reply, by Jingo! There's always toddy on the table when anyone comes.

3RD CITIZEN

I think he just goes off his head now and then.

1ST CITIZEN

Yes, don't they say there's madness in the family?

BILLING

Could be.

4TH CITIZEN

No, it's pure spite. Wants revenge for something or other.

BILLING

He did say something the other day about a rise in salary. But he didn't get it.

ALL THE MEN

(*with one voice*)

Ah, that explains it!

THE DRUNK MAN

(*in the thick of the crowd*)

I want a blue one! And I want a white one too!

SHOUTS

There's the drunk man again! Throw him out!

MORTEN KIIL

(*comes up to* DR. STOCKMANN)

Well, Stockmann, you see now what happens once you start playing monkey tricks?

DR. STOCKMANN

I have done my duty.

MORTEN KIIL

What was that you were saying about the tanneries at Moellerdal?

DR. STOCKMANN
You heard. I said that that's where all the filth comes from.
MORTEN KIIL
From my tannery too?
DR. STOCKMANN
I'm afraid your tannery is the worst of all.
MORTEN KIIL
Are you going to print that in the papers?
DR. STOCKMANN
I shall hide nothing.
MORTEN KIIL
That'll cost you dear, Stockmann. *(Goes)*
A FAT MAN
(goes across to HORSTER, *without greeting the ladies)*
Well, Captain, so you lend your house to enemies of the people?
HORSTER
I reckon I can do what I like with my own property.
FAT MAN
Then you won't object if I do the same with mine?
HORSTER
What do you mean?
FAT MAN
You'll hear from me tomorrow. *(Turns and goes.)*
PETRA
Isn't that the man who owns your ship, Captain Horster?
HORSTER
Yes.
ASLAKSEN
(with the voting papers in his hand, steps up on to the dais and rings his bell)
Gentlemen, allow me to inform you of the result. With only a single dissenting vote—
A YOUNG MAN
That's the drunk man!
ASLAKSEN
With only one dissenting vote, and that of a man not sober, this gathering of citizens unanimously declares the medical officer of the Baths, Dr. Thomas Stockmann, an enemy of the people! *(Shouts and gestures of approval)* Long live our ancient

and noble community! *(More cheers)* Long live our worthy and active Mayor, who has so loyally ignored the ties of blood! *(Cheers)* The meeting is closed. *(He steps down.)*

BILLING

Three cheers for the Chairman!

WHOLE CROWD

Hurrah for Mr. Aslaksen! Hurrah! Hurrah!

DR. STOCKMANN

My hat and coat, Petra. Captain, have you room in your ship for passengers to the new world?

HORSTER

For you and yours, Doctor, I'll make room.

DR. STOCKMANN

(as PETRA *helps him on with coat)*

Good! Come, Catherine! Come, boys! *(He takes his wife by the arm.)*

MRS. STOCKMANN

(quietly)

Thomas, dear, let's go out the back way.

DR. STOCKMANN

No back way for me, Catherine! *(Raises his voice.)* You'll hear from your enemy of the people before he shakes the dust of this town from his feet! I'm not so forgiving as a certain person. I don't say, "I forgive ye, for ye know not what ye do!"

ASLAKSEN

(shouts)

That comparison's a blasphemy, Dr. Stockmann!

BILLING

I'll say it is, by G—! What a dreadful thing for respectable people to hear!

A COARSE VOICE

He's threatening us now!

EXCITED SHOUTS

Let's break the windows! Throw him in the fjord!

A MAN IN THE CROWD

Blow your horn, Evensen! *(He imitates the sound of the horn twice.)*

(Blasts on the horn, whistles, and wild cries. The DOCTOR *goes*

with his family towards the door. HORSTER *clears a way for them.)*

THE WHOLE CROWD
(howling after them as they go)
Enemy of the people! Enemy of the people! Enemy of the people!

BILLING
(as he puts his notes in order)
I'm damned if I'll drink toddy with them tonight, by Jingo!

(THE CROWD *swarms towards the door. The shouting spreads outside. From the street can be heard the cry: "Enemy of the people! Enemy of the people! Enemy of the people!"*)

(Curtain)

ACT 5

DR. STOCKMANN'S *study. Bookshelves and cupboards containing medicine bottles, along the walls. In the background is the exit to the hall; downstage left is the door to the dining room. In the wall on the right are two windows, all the panes of which are smashed. In the middle of the room stands the* DOCTOR'S *desk, covered with books and papers. The room is in disorder. It is morning.*

DR. STOCKMANN, *in dressing gown and slippers and with his smoking cap on his head, is crouched down raking under one of the cupboards with an umbrella. At length he pulls out a stone.*

DR. STOCKMANN
(speaks through the open door into the living room)
Catherine, I've found another!

MRS. STOCKMANN
(from the living room)
Oh, you'll find a lot more yet.

DR. STOCKMANN

(puts the stone among a heap of others on the table)

I shall keep these stones as sacred relics. Eilif and Morten shall see them every day, and when they're grown up they shall inherit them from me. *(Rakes under a bookshelf.)* Hasn't—what the devil's her name—you know, the maid—hasn't she gone for the glazier yet?

MRS. STOCKMANN

(enters)

He said he didn't know if he'd be able to come today.

DR. STOCKMANN

The truth is, he doesn't dare.

MRS. STOCKMANN

Yes, Randine says he daren't because of the neighbors. *(Speaks into the living room.)* What is it, Randine? Very well. *(Goes inside and returns immediately.)* Here's a letter for you, Thomas.

DR. STOCKMANN

Give it to me. *(Opens it and reads.)* I see.

MRS. STOCKMANN

Who's it from?

DR. STOCKMANN

The landlord. He's giving us notice to quit.

MRS. STOCKMANN

Is he really? He seems such a decent man—

DR. STOCKMANN

(looks at the letter)

He daren't do otherwise, he says. He's very sorry, but he daren't do otherwise—his fellow-citizens—respect for public opinion—certain obligation—dare not offend certain persons of influence—

MRS. STOCKMANN

There, Thomas, you see.

DR. STOCKMANN

Yes, yes, I see. They're all cowards in this town. None of them dares do anything for fear of the others. *(Throws the letter on the table.)* But we don't have to worry, Catherine. We're off to the new world now—

MRS. STOCKMANN

Thomas, do you really think it's a good idea, this going away?

DR. STOCKMANN

Am I to stay here when they've pilloried me as an enemy of the people, branded me, broken my windows? And just look at this, Catherine! They've torn my trousers, too!

MRS. STOCKMANN

Oh, no! And they're your best!

DR. STOCKMANN

One should never wear one's best trousers when one goes out to fight for freedom and truth. Oh, I don't mind so much about the trousers—you can always patch them up for me. It's the fact that these riff-raff dare to threaten me as though they were my equals—that's the thing I can't damned well stomach!

MRS. STOCKMANN

Yes, Thomas, they've behaved shockingly to you in this town. But does that mean we have to leave the country?

DR. STOCKMANN

Do you think the rabble aren't just as insolent in other towns? Oh, yes, Catherine. There isn't twopence to choose between them. To hell with the curs, let them yelp. That's not the worst. The worst is that throughout this country all the people are just party slaves. Mind you, they're probably not much better in America. The majority's rampant there too, and liberal public opinion and all the rest of the rubbish. But the context is larger there, you see. They may kill you, but they won't torture you slowly; they don't pin a free man in a vice as they do here. And if you want to, you can stay independent outside it all. (*Walks across the room.*) If only I knew of some primeval forest or a little South Sea island that was going cheap—

MRS. STOCKMANN

But what about the boys, Thomas?

DR. STOCKMANN

(*stops*)

How extraordinary you are, Catherine! Would you rather they grew up in a society like this? You saw for yourself last night that half the people are raving lunatics; and if the other half haven't lost their wits it's only because they're beasts that don't have any wits to lose.

MRS. STOCKMANN

But, Thomas dear, you're so careless about what you say.

DR. STOCKMANN

What! Don't I tell them the truth? Don't they turn every idea upside down? Don't they merge right and wrong so that they can't tell the difference? Don't they call everything a lie which I know to be true? But the maddest thing of all is that you get grown men of liberal inclinations getting together in groups and convincing themselves and other people that they're progressive thinkers! Did you ever hear the like, Catherine?

MRS. STOCKMANN

Yes, yes, it's all very stupid, but—

(PETRA *enters from the living room.*)

MRS. STOCKMANN

Are you back from school already?

PETRA

I've got the sack.

MRS. STOCKMANN

The sack?

DR. STOCKMANN

You too!

PETRA

Mrs. Busk gave me notice. So I thought I'd better leave at once.

DR. STOCKMANN

Quite right, my heaven!

MRS. STOCKMANN

Who'd have thought Mrs. Busk was such a nasty woman?

PETRA

Oh, mother, she's not nasty. It was quite obvious she didn't like doing it. But she said she dared not do otherwise. So I got the sack.

DR. STOCKMANN

(*laughs and rubs his hands*)

Dared not do otherwise! She too! Oh, that's splendid!

MRS. STOCKMANN

Well, after those dreadful scenes last night, you can't—

PETRA

It wasn't only that. Listen to this, father.

DR. STOCKMANN

Yes?

PETRA

Mrs. Busk showed me no less than three letters she'd received this morning—

DR. STOCKMANN

Anonymous, of course?

PETRA

Yes.

DR. STOCKMANN

They daren't even sign their names, Catherine.

PETRA

Two of them stated that a gentleman who frequents this house announced in the Club last night that I held excessively free views on various subjects—

DR. STOCKMANN

I hope you didn't deny that.

PETRA

Not on your life! Mrs. Busk expresses pretty free views herself when we're alone together; but now that this has come out about me, she didn't dare to keep me.

MRS. STOCKMANN

Fancy—"a gentleman who frequents this house"! You see what thanks you get for your hospitality, Thomas!

DR. STOCKMANN

We won't go on living in this jungle any longer. Pack the bags as quickly as you can, Catherine. The sooner we get away from here, the better.

MRS. STOCKMANN

Hush—I think there's someone in the hall. Go and look, Petra.

PETRA

(opens the door)

Oh, is it you, Captain Horster? Please come in.

HORSTER

(from the hall)

Good morning. I felt I had to come along and see how everything was.

DR. STOCKMANN

(shakes his hand)

Thank you. It's extremely good of you.

MRS. STOCKMANN

And thank you for seeing us safely back last night, Captain Horster.

PETRA

How did you manage to get home again?

HORSTER

Oh, I managed; I'm pretty strong, and those fellows bark worse than they bite.

DR. STOCKMANN

Yes, isn't it amazing what wretched cowards they are! Come here, I'll show you something. Look, here are all the stones they threw through our windows. Just look at them! Upon my soul, there aren't more than two decent rocks in the whole lot; the others are just pebbles—mere gravel! And yet they stood out there howling, and swearing they'd beat the life out of me—but action—action—no, you won't see much of that in this town.

HORSTER

Just as well for you on this occasion, Doctor.

DR. STOCKMANN

Of course! But it annoys me all the same; for if it ever comes to a serious fight, in defense of our country, you'll see, Captain Horster—public opinion'll be for safety first, and this sacred majority'll run for their lives like a flock of sheep. That's what's so sad—it really hurts me to think of it—no, damn it, I'm just being stupid! They've said I'm an enemy of the people, so let me be an enemy of the people!

MRS. STOCKMANN

You'll never be that, Thomas.

DR. STOCKMANN

Don't be so sure, Catherine. An ugly word can be like the scratch of a needle on the lung. And that damned phrase—I can't forget it—it's got stuck down here in the pit of my stomach, and it's lying there chafing and corroding me like an acid. And there's no magnesia that will neutralize that.

PETRA

You must just laugh at them, Father.

HORSTER

People will think differently of you in time, Doctor.

MRS. STOCKMANN

Yes, Thomas, that's as sure as you're standing here.

DR. STOCKMANN

Perhaps, when it's too late. Well, it's their funeral! Let them live like beasts; they'll be sorry they drove a patriot into exile. When do you sail, Captain Horster.

HORSTER

Hm—that was what I came to talk to you about, as a matter of fact—

DR. STOCKMANN

Why, has something happened to the ship?

HORSTER

No. It's just that I shan't be going with her.

PETRA

They surely haven't given you the sack?

HORSTER
(smiles)
Indeed they have!

PETRA

You, too!

MRS. STOCKMANN

There, Thomas, you see!

DR. STOCKMANN

And just because I spoke the truth! Oh, if I'd ever dreamed that such a thing could happen—

HORSTER

Don't worry about me. I'll find a job with a company somewhere else.

DR. STOCKMANN

But that boss of yours is a rich man, he's completely independent! Oh, damn, damn!

HORSTER

He's fair enough in the ordinary way. He said himself, he'd have liked to have kept me, if only he'd dared—

DR. STOCKMANN
(laughs)
But he didn't dare! No, of course not!

HORSTER

It isn't so easy, he said, when you belong to a party—

DR. STOCKMANN

That's the truest word he ever uttered! A party is like a mincing machine. It grinds everyone's brains into a pulp, and all you're left with is human sausages, all identical!

MRS. STOCKMANN

Thomas, really!

PETRA

(to HORSTER*)*

If only you hadn't seen us home, this might never have happened.

HORSTER

I don't regret it.

PETRA

(holds out her hand)

Thank you!

HORSTER

(to DR. STOCKMANN*)*

What I wanted to say was, if you still want to go, I have thought of another way—

DR. STOCKMANN

Fine! As long as we can get away quickly—

MRS. STOCKMANN

Hush—wasn't that a knock at the door?

PETRA

I think it's Uncle.

DR. STOCKMANN

Aha! *(Shouts.)* Come in!

MRS. STOCKMANN

Now, Thomas dear, do promise me—

(The MAYOR *enters from the hall.)*

MAYOR

(in the doorway)

Oh, you're engaged. I'll come back later—

DR. STOCKMANN

No, no. Please come in.

MAYOR

I wanted to speak to you privately.

MRS. STOCKMANN
We'll go into the living room.

HORSTER
And I'll come back later.

DR. STOCKMANN
No, you go in too. I want to know more about that—

HORSTER
Right, I'll wait, then.

(He goes with MRS. STOCKMANN *and* PETRA *into the living room. The* MAYOR *says nothing but glances at the windows.)*

DR. STOCKMANN
Do you find it draughty here today? Put your hat on.

MAYOR
Thank you, if I may. *(Does so.)* I think I caught a cold last night. I stood there shivering—

DR. STOCKMANN
Really? I found it warm enough.

MAYOR
I regret that it didn't lie within my power to prevent those nocturnal extravagances.

DR. STOCKMANN
Did you come out here to tell me that?

MAYOR
(takes out a large letter)
I have this document for you, from the Directors of the Baths.

DR. STOCKMANN
Am I dismissed?

MAYOR
From the date of writing. *(Puts the letter on the table.)* It distresses us; but, frankly, we had no choice. Public opinion being what it is, we didn't dare—

DR. STOCKMANN
(smiles)
Didn't dare? I've heard that word before today.

MAYOR
I beg you to realize your position. From now on you can't reckon on having any practice whatever in this town.

DR. STOCKMANN

The devil with the practice! But what makes you so sure?

MAYOR

The Property Owners' Association has drawn up a round robin which it is sending from house to house. All respectable citizens are being urged not to employ you; and I'll guarantee that not a single householder will dare refuse to sign it. They just won't dare.

DR. STOCKMANN

Yes, yes, I don't doubt that. But what then?

MAYOR

My advice would be that you should leave town for a while—

DR. STOCKMANN

Yes, I'm thinking of doing that.

MAYOR

Good. Then, when you've had six months to think the matter over, you might, after mature consideration, possibly reconcile yourself to issuing a short statement admitting your error and expressing your regret—

DR. STOCKMANN

And then, you mean, I might get my job back?

MAYOR

It's not unthinkable.

DR. STOCKMANN

But what about public opinion? You daren't offend that.

MAYOR

Public opinion is very fickle. And, quite frankly, it's important to us that you should publish some such admission.

DR. STOCKMANN

Yes, that'd make you smack your lips, wouldn't it? But, damn it, haven't I told you already what I think of that kind of chicanery?

MAYOR

Your position was somewhat stronger then. You had reason to suppose that the whole town was behind you—

DR. STOCKMANN

And now they're rubbing my face in the dirt! *(Flares up.)* I don't care if I've got the Devil himself and his great-grandmother on my back! Never, I tell you, never!

MAYOR

A man with a family has no right to act as you're doing. You have no right, Thomas!

DR. STOCKMANN

No right! There's only one thing in the world that a free man has no right to do! Do you know what that is?

MAYOR

No.

DR. STOCKMANN

No, of course you don't. But I'll tell you. A free man has no right to befoul himself like a beast. He has no right to get himself into the position where he feels the need to spit in his own face!

MAYOR

That all sounds very plausible—if only there didn't happen to exist another explanation for your stubbornness. But there does.

DR. STOCKMANN

What do you mean by that?

MAYOR

You know perfectly well. But as your brother, and as a man of the world, I would advise you not to put too much trust in expectations that might so easily not be fulfilled.

DR. STOCKMANN

What on earth are you talking about?

MAYOR

Do you seriously expect me to believe that you don't know of the arrangements that Morten Kiil has made in his will?

DR. STOCKMANN

I know that what little he has is to go to a home for retired artisans. But what's that got to do with me?

MAYOR

To begin with, it's not so little. Morten Kiil is a pretty wealthy man.

DR. STOCKMANN

I had no idea—!

MAYOR

Hm—hadn't you really? Then I suppose you also have no idea that a considerable proportion of his money is earmarked for your children, and that you and your wife will be able to enjoy the interest for the rest of your lives. Hasn't he told you?

DR. STOCKMANN

Indeed he has not! On the contrary, he's done nothing but complain about how disgracefully overtaxed he is. But are you quite sure of this, Peter?

MAYOR

I have it from an impeccable source.

DR. STOCKMANN

But, good heavens—that means Catherine's future is secured—and the children's, too! I say, I must tell her! *(Shouts.)* Catherine, Catherine!

MAYOR

(holds him back)
Hush, don't say anything yet.

MRS. STOCKMANN

(opens the door)
What is it?

DR. STOCKMANN

Nothing, my dear. Go back in again.

(MRS. STOCKMANN closes the door.)

DR. STOCKMANN

(paces up and down the room)
Their future secured! I can't believe it! All of them—and for life! Oh, it's a wonderful feeling to know that one's future is secured. Forever!

MAYOR

But that's just what it isn't. Morten Kiil can revoke that will any day or hour that he chooses.

DR. STOCKMANN

But he won't, my dear Peter. The Badger's much too delighted at the embarrassment I've caused to you and your worthy friends.

MAYOR

(starts and looks searchingly at him)
Aha! So that's the explanation!

DR. STOCKMANN

What do you mean?

MAYOR

This whole thing's been a conspiracy. These violent and unprincipled accusations which you've leveled against the authorities in the name of truth were simply your price for being remembered in that vindictive old idiot's will.

DR. STOCKMANN

(almost speechless)

Peter, you are the worst scoundrel I have ever met in all my life!

MAYOR

Things are finished between us now. Your dismissal is final. Now we have a weapon against you. *(He goes.)*

DR. STOCKMANN

The filthy—damn, damn! *(Shouts.)* Catherine! Scrub the floors behind him! Tell her to bring in a bucket—that girl—what the devil's her name?—the one who's always got a dirty nose—

MRS. STOCKMANN

(in the doorway to the living room)

Hush, hush, Thomas, please!

PETRA

(also in the doorway)

Father, Grandfather's here and says, can he speak to you privately?

DR. STOCKMANN

Yes, of course. *(At the door)* Come in, Father.

(MORTEN KIIL *comes in.* DR. STOCKMANN *closes the door behind him.*)

DR. STOCKMANN

Well, what is it? Sit down.

MORTEN KIIL

No, I won't sit. *(Looks around.)* Nice and cosy it looks here today, Stockmann.

DR. STOCKMANN

Yes, doesn't it?

MORTEN KIIL

Very nice. And fresh air too! You've got enough of that oxygen you were talking about last night! Your conscience feels pretty good today, I suppose?

DR. STOCKMANN

Yes, it does.

MORTEN KIIL

I thought it would. *(Thumps himself on the breast.)* But do you know what *I've* got here?

DR. STOCKMANN

A good conscience too, I hope.

MORTEN KIIL

(snorts)

No, something better than that.

(Takes out a thick pocketbook, opens it and shows a wad of papers.)

DR. STOCKMANN

(looks at him in amazement)

Shares in the Baths?

MORTEN KIIL

They weren't hard to come by today.

DR. STOCKMANN

You mean you've been out and bought—?

MORTEN KIIL

As many as I could afford.

DR. STOCKMANN

But, my dear Mr. Kiil—the state those Baths are in now, you—!

MORTEN KIIL

If you act like a sensible man, you'll soon have them on their feet again.

DR. STOCKMANN

You see for yourself I'm doing all I can, but—! The people of this town are quite mad!

MORTEN KIIL

You said last night that the worst of the filth comes from my tannery. But if that were true, then my grandfather and my father before me, and I myself, have been polluting this town for generations like three angels of death. Do you think I'm going to let an imputation like that hang over my head?

DR. STOCKMANN

I'm afraid it looks as though you'll have to.

MORTEN KIIL

No, thank you! I value my name and reputation. People call

me "the Badger," I'm told. A badger's a dirty beast, isn't it? Well, I'll prove them wrong. I intend to live and die clean.

DR. STOCKMANN

And how are you going to go about that?

MORTEN KIIL

You're going to make me clean, Stockmann.

DR. STOCKMANN

I!

MORTEN KIIL

Do you know what money I've used to buy these shares with? No, you can't; but I'll tell you. It's the money Catherine and Petra and the boys are going to inherit when I'm gone. I've managed to put a little aside, you see.

DR. STOCKMANN

(flares up)

You mean you've spent Catherine's money on this?

MORTEN KIIL

Yes, now it's all invested in the Baths. So now we'll see if you're really as daft as you pretend, Stockmann. Every time you say there's vermin coming out of my tannery, it'll be as though you were cutting a pound of flesh from your wife's body, and Petra's and the children. But no self-respecting husband and father would do such a thing—unless he really was mad.

DR. STOCKMANN

(walks up and down)

Yes, but I *am* mad! I *am* mad!

MORTEN KIIL

You can't be that mad when your wife and children are at stake.

DR. STOCKMANN

(stops in front of him)

Why couldn't you have come and spoken to me before you went and bought all this waste paper?

MORTEN KIIL

Actions speak louder than words.

DR. STOCKMANN

(wanders around restlessly)

If only I weren't so sure—! But I *know* I'm right!

MORTEN KIIL

(weighs the pocketbook in his hand)

If you persist in this lunacy, these shares won't be worth much, you know.

(He puts the pocketbook back in his pocket.)

DR. STOCKMANN

But, damn it, science must be able to find some way. A preventative; or a purifier or something—

MORTEN KIIL

You mean something to kill these vermin?

DR. STOCKMANN

Yes, or render them harmless.

MORTEN KIIL

Couldn't you try rat poison?

DR. STOCKMANN

Oh, no, no! But everyone keeps saying it's just a fancy of mine. All right, then, let them have it that way. Those ignorant, narrow-minded curs denounced me as an enemy of the people, didn't they? And all but tore the clothes off my back!

MORTEN KIIL

And smashed your windows.

DR. STOCKMANN

Yes. And then this question of my duty towards my family. I must talk to Catherine. She knows about these things.

MORTEN KIIL

That's a good idea. She's a sensible woman. Follow her advice.

DR. STOCKMANN

(turns on him)

Why did you have to do such a stupid thing? Hazard Catherine's money, and put me in this frightful predicament! When I look at you, I feel as though I was looking at the Devil himself—

MORTEN KIIL

Then I'd best be off. But I want your answer by two o'clock. If it's no, I'm giving these shares to the Old Folks Home—and I'll do it today.

DR. STOCKMANN

And what will Catherine get then?

MORTEN KIIL
   Not a farthing.

   (*The door to the hall is opened.* HOVSTAD *and* ASLAKSEN *are seen there.*)

MORTEN KIIL
   Well! Look whom we have here!
DR. STOCKMANN
   (*stares at them*)
   What the devil—? Do you two still dare to visit me?
HOVSTAD
   Indeed we do.
ASLAKSEN
   We've something we want to talk to you about.
MORTEN KIIL
   (*whispers*)
   Yes or no—by two o'clock!
ASLAKSEN
   (*glances at* HOVSTAD)
   Aha!

   (MORTEN KIIL *goes.*)

DR. STOCKMANN
   Well, what do you want? Make it short.
HOVSTAD
   I dare say you don't feel too kindly towards us in view of the stand we took at last night's meeting—
DR. STOCKMANN
   Stand, you call it! A fine stand indeed! You just lay down like a couple of old women! Damn the pair of you!
HOVSTAD
   Call it what you like; we *couldn't* do otherwise.
DR. STOCKMANN
   You *dared* not do otherwise! Isn't that what you mean?
HOVSTAD
   If you wish.

ASLAKSEN

But why didn't you tip us off? You only needed to drop a hint to Mr. Hovstad or me.

DR. STOCKMANN

Hint? About what?

ASLAKSEN

Why you were doing it.

DR. STOCKMANN

I don't understand.

ASLAKSEN

(nods conspiratorially)

Oh, yes you do, Dr. Stockmann.

HOVSTAD

There's no need to keep it secret any longer.

DR. STOCKMANN

(looks from one to the other)

What the devil—?

ASLAKSEN

Forgive the question, but isn't your father-in-law going 'round the town buying up all the shares in the Baths?

DR. STOCKMANN

He has bought some today. But—

ASLAKSEN

You'd have done wiser to employ someone else. Someone not quite so close to you.

HOVSTAD

And you shouldn't have done all this under your own name. Nobody need have known that the attack on the Baths came from you. You ought to have taken me into your confidence, Dr. Stockmann.

DR. STOCKMANN

(stares straight in front of him. A light seems to dawn on him, and he says as though thunderstruck:)

Is it conceivable? Could such a thing really be *done?*

ASLAKSEN

(smiles)

Apparently. But it ought to be done with a certain subtlety, you know.

HOVSTAD

And there ought to be more than one person in on it. A man doesn't have so much responsibility to bear if he's in partnership.

DR. STOCKMANN

(composedly)

In brief, gentlemen, what do you want?

ASLAKSEN

Mr. Hovstad can explain better than—

HOVSTAD

No, you tell him, Aslaksen.

ASLAKSEN

Well, it's just this really, that now we know how the land lies, we think we might venture to put the *People's Tribune* at your disposal.

DR. STOCKMANN

You think you dare risk it? But what about public opinion? Aren't you afraid we might cause a storm?

HOVSTAD

We shall have to ride that storm.

ASLAKSEN

But you'll have to be quick on the trigger, Doctor. As soon as your campaign has done its job—

DR. STOCKMANN

As soon as my father-in-law and I have got all the shares cheaply, you mean?

HOVSTAD

It is of course principally in the cause of science that you are seeking to gain control of the Baths.

DR. STOCKMANN

Of course. It was in the cause of science that I got the old Badger to come in with me on this. And then we'll tinker a bit with the water system and do a little digging on the beach, and it won't cost the ratepayers half a crown. I think we'll get away with it, don't you? Eh?

HOVSTAD

I think so—if you have the *People's Tribune* behind you.

ASLAKSEN

In a free society the press is a power to be feared, Doctor.

DR. STOCKMANN

Quite. And public opinion, too. Mr. Aslaksen, you'll answer for the Property Owners' Association?

ASLAKSEN

The Property Owners' Association and the Temperance Society. Have no fear.

DR. STOCKMANN

But, gentlemen—I blush to mention the matter, but—what consideration—er—

HOVSTAD

Well, of course we'd like to help you absolutely gratis. But the *People's Tribune* is going through an awkward period; we're having an uphill struggle, and I'm very reluctant to wind things up just now, when there are such splendid causes that need our support.

DR. STOCKMANN

Of course. That'd be a bitter pill for a friend of the people like you to have to swallow. *(Flares up.)* But I—I am an enemy of the people! *(Strides around the room.)* Where's that stick of mine? Where the devil did I put my stick?

HOVSTAD

What do you mean?

ASLAKSEN

You surely aren't thinking of—?

DR. STOCKMANN

(stops)

And suppose I don't give you a penny of my shares? We rich men are pretty close with our money, you must remember.

HOVSTAD

And *you* must remember that this little business of the shares would bear more than one interpretation.

DR. STOCKMANN

Yes, that'd be right up your street, wouldn't it? If I don't come to the aid of the *People's Tribune*, you'll misrepresent my motives—you'll start a witch-hunt, drive me to ground, and throttle the life out of me as a hound throttles a hare!

HOVSTAD

That's the law of nature. Every animal has to fight for survival, you know.

ASLAKSEN

Bread doesn't grow on trees. You must take it where you can find it.

DR. STOCKMANN

Then see if you can find any in the gutter! *(Strides around the room.)* Now, by heaven, we'll see which is the strongest animal of us three! *(Finds his umbrella.)* Aha! *(Swings it.)* Now—!

HOVSTAD

You wouldn't dare to assault us!

ASLAKSEN

Be careful with that umbrella!

DR. STOCKMANN

Out of the window with you, Mr. Hovstad!

HOVSTAD

(at the doorway to the hall)
Are you out of your mind?

DR. STOCKMANN

Get through that window, Mr. Aslaksen! Jump I tell you! Don't dally!

ASLAKSEN

(runs round the desk)
Doctor, Doctor, restrain yourself! I'm a weak man—I can't stand excitement—! *(Screams.)* Help, help!

(MRS. STOCKMANN, PETRA, *and* CAPTAIN HORSTER *enter from the living room.*)

MRS. STOCKMANN

In heaven's name, Thomas, what's going on here?

DR. STOCKMANN

(brandishes the umbrella)
Jump out, I tell you! Down into the gutter!

HOVSTAD

An unprovoked assault! I call you to witness, Captain Horster! *(Runs out through the hall.)*

MRS. STOCKMANN

(holds the DOCTOR*)*
Thomas, for mercy's sake, control yourself!

ASLAKSEN

(desperate)

Restraint, Doctor! Restr— oh, dear! *(Scampers out through the living room.)*

DR. STOCKMANN

(throws away the umbrella)

Damn it, they got away after all!

MRS. STOCKMANN

But what did they want?

DR. STOCKMANN

I'll tell you later. I've other things to think about just now. *(Goes to the table and writes on a visiting card.)* Look at this, Catherine. What do you see here?

MRS. STOCKMANN

"No, no, no"—what does that mean?

DR. STOCKMANN

I'll explain that later, too. *(Holds out the card.)* Here, Petra, tell that smutty-nosed girl to run up to the Badger with this as quickly as she can. Hurry!

(PETRA goes out with the card through the hall.)

DR. STOCKMANN

If I haven't had all the Devil's messengers after me today, I really don't know who's left! But now I'll sharpen my pen against them until it's like a dagger! I'll dip it in gall and venom! I'll fling my inkstand against their stupid skulls!

MRS. STOCKMANN

But Thomas, we're leaving!

(PETRA returns.)

DR. STOCKMANN

Well?

PETRA

She's taken it.

DR. STOCKMANN

Good! Leaving, did you say? No, by God, we're not! We're staying here, Catherine!

PETRA

Staying?

MRS. STOCKMANN

In this town?

DR. STOCKMANN

Yes! This is the chosen battlefield, and it's here that the battle must be fought! And it's here that I shall win! As soon as you've sewn up those trousers of mine, I'll go into town and look for a house. We've got to have a roof over our heads when winter comes.

HORSTER

I can let you have my house.

DR. STOCKMANN

Would you?

HORSTER

Of course. I've plenty of rooms, and I'm hardly ever there.

MRS. STOCKMANN

Oh, Captain Horster, how kind of you!

PETRA

Thank you!

DR. STOCKMANN

(presses his hand)

Thank you, thank you! Well, that problem's behind us! I'll start my campaign this very day! Oh, Catherine, there's so much to be done! But luckily I'll be able to devote my whole time to it. Look at this. I've been sacked from the Baths—

MRS. STOCKMANN

(sighs)

Ah, well. I was expecting that.

DR. STOCKMANN

And they want to take away my practice too! All right, let them! At least I'll keep my poor patients—they're the ones who can't pay—well, heaven knows they're the ones who need me most. But, by God, they'll have to listen to me! I'll preach to them morning, noon, and night.

MRS. STOCKMANN

Oh, Thomas, Thomas! Surely you've seen what good preaching does!

DR. STOCKMANN

You really are absurd, Catherine! Am I to allow myself to be chased from the field by public opinion, and the majority, and such fiddle faddle? No, thank you! What I want is so simple and straightforward and easy! I only want to knock it into the heads of these curs that the liberals are the most insidious enemies of freedom—that party programs strangle every new truth that deserves to live—and that expediency and self-interest turn morality and justice upside down, so that in the end life here becomes intolerable. Well, Captain Horster, don't you think I ought to be able to get people to grasp that?

HORSTER

I dare say. I don't really understand these things.

DR. STOCKMANN

Well, you see, the real point is this! It's the party bosses—they're the ones who've got to be rooted out! A party boss is like a hungry wolf—he needs a certain number of baby lambs to devour every year if he is to survive. Look at Hovstad and Aslaksen! How many innocent and vital young idealists have they knocked on the head! Or else they mangle and maul them till they're fit for nothing but to be property owners or subscribers to the *People's Tribune!* (*Half sits on the table.*) Come here, Catherine! Look how beautifully the sun's shining in through the windows today! And smell this glorious, fresh spring air which is being wafted in to us.

MRS. STOCKMANN

Oh, my dear Thomas, if only we could live on sunshine and spring air!

DR. STOCKMANN

Well, you may have to pinch and scrape a little, but we'll manage. That's the least of my worries. No, the worst is that I don't know of anyone sufficiently free and—*unplebeian* to carry on my work after me.

PETRA

Oh, never mind that, Father. You'll find someone in time. Look, here are the boys!

(EILIF *and* MORTEN *enter from the living room.*)

MRS. STOCKMANN

Have you been given a holiday today?

MORTEN

No—but we had a fight with the other boys in the break, so—

EILIF

That's not true! It was the other boys who fought with us!

MORTEN

Yes. So I said to Dr. Roerlund I thought it would be better if we stayed at home for a few days.

DR. STOCKMANN

(snaps his fingers and jumps from the table)

I've got it! By heaven, I've got it! Neither of you shall ever set foot in that school again!

THE BOYS

Not go to school?

MRS. STOCKMANN

But, Thomas—!

DR. STOCKMANN

Never, I say! I'll teach you myself! You won't learn a damned thing—

MORTEN

Hurray!

DR. STOCKMANN

But I'll make you free men! Aristocrats! Petra, you'll have to help me.

PETRA

Yes, Father, of course.

DR. STOCKMANN

And we'll hold the school in the room where they branded me as an enemy of the people. But we need more pupils. I must have at least twelve to begin with.

MRS. STOCKMANN

You won't find them in this town.

DR. STOCKMANN

We shall see. *(To the boys)* Do you know any street urchins—real guttersnipes—?

EILIF

Oh yes, Father, I know lots!

DR. STOCKMANN

That's fine! Get hold of a few for me. I'm going to experiment with mongrels for once. They have good heads on them sometimes.

EILIF

But what shall we do when we've become free men and aristocrats?

DR. STOCKMANN

Then, my boys, you'll chase all these damned politicians into the Atlantic Ocean!

(EILIF *looks somewhat doubtful.* MORTEN *jumps and cheers.*)

MRS. STOCKMANN

Let's hope it won't be the politicians who'll chase you out, Thomas.

DR. STOCKMANN

Are you quite mad, Catherine? Chase me out? Now, when I am the strongest man in town?

MRS. STOCKMANN

The strongest—now?

DR. STOCKMANN

Yes! I'll go further! I am now one of the strongest men in the whole world.

MORTEN

Hurrah!

DR. STOCKMANN

(lowers his voice)

Hush! You mustn't talk about it yet! But I've made a great discovery!

MRS. STOCKMANN

Not again!

DR. STOCKMANN

Yes—yes! *(Gathers them around him and whispers to them.)* The fact is, you see, that the strongest man in the world is he who stands most alone.

MRS. STOCKMANN

(smiles and shakes her head)

Oh, Thomas—!

PETRA

(warmly, clasps his hands)

Father!

(Curtain)

for discussion

ACT 1

1. Ibsen is famous for having introduced realism into the drama. (For a definition of *realism*, see Glossary, page 547.) How is this apparent in the setting and in the opening scene of the play?
2. The giving of background information early in a play is called *exposition* (see Glossary, page 545). How are the requirements of exposition fulfilled in the opening scenes of *An Enemy of the People?* Specifically, what do you learn about Dr. Stockmann and the town in which he lives?
3. A character in a play is brought to life by what he says, by what he does, and by what other people say about him. Which method does Ibsen employ in his characterization of the Mayor? What kind of person is the Mayor? Cite specific details.
4. Discuss the personality of Dr. Stockmann as it is developed in his scenes with Captain Horster and with the Mayor.
5. Describe the relationship between Dr. Stockmann and his brother. Quote specific lines to support your answer.
6. Why did Ibsen include the cigars-and-toddy scene? What purpose does it serve?
7. After Petra gives her father the letter, what device does Ibsen use to create suspense? Have there been any other attempts to create suspense before this? If so, where?
8. Why is Stockmann so jubilant about the news he receives in the letter? What course of action does he feel the town must now pursue? As Act 1 closes, how does Ibsen dramatize Stockmann's mood?

ACT 2

1. How is Morten Kiil related to Dr. Stockmann? What is Kiil's reaction when Stockmann confirms the news about the polluted water? What does this reveal about Kiil?
2. After Kiil leaves, Hovstad informs Stockmann, "You're a doctor and a man of science, and to you this business of the water is something to be considered in isolation. I think you don't perhaps realize how it's tied up with a lot of other things." To what "other things" is Hovstad referring?

3. Cite the lines in which Hovstad unveils his true purpose. What is Hovstad's ambition, as he now states it?
4. Why has Aslaksen come to the Stockmann home? How does his clothing suggest his character? What prompts him to say, "We mustn't offend authority, Mr. Hovstad!"?
5. In the light of the next scene with the Mayor, why is it ironic that Dr. Stockmann should now exclaim happily to Aslaksen and Hovstad, "How splendid to feel that one stands shoulder to shoulder with one's fellow-citizens in brotherly concord!"?
6. The reason for the Mayor's anger is seemingly his concern for the well-being of the town. What other reasons may there be?
7. What distinction does the Mayor make between his brother's rights as an employee of the government and his rights as a private person. What does Dr. Stockmann think of this distinction? With whom do you agree? Why?
8. What does the Mayor want Dr. Stockmann to do? With what does he threaten the doctor? How do Petra and Mrs. Stockmann react, first to the Mayor's demand and then to his threat? How does Stockmann react?
9. What dramatic effect is achieved by the entrance of Eilif and Morten at the end of the act?

ACT 3

1. What were Dr. Stockmann's original intentions in publishing his report? Referring to specific lines in the scene between Stockmann, Hovstad, and Aslaksen, show how the doctor's intentions now differ from his original ones. In your opinion, what caused this change, or expansion, of intention?
2. Describe the three newspapermen: Billing, Hovstad, and Aslaksen. Which, if any, are men of principle? Explain your answers.
3. Why does Petra visit the newspaper office? What does this scene reveal about her character? What does it reveal about Hovstad's character and about his feelings toward Petra?
4. What is the Mayor's purpose in visiting the newspaper office? How does he accomplish his purpose?
5. Why does Dr. Stockmann return to the newspaper office? Explain why this scene is a highly ironic one.
6. Why does the playwright have Dr. Stockmann march up and down with the Mayor's hat and stick, and eventually relinquish it to his brother. How do these actions symbolize what has happened during the course of Act 3?
7. Aslaksen explains to the doctor that it is not the editors who rule the press but "the subscribers . . . public opinion, the educated

reader, the property owners, and so forth." In light of the opening scenes of this act, how true is this statement? Do you think it is true of the press today? Defend your answer.
8. The three newspapermen are not the only characters to have a change of heart during the course of Act 3. Who else changes? In what way? Cite lines to support your answer.
9. What do you think is the climax of this act? Explain how Ibsen builds to it. How does he maintain interest and suspense after the climax, until the curtain has fallen?

ACT 4

1. What impressions do you get of the citizens in the opening scene of this act? In what spirit have they come to the meeting? How well-informed are they on the issue at stake? How qualified are they to vote on such an issue?
2. The cards are stacked against Dr. Stockmann from the outset of the meeting. How and by whom are the first setbacks administered? How fair is Aslaksen as a chairman? Explain your answer.
3. What reason does the Mayor give for opposing Dr. Stockmann's report? What reasons do Aslaksen and Hovstad give? Show how these reasons are consistent with each of their characters as developed by the playwright in the first three acts of the play.
4. The meeting is constantly interrupted by the protests of a Drunk Man. Why does Ibsen include this character? Your answer should refer to the tone of Act 4 as well as to the theme of the play.
5. Dr. Stockmann had planned to read his report at the meeting, but he decides against it. Explain why he changes his mind.
6. Citing specific lines to support your answer, summarize the main point of Dr. Stockmann's speech. Do you agree or disagree with it? Defend your answer.
7. Describe the people's reaction to Dr. Stockmann's speech. Do you think their behavior is justified or not? Do you think it illustrates the charges against them that Stockmann has just made?
8. Why does Ibsen include the short conversations between Morten Kiil and Dr. Stockmann, and between the Fat Man and Horster at the end of the act?
9. As he is leaving, Dr. Stockmann shouts, "I'm not so forgiving as a certain person. I don't say 'I forgive ye, for ye know not what ye do'!" How does this statement reflect the doctor's mood? Why

An Enemy of the People 135

does Aslaksen accuse him of blasphemy? What is ironic about Billing's response?

ACT 5

1. Like all good dramatists, Ibsen embodies ideas in actions as well as stating them in the dialogue. Show how, at the beginning of this act, Ibsen dramatizes the town's hostility to the Stockmann family.
2. What is the key phrase which recurs in the landlord's letter, in Petra's dismissal, and in Captain Horster's discharge? What does this phrase show about the people of the town? What point is Ibsen making about human nature through these actions? Do you think it is a valid one? Explain your answer.
3. Captain Horster proves to be the one true friend of the Stockmanns. Mention the ways in which he helps them. Reread the cigars-and-toddy scene in the first act (pp. 15-17). In light of what is said there, discuss the irony of Horster's befriending the Stockmann family and Hovstad and Billing's deserting them.
4. The Mayor and Dr. Stockmann part on a note of bitterness and misunderstanding. What is the cause of it? What do the Mayor's suspicions about his brother's motives reveal about his own character?
5. Explain why Morten Kiil wants Dr. Stockmann to publish an admission of error. What does he mean when he says on page 120, "I intend to live and die clean. . . . You're going to make me clean, Stockmann"?
6. Aslaksen and Hovstad come to the doctor because they think they have discovered the real motive for his actions. What is that motive? In light of it, what do they propose to do? How does Stockmann respond to their proposal?
7. The suggestion of the printer and the editor is the last in a series of proposals designed to force Dr. Stockmann to compromise his ideals. Summarize these proposals. Which one do you think is the most difficult for the doctor to reject? Why?
8. As a result of the Aslaksen-Hovstad visit, Dr. Stockmann decides not to leave Norway. Why? What does he propose to do instead? How practical is his final plan? How "right" is it?
9. What does Dr. Stockmann mean when he says, "The fact is, you see, that the strongest man in the world is he who stands most alone." Do you agree? Why or why not? Choose examples from history to support your answer.

viewing the play as a whole

1. What do you consider to be the major theme, or central idea, of *An Enemy of the People?* In your opinion, is this theme as relevant today as it was in 1882, when Ibsen wrote the play? Explain your answer.
2. *An Enemy of the People* has been described as a realistic play. What aspects of the plot, characterizations, dialogue, and setting justify this description? What aspects of the play, if any, appear unrealistic?
3. Discuss the character of Dr. Stockmann. What do you think are his chief strengths? his chief weaknesses? Do you think Dr. Stockmann might have proceeded in a way which would not have incurred the wrath of the whole town? Or do you think the town would have opposed Stockmann no matter how he had proceeded? Explain.
4. Look up the distinction between a dynamic character and a static one (see *character*, page 544). Discuss the following characters in relation to these terms: Dr. Stockmann, Mrs. Stockmann, Petra, Hovstad, the Mayor.
5. In his indictment of society, Dr. Stockmann condemns the majority, the politicians, and the people who claim to be liberal. What specific criticism does he level against each of these groups? Cite passages to support your answers. In terms of what happens in the play, do you think Dr. Stockmann's criticisms are justified?
6. How valid do you think Dr. Stockmann's comparison of people to mongrels and thoroughbreds is? Do you agree with him that only the "thoroughbred" should rule? Defend your answer.
7. During Ibsen's time, what is now termed the "well-made" play was in vogue. The "well-made" play had one central action (with no sub-plots), which built up to a sensational climax, after which all the "loose ends" of the plot were neatly tied together. Chance and coincidence played an important part in the development of the action. In what ways is *An Enemy of the People* a "well-made" play? In what ways does it differ from the standard dramas of Ibsen's time?
8. The pages of history contain the names of many people who, like Dr. Stockmann, tried to reform society. Mention some of them and briefly describe each of their lives. Who do you know in the twentieth century who has given up comfort and security to fight for his beliefs?

for composition

1. Write an essay which discusses one of the themes of *An Enemy of the People*. Be sure to show why, and how, this theme is still relevant.
2. In the second act, the Mayor orders Dr. Stockmann not to publish his report. "As an employee you have no right to any independent conviction. . . . As a private person—well, heaven knows that's another matter." Discuss this distinction, using either the action described in the play, an historical situation, or a personal experience to illustrate your ideas.
3. Write a composition from the point of view of someone in the crowd at the meeting which Dr. Stockmann has called. Describe your reaction to the doctor's speech, and explain why you feel that Stockmann is "an enemy of the people."
4. The function of the press, Hovstad says before the crowd, is not to mold public opinion but rather to reflect it. Do you agree with him? Give reasons for your answer.
5. "The majority is never right! Never, I tell you! That's one of those community lies that free, thinking men have got to rebel against! . . . The ones who are right are a few isolated individuals. . . . The minority is always right!" Write a well-organized essay which supports or criticizes the point of view expressed in these sentences.

cyrano de bergerac

EDMOND ROSTAND
Translated by Brian Hooker

cyrano de bergerac

CHARACTERS

CYRANO DE BERGERAC	A Meddler
CHRISTIAN DE NEUVILLETTE	A Musketeer
ROXANE	Another Musketeer
HER DUENNA	A Spanish Officer
COMTE DE GUICHE	A Cavalier
RAGUENEAU	The Porter
LE BRET	A Citizen
CARBON DE CASTEL-JALOUX	His Son
LIGNIÈRE	A Cut-Purse
VICOMTE DE VALVERT	A Spectator
CUIGY	A Sentry
BRISSAILLE	Bertrandou the Fifer
LISE	A Capuchin
MOTHER MARGUÉRITE DE JESUS	Two Musicians
SISTER MARTHE	The Poets
SISTER CLAIRE	The Pastrycooks
MONTFLEURY	The Pages
BELLEROSE	An Actress
JODELET	A Soubrette
The Cadets	The Flower Girl
A Marquis	
Second Marquis	
Third Marquis	

The Crowd, Citizens, Marquis, Musketeers, Thieves, Pastrycooks, Poets, Cadets of Gascoyne, Actors, Violins, Pages, Children, Spanish Soldiers, Spectators, Intellectuals, Academicians, Nuns.

THE FIRST ACT

A PERFORMANCE AT THE HÔTEL DE BOURGOGNE

The HALL OF THE HÔTEL DE BOURGOGNE *in 1640. A sort of Tennis Court, arranged and decorated for theatrical productions.*

The Hall is a long rectangle; we see it diagonally, in such a way that one side of it forms the back scene, which begins at the First Entrance on the Right and runs up to the Last Entrance on the Left, where it makes a right angle with the Stage which is seen obliquely.

This Stage is provided on either hand with benches placed along the wings. The curtain is formed by two lengths of Tapestry which can be drawn apart. Above a Harlequin cloak, the Royal Arms. Broad steps lead from the Stage down to the floor of the Hall. On either side of these steps, a place for the Musicians. A row of candles serving as footlights. Two tiers of Galleries along the side of the Hall; the upper one divided into boxes.

There are no seats upon the Floor, which is the actual stage of our theatre; but toward the back of the Hall, on the right, a few benches are arranged; and underneath a stairway on the extreme right, which leads up to the galleries, and of which only the lower portion is visible, there is a sort of Sideboard, decorated with little tapers, vases of flowers, bottles and glasses, plates of cake, etcetera.

Farther along, toward the center of our stage is the Entrance to the Hall; a great double door which opens only slightly to admit the Audience. On one of the panels of this door, as also in other places about the Hall, and in particular just over the Sideboard, are Playbills in red, upon which we may read the title LA CLORISE.

As the CURTAIN RISES, *the Hall is dimly lighted and still empty. The Chandeliers are lowered to the floor, in the middle of the Hall, ready for lighting.*

(Sound of voices outside the door. Then a CAVALIER *enters abruptly.)*

THE PORTER
(follows him)
Halloa there!—Fifteen sols!

THE CAVALIER
                    I enter free.

THE PORTER
Why?

THE CAVALIER
     Soldier of the Household of the King!

THE PORTER
(turns to another CAVALIER *who has just entered)*
You?

SECOND CAVALIER
    I pay nothing.

THE PORTER
              Why not?

SECOND CAVALIER
                      Musketeer!

FIRST CAVALIER
(to the Second)
The play begins at two. Plenty of time—
And here's the whole floor empty. Shall we try
Our exercise?

(They fence with the foils which they have brought.)

A LACKEY
(enters)
              —Pst! ... Flanquin! ...

ANOTHER
(already on stage)
                            What, Champagne?

FIRST LACKEY
(showing games which he takes out of his doublet)
Cards. Dice. Come on.
(Sits on the floor.)
SECOND LACKEY
(same action)
Come on, old cock!
FIRST LACKEY
(takes from his pocket a bit of candle, lights it, sets it on the floor)
I have stolen
A little of my master's fire.
A GUARDSMAN
(to a FLOWER GIRL who comes forward)
How sweet
Of you, to come before they light the hall!
(Puts his arm around her.)
FIRST CAVALIER
(receives a thrust of the foil)
A hit!
SECOND LACKEY
A club!
THE GUARDSMAN
(pursuing the girl)
A kiss!
THE FLOWER GIRL
(pushing away from him)
They'll see us!—
THE GUARDSMAN
(draws her into a dark corner)
No danger!
A MAN
(sits on the floor, together with several others who have brought packages of food)
When we come early, we have time to eat.
A CITIZEN
(escorting his son, a boy of sixteen)
Sit here, my son.

FIRST LACKEY
>Mark the Ace!

ANOTHER MAN
(draws a bottle from under his cloak and sits down with the others)
>Here's the spot

For a jolly old sot to suck his Burgundy—
(Drinks.)
Here—in the house of the Burgundians!

THE CITIZEN
(to his son)
Would you not think you were in some den of vice?
(Points with his cane at the drunkard.)
Drunkards—
(In stepping back, one of the cavaliers trips him up.)
>Bullies!—

(He falls between the lackeys.)
>Gamblers!—

THE GUARDSMAN
(behind him as he rises, still struggling with the FLOWER GIRL)
>One kiss—

THE CITIZEN
>Good God!—

(Draws his son quickly away.)
Here!—And to think, my son, that in this hall
They play Rotrou!

THE BOY
>Yes father—and Corneille!

THE PAGES
(dance in, holding hands and singing:)
Tra-la-la-la-la-la-la-la-la-lère . . .

THE PORTER
You pages there—no nonsense!

FIRST PAGE
(with wounded dignity)
>Oh, monsieur!

Really! How could you?
(To the SECOND, the moment the PORTER turns his back)
>Pst!—a bit of string?

SECOND PAGE
(shows fishline with hook)
Yes—and a hook.
FIRST PAGE
Up in the gallery,
And fish for wigs!
A CUT-PURSE
(gathers around him several evil-looking young fellows)
Now then, you picaroons,
Perk up, and hear me mutter. Here's your bout—
Bustle around some cull, and bite his bung ...
SECOND PAGE
(calls to other pages already in the gallery)
Hey! Brought your pea-shooters?
THIRD PAGE
(from above)
And our peas, too!
(Blows, and showers them with peas.)
THE BOY
What is the play this afternoon?
THE CITIZEN
Clorise.
THE BOY
Who wrote that?
THE CITIZEN
Balthasar Baro. What a play! ...
(He takes the BOY's arm and leads him upstage.)
THE CUT-PURSE
(to his pupils)
Lace now, on those long sleeves, you cut it off—
(Gesture with thumb and finger, as if using scissors)
A SPECTATOR
(to another, pointing upward toward the gallery)
Ah, *Le Cid!*—Yes, the first night, I sat there—
THE CUT-PURSE
Watches—
(Gesture as of picking a pocket)
THE CITIZEN
(coming down with his son)
Great actors we shall see today—

THE CUT-PURSE
Handkerchiefs—
(Gesture of holding the pocket with left hand, and drawing out handkerchief with right)
THE CITIZEN
     ˙ Montfleury—

A VOICE
(in the gallery)
         Lights! Light the lights!

THE CITIZEN
Bellerose, l'Épy, Beaupré, Jodelet—

A PAGE
(on the floor)
Here comes the orange girl.

THE ORANGE GIRL
        Oranges, milk,
Raspberry syrup, lemonade—
(Noise at the door)

A FALSETTO VOICE
(outside)
         Make way,
Brutes!

FIRST LACKEY
   What, the Marquis—on the floor?
(The Marquis enter in a little group.)

SECOND LACKEY
          Not long—
Only a few moments; they'll go and sit
On the stage presently.

FIRST MARQUIS
(seeing the hall half empty)
       How now! We enter
Like tradespeople—no crowding, no disturbance!—
No treading on the toes of citizens?
Oh fie! Oh fie!
(He encounters two gentlemen who have already arrived.)
    Cuigy! Brissaille!
(Great embracings)

CUIGY

> The faithful!

(Looks around him.)
We are here before the candles.

FIRST MARQUIS

> Ah, be still!

You put me in a temper.

SECOND MARQUIS

> Console yourself,

Marquis—the lamplighter!

THE CROWD
(applauding the appearance of the lamplighter)

> Ah! . . .

(A group gathers around the chandelier while he lights it. A few people have already taken their place in the gallery. LIGNIÈRE *enters the hall, arm in arm with* CHRISTIAN DE NEUVILLETTE. LIGNIÈRE *is a slightly disheveled figure, dissipated and yet distinguished-looking.* CHRISTIAN, *elegantly but rather unfashionably dressed, appears preoccupied and keeps looking up at the boxes.)*

CUIGY

> Lignière!—

BRISSAILLE
(laughing)
Still sober—at this hour?

LIGNIÈRE
(to CHRISTIAN*)*

> May I present you?

*(*CHRISTIAN *assents.)*
Baron Christian de Neuvillette.
(They salute.)

THE CROWD
(applauding as the lighted chandelier is hoisted into place)

> Ah!—

CUIGY
(aside to BRISSAILLE, *looking at* CHRISTIAN*)*

> Rather

A fine head, is it not? The profile . . .

FIRST MARQUIS
(who has overheard)
                                Peuh!
LIGNIÈRE
(presenting them to CHRISTIAN*)*
Messieurs de Cuigy ... de Brissaille ...
CHRISTIAN
(bows)
                                Enchanted!
FIRST MARQUIS
(to the Second)
He is not ill-looking; possibly a shade
Behind the fashion.
LIGNIÈRE
(to CUIGY*)*
                    Monsieur is recently
From the Touraine.
CHRISTIAN
                    Yes, I have been in Paris
Two or three weeks only. I join the Guards
Tomorrow.
FIRST MARQUIS
(watching the people who come into the boxes)
            Look—Madame la Présidente
Aubry!
THE ORANGE GIRL
            Oranges, milk—
THE VIOLINS
(tuning up)
                    La ... la ...
CUIGY
(to CHRISTIAN, *calling his attention to the increasing crowd)*
                                We have
An audience today!
CHRISTIAN
                    A brilliant one.
FIRST MARQUIS
Oh yes, all our own people—the gay world!

(They name the ladies who enter the boxes elaborately dressed. Bows and smiles are exchanged.)

SECOND MARQUIS
　Madame de Guéméné...
CUIGY
　　　　　　　　De Bois-Dauphin...
FIRST MARQUIS
　Whom we adore—
BRISSAILLE
　　　　　　　　Madame de Chavigny...
SECOND MARQUIS
　Who plays with all our hearts—
LIGNIÈRE
　　　　　　　　　　Why, there's Corneille
Returned from Rouen!
THE BOY
　(to his father)
　　　　　　　　Are the Academy
All here?
THE CITIZEN
　　　　　　I see some of them... there's Boudu—
Boissat—Cureau—Porchères—Colomby—
Bourzeys—Bourdon—Arbaut—
　　　　　　　　　Ah, those great names,
Never to be forgotten!
FIRST MARQUIS
　　　　　　　　Look—at last!
Our Intellectuals! Barthénoide,
Urimédonte, Félixérie...
SECOND MARQUIS
　(languishing)
　　　　　　　　Sweet heaven!
How exquisite their surnames are! Marquis,
You know them all?
FIRST MARQUIS
　　　　　　　　I know them all, Marquis!
LIGNIÈRE
　(draws CHRISTIAN *aside)*
My dear boy, I came here to serve you—Well,
But where's the lady? I'll be going.
CHRISTIAN
　　　　　　　　Not yet—

A little longer! She is always here.
Please! I must find some way of meeting her.
I am dying of love! And you—you know
Everyone, the whole court and the whole town,
And put them all into your songs—at least
You can tell me her name!

THE FIRST VIOLIN

(raps on his desk with his bow)

      Pst—Gentlemen!

(Raises his bow.)

THE ORANGE GIRL

Macaroons, lemonade—

CHRISTIAN

      Then she may be
One of those aesthetes . . . Intellectuals,
You call them—How can I talk to a woman
In that style? I have no wit. This fine manner
Of speaking and of writing nowadays—
Not for me! I am a soldier—and afraid.
That's her box, on the right—the empty one.

LIGNIÈRE

(starts for the door)

I am going.

CHRISTIAN

(restrains him)

   No—wait!

LIGNIÈRE

     Not I. There's a tavern
Not far away—and I am dying of thirst.

THE ORANGE GIRL

(passes with her tray)

Orange juice?

LIGNIÈRE

   No!

THE ORANGE GIRL

    Milk?

LIGNIÈRE

     Pouah!

THE ORANGE GIRL

      Muscatel?

152   *Edmond Rostand*

LIGNIÈRE
  Here! Stop!
  (*To* CHRISTIAN)
            I'll stay a little.
  (*To the* GIRL)
                    Let me see
  Your Muscatel.
  (*He sits down by the sideboard. The* GIRL *pours out wine for him.*)
VOICES
  (*in the crowd about the door, upon the entrance of a spruce little man, rather fat, with a beaming smile*)
            Ragueneau!
LIGNIÈRE
  (*To* CHRISTIAN)
                    Ragueneau,
  Poet and pastrycook—a character!
RAGUENEAU
  (*dressed like a confectioner in his Sunday clothes, advances quickly to* LIGNIÈRE)
  Sir, have you seen Monsieur de Cyrano?
LIGNIÈRE
  (*presents him to* CHRISTIAN)
  Permit me . . . Ragueneau, confectioner,
  The chief support of modern poetry.
RAGUENEAU
  (*bridling*)
  Oh—too much honor!
LIGNIÈRE
                Patron of the Arts—
  Maecenas! Yes, you are—
RAGUENEAU
                    Undoubtedly,
  The poets gather round my hearth.
LIGNIÈRE
                        On credit—
  Himself a poet—
RAGUENEAU
            So they say—

LIGNIÈRE
                    Maintains
  The Muses.
RAGUENEAU
            It is true that for an ode—
LIGNIÈRE
  You give a tart—
RAGUENEAU
              A tartlet—
LIGNIÈRE
                     Modesty!
  And for a triolet you give—
RAGUENEAU
                     Plain bread.
LIGNIÈRE
  (severely)
  Bread and milk! And you love the theater?
RAGUENEAU
  I adore it!
LIGNIÈRE
        Well, pastry pays for all.
  Your place today now—come, between ourselves,
  What did it cost you?
RAGUENEAU
                  Four pies; fourteen cakes.
  (Looking about)
  But— Cyrano not here? Astonishing!
LIGNIÈRE
  Why so?
RAGUENEAU
        Why—Montfleury plays!
LIGNIÈRE
                          Yes, I hear
  That hippopotamus assumes the rôle
  Of Phédon. What is that to Cyrano?
RAGUENEAU
  Have you not heard? Monsieur de Bergerac
  So hates Montfleury, he has forbidden him
  For three weeks to appear upon the stage.

LIGNIÈRE
(who is, by this time, at his fourth glass)
Well?
RAGUENEAU
  Montfleury plays!—
CUIGY
(strolls over to them)
       Yes—what then?
RAGUENEAU
         Ah! That
Is what I came to see.
FIRST MARQUIS
      This Cyrano—
Who is he?
CUIGY
    Oh, he is the lad with the long sword.
SECOND MARQUIS
Noble?
CUIGY
    Sufficiently; he is in the Guards.
(Points to a gentleman who comes and goes about the hall as though seeking for someone.)
His friend Le Bret can tell you more.
(Calls to him.)
        Le Bret!
(LE BRET *comes down to them.*)
Looking for Bergerac?
LE BRET
       Yes. And for trouble.
CUIGY
Is he not an extraordinary man?
LE BRET
The best friend and the bravest soul alive!
RAGUENEAU
Poet—
CUIGY
   Swordsman—
LE BRET
     Musician—

BRISSAILLE

Philosopher—

LIGNIÈRE

Such a remarkable appearance, too!

RAGUENEAU

Truly, I should not look to find his portrait
By the grave hand of Philippe de Champagne.
He might have been a model for Callot—
One of those wild swashbucklers in a masque—
Hat with three plumes, and doublet with six points—
His cloak behind him over his long sword
Cocked, like the tail of strutting Chanticleer—
Prouder than all the swaggering Tamburlaines
Hatched out of Gascony. And to complete
This Punchinello figure—such a nose!—
My lords, there is no such nose as that nose—
You cannot look upon it without crying: "Oh, no,
Impossible! Exaggerated!" Then
You smile, and say: "Of course—I might have known;
Presently he will take it off." But that
Monsieur de Bergerac will never do.

LIGNIÈRE

(grimly)

He keeps it—and God help the man who smiles!

RAGUENEAU

His sword is one half of the shears of Fate!

FIRST MARQUIS

(shrugs)

He will not come.

RAGUENEAU

Will he not? Sir, I'll lay you
A pullet à la Ragueneau!

FIRST MARQUIS

(laughing)

Done!

(Murmurs of admiration; ROXANE *has just appeared in her box. She sits at the front of the box, and her* DUENNA *takes a seat toward the rear.* CHRISTIAN, *busy paying the* ORANGE GIRL, *does not see her at first.)*

SECOND MARQUIS
(*with little excited cries*)
Ah!
Oh! Oh! Sweet sirs, look yonder! Is she not
Frightfully ravishing?
FIRST MARQUIS
Bloom of the peach—
Blush of the strawberry—
SECOND MARQUIS
So fresh—so cool,
That our hearts, grown all warm with loving her,
May catch their death of cold!
CHRISTIAN
(*Looks up, sees* ROXANE, *and seizes* LIGNIÈRE *by the arm*)
There! Quick—up there—
In the box! Look!—
LIGNIÈRE
(*coolly*)
Herself?
CHRISTIAN
Quickly—her name?
LIGNIÈRE
(*sipping his wine, and speaking between sips*)
Madeleine Robin, called Roxane . . . refined . . .
Intellectual . . .
CHRISTIAN
Ah!—
LIGNIÈRE
Unmarried . . .
CHRISTIAN
Oh!—
LIGNIÈRE
No title . . . rich enough . . . an orphan . . . cousin
To Cyrano . . . of whom we spoke just now . . .

(*At this point, a very distinguished-looking gentleman, the
Cordon Bleu around his neck, enters the box, and stands a
moment talking with* ROXANE.)

CHRISTIAN
(starts)
And the man? . . .

LIGNIÈRE
(beginning to feel his wine a little; cocks his eye at them.)
Oho! That man? . . . Comte de Guiche . . .
In love with her . . . married himself, however,
To the niece of the Cardinal—Richelieu . . .
Wishes Roxane, therefore, to marry one
Monsieur de Valvert . . . Vicomte . . . friend of his . . .
A somewhat melancholy gentleman . . .
But . . . well, accommodating! . . . She says No . . .
Nevertheless, de Guiche is powerful . . .
Not above persecuting . . .
(He rises, swaying a little, and very happy.)
I have written
A little song about his little game . . .
Good little song, too . . . Here, I'll sing it for you . . .
Make de Guiche furious . . . naughty little song . . .
Not so bad, either—Listen! . . .
(He stands with his glass held aloft, ready to sing.)

CHRISTIAN
No. Adieu.

LIGNIÈRE
Whither away?

CHRISTIAN
To Monsieur de Valvert!

LIGNIÈRE
Careful! The man's a swordsman . . .
(Nods toward ROXANE, *who is watching* CHRISTIAN.)
Wait! Someone
Looking at you—

CHRISTIAN
Roxane! . . .

(He forgets everything, and stands spellbound, gazing toward ROXANE. *The* CUT-PURSE *and his crew, observing him transfixed, his eyes raised and his mouth half open, begin edging in his direction.)*

LIGNIÈRE
                    Oh! Very well,
Then I'll be leaving you ... Good day ... Good day! ...
(CHRISTIAN *remains motionless.*)
Everywhere else, they like to hear me sing!—
Also, I am thirsty.

(*He goes out, navigating carefully.* LE BRET, *having made the circuit of the hall, returns to* RAGUENEAU, *somewhat reassured.*)

LE BRET
                    No sign anywhere
Of Cyrano!
RAGUENEAU
(*incredulous*)
                    Wait and see!
LE BRET
                    Humph! I hope
He has not seen the bill.
THE CROWD
                    The play!—The play!—
FIRST MARQUIS
(*observing* DE GUICHE, *as he descends from* ROXANE'S *box and crosses the floor, followed by a knot of obsequious gentlemen, the* VICOMTE DE VALVERT *among them*)
This man de Guiche—what ostentation!
SECOND MARQUIS
                    Bah!—
Another Gascon!
FIRST MARQUIS
                    Gascon, yes—but cold
And calculating—certain to succeed—
My word for it. Come, shall we make our bow?
We shall be none the worse, I promise you ...
(*They go toward* DE GUICHE.)
SECOND MARQUIS
Beautiful ribbons, Count! That color, now,
What is it—"Kiss-me-Dear" or "Startled-Fawn"?

DE GUICHE
  I call that shade "The Dying Spaniard."
FIRST MARQUIS
                              Ha!
  And no false colors either—thanks to you
  And your brave troops, in Flanders before long
  The Spaniard will die daily.
DE GUICHE
                      Shall we go
  And sit upon the stage? Come, Valvert.
CHRISTIAN
  (starts at the name)
                                  Valvert!—
  The Vicomte—Ah, that scoundrel! Quick—my glove—
  I'll throw it in his face—
  (Reaching into his pocket for his glove, he catches the hand of the CUT-PURSE.*)*
THE CUT-PURSE
                      Oh!—
CHRISTIAN
  (holding fast to the man's wrist)
                              Who are you?
  I was looking for a glove—
THE CUT-PURSE
  (cringing)
                          You found a hand.
  (Hurriedly)
  Let me go—I can tell you something—
CHRISTIAN
  (still holding him)
                              Well?
THE CUT-PURSE
  Lignière—that friend of yours—
CHRISTIAN
  (same business)
                              Well?
THE CUT-PURSE
                                  Good as dead—
  Understand? Ambuscaded. Wrote a song

About—no matter. There's a hundred men
Waiting for him tonight—I'm one of them.
CHRISTIAN

A hundred? Who arranged this?

THE CUT-PURSE

Secret.

CHRISTIAN

Oh!

THE CUT-PURSE
(with dignity)
Professional secret.

CHRISTIAN

Where are they to be?

THE CUT-PURSE

Porte de Nesle. On his way home. Tell him so.
Save his life.

CHRISTIAN
(releases the man)

Yes, but where am I to find him?

THE CUT-PURSE

Go round the taverns. There's the Golden Grape,
The Pineapple, the Bursting Belt, the Two
Torches, the Three Funnels—in every one
You leave a line of writing—understand?
To warn him.

CHRISTIAN
(starts for the door)

I'll go! God, what a swine—a hundred
Against one man! . . .
(Stops and looks longingly at ROXANE.*)*

Leave *her* here!—
(Savagely, turning toward VALVERT*)*

And leave *him!*—
(Decidedly)
I must save Lignière!
(Exit)

(DE GUICHE, VALVERT, *and all the* MARQUIS *have disappeared through the curtains, to take their seats upon the stage. The floor is entirely filled; not a vacant seat remains in the gallery or in the boxes.)*

THE CROWD

>The play! The play!

Begin the play!

A CITIZEN

(as his wig is hoisted into the air on the end of a fishline, in the hands of a page in the gallery)

>My wig!!

CRIES OF JOY

>He's bald! Bravo,

You pages! Ha ha ha!

THE CITIZEN

(furious, shakes his fist at the boy)

>Here, you young villain!

CRIES OF LAUGHTER

(beginning very loud, then suddenly repressed)
HA HA! Ha Ha! ha ha ...
(Complete silence)

LE BRET

(surprised)

>That sudden hush? ...

(A SPECTATOR whispers in his ear.)
Yes?

THE SPECTATOR

I was told on good authority ...

MURMURS

(here and there)
What? ... Here? ... No ... Yes ... Look—in the latticed box—
The Cardinal! ... The Cardinal! ...

A PAGE

>The Devil!

Now we shall all have to behave ourselves!
(Three raps on the stage. The audience becomes motionless. Silence)

THE VOICE OF A MARQUIS

(from the stage, behind the curtains)
Snuff that candle!

ANOTHER MARQUIS
(puts his head out through the curtains)
A chair! ...

(A chair is passed from hand to hand over the heads of the crowd. He takes it, and disappears behind the curtains, not without having blown a few kisses to the occupants of the boxes.)

A SPECTATOR
Silence!

VOICES
Hssh! ... Hssh! ...

(Again the three raps on the stage. The curtains part. TABLEAU: *The* MARQUIS *seated on their chairs to right and left of the stage, insolently posed. Back drop representing a pastoral scene, bluish in tone. Four little crystal chandeliers light up the stage. The violins play softly.)*

LE BRET
(in a low tone, to RAGUENEAU*)*
Montfleury enters now?

RAGUENEAU
(nods)
Opens the play.

LE BRET
(much relieved)
Then Cyrano is not here!

RAGUENEAU
I lose ...

LE BRET
Humph!—
So much the better!

(The melody of a Musette is heard. MONTFLEURY *appears upon the scene, a ponderous figure in the costume of a rustic shepherd, a hat garlanded with roses tilted over one ear, playing upon a beribboned pastoral pipe.)*

THE CROWD
(applauds)
Montfleury! ... Bravo! ...

MONTFLEURY
(after bowing to the applause, begins the rôle of Phédon)
"Thrice happy he who hides from pomp and power
In sylvan shade or solitary bower;
Where balmy zephyrs fan his burning cheeks—"

A VOICE
(from the midst of the hall)
Wretch. Have I not forbade you these three weeks?
(Sensation. Everyone turns to look. Murmurs.)

SEVERAL VOICES
What? ... Where? ... Who is it? ...

CUIGY
Cyrano!

LE BRET
(in alarm)
Himself!

THE VOICE
King of clowns! Leave the stage—*at once!*

THE CROWD
Oh!—

MONTFLEURY
Now, Now, now—

THE VOICE
You disobey me?

SEVERAL VOICES
(from the floor, from the boxes)
Hsh! Go on—
Quiet—Go on, Montfleury!—Who's afraid?—

MONTFLEURY
(in a voice of no great assurance)
"Thrice happy he who hides from ..."

THE VOICE
(more menacingly)
Well? Well? Well? ...

Monarch of mountebanks! Must I come and plant
A forest on your shoulders?

(A cane at the end of a long arm shakes above the heads of the crowd.)

MONTFLEURY
  (in a voice increasingly feeble)
                              "Thrice hap—"
  (The cane is violently agitated.)
THE VOICE
                              GO!!!

THE CROWD
                    Ah...

CYRANO
  (arises in the center of the floor, erect upon a chair, his arms folded, his hat cocked ferociously, his mustache bristling, his nose terrible)
              Presently I shall grow angry!
  (Sensation at his appearance)
MONTFLEURY
  (to the Marquis)
                                        Messieurs,

If you protect me—
A MARQUIS
  (nonchalantly)
              Well—proceed!
CYRANO
                              Fat swine!
If you dare breathe one balmy zephyr more,
I'll fan your cheeks for you!
THE MARQUIS
                    Quiet down there!
CYRANO
  Unless these gentlemen retain their seats,
  My cane may bite their ribbons!
ALL THE MARQUIS
  (on their feet)
                              That will do!—

  Montfleury—

CYRANO

              Fly, goose! Shoo! Take to your wings,
Before I pluck your plumes, and draw your gorge!

A VOICE

See here—

CYRANO

          Off stage!!

ANOTHER VOICE

                    One moment—

CYRANO

                            What—still there?
(Turns back his cuffs deliberately.)
Very good—then I enter—*Left—with knife—*
To carve this large Italian sausage.

MONTFLEURY

(desperately attempting dignity)
                                Sir,
When you insult me, you insult the Muse!

CYRANO

(with great politeness)
Sir, if the Muse, who never knew your name,
Had the honor to meet you—then be sure
That after one glance at that face of yours,
That figure of a mortuary urn—
She would apply her buskin—toward the rear!

THE CROWD

Montfleury! . . . Montfleury! . . . The play! The play!

CYRANO

(to those who are shouting and crowding about him)
Pray you, be gentle with my scabbard here—
She'll put her tongue out at you presently!—
(The circle enlarges.)

THE CROWD

(recoiling)
Keep back—

CYRANO

(to MONTFLEURY*)*
              Begone!

THE CROWD
(pushing in closer, and growling)
                    Ahr! ... ahr! ...

CYRANO
(turns upon them)
                              Did someone speak?

(They recoil again.)

A VOICE
(in the back of the hall, sings)
Monsieur de Cyrano
  Must be another Caesar—
Let Brutus lay him low,
  And play us *La Clorise!*

ALL THE CROWD
(singing)
                    La Clorise! La Clorise!

CYRANO
Let me hear one more word of that same song,
And I destroy you all!

A CITIZEN
                    Who might you be?
Samson?—

CYRANO
          Precisely. Would you kindly lend me
Your jawbone?

A LADY
(in one of the boxes)
                    What an outrage!

A NOBLE
                              Scandalous!

A CITIZEN
  Annoying!

A PAGE
          What a game!

THE CROWD
                    Kss! Montfleury!

  Cyrano!

CYRANO
      Silence!

THE CROWD
(delirious)
> Woof! Woof! Baaa! Cockadoo!

CYRANO
I—

A PAGE
Meow!

CYRANO
> I say be silent!—
(His voice dominates the uproar. Momentary hush.)
> And I offer
> One universal challenge to you all!
> Approach, young heroes—I will take your names.
> Each in his turn—no crowding! One, two, three—
> Come, get your numbers—who will head the list—
> You sir? No— You? Ah, no. To the first man
> Who falls I'll build a monument! . . . Not one?
> Will all who wish to die, please raise their hands? . . .
> I see. You are so modest, you might blush
> Before a sword naked. Sweet innocence! . . .
> Not one name? Not one finger? . . . Very well,
> Then I go on:
(Turning back towards the stage, where MONTFLEURY waits in despair)
> I'd have our theater cured
> Of this carbuncle. Or if not, why then—
(His hand on his sword hilt)
> The lancet!

MONTFLEURY
I—

CYRANO
(descends from his chair, seats himself comfortably in the center of the circle which has formed around him, and makes himself quite at home)
> Attend to me—full moon!
> I clap my hands, three times—thus. At the third
> You will eclipse yourself.

THE CROWD
(amused)
> Ah!

CYRANO
>   Ready? One!

MONTFLEURY
>   I—

A VOICE
(from the boxes)
No!

THE CROWD
>   He'll go— He'll stay—

MONTFLEURY
>   I really think,

Gentlemen—

CYRANO
>   Two!

MONTFLEURY
>   Perhaps I had better—

CYRANO
>   Three!

(MONTFLEURY *disappears, as if through a trapdoor. Tempest of laughter, hoots and hisses*)

THE CROWD
Yah!—Coward— Come back—

CYRANO
(beaming, drops back in his chair and crosses his legs)
>   Let him—if he dare!

A CITIZEN
The Manager! Speech! Speech!
(BELLEROSE *advances and bows.*)

THE BOXES
>   Ah! Bellerose!

BELLEROSE
(with elegance)
Most noble—most fair—

THE CROWD
>   No! The Comedian—

Jodelet!—

JODELET
(advances, and speaks through his nose)
>   Lewd fellows of the baser sort—

THE CROWD
　Ha! Ha! Not bad! Bravo!
JODELET
　　　　　　　　　　No bravos here!
Our heavy tragedian with the voluptuous bust
Was taken suddenly—
THE CROWD
　　　　　　　　Yah! Coward!
JODELET
　　　　　　　　　　　　I mean . . .
He had to be excused—
THE CROWD
　　　　　　　　Call him back— No!—
Yes!—
THE BOY
　(to CYRANO*)*
　　　　After all, Monsieur, what reason have you
　To hate this Montfleury?
CYRANO
　(graciously, still seated)
　　　　　　　　　　　My dear, young man,
I have two reasons, either one alone
Conclusive. *Primo:* a lamentable actor,
Who mouths his verse and moans his tragedy,
And heaves up— Ugh!—like a hod-carrier, lines
That ought to soar on their own wings. *Secundo:*—
Well—that's my secret.
THE OLD CITIZEN
　(behind him)
　　　　　　　　　But you close the play—
La Clorise—by Baro! Are we to miss
Our entertainment, merely—
CYRANO
　(respectfully, turns his chair toward the old man)
　　　　　　　　　　　My dear old boy,
The poetry of Baro being worth
Zero, or less, I feel that I have done
Poetic justice!

THE INTELLECTUALS
(in the boxes)
> Really!—our Baro!—
My dear!—Who ever?—Ah, dieu! The idea!—

CYRANO
(gallantly, turns his chair toward the boxes)
Fair ladies—shine upon us like the sun,
Blossom like the flowers around us—be our songs,
Heard in a dream— Make sweet the hour of death,
Smiling upon us as you close our eyes—
Inspire, but do not try to criticize!

BELLEROSE
Quite so!—and the mere money—possibly
You would like that returned— Yes?

CYRANO
> Bellerose,
You speak the first word of intelligence!
I will not wound the mantle of the Muse—
Here, catch!—
(Throws him a purse.)
> And hold your tongue.

THE CROWD
(astonished)
> Ah! Ah!

JODELET
(deftly catches the purse, weighs it in his hand)
> Monsieur,
You are hereby authorized to close our play
Every night, on the same terms.

THE CROWD
> Boo!

JODELET
> And welcome!
Let us be booed together, you and I!

BELLEROSE
Kindly pass out quietly . . .

JODELET
(burlesquing BELLEROSE)
> Quietly . . .

(They begin to go out, while CYRANO *looks about him with satisfaction. But the exodus ceases presently during the ensuing scene. The ladies in the boxes who have already risen and put on their wraps, stop to listen, and finally sit down again.)*

LE BRET
(To CYRANO*)*
Idiot!

A MEDDLER
(hurries up to CYRANO*)*
But what a scandal! Montfleury—
The great Montfleury! Did you know the Duc de Candale was
His patron? Who is yours?

CYRANO
No one.

THE MEDDLER
No one—no patron?

CYRANO
I said no.

THE MEDDLER
What, no great lord, to cover with his name—

CYRANO
(with visible annoyance)
No, I have told you twice. Must I repeat?
No sir, no patron—
(His hand on his sword)
But a patroness!

THE MEDDLER
And when do you leave Paris?

CYRANO
That's as may be.

THE MEDDLER
The Duc de Candale has a long arm.

CYRANO
(drawing his sword)
Mine
Is longer by three feet of steel.

THE MEDDLER
Yes, yes,
But do you dream of daring—

CYRANO

                                     I do dream
Of daring . . .

THE MEDDLER
           But—

CYRANO
                  You may go now.

THE MEDDLER
                         But—

CYRANO
                                  You may go—
Or tell me why you are staring at my nose!

THE MEDDLER
(in confusion)
No—I—

CYRANO
(stepping up to him)
      Does it astonish you?

THE MEDDLER
(drawing back)
                        Your grace
Misunderstands my—

CYRANO
                 Is it long and soft
And dangling, like a trunk?

THE MEDDLER
(same business)
                      I never said—

CYRANO
Or crooked, like an owl's beak?

THE MEDDLER
                      I—

CYRANO
                      Perhaps
A pimple ornaments the end of it?

THE MEDDLER
No—

CYRANO
    Or a fly parading up and down?
What is this portent?

THE MEDDLER
> Oh!—

CYRANO
> This phenomenon?

THE MEDDLER
But I have been careful not to look—

CYRANO
> And why

Not, if you please?

THE MEDDLER
> Why—

CYRANO
> It disgusts you, then?

THE MEDDLER
My dear sir—

CYRANO
> Does its color appear to you

Unwholesome?

THE MEDDLER
> Oh, by no means!

CYRANO
> Or its form

Obscene?

THE MEDDLER
> Not in the least—

CYRANO
> Then why assume

This deprecating manner? Possibly
You find it just a trifle large?

THE MEDDLER
(babbling)
> Oh no!—

Small, very small, infinitesimal—

CYRANO
(roars)
> What?

How? You accuse me of absurdity?
Small—*my nose?* Why—

THE MEDDLER
(breathless)

My God!—

CYRANO

Magnificent,
My nose! ... You pug, you knob, you buttonhead,
Know that I glory in this nose of mine,
For a great nose indicates a great man—
Genial, courteous, intellectual,
Virile, courageous—as I am—and such
As you—poor wretch—will never dare to be
Even in imagination. For that face—
That blank, inglorious concavity
Which my right hand finds—
(He strikes him.)

THE MEDDLER

Ow!

CYRANO

—on top of you,
Is as devoid of pride, of poetry,
Of soul, of picturesqueness, of contour,
Of character, of NOSE in short—as that
(Takes him by the shoulders and turns him around, suiting the action to the word)
Which at the end of that limp spine of yours
My left foot—

THE MEDDLER
(escaping)

Help! The Guard!

CYRANO

Take notice, all
Who find this feature of my countenance
A theme for comedy! When the humorist
Is noble, then my custom is to show
Appreciation proper to his rank—
More heartfelt ... and more pointed. ...

DE GUICHE
(who has come down from the stage, surrounded by the MARQUIS)

Presently

This fellow will grow tiresome.
VALVERT
(shrugs)

Oh, he blows

His trumpet!
DE GUICHE

Well—will no one interfere?
VALVERT

No one?
(Looks around.)

Observe. I myself will proceed
To put him in his place:
(He walks up to CYRANO, *who has been watching him, and stands there, looking him over with an affected air.)*

Ah . . . your nose . . . hem! . . .
Your nose is . . . rather large!
CYRANO
(gravely)

Rather.

VALVERT
(simpering)

Oh well—

CYRANO
(coolly)
Is that all?
VALVERT
(turns away with a shrug)

Well, of course—
CYRANO

Ah, no, young sir!
You are too simple. Why, you might have said—
Oh, a great many things! Mon dieu, why waste
Your opportunity? For example, thus:—
AGGRESSIVE: I, sir, if that nose were mine,
I'd have it amputated—on the spot!
FRIENDLY: How do you drink with such a nose?
You ought to have a cup made specially.

DESCRIPTIVE: 'Tis a rock—a crag—a cape—
A cape? say rather, a peninsula!
INQUISITIVE: What is that receptacle—
A razor-case or a portfolio?
KINDLY: Ah, do you love the little birds
So much that when they come and sing to you,
You give them this to perch on? INSOLENT:
Sir, when you smoke, the neighbors must suppose
Your chimney is on fire. CAUTIOUS: Take care—
A weight like that might make you topheavy.
THOUGHTFUL: Somebody fetch my parasol—
Those delicate colors fade so in the sun!
PEDANTIC: Does not Aristophanes
Mention a mythologic monster called
Hippocampelephantocamelos?
Surely we have here the original!
FAMILIAR: Well, old torchlight! Hang your hat
Over that chandelier—it hurts my eyes.
ELOQUENT: When it blows, the typhoon howls,
And the clouds darken. DRAMATIC: When it bleeds—
The Red Sea! ENTERPRISING: What a sign
For some perfumer! LYRIC: Hark—the horn
Of Roland calls to summon Charlemagne!—
SIMPLE: When do they unveil the monument?
RESPECTFUL: Sir, I recognize in you
A man of parts, a man of prominence—
RUSTIC: Hey? What? Call that a nose? Na na—
I be no fool like what you think I be—
That there's a blue cucumber! MILITARY:
Point against cavalry! PRACTICAL: Why not
A lottery with this for the grand prize?
Or—parodying Faustus in the play—
"Was this the nose that launched a thousand ships
And burned the topless towers of Ilium?"
These, my dear sir, are things you might have said
Had you some tinge of letters or of wit
To color your discourse. But wit,—not so,
You never had an atom—and of letters,
You need but three to write you down—an Ass.

Moreover,—if you had the invention, here
Before these folks to make a jest of me—
Be sure you would not then articulate
The twentieth part of half a syllable
Of the beginning! For I say these things
Lightly enough myself, about myself,
But I allow none else to utter them.

DE GUICHE

(tries to lead away the amazed VALVERT*)*
Vicomte—come.

VALVERT

(choking)

        Oh— These arrogant grand airs!—
A clown who—look at him—not even gloves!
No ribbons—no lace—no buckles on his shoes—

CYRANO

I carry my adornments on my soul.
I do not dress up like a popinjay;
But inwardly, I keep my daintiness.
I do not bear with me, by any chance,
An insult not yet washed away—a conscience
Yellow with unpurged bile—an honor frayed
To rags, a set of scruples badly worn.
I go caparisoned in gems unseen,
Trailing white plumes of freedom, garlanded
With my good name—no figure of a man,
But a soul clothed in shining armor, hung
With deeds for decorations, twirling—thus—
A bristling wit, and swinging at my side
Courage, and on the stones of this old town
Making the sharp truth ring, like golden spurs!

VALVERT

But—

CYRANO

    But I have no gloves! A pity too!
I had one—the last one of an old pair—
And lost that. Very careless of me. Some
Gentleman offered me an impertinence.
I left it—in his face.

VALVERT
>Dolt, bumpkin, fool,
Insolent puppy, jobbernowl!

CYRANO
(removes his hat and bows)
>Ah, yes?

And I—Cyrano-Savinien-Hercule
De Bergerac!

VALVERT
(turns away)
>Buffoon!

CYRANO
(cries out as if suddenly taken with a cramp)
>Oh!

VALVERT
(turns back)
>Well, what now?

CYRANO
(with grimaces of anguish)
I must do something to relieve these cramps—
This is what comes of lack of exercise—
Ah!—

VALVERT
>What is all this?

CYRANO
>My sword has gone to sleep?

VALVERT
(draws)
So be it!

CYRANO
>You shall die exquisitely.

VALVERT
(contemptuously)
Poet!

CYRANO
>Why yes, a poet if you will;
So while we fence, I'll make you a Ballade
Extempore.

VALVERT
        A Ballade?
CYRANO
                Yes. You know
  What that is?
VALVERT
            I—
CYRANO
              The Ballade, sir, is formed
  Of three stanzas of eight lines each—
VALVERT
                        Oh, come!
CYRANO
  And a refrain of four.
VALVERT
            You—
CYRANO
                I'll compose
  One, while I fight with you; and at the end
  Of the last line—thrust home!
VALVERT
              Will you?
CYRANO
                    I will.
  (declaims)
  "Ballade of the duel at the Hôtel de Bourgogne
  Between de Bergerac and a Boeotian."
VALVERT
  (sneering)
  What do you mean by that?
CYRANO
              Oh, that? The title.
THE CROWD
  (excited)
  Come on—
        A circle—
              Quiet—
                  Down in front!

(TABLEAU: *A ring of interested spectators in the center of the floor, the Marquis and the Officers mingling with the citizens and common folk. Pages swarming up on men's shoulders to see better; the Ladies in the boxes standing and leaning over. To the right,* DE GUICHE *and his following; to the left,* LE BRET, CUIGY, RAGUENEAU, *and others of* CYRANO'S *friends.)*

CYRANO
(closes his eyes for an instant)
Stop . . . Let me choose my rimes. . . . Now!
   Here we go—

(He suits the action to the word, throughout the following:)

Lightly I toss my hat away,
   Languidly over my arm let fall
The cloak that covers my bright array—
   Then out swords, and to work withal!
   A Launcelot, in his Lady's hall . . .
A Spartacus, at the Hippodrome! . . .
   I dally awhile with you, dear jackal,
Then, as I end the refrain, thrust home!

(The swords cross—the fight is on.)

Where shall I skewer my peacock? . . . Nay,
   Better for you to have shunned this brawl!—
Here, in the heart, thro' your ribbons gay?
   —In the belly, under your silken shawl?
   Hark, how the steel rings musical!
Mark how my point floats, light as the foam,
   Ready to drive you back to the wall,
Then, as I end the refrain, thrust home!

Ho, for a rime! . . . You are white as whey—
   You break, you cower, you cringe, you . . . crawl!
Tac!—and I parry your last essay:
   So may the turn of a hand forestall

Life with its honey, death with its gall;
So may the turn of my fancy roam
  Free, for a time, till the rimes recall,
Then, as I end the refrain, thrust home!

(He announces solemnly.)

Refrain:
  Prince! Pray God, that is Lord of all,
Pardon your soul, for your time has come!
  Beat—pass—fling you aslant, asprawl—
Then, as I end the refrain . . .
(He lunges; VALVERT *staggers back and falls into the arms of his friends.* CYRANO *recovers, and salutes.)*
                    —Thrust home!

(Shouts. Applause from the boxes. Flowers and handkerchiefs come fluttering down. The Officers surround CYRANO *and congratulate him.* RAGUENEAU *dances for joy.* LE BRET *is unable to conceal his enthusiasm. The friends of* VALVERT *hold him up and help him away.)*

THE CROWD
  (in one long cry)
  Ah-h!
A CAVALIER
        Superb!
A WOMAN
              Simply sweet!
RAGUENEAU
                    Magnelephant!
A MARQUIS
  A novelty!
LE BRET
        Bah!
THE CROWD
  (thronging around CYRANO*)*
              Compliments—regards—
  Bravo!—

A WOMAN'S VOICE
> Why, he's a hero!

A MUSKETEER
(advances quickly to CYRANO, *with outstretched hands)*
> Monsieur, will you

Permit me?—It was altogether fine!
I think I may appreciate these things—
Moreover, I have been stamping for pure joy!
(He retires quickly.)

CYRANO
(to CUIGY*)*
What was that gentleman's name?

CUIGY
> Oh . . . D'Artagnan.

LE BRET
(takes CYRANO's *arm)*
Come here and tell me—

CYRANO
> Let this crowd go first—

(To BELLEROSE*)*
May we stay?

BELLEROSE
(with great respect)
> Certainly!
(Cries and cat-calls offstage)

JODELET
(comes down from the door where he has been looking out)
> Hark!— Montfleury—

They are hooting him.

BELLEROSE
(solemnly)
> "Sic transit gloria!"
(Changes his tone and shouts to the PORTER *and the* LAMP-LIGHTER.*)*
—Strike! . . . Close the house! . . . Leave the lights—
We rehearse
The new farce after dinner.

*(*JODELET *and* BELLEROSE *go out after elaborately saluting* CYRANO.*)*

THE PORTER
(to CYRANO*)*
>You do not dine?

CYRANO
I?— No!
(The PORTER *turns away.)*

LE BRET
>Why not?

CYRANO
(haughtily)
>Because—
(Changing his tone when he sees the PORTER *has gone)*
>Because I have
No money.

LE BRET
(gesture of tossing)
>But—the purse of gold?

CYRANO
>Farewell,
Paternal pension!

LE BRET
>So you have, until
The first of next month—?

CYRANO
>Nothing.

LE BRET
>What a fool!—

CYRANO
But—what a gesture!

THE ORANGE GIRL
(behind her little counter; coughs)
>Hem!
(CYRANO *and* LE BRET *look around; she advances timidly.)*
>Pardon, monsieur...
A man ought never to go hungry...
(Indicating the sideboard)
>See,
I have everything here...
(Eagerly)
>Please!—

CYRANO
(uncovers)

                      My dear child,
I cannot bend this Gascon pride of mine
To accept such a kindness— Yet, for fear
That I may give you pain if I refuse,
I will take . . .
(He goes to the sideboard and makes his selection.)
              Oh, not very much! A grape . . .
(She gives him the bunch; he removes a single grape.)
One only! And a glass of water . . .
(She starts to pour wine into it; he stops her.)
                              Clear!
And . . . half a macaroon!
(He gravely returns the other half.)

LE BRET
                Old idiot!

THE ORANGE GIRL
  Please!— Nothing more?

CYRANO
                  Why yes— Your hand to kiss.
(He kisses the hand which she holds out, as he would the hand of a princess.)

THE ORANGE GIRL
  Thank you, sir.
(She curtseys.)
           Good night.
(She goes out.)

CYRANO
                  Now, I am listening.
(Plants himself before the sideboard and arranges thereon—)
Dinner!—
(—the macaroon)
      Drink!—
(—the glass of water)
             Dessert!—
(—the grape)
                    There—now I'll sit down.
(Seats himself.)

Lord, I was hungry! Abominably!
(Eating)

                        Well?

LE BRET

These fatheads with the bellicose grand airs
Will have you ruined if you listen to them;
Talk to a man of sense and hear how all
Your swagger impresses him.

CYRANO

(finishes his macaroon)

                      Enormously.

LE BRET

The Cardinal—

CYRANO

(beaming)

           Was he there?

LE BRET

                          He must have thought you—

CYRANO

Original.

LE BRET

    Well, but—

CYRANO

            He is himself
A playwright. He will not be too displeased
That I have closed another author's play.

LE BRET

But look at all the enemies you have made!

CYRANO

(begins on the grape)
How many—do you think?

LE BRET

                   Just forty-eight
Without the women.

CYRANO

           Count them.

LE BRET

                Montfleury,
Baro, de Guiche, the Vicomte, the Old Man,
All the Academy—

CYRANO
                    Enough! You make me
Happy!
LE BRET
          But where is all this leading you?
What is your plan?
CYRANO
                         I have been wandering—
Wasting my force upon too many plans.
Now I have chosen one.
LE BRET
                    What one?

CYRANO
                              The simplest—
To make myself in all things admirable!
LE BRET
     Hmph!— Well, then, the real reason why you hate
Montfleury—Come, the truth, now!
CYRANO
     (rises)
                              That Silenus,
Who cannot hold his belly in his arms,
Still dreams of being sweetly dangerous
Among the women—sighs and languishes,
Making sheeps' eyes out of his great frog's face—
I hate him ever since one day he dared
Smile upon—
               Oh, my friend, I seemed to see
Over some flower a great snail crawling!
LE BRET
     (amazed)
                              How,
What? Is it possible?—
CYRANO
     (with a bitter smile)
                         For me to love? ...
     (Changing his tone; seriously)
     I love.
LE BRET
          May I know? You have never said—

CYRANO

Whom I love? Think a moment. Think of me—
Me, whom the plainest woman would despise—
Me, with this nose of mine that marches on
Before me by a quarter of an hour!
Whom should I love? Why—of course—it must be
The woman in the world most beautiful.

LE BRET

Most beautiful?

CYRANO

In all this world—most sweet;
Also most wise; most witty; and most fair!

LE BRET

Who and what is this woman?

CYRANO

Dangerous
Mortally, without meaning; exquisite
Without imagining. Nature's own snare
To allure manhood. A white rose wherein
Love lies in ambush for his natural prey.
Who knows her smile has known a perfect thing.
She creates grace in her own image, brings
Heaven to earth in one movement of her hand—
Nor thou, O Venus! balancing thy shell
Over the Mediterranean blue, nor thou,
Diana! marching through broad, blossoming woods,
Art so divine as when she mounts her chair,
And goes abroad through Paris!

LE BRET

Oh, well—of course,
That makes everything clear!

CYRANO

Transparently.

LE BRET

Madeleine Robin—your cousin?

CYRANO

Yes; Roxane.

LE BRET

And why not? If you love her, tell her so!
You have covered yourself with glory in her eyes
This very day.

CYRANO

               My old friend—look at me,
And tell me how much hope remains for me
With this protuberance! Oh I have no more
Illusions! Now and then—bah! I may grow
Tender, walking alone in the blue cool
Of evening, through some garden fresh with flowers
After the benediction of the rain;
My poor big devil of a nose inhales
April . . . and so I follow with my eyes
Where some boy, with a girl upon his arm,
Passes a patch of silver . . . and I feel
Somehow, I wish I had a woman too,
Walking with little steps under the moon,
And holding my arm so, and smiling. Then
I dream—and I forget. . . .
                            And then I see
The shadow of my profile on the wall!

LE BRET

My friend! . . .

CYRANO

              My friend, I have my bitter days,
Knowing myself so ugly, so alone.
Sometimes—

LE BRET

        You weep?

CYRANO

(quickly)

               Oh, not that ever! No,
That would be too grotesque—tears trickling down
All the long way along this nose of mine?
I will not so profane the dignity
Of sorrow. Never any tears for me!
Why, there is nothing more sublime than tears,
Nothing!—Shall I make them ridiculous
In my poor person?

LE BRET

                Love's no more than chance!

CYRANO

(shakes his head)
No. I love Cleopatra; do I appear
Caeser? I adore Beatrice; have I
The look of Dante?

LE BRET

                  But your wit—your courage—
Why, that poor child who offered you just now
Your dinner! She—you saw with your own eyes,
Her eyes did not avoid you.

CYRANO

(thoughtful)
                  That is true . . .

LE BRET

Well then! Roxane herself, watching your duel,
Paler than—

CYRANO

    Pale?—

LE BRET

           Her lips parted, her hand
Thus, at her breast— I saw it! Speak to her
Speak, man!

CYRANO

         Through my nose? She might laugh at me;
That is the one thing in this world I fear!

THE PORTER

(followed by the DUENNA, *approaches* CYRANO *respectfully)*
A lady asking for Monsieur.

CYRANO

               Mon dieu . . .

Her Duenna!—

THE DUENNA

(a sweeping curtsey)
       Monsieur . . .
                A message for you:
From our good cousin we desire to know
When and where we may see him privately.

CYRANO

(amazed)
To see me?

THE DUENNA
(an elaborate reverence)
     To see you. We have certain things
To tell you.
CYRANO
     Certain—
THE DUENNA
       Things.
CYRANO
(trembling)
       Mon dieu! . . .
THE DUENNA
         We go
Tomorrow, at the first flush of the dawn,
To hear Mass at St. Roch. Then afterwards,
Where can we meet and talk a little?
CYRANO
(catching LE BRET'S *arm)*
        Where?—
I—Ah, mon dieu! . . . mon dieu! . . .
THE DUENNA
       Well?
CYRANO
        I am thinking . . .
THE DUENNA
And you think?
CYRANO
     I . . . The shop of Ragueneau . . .
Ragueneau—pastrycook . . .
THE DUENNA
      Who dwells?—
CYRANO
       Mon dieu! . . .
Oh, yes . . . Ah, mon dieu! . . . Rue St.-Honoré.
THE DUENNA
We are agreed. Remember—seven o'clock.
(Reverence)
Until then—

CYRANO
                I'll be there.
(The DUENNA *goes out.)*
CYRANO
(falls into the arms of LE BRET*)*
                    Me . . . to see me! . . .
LE BRET
You are not quite so gloomy.
CYRANO
                    After all,
She knows that I exist—no matter why!
LE BRET
So now, you are going to be happy.
CYRANO
                     Now! . . .
(beside himself)
I—I am going to be a storm—a flame—
I need to fight whole armies all alone;
I have ten hearts; I have a hundred arms; I feel
Too strong to war with mortals—
(He shouts at the top of his voice.)
                        Bring me giants!

(A moment since, the shadows of the COMEDIANS *have been visible moving and posturing upon the stage. The* VIOLINS *have taken their places.)*

A VOICE
(from the stage)
Hey—pst—less noise! We are rehearsing here!
CYRANO
(laughs)
We are going.

(He turns upstage. Through the street door enter CUIGY, BRISSAILLE, *and a number of* OFFICERS, *supporting* LIGNIÈRE, *who is now thoroughly drunk.)*

CUIGY
>	Cyrano!

CYRANO
>	What is it?

CUIGY
>	Here—

Here's your stray lamb!

CYRANO
(recognizes LIGNIÈRE)
>	Lignière—What's wrong with him?

CUIGY

He wants you.

BRISSAILLE
>	He's afraid to go home.

CYRANO
>	Why?

LIGNIÈRE

(showing a crumpled scrap of paper and speaking with the elaborate logic of profound intoxication)
This letter—hundred against one—that's me—
I'm the one—all because of little song—
Good song— Hundred men, waiting, understand?
Porte de Nesle—way home— Might be dangerous—
Would you permit me spend the night with you?

CYRANO

A hundred—is that all? You are going home!

LIGNIÈRE

(astonished)
Why—

CYRANO

(in a voice of thunder, indicating the lighted lantern which the PORTER holds up curiously as he regards the scene)
>	Take that lantern!

(LIGNIÈRE precipitately seizes the lantern.)
>	Forward march! I say

I'll be the man tonight that sees you home.
(To the OFFICERS)
You others follow—I want an audience!

CUIGY

A hundred against one—

CYRANO

      Those are the odds
Tonight!

(The COMEDIANS *in their costumes are descending from the stage and joining the group.)*

LE BRET

   But why help this—

CYRANO

       There goes Le Bret
Growling!

LE BRET

  —This drunkard here?

CYRANO

(his hand on LE BRET'S *shoulder)*

       Because this drunkard—
This tun of sack, this butt of Burgundy—
Once in his life has done one lovely thing:
After the Mass, according to the form,
He saw, one day, the lady of his heart
Take holy water for a blessing. So
This one, who shudders at a drop of rain,
This fellow here—runs headlong to the font
Bends down and drinks it dry!

A SOUBRETTE

      I say that was
A pretty thought!

CYRANO

    Ah, was it not?

THE SOUBRETTE

(to the others)

      But why
Against one poor poet, a hundred men?

CYRANO

March!

(To the OFFICERS*)*

  And you gentlemen, remember now,
No rescue— Let me fight alone.

COMEDIENNE
(jumps down from the stage)
                              Come on!
I'm going to watch—
CYRANO
                    Come along!
ANOTHER COMEDIENNE
(jumps down, speaks to a COMEDIAN *costumed as an old man)*
                                        You, Cassandre?
CYRANO
Come all of you—the Doctor, Isabelle,
Léandre—the whole company—a swarm
Of murmuring, golden bees—we'll parody
Italian farce and Tragedy-of-Blood;
Ribbons for banners, masks for blazonry,
And tambourines to be our rolling drums!
ALL THE WOMEN
(jumping for joy)
Bravo!—My hood— My cloak— Hurry!
JODELET
(mock heroic)
                              Lead on!—
CYRANO
(to the VIOLINS*)*
You violins—play us an overture—
(The VIOLINS *join the procession which is forming. The lighted candles are snatched from the stage and distributed; it becomes a torchlight procession.)*
Bravo!—Officers— Ladies in costume—
And twenty paces in advance . . .
(He takes his station as he speaks.)
                                    Myself,
Alone, with glory fluttering over me,
Alone as Lucifer at war with heaven!
Remember—no one lifts a hand to help—
Ready there? One . . . two . . . three! Porter, the doors! . . .
(The PORTER *flings wide the great doors. We see in the dim moonlight a corner of old Paris, purple and picturesque.)*
Look—Paris dreams—nocturnal, nebulous,

Under blue moonbeams hung from wall to wall—
Nature's own setting for the scene we play!—
Yonder, behind her veil of mist, the Seine,
Like a mysterious and magic mirror
Trembles—
        And you shall see what you shall see!

ALL

To the Porte de Nesle!

CYRANO

(erect upon the threshold)
To the Porte de Nesle!
(He turns back for a moment to the SOUBRETTE.*)*
Did you not ask, my dear, why against one
Singer they send a hundred swords?
(Quietly, drawing his own sword)
                  Because
They know this one man for a friend of mine!

(He goes out. The procession follows: LIGNIÈRE *zigzagging at its head, then the* COMEDIENNES *on the arms of the* OFFICERS, *then the* COMEDIANS, *leaping and dancing as they go. It vanishes into the night to the music of the violins, illuminated by the flickering glimmer of the candles.)*

(Curtain)

THE SECOND ACT

THE BAKERY OF THE POETS

THE SHOP OF RAGUENEAU, *Baker and Pastrycook: a spacious affair at the corner of the Rue St.-Honoré and the Rue de l'Arbre Sec. The street, seen vaguely through the glass panes in the door at the back, is gray in the first light of dawn.*

In the foreground, at the Left, a Counter is surmounted by a Canopy of wrought iron from which are hanging ducks, geese, and white peacocks. Great crockery jars hold bouquets of common flowers, yellow sunflowers in particular. On the same side farther back, a huge fireplace; in front of it, between great andirons, of which each one supports a little saucepan, roast fowls revolve and weep into their dripping pans. To the Right at the First Entrance, a door. Beyond it, Second Entrance, a staircase leads up to a little dining room under the eaves, its interior visible through open shutters. A table is set there and a tiny Flemish candlestick is lighted; there one may retire to eat and drink in private. A wooden gallery, extending from the head of the stairway, seems to lead to other little dining rooms.

In the center of the shop, an iron ring hangs by a rope over a pulley so that it can be raised or lowered; adorned with game of various kinds hung from it by hooks, it has the appearance of a sort of gastronomic chandelier.

In the shadow under the staircase, ovens are glowing. The spits revolve; the copper pots and pans gleam ruddily. Pastries in pyramids. Hams hanging from the rafters. The morning baking is in progress: a bustle of tall cooks and timid scullions and scurrying apprentices; a blossoming of white caps adorned with cock's feathers or the wings of guinea fowl. On wicker trays or on great metal platters they bring in rows of pastries and fancy dishes of various kinds.

Tables are covered with trays of cakes and rolls; others with chairs placed about them are set for guests.

One little table in a corner disappears under a heap of papers. At the CURTAIN RISE, RAGUENEAU *is seated there. He is writing poetry.*

A PASTRYCOOK

(brings in a dish)

Fruits en gelée!

SECOND PASTRYCOOK

(brings dish)

     Custard!

THIRD PASTRYCOOK

(brings roast peacock ornamented with feathers)

     Peacock rôti!

FOURTH PASTRYCOOK

(brings tray of cakes)

Cakes and confections!

FIFTH PASTRYCOOK

(brings earthen dish)

     Beef en casserole!

RAGUENEAU

(raises his head; returns to mere earth)

Over the coppers of my kitchen flows
The frosted-silver dawn. Silence awhile
The god who sings within thee, Ragueneau!
Lay down the lute—the oven calls for thee!
(Rises; goes to one of the cooks.)
Here's a hiatus in your sauce; fill up
The measure.

THE COOK

    How much?

RAGUENEAU

(measures on his finger)

     One more dactyl.

THE COOK

       Huh? . . .

FIRST PASTRYCOOK

Rolls!

SECOND PASTRYCOOK

 Roulades!

RAGUENEAU
(before the fireplace)
                    Veil, O Muse, thy virgin eyes
From the lewd gleam of these terrestrial fires!
(To FIRST PASTRYCOOK*)*
Your rolls lack balance. Here's the proper form—
An equal hemistich on either side,
And the caesura in between.
(To another, pointing out an unfinished pie)
                                   Your house
Of crust should have a roof upon it.
(To another, who is seated on the hearth, placing poultry on a spit)
                                        And you—
Along the interminable spit, arrange
The modest pullet and the lordly Turk
Alternately, my son—as great Malherbe
Alternates male and female rimes. Remember,
A couplet, or a roast, should be well turned.

AN APPRENTICE
(advances with a dish covered by a napkin)
Master, I thought of you when I designed
This, hoping it might please you.

RAGUENEAU
                         Ah! a lyre—

THE APPRENTICE
 In puff-paste—

RAGUENEAU
                 And the jewels—candied fruit!

THE APPRENTICE
 And the strings, barley-sugar!

RAGUENEAU
(gives him money)
                          Go and drink
My health.
*(*LISE *enters.)*
            St!—My wife— Circulate, and hide
That money!
(Shows the lyre to LISE, *with a languid air.)*
             Graceful—yes?

LISE

Ridiculous!

(She places on the counter a pile of paper bags.)

RAGUENEAU

Paper bags? Thank you . . .
(He looks at them.)

Ciel! My manuscripts!
The sacred verses of my poets—rent
Asunder, limb from limb—butchered to make
Base packages of pastry! Ah, you are one
Of those insane Bacchantes who destroyed
Orpheus!

LISE

Your dirty poets left them here
To pay for eating half our stock-in-trade:
We ought to make some profit out of them!

RAGUENEAU

Ant! Would you blame the locust for his song?

LISE

I blame the locust for his appetite!
There used to be a time—before you had
Your hungry friends—you never called me Ant—
No, nor Bacchantes!

RAGUENEAU

What a way to use
Poetry!

LISE

Well, what is the use of it?

RAGUENEAU

But, my dear girl, what would you do with prose?
(Two children enter.)
Well, dears?

A CHILD

Three little patties.

RAGUENEAU

(serves them)

There we are!
All hot and brown.

THE CHILD

Would you mind wrapping them?

RAGUENEAU

One of my paper bags! ...

                  Oh, certainly.

(Reads from the bag, as he is about to wrap the patties in it.)
"Ulysses, when he left Penelope"—
Not that one!
(Takes another bag; reads.)
            "Phoebus, golden-crowned"—

                            Not that one.

LISE

Well? They are waiting!

RAGUENEAU

                Very well, very well!—
The Sonnet to Phyllis ...
                Yet—it does seem hard ...

LISE

Made up your mind—at last! Mph!—Jack-o'-Dreams!

RAGUENEAU

(as her back is turned, calls back the children, who are already at the door)
Pst!—Children— Give me back the bag. Instead
Of three patties, you shall have six of them!
(Makes the exchange. The children go out. He reads from the bag, as he smooths it out tenderly.)
"Phyllis"—
        A spot of butter on her name!—
"Phyllis"—

CYRANO

(enters hurriedly)
        What is the time?

RAGUENEAU

              Six o'clock.

CYRANO

                        One
Hour more ...

RAGUENEAU

          Felicitations!

CYRANO

                And for what?

RAGUENEAU
   Your victory! I saw it all—
CYRANO
                    Which one?
RAGUENEAU
   At the Hôtel de Bourgogne.
CYRANO
                    Oh—the duel!
RAGUENEAU
   The duel in Rime!
LISE
                He talks of nothing else.
CYRANO
   Nonsense!
RAGUENEAU
   (fencing and foiling with a spit, which he snatches up from the hearth)
        "Then, as I end the refrain, thrust home!"
   "Then, as I end the refrain"—
                        Gods! What a line!
   "Then, as I end"—
CYRANO
                What time now, Ragueneau?
RAGUENEAU
   (petrified at the full extent of a lunge, while he looks at the clock)
   Five after six—
   (Recovers)
            "—thrust home!"
                        A Ballade, too!
LISE
   (to CYRANO, *who in passing has mechanically shaken hands with her)*
   Your hand—what have you done?
CYRANO
                        Oh, my hand?—Nothing.
RAGUENEAU
   What danger now—

CYRANO
>   No danger.

LISE
>   I believe

He is lying.

CYRANO
>   Why? Was I looking down my nose?

That must have been a devil of a lie!
(Changing his tone; to RAGUENEAU*)*
I expect someone. Leave us here alone,
When the time comes.

RAGUENEAU
>   How can I? In a moment,

My poets will be here.

LISE
>   To break their ... fast!

CYRANO
Take them away, then, when I give the sign.
—What time?

RAGUENEAU
>   Ten minutes after.

CYRANO
>   Have you a pen?

RAGUENEAU
(offers him a pen)
An eagle's feather!

A MUSKETEER
(enters, and speaks to LISE *in a stentorian voice)*
>   Greeting!

CYRANO
(to RAGUENEAU*)*
>   Who is this?

RAGUENEAU
My wife's friend. A terrific warrior,
So he says.

CYRANO
>   Ah—I see.

(Takes up the pen; waves RAGUENEAU *away.)*
>   Only to write—

To fold— To give it to her—and to go . . .
(Throws down the pen.)
Coward! And yet—the Devil take my soul
If I dare speak one word to her . . .
(To RAGUENEAU)

                        What time now?

RAGUENEAU
  A quarter after six.
CYRANO
  (striking his breast)
            —One little word
Of all the many thousand I have here!
Whereas in writing . . .
(Takes up the pen.)
            Come, I'll write to her
That letter I have written on my heart,
Torn up, and written over many times—
So many times . . . that all I have to do
Is to remember, and to write it down.

(He writes. Through the glass of the door appear vague and hesitating shadows. The POETS enter, clothed in rusty black and spotted with mud.)

LISE
  (to RAGUENEAU)
  Here come your scarecrows!
FIRST POET
                 Comrade!
SECOND POET
  (takes both RAGUENEAU's hands)
                     My dear brother!
THIRD POET
  (sniffing)
  O Lord of Roasts, how sweet thy dwellings are!
FOURTH POET
  Phoebus Apollo of the Silver Spoon!
FIFTH POET
  Cupid of Cookery!

RAGUENEAU
  (surrounded, embraced, beaten on the back)
                    These geniuses,
 They put one at one's ease!
FIRST POET
                         We were delayed
 By the crowd at the Porte de Nesle.
SECOND POET
                                   Dead men
 All scarred and gory, scattered on the stones,
 Villainous-looking scoundrels—eight of them.
CYRANO
  (looks up an instant)
 Eight? I thought only seven—
RAGUENEAU
                         Do you know
 The hero of this hecatomb?
CYRANO
                    I? ... No.

LISE
  (to the MUSKETEER*)*
 Do you?
THE MUSKETEER
         Hmm—perhaps!
FIRST POET
                    They say one man alone
 Put to flight all this crowd.
SECOND POET
                         Everywhere lay
 Swords, daggers, pikes, bludgeons—
CYRANO
  (writing)
                              "Your eyes ..."
THIRD POET
                                         As far
 As the Quai des Orfevres, hats and cloaks—
FIRST POET
 Why, that man must have been the devil!
CYRANO
                              "Your lips ..."

FIRST POET

Some savage monster might have done this thing!

CYRANO

"Looking upon you, I grow faint with fear . . ."

SECOND POET

What have you written lately, Ragueneau?

CYRANO

"Your Friend—Who loves you . . ." So. No signature;
I'll give it to her myself.

RAGUENEAU

A Recipe

In Rime.

THIRD POET

Read us your rimes!

FOURTH POET

Here's a brioche

Cocking its hat at me.
(He bites off the top of it.)

FIRST POET

Look how those buns
Follow the hungry poet with their eyes—
Those almond eyes!

SECOND POET

We are listening—

THIRD POET

See this cream-puff—
Fat little baby, drooling while it smiles!

SECOND POET

(nibbling at the pastry lyre)
For the first time, the lyre is my support.

RAGUENEAU

(coughs, adjusts his cap, strikes an attitude)
A Recipe in Rime—

SECOND POET

(gives FIRST POET a dig with his elbow)
Your breakfast?

FIRST POET

Dinner!

RAGUENEAU
(declaims)
A Recipe for Making Almond Tarts

Beat your eggs, the yolk and white,
    Very light;
Mingle with their creamy fluff
    Drops of lime juice, cool and green;
        Then pour in
Milk of Almonds, just enough.

Dainty patty-pans, embraced
    In puff-paste—
Have these ready within reach;
    With your thumb and finger, pinch
        Half an inch
Up around the edge of each—

Into these, a score or more,
    Slowly pour
All your store of custard; so
    Take them, bake them golden-brown—
        Now sit down! . . .
Almond tartlets, Ragueneau!

THE POETS
Delicious! Melting!

A POET
(chokes)
                Humph!

CYRANO
(to RAGUENEAU*)*
                Do you not see
Those fellows fattening themselves?—

RAGUENEAU
                        I know.
I would not look—it might embarrass them—
You see, I love a friendly audience.
Besides—another vanity—I am pleased
When they enjoy my cooking.

CYRANO

(slaps him on the back)

                       Be off with you!—

(RAGUENEAU *goes upstage.*)
Good little soul!
(Calls to LISE.*)*

              Madame!—

(She leaves the MUSKETEER *and comes down to him.*)

                      This musketeer—

He is making love to you?

LISE

(haughtily)

                       If any man
Offends my virtue—all I have to do
Is look at him—once!

CYRANO

(looks at her gravely; she drops her eyes.)

                  I do not find

Those eyes of yours unconquerable.

LISE

(panting)

                       —Ah!

CYRANO

(raising his voice a little)
Now listen— I am fond of Ragueneau;
I allow no one—do you understand?—
To . . . take his name in vain!

LISE

                You think—

CYRANO

(ironic emphasis)

                     I think

I interrupt you.

(He salutes the MUSKETEER, *who has heard without daring to resent the warning.* LISE *goes to the* MUSKETEER *as he returns* CYRANO's *salute.*)

LISE

    You—you swallow that?—
You ought to have pulled his nose!

THE MUSKETEER

        His nose?—His nose! . . .

(He goes out hurriedly. ROXANE *and the* DUENNA *appear outside the door.)*

CYRANO
(nods to RAGUENEAU*)*
Pst!—

RAGUENEAU
(to the POETS*)*
  Come inside—

CYRANO
(impatient)

      Pst! . . . Pst! . . .

RAGUENEAU

        We shall be more
Comfortable . . .
(He leads the POETS *into inner room.)*

FIRST POET
    The cakes!

SECOND POET
Bring them along!
(They go out.)

CYRANO
If I can see the faintest spark of hope,
Then—
(Throws door open—bows.)
  Welcome!
*(*ROXANE *enters, followed by the* DUENNA, *whom* CYRANO *detains.)*
    Pardon me—one word—

THE DUENNA

        Take two.

CYRANO
Have you a good digestion?

THE DUENNA
>   Wonderful!

CYRANO
Good. Here are two sonnets, by Benserade—
THE DUENNA
Euh!
CYRANO
> Which I fill for you with éclairs.

THE DUENNA
>   Ooo!

CYRANO
Do you like cream-puffs?
THE DUENNA
>   Only with whipped cream.

CYRANO
Here are three . . . six—embosomed in a poem
By Saint-Amant. This ode of Chapelin
Looks deep enough to hold—a jelly roll.
—Do you love Nature?
THE DUENNA
>   Mad about it.

CYRANO
>   Then
Go out and eat these in the street. Do not
Return—
THE DUENNA
> Oh, but—

CYRANO
>   Until you finish them.

(Down to ROXANE)
Blessed above all others be the hour
When you remembered to remember me,
And came to tell me . . . what?
ROXANE
(takes off her mask)
>   First let me thank you
Because . . . that man . . . that creature, whom your sword
Made sport of yesterday— His patron, one—
CYRANO
De Guiche?—

ROXANE

     —who thinks himself in love with me
Would have forced that man upon me for—
a husband—

CYRANO

 I understand—so much the better then!
I fought, not for my nose, but your bright eyes.

ROXANE

 And then, to tell you—but before I can
Tell you— Are you, I wonder, still the same
Big brother—almost—that you used to be
When we were children, playing by the pond
In the old garden down there—

CYRANO

        I remember—
Every summer you came to Bergerac! ...

ROXANE

 You used to make swords out of bulrushes—

CYRANO

 Your dandelion-dolls with golden hair—

ROXANE

 And those green plums—

CYRANO

       And those black mulberries—

ROXANE

 In those days, you did everything I wished!

CYRANO

 Roxane, in short skirts, was called Madeleine.

ROXANE

 Was I pretty?

CYRANO

    Oh—not too plain!

ROXANE

       Sometimes
When you had hurt your hand you used to come
Running to me—and I would be your mother,
And say— Oh, in a very grown-up voice:
(She takes his hand.)
"Now, what have you been doing to yourself?

Let me see—"
(She sees the hand—starts.)
　　　　　Oh!—
　　　　　　　　Wait— I said, "Let me see!"
Still—at your age! How did you do that?

CYRANO
　　　　　　　　　　　Playing
With the big boys, down by the Porte de Nesle.

ROXANE
(sits at a table and wets her handkerchief in a glass of water)
Come here to me.

CYRANO
　　　　　　—Such a wise little mother!

ROXANE
And tell me, while I wash this blood away,
How many you—played with?

CYRANO
　　　　　　　　　　Oh, about a hundred.

ROXANE
Tell me.

CYRANO
　　　No. Let me go. Tell me what you
Were going to tell me—if you dared?

ROXANE
(still holding his hand)
　　　　　　　　　　　I think
I do dare—now. It seems like long ago
When I could tell you things. Yes—I dare ...
Listen:
I ... love someone.

CYRANO
　　　　　Ah! ...

ROXANE
　　　　　　　　　Someone who does not know.

CYRANO
Ah! ...

ROXANE
　　　At least—not yet.

CYRANO
                    Ah! ...
ROXANE
                            But he will know
Some day.
CYRANO
        Ah! ...
ROXANE
                        A big boy who loves me too,
And is afraid of me, and keeps away,
And never says one word.
CYRANO
                    Ah! ...
ROXANE
                            Let me have
Your hand a moment—why how hot it is!—
I know. I see him trying ...
CYRANO
                    Ah! ...
ROXANE
                            There now!
Is that better?—
(She finishes bandaging the hand with her handkerchief.)
                Besides—only to think—
(This is a secret.) He is a soldier too,
In your own regiment—
CYRANO
                    Ah! ...
ROXANE
                        Yes, in the Guards,
Your company too.
CYRANO
            Ah! ...
ROXANE
                            And such a man!—
He is proud—noble—young—brave—beautiful—
CYRANO
  (turns pale; rises)
Beautiful!—

ROXANE
>What's the matter?

CYRANO
(smiling)
>Nothing—this—

My sore hand!

ROXANE
>Well, I love him. That is all.

Oh—and I never saw him anywhere
Except at the *Comédie.*

CYRANO
>You have never spoken?—

ROXANE
Only our eyes ...

CYRANO
>Why, then— How do you know?—

ROXANE
People talk about people; and I hear
Things ... and I know.

CYRANO
>You say he is in the Guards:

His name?

ROXANE
>Baron Christian de Neuvillette.

CYRANO
He is not in the Guards.

ROXANE
>Yes. Since this morning.

Captain Carbon de Castel-Jaloux.

CYRANO
>So soon! ...

So soon we lose our hearts!—
>But, my dear child,—

THE DUENNA
(opens the door)
I have eaten the cakes, Monsieur de Bergerac!

CYRANO
Good! Now go out and read the poetry!
(The DUENNA *disappears.)*

—But, my dear child! You, who love only words,
Wit, the grand manner— Why, for all you know,
The man may be a savage, or a fool.

ROXANE

His curls are like a hero from D'Urfé.

CYRANO

His mind may be as curly as his hair.

ROXANE

Not with such eyes. I read his soul in them.

CYRANO

Yes, all our souls are written in our eyes!
But—if he be a bungler?

ROXANE

                Then I shall die—
There!

CYRANO

(after a pause)
        And you brought me here to tell me this?
I do not yet quite understand, Madame,
The reason for your confidence.

ROXANE

                        They say
That in your company— It frightens me—
You are all Gascons . . .

CYRANO

                And we pick a quarrel
With any flat-foot who intrudes himself,
Whose blood is not pure Gascon like our own?
Is this what you have heard?

ROXANE

                     I am so afraid
For him!

CYRANO

(between his teeth)
       Not without reason!—

ROXANE

                    And I thought
You . . . You were so brave, so invincible

Yesterday, against all those brutes!—If you,
Whom they all fear—

CYRANO

                Oh well— I will defend
Your little Baron.

ROXANE

                Will you? Just for me?
Because I have always been—your friend!

CYRANO

                              Of course . . .

ROXANE

Will you be *his* friend?

CYRANO

                I will be his friend.

ROXANE

And never let him fight a duel?

CYRANO

                No—never.

ROXANE

Oh, but you are a darling!—I must go—
You never told me about last night— Why,
You must have been a hero! Have him write
And tell me all about it—will you?

CYRANO

                Of course . . .

ROXANE

(kisses her hand)
I always did love you!—A hundred men
Against one— Well. . . . Adieu. We are great friends,
Are we not?

CYRANO

      Of course . . .

ROXANE

              He *must* write to me—
A hundred— You shall tell me the whole story
Some day, when I have time. A hundred men—
What courage—

CYRANO
(salutes as she goes out)
                Oh . . . I have done better since!

(The door closes after her. CYRANO *remains motionless, his eyes on the ground. Pause. The other door opens;* RAGUENEAU *puts in his head.)*

RAGUENEAU
May I come in?
CYRANO
(without moving)
                Yes . . .

*(*RAGUENEAU *and his friends re-enter. At the same time,* CARBON DE CASTEL-JALOUX *appears at the street door in uniform as Captain of the Guards; recognizes* CYRANO *with a sweeping gesture.)*

CARBON
                Here he is!—Our hero!
CYRANO
(raises his head and salutes)
Our Captain!
CARBON
            We know! All our company
Are here—
CYRANO
(recoils)
        No—
CARBON
            Come! They are waiting for you.
CYRANO
                            No!
CARBON
(tries to lead him out)
Only across the street—Come!
CYRANO
                Please—

CARBON
(goes to the door and shouts in a voice of thunder)
                                        Our champion
Refuses! He is not feeling well today!

A VOICE OUTSIDE
Ah! Sandious!
(Noise outside of swords and trampling feet approaching)

CARBON
            Here they come now!

THE CADETS
(entering the shop)
                                    Mille dious!—
Mordious!—Capdedious!—Pocapdedious!

RAGUENEAU
(in astonishment)
                            Gentlemen—
You are all Gascons?

THE CADETS
            All!

FIRST CADET
(to CYRANO)
                    Bravo!

CYRANO
                    Baron!

ANOTHER CADET
(takes both his hands)
Vivat!

CYRANO
    Baron!

THIRD CADET
            Come to my arms!

CYRANO
                    Baron!

OTHERS
To mine!—To mine!—

CYRANO
                Baron ... Baron ... Have mercy—

RAGUENEAU
You are all Barons too?

THE CADETS
      Are we?
RAGUENEAU
         Are they? . . .
FIRST CADET
Our coronets would star the midnight sky!
LE BRET
(enters; hurries to CYRANO*)*
The whole town's looking for you! Raving mad—
A triumph! Those who saw the fight—
CYRANO
            I hope
You have not told them where I—
LE BRET
(rubbing his hands)
          Certainly
I told them!
CITIZEN
(enters, followed by a group)
    Listen! Shut the door!—Here comes
All Paris!

(The street outside fills with a shouting crowd. Chairs and carriages stop at the door.)

LE BRET
(aside to CYRANO, *smiling)*
    And Roxane?
CYRANO
(quickly)
       Hush!
THE CROWD OUTSIDE
      Cyrano!

(A mob bursts into the shop. Shouts, acclamations, general disturbance)

RAGUENEAU
(standing on a table)
My shop invaded— They'll break everything—
Glorious!

SEVERAL MEN
(crowding about CYRANO)
My friend! ... My friend! ...

CYRANO
Why, yesterday
I did not have so many friends!

LE BRET
Success
At last!

A MARQUIS
(runs to CYRANO, with outstretched hands)
My dear—really!—

CYRANO
(coldly)
So? And how long
Have I been dear to you?

ANOTHER MARQUIS
One moment—pray!
I have two ladies in my carriage here;
Let me present you—

CYRANO
Certainly! And first,
Who will present you, sir,—to me?

LE BRET
(astounded)
Why, what
The devil?—

CYRANO
Hush!

A MAN OF LETTERS
(with a portfolio)
May I have the details? ...

CYRANO
You may not.

LE BRET
  (plucking CYRANO's *sleeve)*
                Theophraste Renaudot!—Editor
  Of the *Gazette*—your reputation! . . .
CYRANO
                                No!
A POET
  (advances)
  Monsieur—
CYRANO
        Well?
THE POET
                Your full name? I will compose
  A pentacrostic—
ANOTHER
                Monsieur—
CYRANO
                        That will do!

(Movement. The crowd arranges itself. DE GUICHE *appears, escorted by* CUIGY, BRISSAILLE, *and the other officers who were with* CYRANO *at the close of the First Act.)*

CUIGY
  (goes to CYRANO*)*
  Monsieur de Guiche!—
  (Murmur. Everyone moves.)
                        A message from the Marshal
  De Gassion—
DE GUICHE
  (saluting CYRANO*)*
                Who wishes to express
  Through me his admiration. He has heard
  Of your affair—
THE CROWD
                Bravo!
CYRANO
  (bowing)
                        The Marshal speaks
  As an authority.

DE GUICHE
                He said just now
The story would have been incredible
Were it not for the witness—
CUIGY
                         Of our eyes!

LE BRET
(aside to CYRANO*)*
What is it?
CYRANO
      Hush!—
LE BRET
              Something is wrong with you;
Are you in pain?
CYRANO
(recovering himself)
            In pain? Before this crowd?
(His mustache bristles. He throws out his chest.).
I? In pain? You shall see!
DE GUICHE
(to whom CUIGY *has been whispering)*
                  Your name is known
Already as a soldier. You are one
Of those wild Gascons, are you not?
CYRANO
                    The Guards,
Yes. A Cadet.
A CADET
(in a voice of thunder)
          One of ourselves!
DE GUICHE
                    Ah! So—
Then all these gentlemen with the haughty air,
These are the famous—
CARBON
           Cyrano!
CYRANO
              Captain?
CARBON
Our troop being all present, be so kind

As to present them to the Comte de Guiche!

CYRANO

(with a gesture presenting the Cadets to DE GUICHE, *declaims)*
The Cadets of Gascoyne—the defenders
   of Carbon de Castel-Jaloux:
Free fighters, free lovers, free spenders—
The Cadets of Gascoyne—the defenders
Of old homes, old names, and old splendors—
   A proud and a pestilent crew!
The Cadets of Gascoyne, the defenders
   Of Carbon de Castel-Jaloux.

Hawk-eyed, they stare down all contenders—
   The wolf bares his fangs as they do—
Make way there, you fat money-lenders!
(Hawk-eyed, they stare down all contenders)
Old boots that have been to the menders,
   Old cloaks that are worn through and through—
Hawk-eyed, they stare down all contenders—
   The wolf bares his fangs as they do!

Skull-breakers they are, and sword-benders;
   Red blood is their favorite brew;
Hot haters and loyal befrienders,
Skull-breakers they are, and sword-benders.
Wherever a quarrel engenders,
   They're ready and waiting for you!
Skull-breakers they are, and sword-benders;
   Red blood is their favorite brew!

Behold them—our Gascon defenders
   Who win every woman they woo!
There's never a dame but surrenders—
Behold them, our Gascon defenders!
Young wives who are clever pretenders—
   Old husbands who house the cuckoo—
Behold them—our Gascon defenders
   Who win every woman they woo!

DE GUICHE
(languidly, sitting in a chair)
Poets are fashionable nowadays
To have about one. Would you care to join
My following?

CYRANO
              No, sir. I do not follow.

DE GUICHE
Your duel yesterday amused my uncle
The Cardinal. I might help you there.

LE BRET
                        Grand Dieu!

DE GUICHE
I suppose you have written a tragedy—
They all have.

LE BRET
(aside to CYRANO*)*
              Now at last you'll have it played—
Your *Agrippine!*

DE GUICHE
              Why not? Take it to him.

CYRANO
(tempted)
Really—

DE GUICHE
       He is himself a dramatist;
Let him rewrite a few lines here and there,
And he'll approve the rest.

CYRANO
(his face falls again)
                    Impossible.
My blood curdles to think of altering
One comma.

DE GUICHE
           Ah, but when he likes a thing
He pays well.

CYRANO
            Yes—but not so well as I—

When I have made a line that sings itself
So that I love the sound of it—I pay
Myself a hundred times.

DE GUICHE

                You are proud, my friend.

CYRANO

You have observed that?

A CADET

(enters with a drawn sword, along the whole blade of which is transfixed a collection of disreputable hats, their plumes draggled, their crowns cut and torn)

                Cyrano! See here—
Look what we found this morning in the street—
The plumes dropped in their flight by those fine birds
Who showed the white feather!

CARBON

                Spoils of the hunt—
Well mounted!

THE CROWD

       Ha-ha-ha!

CUIGY

                Whoever hired
Those rascals, he must be an angry man
Today!

BRISSAILLE

   Who was it? Do you know?

DE GUICHE

                Myself!—
(The laughter ceases.)
I hired them to do the sort of work
We do not soil our hands with—punishing
A drunken poet. . . .
(Uncomfortable silence)

THE CADET

(to CYRANO)

              What shall we do with them?
They ought to be preserved before they spoil—

CYRANO

(takes the sword, and in the gesture of saluting DE GUICHE with

it, makes all the hats slide off at his feet)
Sir, will you not return these to your friends?

DE GUICHE

My chair—my porters here—immediately!
(To CYRANO *violently)*
—As for you, sir!—

A VOICE

(in the street)
>The chair of Monseigneur

Le Comte de Guiche!—

DE GUICHE

(who has recovered his self-control; smiling)
>Have you read *Don Quixote?*

CYRANO

I have—and found myself the hero.

A PORTER

(appears at the door)
>Chair

Ready!

DE GUICHE

>Be so good as to read once more

The chapter of the windmills.

CYRANO

(gravely)
>Chapter Thirteen.

DE GUICHE

Windmills, remember, if you fight with them—

CYRANO

My enemies change, then, with every wind?

DE GUICHE

—May swing round their huge arms and cast you down
Into the mire.

CYRANO

>Or up—among the stars!

(DE GUICHE *goes out. We see him get into the chair. The* OFFICERS *follow, murmuring among themselves.* LE BRET *goes up with them. The crowd goes out.)*

CYRANO

(saluting with burlesque politeness, those who go out without daring to take leave of him)

Gentlemen.... Gentlemen....

LE BRET

(as the door closes, comes down, shaking his clenched hands to heaven)

    You have done it now—
You have made your fortune!

CYRANO

    There you go again,
Growling!—

LE BRET

    At least this latest pose of yours—
Ruining every chance that comes your way—
Becomes exaggerated—

CYRANO

    Very well,
Then I exaggerate!

LE BRET

(triumphantly)

    Oh, you do!

CYRANO

    Yes;
On principle. There are things in this world
A man does well to carry to extremes.

LE BRET

Stop trying to be Three Musketeers in one!
Fortune and glory—

CYRANO

    What would you have me do?
Seek for the patronage of some great man,
And like a creeping vine on a tall tree
Crawl upward, where I cannot stand alone?
No thank you! Dedicate, as others do,
Poems to pawnbrokers? Be a buffoon
In the vile hope of teasing out a smile
On some cold face? No thank you! Eat a toad
For breakfast every morning? Make my knees
Callous, and cultivate a supple spine,—

Wear out my belly groveling in the dust?
No thank you! Scratch the back of any swine
That roots up gold for me? Tickle the horns
Of Mammon with my left hand, while my right
Too proud to know his partner's business,
Takes in the fee? No thank you! Use the fire
God gave me to burn incense all day long
Under the nose of wood and stone? No thank you!
Shall I go leaping into ladies' laps
And licking fingers?—or—to change the form—
Navigating with madrigals for oars,
My sails full of the sighs of dowagers?
No thank you! Publish verses at my own
Expense? No thank you! Be the patron saint
Of a small group of literary souls
Who dine together every Tuesday? No
I thank you! Shall I labor night and day
To build a reputation on one song,
And never write another? Shall I find
True genius only among Geniuses,
Palpitate over little paragraphs,
And struggle to insinuate my name
In the columns of the *Mercury?*
No thank you! Calculate, scheme, be afraid,
Love more to make a visit than a poem,
Seek introductions, favors, influences?—
No thank you! No, I thank you! And again
I thank you!—But . . .
                To sing, to laugh, to dream,
To walk in my own way and be alone,
Free, with an eye to see things as they are,
A voice that means manhood—to cock my hat
Where I choose— At a word, a *Yes*, a *No*,
To fight—or write. To travel any road
Under the sun, under the stars, nor doubt
If fame or fortune lie beyond the bourne—
Never to make a line I have not heard
In my own heart; yet, with all modesty
To say: "My soul, be satisfied with flowers,

With fruit, with weeds even; but gather them
In the one garden you may call your own."
So, when I win some triumph, by some chance,
Render no share to Caesar—in a word,
I am too proud to be a parasite,
And if my nature wants the germ that grows
Towering to heaven like the mountain pine,
Or like the oak, sheltering multitudes—
I stand, not high it may be—but alone!

LE BRET

Alone, yes!—But why stand against the world?
What devil has possessed you now, to go
Everywhere making yourself enemies?

CYRANO

Watching you other people making friends
Everywhere—as a dog makes friends! I mark
The manner of these canine courtesies
And think: "My friends are of a cleaner breed;
Here comes—thank God! another enemy!"

LE BRET

But this is madness!

CYRANO

              Method, let us say.
It is my pleasure to displease. I love
Hatred. Imagine how it feels to face
The volley of a thousand angry eyes—
The bile of envy and the froth of fear
Spattering little drops about me— You—
Good nature all around you, soft and warm—
You are like those Italians, in great cowls
Comfortable and loose— Your chin sinks down
Into the folds, your shoulders droop. But I—
The Spanish ruff I wear around my throat
Is like a ring of enemies; hard, proud,
Each point another pride, another thorn—
So that I hold myself erect perforce
Wearing the hatred of the common herd
Haughtily, the harsh collar of Old Spain,
At once a fetter and—a halo!

LE BRET

Yes . . .
(After a silence, draws CYRANO's *arm through his own.)*
Tell this to all the world— And then to me
Say very softly that . . . She loves you not.

CYRANO

(quickly)
Hush!

(A moment since, CHRISTIAN *has entered and mingled with the* CADETS, *who do not offer to speak to him. Finally, he sits down alone at a small table, where he is served by* LISE.*)*

A CADET

(rises from a table upstage, his glass in his hand)
Cyrano!—Your story!

CYRANO

Presently . . .

(He goes up, on the arm of LE BRET, *talking to him. The* CADET *comes downstage.)*

THE CADET

The story of the combat! An example
For—
(He stops by the table where CHRISTIAN *is sitting.)*
—this young tadpole here.

CHRISTIAN

(looks up)

Tadpole?

ANOTHER CADET

Yes, you!—
You narrow-gutted Northerner!

CHRISTIAN

Sir?

FIRST CADET

Hark ye,
Monsieur de Neuvillette: You are to know
There is a certain subject—I would say,

A certain object—never to be named
Among us: utterly unmentionable!

CHRISTIAN
And that is?

THIRD CADET
(in an awful voice)
            Look at me! ...
(He strikes his nose three times with his finger, mysteriously.)
                    You understand?

CHRISTIAN
Why, yes; the—

FOURTH CADET
            Sh! ... We never speak that word—
(Indicating CYRANO *by a gesture)*
To breathe it is to have to do with HIM!

FIFTH CADET
(speaks through his nose)
He has exterminated several
Whose tone of voice suggested ...

SIXTH CADET
(in a hollow tone; rising from under the table on all fours)
                    Would you die
Before your time? Just mention anything
Convex ... or cartilaginous ...

SEVENTH CADET
(his hand on CHRISTIAN's *shoulder)*
                    One word—
One syllable—one gesture—nay, one sneeze—
Your handkerchief becomes your winding sheet!

(Silence. In a circle around CHRISTIAN, *arms crossed, they regard him expectantly.)*

CHRISTIAN
(rises and goes to CARBON, *who is conversing with an officer, and pretending not to see what is taking place)*
Captain!

CARBON
(turns, and looks him over)
            Sir?

CHRISTIAN
>   What is the proper thing to do
> When Gascons grow too boastful?

CARBON
>   Prove to them
> That one may be a Norman, and have courage.
> *(Turns his back.)*

CHRISTIAN
> I thank you.

FIRST CADET
(to CYRANO)
>   Come—the story!

ALL
>   The story!

CYRANO
(comes down)
>   Oh,
> My story? Well ...
> *(They all draw up their stools and group themselves around him, eagerly. CHRISTIAN places himself astride of a chair, his arms on the back of it.)*
>   I marched on, all alone
> To meet those devils. Overhead, the moon
> Hung like a gold watch at the fob of heaven,
> Till suddenly some Angel rubbed a cloud,
> As it might be his handkerchief, across
> The shining crystal, and—the night came down.
> No lamps in those back streets— It was so dark—
> Mordious! You could not see beyond—

CHRISTIAN
>   Your nose.

(Silence. Every man slowly rises to his feet. They look at CYRANO almost with terror. He has stopped short, utterly astonished. Pause.)

CYRANO
> Who is that man there?

A CADET
 (in a low voice)
        A recruit—arrived
This morning.
CYRANO
 (takes a step toward CHRISTIAN*)*
      A recruit—
CARBON
 (in a low voice)
          His name is Christian
De Neuvil—
CYRANO
 (suddenly motionless)
      Oh . . .
 (He turns pale, flushes, makes a movement as if to throw himself upon CHRISTIAN.*)*
        I—
 (Controls himself, and goes on in a choking voice.)
        I see. Very well,
As I was saying—
 (With a sudden burst of rage)
       Mordious! . . .
 (He goes on in a natural tone.)
           It grew dark,
You could not see your hand before your eyes.
I marched on, thinking how, all for the sake
Of one old souse
 (They slowly sit down, watching him.)
      who wrote a bawdy song
Whenever he took—
CHRISTIAN
      A noseful—

 (Everyone rises. CHRISTIAN *balances himself on two legs of his chair.)*

CYRANO
 (half strangled)
          —Took a notion.

Whenever he took a notion— For his sake,
I might antagonize some dangerous man,
One powerful enough to make me pay—
CHRISTIAN

Through the nose—
CYRANO

(wipes the sweat from his forehead)
       —Pay the Piper. After all,
I thought, why am I putting in my—
CHRISTIAN

              Nose—

CYRANO

—My oar ... Why am I putting in my oar?
The quarrel's none of mine. However—now
I am here, I may as well go through with it.
Come Gascon—do your duty!—Suddenly
A sword flashed in the dark. I caught it fair—
CHRISTIAN

On the nose—
CYRANO

     On my blade. Before I knew it,
There I was—
CHRISTIAN

    Rubbing noses—

CYRANO

(pale and smiling)
          Crossing swords
With half a score at once. I handed one—
CHRISTIAN

A nosegay—
CYRANO

(leaping at him)
    Ventre-Saint-Gris! ...

(The GASCONS *tumble over each other to get a good view. Arrived in front of* CHRISTIAN, *who has not moved an inch,* CYRANO *masters himself again, and continues.)*

         He went down;
The rest gave way; I charged—

CHRISTIAN
>   Nose in the air—

CYRANO
I skewered two of them—disarmed a third—
Another lunged— Paf! and I countered—

CHRISTIAN
>   Pif!

CYRANO
(bellowing)
Tonnerre! Out of here!—All of you!
(All the CADETS *rush for the door.)*

FIRST CADET
>   At last—

The old lion wakes!

CYRANO
>   All of you! Leave me here

Alone with that man!

(The lines following are heard brokenly in the confusion of getting through the door.)

SECOND CADET
>   Bigre! He'll have the fellow

Chopped into sausage—

RAGUENEAU
>   Sausage?—

THIRD CADET
>   Mince-meat, then—

One of your pies!—

RAGUENEAU
>   Am I pale? You look white

As a fresh napkin—

CARBON
(at the door)
>   Come!

FOURTH CADET
>   He'll never leave

Enough of him to—

FIFTH CADET
                Why, it frightens ME
To think of what will—
SIXTH CADET
(closing the door)
                     Something horrible
Beyond imagination . . .

(They are all gone: some through the street door, some by the inner doors to right and left. A few disappear up the staircase. CYRANO and CHRISTIAN stand face to face a moment, and look at each other.)

CYRANO
  To my arms!
CHRISTIAN
  Sir? . . .
CYRANO
        You have courage!
CHRISTIAN
                  Oh, that! . . .
CYRANO
                          You are brave—
That pleases me.
CHRISTIAN
         You mean? . . .
CYRANO
                 Do you not know
I am her brother? Come!
CHRISTIAN
          Whose?—
CYRANO
                Hers—Roxane!
CHRISTIAN
  Her . . . brother? You?
  (Hurries to him.)
CYRANO
              Her cousin. Much the same.

CHRISTIAN
  And she has told you? ...
CYRANO
                    Everything.
CHRISTIAN
                              She loves me?
CYRANO
  Perhaps.
CHRISTIAN
  (takes both his hands)
          My dear sir—more than I can say,
  I am honored—
CYRANO
              This is rather sudden.
CHRISTIAN
                              Please
  Forgive me—
CYRANO
  (holds him at arm's length, looking at him)
          Why, he is a handsome devil,
  This fellow!
CHRISTIAN
          On my honor—if you knew
  How much I have admired—
CYRANO
                    Yes, yes—and all
  Those Noses which—
CHRISTIAN
              Please! I apologize.
CYRANO
  (change of tone)
  Roxane expects a letter—
CHRISTIAN
                    Not from me?—
CYRANO
  Yes. Why not?
CHRISTIAN
          Once I write, that ruins all!

CYRANO
  And why?
CHRISTIAN
            Because . . . because I am a fool!
  Stupid enough to hang myself!
CYRANO
                              But no—
  You are no fool; you call yourself a fool,
  There's proof enough in that. Besides, you did not
  Attack me like a fool.
CHRISTIAN
                    Bah! Anyone
  Can pick a quarrel. Yes, I have a sort
  Of rough and ready soldier's tongue. I know
  That. But with any woman—paralyzed,
  Speechless, dumb. I can only look at them.
  Yet sometimes, when I go away, their eyes . . .
CYRANO
  Why not their hearts, if you should wait and see?
CHRISTIAN
  No. I am one of those— I know—those men
  Who never can make love.
CYRANO
                        Strange. . . . Now it seems
  I, if I gave my mind to it, I might
  Perhaps make love well.
CHRISTIAN
                      Oh, if I had words
  To say what I have here!
CYRANO
                        If I could be
  A handsome little Musketeer with eyes!—
CHRISTIAN
  Besides—you know Roxane—how sensitive—
  One rough word, and the sweet illusion—gone!
CYRANO
  I wish you might be my interpreter.
CHRISTIAN
  I wish I had your wit—

CYRANO
                    Borrow it, then!—
Your beautiful young manhood—lend me that,
And we two make one hero of romance!
CHRISTIAN
  What?
CYRANO
            Would you dare repeat to her the words
I gave you, day by day?
CHRISTIAN
                    You mean?
CYRANO
                                I mean
Roxane shall have no disillusionment!
Come, shall we win her both together? Take
The soul within this leathern jack of mine,
And breathe it into you?
(Touches him on the breast.)
                    So—there's my heart
Under your velvet, now!
CHRISTIAN
                    But— Cyrano!—
CYRANO
  But— Christian, why not?
CHRISTIAN
                    I am afraid—
CYRANO
                                I know—
Afraid that when you have her all alone,
You lose all. Have no fear. It is yourself
She loves—give her yourself put into words—
My words, upon your lips!
CHRISTIAN
                    But . . . but your eyes! . . .
They burn like—
CYRANO
            Will you? . . . Will you?

CHRISTIAN
                          Does it mean
So much to you?
CYRANO
(beside himself)
              It means—
(Recovers, changes tone.)
                    A Comedy,
A situation for a poet! Come.
Shall we collaborate? I'll be your cloak
Of darkness, your enchanted sword, your ring
To charm the fairy Princess!
CHRISTIAN
                      But the letter—
I cannot write—
CYRANO
         Oh yes, the letter.
(He takes from his pocket the letter which he has written.)
                        Here.
CHRISTIAN
What is this?
CYRANO
          All there; all but the address.
CHRISTIAN
I—
CYRANO
  Oh, you may send it. It will serve.
CHRISTIAN
                        But why
Have you done this?
CYRANO
             I have amused myself
As we all do, we poets—writing vows
To Chloris, Phyllis—any pretty name—
You might have had a pocketful of them!
Take it, and turn to facts my fantasies—
I loosed these loves like doves into the air;
Give them a habitation and a home.

Here, take it— You will find me all the more
Eloquent, being insincere! Come!
CHRISTIAN
        First,
There must be a few changes here and there—
Written at random, can it fit Roxane?
CYRANO
 Like her own glove.
CHRISTIAN
        No, but—
CYRANO
           My son, have faith—
Faith in the love of women for themselves—
Roxane will know this letter for her own!
CHRISTIAN
(throws himself into the arms of CYRANO; *they stand embraced)*
My friend!
(The door upstage opens a little. A CADET *steals in.)*
THE CADET
      Nothing. A silence like the tomb . . .
I hardly dare look—*(He sees the two.)*
        Wha-at?
(The other CADETS *crowd in behind him and see.)*
THE CADETS
       No!—No!
SECOND CADET
          Mon dieu!
THE MUSKETEER
 (slaps his knee)
 Well, well, well!
CARBON
       Here's our devil . . . Christianized!
Offend one nostril, and he turns the other.
THE MUSKETEER
Now we are allowed to talk about his nose!
(Calls.)
Hey, Lise! Come here— *(Affectedly)*
       Snf! What a horrid smell!

What is it? . . .
(Plants himself in front of CYRANO, *and looks at his nose in an impolite manner.)*
You ought to know about such things;
What seems to have died around here?

CYRANO
(knocks him backward over a bench)
Cabbage-heads!

(Joy. The CADETS *have found their old* CYRANO *again. General disturbance.)*

(Curtain)

THE THIRD ACT

ROXANE'S KISS

A little square in the old Marais: old houses, and a glimpse of narrow streets. On the Right, THE HOUSE OF ROXANE *and her garden wall, overhung with tall shrubbery. Over the door of the house a balcony and a tall window; to one side of the door, a bench.*

Ivy clings to the wall; jasmine embraces the balcony, trembles, and falls away.

By the bench and the jutting stonework of the wall one might easily climb up to the balcony.

Opposite, an ancient house of the like character, brick and stone, whose front door forms an Entrance. The knocker on this door is tied up in linen like an injured thumb.

At the CURTAIN RISE *the* DUENNA *is seated on the bench beside the door. The window is wide open on* ROXANE'S *balcony; a light within suggests that it is early evening. By the* DUENNA *stands* RAGUENEAU *dressed in what might be the livery of one attached to the household. He is by way of telling her something, and wiping his eyes meanwhile.*

RAGUENEAU
—And so she ran off with a Musketeer!
I was ruined—I was alone— Remained
Nothing for me to do but hang myself,
So I did that. Presently along comes
Monsieur de Bergerac, and cuts me down,
And makes me steward to his cousin.

THE DUENNA
                              Ruined?—
I thought your pastry was a great success!

RAGUENEAU
(shakes his head)
Lise loved the soldiers, and I loved the poets—
Mars ate up all the cakes Apollo left;
It did not take long....

THE DUENNA
(calls up to window)
                    Roxane! Are you ready?
We are late!

VOICE OF ROXANE
(within)
            Putting on my cape—

THE DUENNA
(to RAGUENEAU, *indicating the house opposite)*
                        Clomire
Across the way receives on Thursday nights—
We are to have a psycho-colloquy
Upon the Tender Passion.

RAGUENEAU
                    Ah—the Tender...

THE DUENNA
(sighs)
—Passion!...
(Calls up to window.)
            Roxane!—Hurry, dear—we shall miss
The Tender Passion!

ROXANE
            Coming!—
(Music of stringed instruments offstage approaching)

THE VOICE OF CYRANO
  (singing)
                              La, la, la!—
THE DUENNA
  A serenade?—How pleasant—
CYRANO
                              No, no, no!—
  F natural, you natural born fool!
  (Enters, followed by two PAGES, *carrying theorbos.)*
FIRST PAGE
  (ironically)
  No doubt your honor knows F natural
  When he hears—
CYRANO
                    I am a musician, infant!—
  A pupil of Gassendi.
THE PAGE
  (plays and sings)
                        La, la,—
CYRANO
                              Here—
  Give me that—
  (He snatches the instrument from the PAGE *and continues the tune.)*
                        La, la, la, la—
ROXANE
  (appears on the balcony)
                                  Is that you,
  Cyrano?
CYRANO
  (singing)
         I, who praise your lilies fair,
  But long to love your ro . . . ses!
ROXANE
                                    I'll be down—
  Wait—
  (Goes in through window.)
THE DUENNA
          Did you train these virtuosi?

CYRANO

No—
I won them on a bet from D'Assoucy.
We were debating a fine point of grammar
When, pointing out these two young nightingales
Dressed up like peacocks, with their instruments,
He cries: "No, but I KNOW! I'll wager you
A day of music." Well, of course he lost;
And so until tomorrow they are mine,
My private orchestra. Pleasant at first,
But they become a trifle—
(To the PAGES*)*

Here! Go play
A minuet to Montfleury—and tell him
I sent you!
(The PAGES *go up to the exit.* CYRANO *turns to the* DUENNA.*)*
I came here as usual
To inquire after our friend—
(To PAGES*)*

Play out of tune.
And keep on playing!
(The PAGES *go out. He turns to the* DUENNA.*)*
Our friend with the great soul.

ROXANE

(enters in time to hear the last words)
He is beautiful and brilliant—and I love him!

CYRANO

Do you find Christian . . . intellectual?

ROXANE

More so than you, even.

CYRANO

I am glad.

ROXANE

No man
Ever so beautifully said those things—
Those pretty nothings that are everything.
Sometimes he falls into a reverie;
His inspiration fails—then all at once,
He will say something absolutely . . . Oh! . . .

CYRANO

Really!

ROXANE

How like a man! You think a man
Who has a handsome face must be a fool.

CYRANO

He talks well about . . . matters of the heart?

ROXANE

He does not *talk;* he rhapsodizes . . . dreams . . .

CYRANO

(twisting his mustache)
He . . . writes well?

ROXANE

Wonderfully. Listen now:
(Reciting as from memory)
"Take my heart; I shall have it all the more;
Plucking the flowers, we keep the plant in bloom—"
Well?

CYRANO

Pooh!

ROXANE

And this:
"Knowing you have in store
More heart to give than I find heart-room—"

CYRANO

First he has too much, then too little; just
How much heart does he need?

ROXANE

(tapping her foot)

You are teasing me!
You are jealous!

CYRANO

(startled)

Jealous?

ROXANE

Of his poetry—
You poets are like that . . .
And these last lines
Are they not the last word in tenderness?—

"There is no more to say: only believe
That unto you my whole heart gives one cry,
And writing, writes down more than you receive;
Sending you kisses through my fingertips—
Lady, O read my letter with your lips!"

CYRANO

H'm, yes— those last lines . . . but he overwrites!

ROXANE

Listen to this—

CYRANO

                You know them all by heart?

ROXANE

Every one!

CYRANO

(twisting his mustache)
              I may call that flattering . . .

ROXANE

He is a master!

CYRANO

              Oh—come!

ROXANE

                      Yes—a master!

CYRANO

(bowing)
A master—if you will!

THE DUENNA

(comes downstage quickly)
                      Monsieur de Guiche!—
(To CYRANO, *pushing him toward the house)*
Go inside— If he does not find you here,
It may be just as well. He may suspect—

ROXANE

—My secret! Yes; he is in love with me
And he is powerful. Let him not know—
One look would frost my roses before bloom.

CYRANO

(going into house)
Very well, very well!

ROXANE
(to DE GUICHE, *as he enters)*
                          We were just going—
DE GUICHE
  I came only to say farewell.
ROXANE
                          You leave
  Paris?
DE GUICHE
        Yes—for the front.
ROXANE
                          Ah!
DE GUICHE
                          And tonight!
ROXANE
  Ah!
DE GUICHE
        We have orders to besiege Arras.
ROXANE
  Arras?
DE GUICHE
        Yes. My departure leaves you . . . cold?
ROXANE
  (politely)
  Oh! Not that.
DE GUICHE
              It has left me desolate—
  When shall I see you? Ever? Did you know
  I was made Colonel?
ROXANE
  (indifferent)
                          Bravo.
DE GUICHE
                          Regiment
  Of the Guards.
ROXANE
  (catching her breath)
                Of the Guards?—

DE GUICHE

                            His regiment
Your cousin, the mighty man of words!—
(Grimly)

                                   Down there
We may have an accounting!

ROXANE

(suffocating)

                           Are you sure
The Guards are ordered?

DE GUICHE

                      Under my command!

ROXANE

(sinks down, breathless, on the bench; aside)
Christian!—

DE GUICHE

        What is it?

ROXANE

(losing control of herself)

                  To the war—perhaps
Never again to— When a woman cares,
Is that nothing?

DE GUICHE

(surprised and delighted)

            You say this now—to me—
Now, at the very moment?—

ROXANE

(recovers—changes her tone)

                     Tell me something:
My cousin— You say you mean to be revenged
On him. Do you mean that?

DE GUICHE

(smiles)

                    Why? Would you care?

ROXANE

Not for him.

DE GUICHE

      Do you see him?

ROXANE

              Now and then.

DE GUICHE
    He goes about everywhere nowadays
    With one of the Cadets—de Neuve—Neuville—
    Neuvillers—
ROXANE
    (coolly)
                A tall man?—
DE GUICHE
                            Blond—
ROXANE
                                    Rosy cheeks?—
DE GUICHE
    Handsome!—
ROXANE
            Pooh!—
DE GUICHE
                And a fool.
ROXANE
    (languidly)
                            So he appears ...
    (Animated)
    But Cyrano? What will you do to him?
    Order him into danger? He loves that!
    I know what *I* should do.
DE GUICHE
                What?
ROXANE
                        Leave him here
    With his Cadets, while all the regiment
    Goes on to glory! That would torture him—
    To sit all through the war with folded arms—
    I know his nature. If you hate that man,
    Strike at his self-esteem.
DE GUICHE
                    Oh woman—woman!
    Who but a woman would have thought of this?
ROXANE
    He'll eat his heart out, while his Gascon friends
    Bite their nails all day long in Paris here.
    And you will be avenged!

DE GUICHE

                    You love me then,
A little? ...
(She smiles.)
        Making my enemies your own,
Hating them—I should like to see in that
A sign of love, Roxane.

ROXANE

                Perhaps it is one ...

DE GUICHE

(shows a number of folded dispatches)
Here are the orders—for each company—
Ready to send ...
(Selects one.)
        So— This is for the Guards—
I'll keep that. Aha, Cyrano!
(To ROXANE*)*
                    You too,
You play your little games, do you?

ROXANE

(watching him)
                    Sometimes ...

DE GUICHE

(close to her, speaking hurriedly)
And you!—Oh, I am mad over you!—
                        Listen—
I leave tonight—but—let you through my hands
Now, when I feel you trembling?—Listen— Close by,
In the Rue d'Orléans, the Capuchins
Have their new convent. By their law, no layman
May pass inside those walls. I'll see to that—
Their sleeves are wide enough to cover me—
The servants of my Uncle-Cardinal
Will fear his nephew. So—I'll come to you
Masked, after everyone knows I have gone—
Oh, let me wait one day!—

ROXANE

                If this be known,
Your honor—

DE GUICHE

>Bah!

ROXANE

>The war—your duty—

DE GUICHE
(blows away an imaginary feather)

>>Phoo!—

Only say yes!

ROXANE

>No!

DE GUICHE

>Whisper . . .

ROXANE
(tenderly)

>>I ought not

To let you . . .

DE GUICHE

>Ah! . . .

ROXANE
(pretends to break down)

>Ah, go!

(Aside)

>>—Christian remains—

(Aloud—heroically)
I must have you a hero—Antoine . . .

DE GUICHE

>>Heaven! . . .

So you can love—

ROXANE

>One for whose sake I fear.

DE GUICHE
(triumphant)
I go!
    Will that content you?
(Kisses her hand.)

ROXANE

>Yes—my friend!

(He goes out.)

THE DUENNA
(as DE GUICHE *disappears, making a deep curtsey behind his back, and imitating* ROXANE'S *intense tone)*
Yes—my friend!
ROXANE
(quickly, close to her)
     Not a word to Cyrano—
He would never forgive me if he knew
I stole his war!
(She calls toward the house.)
    Cousin!
(CYRANO *comes out of the house; she turns to him, indicating the house opposite.)*
      We are going over—
Alcandre speaks tonight—and Lysimon.
THE DUENNA
(puts finger in her ear)
My little finger says we shall not hear
Everything.
CYRANO
    Never mind me—
THE DUENNA
(across the street)
        Look— Oh, look!
The knocker tied up in a napkin—Yes,
They muzzled you because you bark too loud
And interrupt the lecture—little beast!
ROXANE
(as the door opens)
Enter . . .
(To CYRANO*)*
   If Christian comes, tell him to wait.
CYRANO
Oh—
*(*ROXANE *returns.)*
  When he comes, what will you talk about?
You always know beforehand.
ROXANE
       About . . .

CYRANO

                              Well?

ROXANE

You will not tell him, will you?

CYRANO

                       I am dumb.

ROXANE

About nothing! Or about everything—
I shall say: "Speak of love in your own words—
Improvise! Rhapsodize! Be eloquent!"

CYRANO

(smiling)
Good!

ROXANE

    Sh!—

CYRANO

        Sh!—

ROXANE

            Not a word!
(She goes in; the door closes.)

CYRANO

(bowing)

                      Thank you so much—

ROXANE

(opens door and puts out her head)
He must be unprepared—

CYRANO

               Of course!

ROXANE

                    Sh!—

(Goes in again.)

CYRANO

(calls)

                           Christian!

(CHRISTIAN enters.)
I have your theme—bring on your memory!—
Here is your chance now to surpass yourself,
No time to lose— Come! Look intelligent—
Come home and learn your lines.

CHRISTIAN
                    No.
CYRANO
                        What?
CHRISTIAN
                                I'll wait
Here for Roxane.
CYRANO
            What lunacy is this?
Come quickly!
CHRISTIAN
                No, I say! I have had enough—
Taking my words, my letters, all from you—
Making our love a little comedy!
It was a game at first; but now—she cares . . .
Thanks to you. I am not afraid. I'll speak
For myself now.
CYRANO
            Undoubtedly!
CHRISTIAN
                    I will!
Why not? I am no such fool—you shall see!
Besides—my dear friend—you have taught me much.
I ought to know something. . . . By God, I know
Enough to take a woman in my arms!
(ROXANE *appears in the doorway, opposite.*)
There she is now . . . Cyrano, wait! Stay here!
CYRANO
(bows)
Speak for yourself, my friend!
(He goes out.)
ROXANE
(taking leave of the company)
                        —Barthénoide!
Alcandre! . . . Grémione! . . .
THE DUENNA
                    I told you so—
We missed the Tender Passion!
(She goes into ROXANE's *house.)*

ROXANE
                    Urimédonte!—
Adieu!
(As the guests disappear down the street, she turns to CHRISTIAN.*)*
        Is that you, Christian? Let us stay
Here, in the twilight. They are gone. The air
Is fragrant. We shall be alone. Sit down
There—so . . .
(They sit on the bench.)
            Now tell me things.

CHRISTIAN
(after a silence)
                        I love you.

ROXANE
(closes her eyes)
                            Yes,
Speak to me about love . . .

CHRISTIAN
                I love you.

ROXANE
                        Now
Be eloquent! . . .

CHRISTIAN
            I love—

ROXANE
(opens her eyes)
                You have your theme—
Improvise! Rhapsodize!

CHRISTIAN
                I love you so!

ROXANE
Of course. And then? . . .

CHRISTIAN
                And then . . . Oh, I should be
So happy if you loved me too! Roxane,
Say that you love me too!

ROXANE
(making a face)

I ask for cream
You give me milk and water. Tell me first
A little, how you love me.
CHRISTIAN
Very much.
ROXANE
Oh—tell me how you *feel!*
CHRISTIAN
(coming nearer, and devouring her with his eyes)
Your throat . . . If only
I might . . . kiss it—
ROXANE
Christian!
CHRISTIAN
I love you so!
ROXANE
(makes as if to rise)
Again?
CHRISTIAN
(desperately, restraining her)
No, not again— I do not love you—
ROXANE
(settles back)
That is better . . .
CHRISTIAN
I adore you!
ROXANE
Oh!—
(Rises and moves away.)
CHRISTIAN
I know;
I grow absurd.
ROXANE
(coldly)
And that displeases me
As much as if you had grown ugly.
CHRISTIAN
I—
ROXANE
Gather your dreams together into words!

CHRISTIAN
I love—
ROXANE
    I know; you love me. Adieu.
(She goes to the house.)
CHRISTIAN
                            No,
But wait—please—let me— I was going to say—
ROXANE
(pushes the door open)
That you adore me. Yes; I know that too.
No! . . . Go away! . . .
(She goes in and shuts the door in his face.)
CHRISTIAN
              I . . . I . . .

CYRANO
(enters)
                     A great success!

CHRISTIAN
Help me!
CYRANO
    Not I.
CHRISTIAN
        I cannot live unless
She loves me—now, this moment!
CYRANO
                    How the devil
Am I to teach you now—this moment?
CHRISTIAN
(catches him by the arm)
                      —Wait!—
Look! Up there!—Quick—
(The light shows in ROXANE'S *window.)*
CYRANO
                Her window—
CHRISTIAN
(wailing)
                      I shall die!—
CYRANO
Less noise!

CHRISTIAN
>Oh, I—

CYRANO
>It does seem fairly dark—

CHRISTIAN
(excitedly)
Well?—Well?—Well?—

CYRANO
>Let us try what can be done;
It is more than you deserve—stand over there,
Idiot—there!—before the balcony—
Let me stand underneath. I'll whisper you
What to say.

CHRISTIAN
>She may hear—she may—

CYRANO
>Less noise!

(The PAGES appear upstage.)

FIRST PAGE
Hep!—

CYRANO
(finger to lips)
Sh!—

FIRST PAGE
(low voice)
>We serenaded Montfleury!—
What next?

CYRANO
>Down to the corner of the street—
One this way—and the other over there—
If anybody passes, play a tune!

PAGE
What tune, O musical Philosopher?

CYRANO
Sad for a man, or merry for a woman—
Now go!
(The PAGES disappear, one toward each corner of the street.)

CYRANO
(to CHRISTIAN)

Call her!
CHRISTIAN
Roxane!
CYRANO
Wait...
(Gathers up a handful of pebbles.)
Gravel...
(Throws it at the window.)
There!—
ROXANE
(opens the window)
Who is calling?
CHRISTIAN
I—
ROXANE
Who?
CHRISTIAN
Christian.
ROXANE
You again?
CHRISTIAN
I had to tell you—
CYRANO
(under the balcony)
Good— Keep your voice down.
ROXANE
No. Go away. You tell me nothing.
CHRISTIAN
Please!—
ROXANE
You do not love me any more—
CHRISTIAN
(to whom CYRANO whispers his words)
No—no—
Not any more— I love you ... evermore ...
And ever ... more and more!
ROXANE
(about to close the window—pauses)
A little better...

CHRISTIAN
(same business)
Love grows and struggles like . . . an angry child . . .
Breaking my heart . . . his cradle . . .

ROXANE
(coming out on the balcony)
                                          Better still—
But . . . such a babe is dangerous; why not
Have smothered it newborn?

CHRISTIAN
(same business)
                          And so I do . . .
And yet he lives . . . I found . . . as you shall find . . .
This newborn babe . . . an infant . . . Hercules!

ROXANE
(further forward)
Good!—

CHRISTIAN
(same business)
                  Strong enough . . . at birth . . . to strangle those
Two serpents—Doubt and . . . Pride.

ROXANE
(leans over balcony)
                                  Why, very well!
Tell me now why you speak so haltingly—
Has your imagination gone lame?

CYRANO
(thrusts CHRISTIAN under the balcony, and stands in his place)
                            Here—
This grows too difficult!

ROXANE
                     Your words tonight
Hesitate. Why?

CYRANO
(in a low tone, imitating CHRISTIAN)
                Through the warm summer gloom
They grope in darkness toward the light of you.

ROXANE
My words, well aimed, find you more readily.

CYRANO

My heart is open wide and waits for them—
Too large a mark to miss! My words fly home,
Heavy with honey like returning bees,
To your small secret ear. Moreover—yours
Fall to me swiftly. Mine more slowly rise.

ROXANE

Yet not so slowly as they did at first.

CYRANO

They have learned the way, and you have welcomed them.

ROXANE

(softly)

Am I so far above you now?

CYRANO

So far—
If you let fall upon me one hard word,
Out of that height—you crush me!

ROXANE

(turns)

I'll come down—

CYRANO

(quickly)

No!

ROXANE

(points out the bench under the balcony)

Stand you on the bench. Come nearer!

CYRANO

(recoils into the shadow)

No!—

ROXANE

And why—so great a *No?*

CYRANO

(more and more overcome by emotion)

Let me enjoy
The one moment I ever—my one chance
To speak to you . . . unseen!

ROXANE

Unseen?—

CYRANO
                              Yes!—yes . . .
Night, making all things dimly beautiful,
One veil over us both— You only see
The darkness of a long cloak in the gloom,
And I the whiteness of a summer gown—
You are all light—I am all shadow! . . . How
Can you know what this moment means to me?
If I was ever eloquent—

ROXANE
                    You were

Eloquent—
CYRANO
           —You have never heard till now
My own heart speaking!
ROXANE
                Why not?
CYRANO
                              Until now,
I spoke through . . .
ROXANE
               Yes?—
CYRANO
                         —through that sweet drunkenness
You pour into the world out of your eyes!
But tonight . . . but tonight, I indeed speak
For the first time!
ROXANE
                For the first time— Your voice,
Even, is not the same.
CYRANO
(passionately; moves nearer)
                      How should it be?
I have another voice—my own,
Myself, daring—
(He stops, confused; then tries to recover himself.)
                    Where was I? . . . I forget! . . .
Forgive me. This is all sweet like a dream . . .
Strange—like a dream . . .

ROXANE
>How, strange?

CYRANO
>Is it not so
To be myself to you, and have no fear
Of moving you to laughter?

ROXANE
>Laughter—why?

CYRANO
(struggling for an explanation)
Because... What am I... What is any man,
That he dare ask for you? Therefore my heart
Hides behind phrases. There's a modesty
In these things too— I come here to pluck down
Out of the sky the evening star—then smile,
And stoop to gather little flowers.

ROXANE
>Are they
Not sweet, those little flowers?

CYRANO
>Not enough sweet
For you and me, tonight!

ROXANE
(breathless)
>You never spoke
To me like this...

CYRANO
>Little things, pretty things—
Arrows and hearts and torches—roses red,
And violets blue—are these all? Come away,
And breathe fresh air! Must we keep on and on
Sipping stale honey out of tiny cups
Decorated with golden tracery,
Drop by drop, all day long? We are alive;
We thirst— come away, plunge, and drink, and drown
In the great river flowing to the sea!

ROXANE
But... Poetry?

CYRANO
                    I have made rimes for you—
Not now— Shall we insult Nature, this night,
These flowers, this moment—shall we set all these
To phrases from a letter by Voiture?
Look once at the high stars that shine in heaven,
And put off artificiality!
Have you not seen great gaudy hothouse flowers,
Barren, without fragrance?—Souls are like that:
Forced to show all, they soon become all show—
The means to Nature's end ends meaningless!

ROXANE
  But . . . Poetry?

CYRANO
               Love hates that game of words!
It is a crime to fence with life— I tell you,
There comes one moment, once—and God help those
Who pass that moment by!—when Beauty stands
Looking into the soul with grave, sweet eyes
That sicken at pretty words!

ROXANE
                        If that be true—
And when that moment comes to you and me—
What words will you? . . .

CYRANO
                    All those, all those, all those
That blossom in my heart, I'll fling to you—
Armfuls of loose bloom! Love, I love beyond
Breath, beyond reason, beyond love's own power
Of loving! Your name is like a golden bell
Hung in my heart; and when I think of you,
I tremble, and the bell swings and rings—
                                    "Roxane!" . . .
"Roxane!" . . . along my veins, "Roxane!" . . .
                                        I know
All small forgotten things that once meant You—
I remember last year, the First of May,
A little before noon, you had your hair
Drawn low, that one time only. Is that strange?

You know how, after looking at the sun,
One sees red suns everywhere—so, for hours
After the flood of sunshine that you are,
My eyes are blinded by your burning hair!

ROXANE
(very low)
Yes . . . that is . . . Love—

CYRANO
                Yes, that is Love—that wind
Of terrible and jealous beauty, blowing
Over me—that dark fire, that music . . .
                              Yet
Love seeketh not his own! Dear, you may take
My happiness to make you happier,
Even though you never know I gave it you—
Only let me hear sometimes, all alone,
The distant laughter of your joy! . . .
                             I never
Look at you, but there's some new virtue born
In me, some new courage. Do you begin
To understand, a little? Can you feel
My soul, there in the darkness, breathe on you?
—Oh, but tonight, now, I dare say these things—
I . . . to you . . . and you hear them! . . . It is too much!
In my most sweet unreasonable dreams,
I have not hoped for this! Now let me die,
Having lived. It is my voice, mine, my own,
That makes you tremble there in the green gloom
Above me—for you do tremble, as a blossom
Among the leaves— You tremble, and I can feel,
All the way down along these jasmine branches,
Whether you will or no, the passion of you
Trembling . . .
(He kisses wildly the end of a drooping spray of jasmine.)

ROXANE
                Yes, I do tremble . . . and I weep . . .
And I love you . . . and I am yours . . . and you
Have made me thus!

CYRANO
   (after a pause; quietly)
                     What is death like, I wonder?
   I know everything else now . . .
                                 I have done
   This, to you—I, myself . . .
                           Only let me
   Ask one thing more—
CHRISTIAN
   (under the balcony)
                           One kiss!
ROXANE
   (startled)
                                 One?—
CYRANO
   (to CHRISTIAN)
                                       You! . . .
ROXANE
                                       You ask me
   For—
CYRANO
      I . . . Yes, but—I mean—
   (to CHRISTIAN)
                           You go too far!
CHRISTIAN
   She is willing!—Why not make the most of it?
CYRANO
   (to ROXANE)
   I did ask . . . but I know I ask too much . . .
ROXANE
   Only one— Is that all?
CYRANO
                           All!—How much more
   Than all!—I know—I frighten you—I ask . . .
   I ask you to refuse—
CHRISTIAN
   (to CYRANO)
                     But why? Why? Why?
CYRANO
   Christian, be quiet!

ROXANE

(leaning over)

What is that you say
To yourself?

CYRANO

I am angry with myself
Because I go too far, and so I say
To myself: "Christian, be quiet!"—

(The theorbos begin to play.)

Hark—someone
Is coming—

(ROXANE closes her window. CYRANO listens to the theorbos, one of which plays a gay melody, the other a mournful one.)

A sad tune, a merry tune—
Man, woman, what do they mean?—

(A CAPUCHIN enters; he carries a lantern, and goes from house to house, looking at the doors.)

Aha!—a priest!

(To the CAPUCHIN)
What is this new game of Diogenes?

THE CAPUCHIN

I am looking for the house of Madame—

CHRISTIAN

(impatient)

Bah!—

THE CAPUCHIN

Madeleine Robin—

CHRISTIAN

What does he want?

CYRANO

(to the CAPUCHIN; points out a street)

This way—
To the right—keep to the right—

THE CAPUCHIN

I thank you, sir!—
I'll say my beads for you to the last grain.

CYRANO

Good fortune, father, and my service to you!

(The CAPUCHIN goes out.)

CHRISTIAN
 Win me that kiss!
CYRANO
                    No.
CHRISTIAN
                              Sooner or later—
CYRANO
                                        True . . .
 That is true . . . Soon or late, it will be so
 Because you are young and she is beautiful—
 (To himself)
 Since it must be, I had rather be myself
 (The window re-opens. CHRISTIAN *hides under the balcony.)*
 The cause of . . . what must be.
ROXANE
 (out on the balcony)
                              Are you still there?
 We were speaking of—
CYRANO
                    A kiss. The word is sweet—
 What will the deed be? Are your lips afraid
 Even of its burning name? Not much afraid—
 Not too much! Have you not unwittingly
 Laid aside laughter, slipping beyond speech
 Insensibly, already, without fear,
 From words to smiles . . . from smiles to sighs . . . from
    sighing,
 Even to tears? One step more—only one—
 From a tear to a kiss—one step, one thrill!
ROXANE
 Hush—
CYRANO
         And what is a kiss, when all is done?
 A promise given under seal—a vow
 Taken before the shrine of memory—
 A signature acknowledged—a rosy dot
 Over the i of Loving—a secret whispered
 To listening lips apart—a moment made

Immortal, with a rush of wings unseen—
A sacrament of blossoms, a new song
Sung by two hearts to an old simple tune—
The ring of one horizon around two souls
Together, all alone!

ROXANE

     Hush! . . .

CYRANO

         Why, what shame?—
There was a Queen of France, not long ago,
And a great lord of England—a queen's gift,
A crown jewel!

ROXANE

     Indeed!

CYRANO

       Indeed, like him,
I have my sorrows and my silences;
Like her, you are the queen I dare adore;
Like him I am faithful and forlorn—

ROXANE

         Like him,
Beautiful—

CYRANO

(aside)

  So I am—I forgot that!

ROXANE

Then— Come; . . . Gather your sacred blossom . . .

CYRANO

(to CHRISTIAN*)*

            Go!—

ROXANE

Your crown jewel . . .

CYRANO

     Go on!—

ROXANE

        Your old new song . . .

CYRANO

Climb!—

CHRISTIAN
(hesitates)
          No— Would you? not yet—
ROXANE
                          Your moment made
Immortal...
CYRANO
(pushing him)
            Climb up, animal!

(CHRISTIAN springs on the bench, and climbs by the pillars, the branches, the vines, until he bestrides the balcony railing.)

CHRISTIAN
                    Roxane!...
(He takes her in his arms and bends over her.)
CYRANO
(very low)
Ah!... Roxane!...
                 I have won what I have won—
The feast of love—and I am Lazarus!
Yet... I have something that is mine now
And what was not mine before I spoke the words
That won her—not for me!... Kissing my words
My words, upon your lips!
(The theorbos begin to play.)
                        A merry tune—
A sad tune— So! The Capuchin!
(He pretends to be running, as if he had arrived from a distance; then calls up to the balcony.)
                      Hola!
ROXANE
Who is it?
CYRANO
    I. Is Christian there with you?
CHRISTIAN
(astonished)
Cyrano!
ROXANE
    Good morrow, Cousin!

CYRANO
>   Cousin, . . . good morrow!

ROXANE
I am coming down.
(She disappears into the house. The CAPUCHIN *enters upstage.)*

CHRISTIAN
(sees him)
>   Oh—again!

THE CAPUCHIN
(to CYRANO*)*
>   She lives *here*,

Madeleine Robin!

CYRANO
>   You said Ro-LIN.

THE CAPUCHIN
>   No—

R-O-B-I-N

ROXANE
(appears on the threshold of the house, followed by RAGUENEAU *with a lantern, and by* CHRISTIAN*)*
>   What is it?

THE CAPUCHIN
>   A letter.

CHRISTIAN
>   Oh! . . .

THE CAPUCHIN
(to ROXANE*)*
Some matter profitable to the soul—
A very noble lord gave it to me!

ROXANE
(to CHRISTIAN*)*
De Guiche!

CHRISTIAN
>   He dares?—

ROXANE
>   It will not be for long;

When he learns that I love you . . .
(By the light of the lantern which RAGUENEAU *holds, she reads the letter in a low tone, as if to herself.)*
>   "Mademoiselle

The drums are beating, and the regiment
Arms for the march. Secretly I remain
Here, in the Convent. I have disobeyed;
I shall be with you soon. I send this first
By an old monk, as simple as a sheep,
Who understands nothing of this. Your smile
Is more than I can bear, and seek no more.
Be alone tonight, waiting for one who dares
To hope you will forgive . . .—" etcetera—
(To the CAPUCHIN*)*
Father, this letter concerns you . . .
(To CHRISTIAN*)*

                              —and you.
Listen:
(The others gather around her. She pretends to read from the letter, aloud.)
    "Mademoiselle:
              The Cardinal
Will have his way, although against your will;
That is why I am sending this to you
By a most holy man, intelligent,
Discreet. You will communicate to him
Our order to perform, here and at once
The rite of . . .
(Turns the page.)
        —Holy Matrimony. You
And Christian will be married privately
In your house. I have sent him to you. I know
You hesitate. Be resigned, nevertheless,
To the Cardinal's command, who sends herewith
His blessing. Be assured also of my own
Respect and high consideration—*signed*,
Your very humble and—etcetera—"

THE CAPUCHIN
    A noble lord! I said so—never fear—
    A worthy lord!—a very worthy lord!—

ROXANE
    (to CHRISTIAN*)*
    Am I a good reader of letters?

CHRISTIAN
(motions toward the CAPUCHIN*)*
                              Careful!—

ROXANE
(in a tragic tone)
Oh, this is terrible!

THE CAPUCHIN
(turns the lights of his lantern on CYRANO*)*
                    You are to be—

CHRISTIAN
I am the bridegroom!

THE CAPUCHIN
(turns his lantern upon CHRISTIAN*; then as if some suspicion crossed his mind, upon seeing the young man so handsome)*
              Oh—why, *you* . . .

ROXANE
(quickly)
                              Look here—
"Postscript: Give to the Convent in my name
One hundred and twenty pistoles"—

THE CAPUCHIN
                              Think of it!
A worthy lord—a worthy lord! . . .
(To ROXANE, *solemnly)*
Daughter, resign yourself!

ROXANE
(with an air of martyrdom)
                         I am resigned . . .
(While RAGUENEAU *opens the door for the* CAPUCHIN *and* CHRISTIAN *invites him to enter, she turns to* CYRANO.*)*
De Guiche may come. Keep him out here with you.
Do not let him—

CYRANO
              I understand!
(To the CAPUCHIN*)*
                         How long
Will you be?—

THE CAPUCHIN
              Oh, a quarter of an hour.

CYRANO
(hurrying them into the house)
Hurry—I'll wait here—
ROXANE
(to CHRISTIAN*)*
                        Come!
(They go into the house.)
CYRANO
                        Now then, to make
His Grace delay that quarter of an hour . . .
I have it!—up here—
(He steps on the bench, and climbs up the wall toward the balcony. The theorbos begin to play a mournful melody.)
                 Sad music— Ah, a man! . . .
(The music pauses on a sinister tremolo.)
Oh—Very much a man!
(He sits astride of the railing and, drawing toward him a long branch of one of the trees which border the garden wall, he grasps it with both hands, ready to swing himself down.)
                 So—not too high—
(He peers down at the ground.)
I must float gently through the atmosphere—
DE GUICHE
(enters, masked, groping in the dark toward the house)
Where is that cursed, bleating Capuchin?
CYRANO
What if he knows my voice?—the devil!—Tic-tac,
Bergerac—we unlock our Gascon tongue;
A good strong accent—
DE GUICHE
                     Here is the house—all dark—
Damn this mask!—
(As he is about to enter the house, CYRANO *leaps from the balcony, still holding fast to the branch, which bends and swings him between* DE GUICHE *and the door; then he releases the branch and pretends to fall heavily as though from a height. He lands flatly on the ground, where he lies motionless, as if stunned.* DE GUICHE *leaps back.)*

What is that?
(When he lifts his eyes, the branch has sprung back into place. He can see nothing but the sky; he does not understand.)
Why . . . where did this man
Fall from?
CYRANO
(sits up, and speaks with a strong accent)
—The moon!
DE GUICHE
You—
CYRANO
From the moon, the moon!
I fell out of the moon!
DE GUICHE
The fellow is mad—
CYRANO
(dreamily)
Where am I?
DE GUICHE
Why—
CYRANO
What time is it? What place
Is this? What day? What season?
DE GUICHE
You—
CYRANO
I am stunned!
DE GUICHE
My dear sir—
CYRANO
Like a bomb—a bomb—I fell
From the moon!
DE GUICHE
Now, see here—
CYRANO
(rising to his feet, and speaking in a terrible voice)
I say, the moon!

DE GUICHE
  (recoils)
  Very well—if you say so—
  (Aside)
                    Raving mad!—

CYRANO
  (advancing upon him)
  I am not speaking metaphorically!
DE GUICHE
  Pardon.
CYRANO
          A hundred years—an hour ago—
  I really cannot say how long I fell—
  I was in yonder shining sphere—
DE GUICHE
  (shrugs)
                    Quite so.
  Please let me pass.
CYRANO
  (interposes himself)
                Where am I? Tell the truth—
  I can bear it. In what quarter of the globe
  Have I descended like a meteorite?
DE GUICHE
  Morbleu!
CYRANO
          I could not choose my place to fall—
  The earth spun round so fast— Was it the Earth,
  I wonder?—Or is this another world?
  Another moon? Whither have I been drawn
  By the dead weight of my posterior?
DE GUICHE
  Sir. I repeat—
CYRANO
  (with a sudden cry, which causes DE GUICHE *to recoil again)*
              His face! My God—black!
DE GUICHE
  (carries his hand to his mask)
                    Oh!—

CYRANO
(terrified)
Are you a native? Is this Africa?
DE GUICHE
—This mask!
CYRANO
(somewhat reassured)
                Are we in Venice? Genoa?
DE GUICHE
(tries to pass him)
A lady is waiting for me.
CYRANO
(quite happy again)
                        So this is Paris!
DE GUICHE
(smiling in spite of himself)
This fool becomes amusing.
CYRANO
                          Ah! You smile?
DE GUICHE
I do. Kindly permit me—
CYRANO
(delighted)
                      Dear old Paris—
Well, well!—
(Wholly at his ease, smiles, bows, arranges his dress.)
                    Excuse my appearance. I arrive
By the last thunderbolt—a trifle singed
As I came through the ether. These long journeys—
You know! There are so few conveniences!
My eyes are full of star dust. On my spurs,
Some sort of fur . . . Planet's apparently . . .
(Plucks something from his sleeve.)
Look—on my doublet— That's a Comet's hair!
(He blows something from the back of his hand.)
Phoo!
DE GUICHE
(grows angry)
      Monsieur—

CYRANO
>(*as* DE GUICHE *is about to push past, thrusts his leg in the way*)
>>Here's a tooth, stuck in my boot,
>From the Great Bear. Trying to get away,
>I tripped over the Scorpion and came down
>Slap, into one scale of the Balances—
>The pointer marks my weight this moment . . .
>(*Pointing upward*)
>>>See?
>
>(DE GUICHE *makes a sudden movement.* CYRANO *catches his arm.*)
>Be careful! If you struck me on the nose,
>It would drip milk!

DE GUICHE
>>Milk?

CYRANO
>>From the Milky Way!

DE GUICHE
>Hell!

CYRANO
>No, no—Heaven.
>(*Crossing his arms*)
>>Curious place up there—
>Did you know Sirius wore a nightcap? True!
>(*Confidentially*)
>The Little Bear is still too young to bite.
>(*Laughing*)
>My foot caught in the Lyre, and broke a string.
>(*Proudly*)
>Well—when I write my book, and tell the tale
>Of my adventures—all these little stars
>That shake out of my cloak—I must save those
>To use for asterisks!

DE GUICHE
>>That will do now—
>I wish—

CYRANO
>>Yes, yes—I know—

DE GUICHE
>	Sir—

CYRANO
>	You desire
To learn from my own lips the character
Of the moon's surface—its inhabitants
If any—

DE GUICHE
(loses patience and shouts)
>	I desire no such thing! I—

CYRANO
(rapidly)
You wish to know by what mysterious means
I reached the moon?—well—confidenitally—
It was a new invention of my own.

DE GUICHE
(discouraged)
Drunk too—as well as mad!

CYRANO
>	I scourned the eagle
Of Regiomontanus, and the dove
Of Archytas!

DE GUICHE
>	A learned lunatic!—

CYRANO
I imitated no one. I myself
Discovered not one scheme merely, but six—
Six ways to violate the virgin sky!

(DE GUICHE *has succeeded in passing him, and moves toward the door of* ROXANE'S *house.* CYRANO *follows, ready to use violence if necessary.*)

DE GUICHE
(looks around)
Six?

CYRANO
(with increasing volubility)
>	As for instance—Having stripped myself

Bare as a wax candle, adorn my form
With crystal vials filled with morning dew,
And so be drawn aloft, as the sun rises
Drinking the mist of dawn!

DE GUICHE

(takes a step toward CYRANO*)*
                              Yes—that makes one.

CYRANO

(draws back to lead him away from the door; speaks faster and faster)
Or, sealing up the air in a cedar chest,
Rarefy it by means of mirrors, placed
In an icosahedron.

DE GUICHE

(takes another step)
                    Two.

CYRANO

(still retreating)
                          Again,
I might construct a rocket, in the form
Of a huge locust, driven by impulses
Of villainous saltpeter from the rear,
Upward, by leaps and bounds.

DE GUICHE

(interested in spite of himself, and counting on his fingers)
                                      Three.

CYRANO

(same business)
                              Or again,
Smoke having a natural tendency to rise,
Blow in a globe enough to raise me.

DE GUICHE

(same business, more and more astonished)
                                Four!

CYRANO

Or since Diana, as old fables tell,
Draws forth to fill her crescent horn, the marrow
Of bulls and goats—to anoint myself therewith.

DE GUICHE
(hypnotized)
Five!—

CYRANO
(has by this time led him all the way across the street, close to a bench)
    Finally—seated on an iron plate,
To hurl a magnet in the air—the iron
Follows—I catch the magnet—throw again—
And so proceed indefinitely.

DE GUICHE
                    Six!—
All excellent—and which did you adopt?

CYRANO
(coolly)
Why, none of them. . . . A seventh.

DE GUICHE
                          Which was?—

CYRANO
                                Guess!—

DE GUICHE
An interesting idiot, this!

CYRANO
(imitates the sound of waves with his voice, and their movement by large, vague gestures)
                    Hoo! . . . Hoo! . . .

DE GUICHE
Well?

CYRANO
      Have you guessed it yet?

DE GUICHE
                    Why, no.

CYRANO
(grandiloquent)
                          The ocean! . . .
What hour its rising tide seeks the full moon,
I laid me on the strand, fresh from the spray,
My head fronting the moonbeams, since the hair
Retains moisture—and so I slowly rose

As upon angels' wings, effortlessly,
Upward—then suddenly I felt a shock!—
And then . . .
DE GUICHE
(overcome by curiosity, sits down on the bench)
     And then?
CYRANO
         And then—
(Changes abruptly to his natural voice.)
            The time is up!—
Fifteen minutes, your Grace!—You are now free;
And—they are bound—in wedlock.
DE GUICHE
(leaping up)
         Am *I* drunk?
That voice . . .
(The door of ROXANE'S *house opens; lackeys appear, bearing lighted candles. Lights up.* CYRANO *removes his hat.)*
     And that nose!—Cyrano!
CYRANO
(saluting)
           Cyrano! . . .
This very moment, they have exchanged rings.
DE GUICHE
Who?
(He turns up stage. TABLEAU: *Between the lackeys,* ROXANE *and* CHRISTIAN *appear, hand in hand. The* CAPUCHIN *follows them, smiling.* RAGUENEAU *holds aloft a torch. The* DUENNA *brings up the rear, in a negligée, and a pleasant flutter of emotion.)*
   Zounds!
(To ROXANE*)*
     You?—
(Recognizes CHRISTIAN*)*
     He?—
(Saluting ROXANE*)*
       My sincere compliments!
(To CYRANO*)*
You also, my inventor of machines!

Your rigmarole would have detained a saint
Entering Paradise—decidedly
You must not fail to write that book some day!
CYRANO
(bowing)
Sir, I engage myself to do so.
(The CAPUCHIN *leads the bridal pair down to* DE GUICHE *and strokes with great satisfaction his long white beard.)*
THE CAPUCHIN
                     My lord,
The handsome couple you—and God—have joined
Together!
DE GUICHE
(regarding him with a frosty eye)
      Quite so.
(Turns to ROXANE.*)*
                Madame, kindly bid
Your ... husband farewell.
ROXANE
                Oh!—
DE GUICHE
(to CHRISTIAN*)*
                Your regiment
Leaves tonight, sir. Report at once!
ROXANE
                You mean
For the front? The war?
DE GUICHE
            Certainly!
ROXANE
              I thought
The Cadets were not going—
DE GUICHE
            Oh yes, they are!
(Taking out the dispatch from his pocket.)
Here is the order—
(To CHRISTIAN*)*
            Baron! Deliver this.

ROXANE
(throws herself into CHRISTIAN'S *arms)*
Christian!
DE GUICHE
(to CYRANO, *sneering)*
   The bridal night is not so near!
CYRANO
(aside)
Somehow that news fails to disquiet me.
CHRISTIAN
(to ROXANE*)*
Your lips again . . .
CYRANO
     There . . . That will do now— Come!
CHRISTIAN
(still holding ROXANE*)*
You do not know how hard it is—
CYRANO
(tries to drag him away)
        I know!
(The beating of drums is heard in the distance.)
DE GUICHE
(upstage)
The regiment—on the march!
ROXANE
(as CYRANO *tries to lead* CHRISTIAN *away, follows, and detains them)*
      Take care of him
For me—*(appealingly)*
   Promise me never to let him do
Anything dangerous!
CYRANO
     I'll do my best—
I cannot promise—
ROXANE
(same business)
    Make him be careful!
CYRANO
        Yes—
I'll try—

ROXANE
(same business)
>Be sure to keep him dry and warm!

CYRANO
Yes, yes—if possible—

ROXANE
(same business; confidentially, in his ear)
>See that he remains

Faithful!—

CYRANO
>Of course! If—

ROXANE
(same business)
>And have him write to me

Every single day!

CYRANO
(stops)
>That, I promise you!

(Curtain)

THE FOURTH ACT

THE CADETS OF GASCOYNE

THE POST *occupied by the Company of* CARBON DE CASTEL-JALOUX *at* THE SIEGE OF ARRAS.

In the background, a Rampart traversing the entire scene; beyond this, and apparently below, a Plain stretches away to the horizon. The country is cut up with earthworks and other suggestions of the siege. In the distance against the skyline, the houses and the walls of Arras.

Tents; scattered Weapons; Drums, etcetera. It is near daybreak and the East is yellow with approaching dawn. Sentries at intervals. Campfires.

CURTAIN RISE *discovers the* CADETS *asleep, rolled in their cloaks.* CARBON DE CASTEL-JALOUX *and* LE BRET *keep watch. They are both very thin and pale.* CHRISTIAN *is asleep among the others, wrapped in his cloak, in the foreground, his face lighted by the flickering fire. Silence.*

LE BRET
Horrible!
CARBON
   Why, yes. All of that.
LE BRET
        Mordious!
CARBON
(gesture toward the sleeping CADETS*)*
Swear gently— You might wake them.
(To CADETS*)*
          Go to sleep—

Hush!
(To LE BRET*)*
   Who sleeps dines.
LE BRET
      I have insomnia.
God! What a famine.
(Firing offstage)
CARBON
      Curse that musketry!
They'll wake my babies.
(To the men)
      Go to sleep!—
A CADET
(rouses)
        Diantre!

Again?
CARBON
  No—only Cyrano coming home.
(The heads which have been raised sink back again.)
A SENTRY
(offstage)
Halt! Who goes there?

VOICE OF CYRANO
>Bergerac!

THE SENTRY ON THE PARAPET
>Halt! Who goes?—

CYRANO

(appears on the parapet)
Bergerac, idiot!

LE BRET

(goes to meet him)
>Thank God again!

CYRANO

(signs to him not to wake anyone)
Hush!

LE BRET
>Wounded?—

CYRANO
>No— They always miss me—quite

A habit by this time!

LE BRET
>Yes— Go right on—

Risk your life every morning before breakfast
To send a letter!

CYRANO

(stops near CHRISTIAN*)*
>I promised he should write

Every single day . . .
(Looks down at him.)
>Hm— The boy looks pale

When he is asleep—thin too—starving to death—
If that poor child knew! Handsome, none the less . . .

LE BRET

Go and get some sleep!

CYRANO

(affectionately)
>Now, now—you old bear,

No growling!—I am careful—you know I am—
Every night, when I cross the Spanish lines
I wait till they are all drunk.

LE BRET

                          You might bring
Something with you.

CYRANO

                    I have to travel light
To pass through—By the way, there will be news
For you today: the French will eat or die,
If what I saw means anything.

LE BRET

                        Tell us!

CYRANO

                            No—
I am not sure—we shall see!

CARBON

                    What a war,
When the besieger starves to death!

LE BRET

                            Fine war—
Fine situation! We besiege Arras—
The Cardinal Prince of Spain besieges us—
And—here we are!

CYRANO

                Someone might besiege *him*.

CARBON

  A hungry joke!

CYRANO

                Ho, ho!

LE BRET

                  Yes, you can laugh—
Risking a life like yours to carry letters—
Where are you going now?

CYRANO

  (at the tent door)

                    To write another.

(Goes into tent.)

(A little more daylight. The clouds redden. The town of Arras shows on the horizon. A cannon shot is heard, followed immediately by a roll of drums, far away to the left. Other drums

beat a little nearer. The drums go on answering each other here and there, approach, beat loudly almost on the stage, and die away toward the right, across the camp. The camp awakes. Voices of officers in the distance.)

CARBON
(sighs)
Those drums!—another good nourishing sleep
Gone to the devil.
(The CADETS *rouse themselves.)*
      Now then!—

FIRST CADET
(sits up, yawns)
        God! I'm hungry!

SECOND CADET
 Starving!

ALL
(groan)
   Aoh!

CARBON
    Up with you!

THIRD CADET
       Not another step!

FOURTH CADET
 Not another movement!

FIRST CADET
        Look at my tongue—
I said this air was indigestible!

FIFTH CADET
 My coronet for half a pound of cheese!

SIXTH CADET
 I have no stomach for this war—I'll stay
In my tent—like Achilles.

ANOTHER
      Yes—no bread,
 No fighting—

CARBON
    Cyrano!

OTHERS

> May as well die—

CARBON

Come out here!—You know how to talk to them.
Get them laughing—

SECOND CADET

(rushes up to FIRST CADET *who is eating something)*
> What are you gnawing there?

FIRST CADET

Gun wads and axle grease. Fat country this
Around Arras.

ANOTHER

(enters)
> I have been out hunting!

ANOTHER

(enters)
Went fishing, in the Scarpe!

ALL

(leaping up and surrounding the newcomers)
> Find anything?

Any fish? Any game? Perch? Partridges?
Let me look!

THE FISHERMAN

> Yes—one gudgeon.

(Shows it.)

THE HUNTER

> One fat . . . sparrow.

(Shows it.)

ALL

Ah!—See here, this—mutiny!—

CARBON

> Cyrano!

Come and help!

CYRANO

(enters from tent)
> Well?

(Silence. To the FIRST CADET *who is walking away, with his chin on his chest.)*
> You there, with the long face?

FIRST CADET

I have something on my mind that troubles me.

CYRANO

What is that?

FIRST CADET

    My stomach.

CYRANO

        So have I.

FIRST CADET

            No doubt

You enjoy this!

CYRANO

(tightens his belt)

    It keeps me looking young.

SECOND CADET

My teeth are growing rusty.

CYRANO

        Sharpen them!

THIRD CADET

My belly sounds as hollow as a drum.

CYRANO

Beat the long roll on it!

FOURTH CADET

      My ears are ringing.

CYRANO

Liar! A hungry belly has no ears.

FIFTH CADET

Oh for a barrel of good wine!

CYRANO

(offers him his own helmet)

        Your casque.

SIXTH CADET

I'll swallow anything!

CYRANO

(throws him the book which he has in his hand)

    Try the *Iliad*.

SEVENTH CADET

The Cardinal, he has four meals a day—
What does he care!

CYRANO
      Ask him; he really ought
To send you . . . a spring lamb out of his flock,
Roasted whole—
THE CADET
      Yes, and a bottle—
CYRANO
(exaggerates the manner of one speaking to a servant)
          If you please,
Richelieu—a little more of the Red Seal . . .
Ah, thank you!
THE CADET
      And the salad—
CYRANO
        Of course—Romaine!
ANOTHER CADET
(shivering)
I am as hungry as a wolf.
CYRANO
(tosses him a cloak)
      Put on
Your sheep's clothing.
FIRST CADET
(with a shrug)
      Always the clever answer!
CYRANO
Always the answer—yes! Let me die so—
Under some rosy-golden sunset, saying
A good thing, for a good cause! By the sword,
The point of honor—by the hand of one
Worthy to be my foeman, let me fall—
Steel in my heart, and laughter on my lips!
VOICES HERE AND THERE
All very well— We are hungry!
CYRANO
      Bah! You think
Of nothing but yourselves.
(His eye singles out the old FIFER *in the background.)*
      Here, Bertrandou,

You were a shepherd once— Your pipe now! Come,
Breathe, blow,— Play to those belly-worshipers
The old airs of the South—
                    "Airs with a smile in them,
Airs with a sigh in them, airs with the breeze
And the blue of the sky in them—"
                    Small, demure tunes
Whose every note is like a little sister—
Songs heard only in some long silent voice
Not quite forgotten— Mountain melodies
Like thin smoke rising from brown cottages
In the still noon, slowly— Quaint lullabies,
Whose very music has a Southern tongue—
(The OLD MAN *sits down and prepares his fife.)*
Now, let the fife, that dry old warrior,
Dream, while over the stops your fingers dance
A minuet of little birds—let him
Dream beyond ebony and ivory;
Let him remember he was once a reed
Out of the river, and recall the spirit
Of innocent, untroubled country days . . .
(The FIFER *begins to play a Provençal melody.)*
Listen, you Gascons! Now it is no more
The shrill fife— It is the flute, through woodlands far
Away, calling—no longer the hot battle cry,
But the cool, quiet pipe our goatherds play!
Listen—the forest glens . . . the hills . . . the downs . . .
The green sweetness of night on the Dordogne . . .
Listen, you Gascons! It is all Gascoyne! . . .

(Every head is bowed; every eye cast down. Here and there a tear is furtively brushed away with the back of a hand, the corner of a cloak.)

CARBON
(softly to CYRANO*)*
You make them weep—
CYRANO
                    For homesickness—a hunger

More noble than that hunger of the flesh;
It is their hearts now that are starving.
CARBON
            Yes,
But you melt down their manhood.
CYRANO
(motions the drummer to approach)
             You think so?
Let them be. There is iron in their blood
Not easily dissolved in tears. You need
Only—
(He makes a gesture; the drum beats.)
ALL
(spring up and rush toward their weapons)
   What's that? Where is it?—What?—
CYRANO
(smiles)
              You see—
Let Mars snore in his sleep once—and farewell
Venus—sweet dreams—regrets—dear thoughts of home—
All the fife lulls to rest wakes at the drums!
A CADET
(looks upstage)
Aha— Monsieur de Guiche!
THE CADETS
(mutter among themselves)
            Ugh! . . .
CYRANO
(smiles)
           Flattering
Murmur!
A CADET
    He makes me weary!
ANOTHER
         With his collar
Of lace over his corselet—
ANOTHER
        Like a ribbon
Tied round a sword!

ANOTHER
> Bandages for a boil

On the back of his neck—

SECOND CADET
> A courtier always!

ANOTHER

The Cardinal's nephew!

CARBON
> None the less—a Gascon.

FIRST CADET

A counterfeit! Never you trust that man—
Because we Gascons, look you, are all mad—
This fellow is reasonable—nothing more
Dangerous than a reasonable Gascon!

LE BRET

He looks pale.

ANOTHER
> Oh, he can be hungry too,

Like any other poor devil—but he wears
So many jewels on that belt of his
That his cramps glitter in the sun!

CYRANO

(quickly)
> Is he

To see us looking miserable? Quick—
Pipes!—Cards!—Dice!—

(They all hurriedly begin to play, on their stools, on the drums, or on their cloaks spread on the ground, lighting their long pipes meanwhile.)
> As for me, I read Descartes.

(He walks up and down, reading a small book which he takes from his pocket. TABLEAU: DE GUICHE *enters, looking pale and haggard. All are absorbed in their games. General air of contentment.* DE GUICHE *goes to* CARBON. *They look at each other askance, each observing with satisfaction the condition of the other.)*

DE GUICHE
  Good morning!
  (Aside)
                    He looks yellow.
CARBON
  (same business)
                          He is all eyes.
DE GUICHE
  (looks at the CADETS*)*
  What have we here? Black looks? Yes, gentlemen—
  I am informed I am not popular;
  The hill-nobility, barons of Béarn,
  The pomp and pride of Périgord—I learn
  They disapprove their colonel; call him courtier,
  Politician—they take it ill that I
  Cover my steel with lace of Genoa.
  It is a great offense to be a Gascon
  And not to be a beggar!
  (Silence. They smoke. They play.)
                    Well—Shall I have
  Your captain punish you? ... No.
CARBON
                          As to that,
  It would be impossible.
DE GUICHE
                    Oh?
CARBON
                          I am free;
  I pay my company; it is my own;
  I obey military orders.
DE GUICHE
                    Oh!
  That will be quite enough.
  (To the CADETS*)*
                    I can afford
  Your little hates. My conduct under fire
  Is well known. It was only yesterday
  I drove the Count de Bucquoi from Bapaume,
  Pouring my men down like an avalanche,
  I myself led the charge—

CYRANO
(without looking up from his book)
                    And your white scarf?
DE GUICHE
(surprised and gratified)
You heard that episode? Yes—rallying
My men for the third time, I found myself
Carried among a crowd of fugitives
Into the enemy's lines. I was in danger
Of being shot or captured; but I thought
Quickly—took off and flung away the scarf
That marked my military rank—and so
Being inconspicuous, escaped among
My own force, rallied them, returned again
And won the day! . . .
(The CADETS *do not appear to be listening, but here and there the cards and the dice boxes remain motionless, the smoke is retained in their cheeks.)*
                    What do you say to that?
Presence of mind—yes?
CYRANO
            Henry of Navarre
Being outnumbered, never flung away
His white plume.

(Silent enjoyment. The cards flutter, the dice roll, the smoke puffs out.)

DE GUICHE
            My device was a success,
However!

(Same attentive pause, interrupting the games and the smoking.)

CYRANO
        Possibly . . . An officer
Does not lightly resign the privilege
Of being a target.

(*Cards, dice, and smoke fall, roll, and float away with increasing satisfaction.*)

Now, if I had been there—
Your courage and my own differ in this—
When your scarf fell, I should have put it on.

DE GUICHE
Boasting again!

CYRANO
Boasting? Lend it to me
Tonight; I'll lead the first charge, with your scarf
Over my shoulder!

DE GUICHE
Gasconnade once more!
You are safe making that offer, and you know it—
My scarf lies on the river bank between
The lines, a spot swept by artillery
Impossible to reach alive!

CYRANO
(*produces the scarf from his pocket*)
Yes. Here . . .

(*Silence. The* CADETS *stifle their laughter behind their cards and their dice boxes.* DE GUICHE *turns to look at them. Immediately they resume their gravity and their game. One of them whistles carelessly the mountain air which the fifer was playing.*)

DE GUICHE
(*takes the scarf*)
Thank you! That bit of white is what I need
To make a signal. I was hesitating—
You have decided me.

(*He goes up to the parapet, climbs upon it, and waves the scarf at arm's length several times.*)

ALL
What is he doing?—
What?—

THE SENTRY ON THE PARAPET
There's a man down there running away!

DE GUICHE
(descending)
A Spaniard. Very useful as a spy
To both sides. He informs the enemy
As I instruct him. By his influence
I can arrange their dispositions.

CYRANO

      Traitor!

DE GUICHE
(folding the scarf)
A traitor, yes; but useful . . .

      We were saying? . . .
Oh, yes— Here is a bit of news for you:
Last night we had hopes of reprovisioning
The Army. Under cover of the dark,
The Marshal moved to Dourlens. Our supplies
Are there. He may reach them. But to return
Safely, he needs a large force—at least half
Our entire strength. At present, we have here
Merely a skeleton.

CARBON

      Fortunately,
The Spaniards do not know that.

DE GUICHE

      Oh, yes; they know
They will attack.

CARBON

    Ah!

DE GUICHE

      From that spy of mine
I learned of their intention. His report
Will determine the point of their advance.
The fellow asked me what to say! I told him:
"Go out between the lines; watch for my signal;
Where you see that, let them attack there."

CARBON
(to the CADETS*)*

      Well,
Gentlemen!
(All rise. Noise of sword belts and breastplates being buckled on.)

DE GUICHE
>>You may have perhaps an hour.

FIRST CADET
Oh— An hour!

(They all sit down and resume their games once more.)

DE GUICHE
(to CARBON*)*
>>The great thing is to gain time.
Any moment the Marshal may return.

CARBON
And to gain time?

DE GUICHE
>>You will all be so kind
As to lay down your lives!

CYRANO
>>Ah! Your revenge?

DE GUICHE
I make no great pretense of loving you!
But—since you gentlemen esteem yourselves
Invincible, the bravest of the brave,
And all that—why need we be personal?
I serve the king in choosing . . . as I choose!

CYRANO
(salutes)
Sir, permit me to offer—all our thanks.

DE GUICHE
(returns the salute)
You love to fight a hundred against one;
Here is your opportunity!
(He goes upstage with CARBON.*)*

CYRANO
(to the CADETS*)*
>>My friends,
We shall add now to our Gascon arms
With their six chevrons, blue and gold, a seventh—
Blood-red!

(DE GUICHE *talks in a low tone to* CARBON *upstage. Orders are given. The defense is arranged.* CYRANO *goes to* CHRISTIAN, *who has remained motionless with folded arms. He lays a hand on his shoulder.*)

CHRISTIAN
(shakes his head)
                    Roxane . . .

CYRANO
                           Yes.

CHRISTIAN
                                I should like
To say farewell to her, with my whole heart
Written for her to keep.

CYRANO
                      I thought of that—
(Takes a letter from his doublet.)
I have written your farewell.

CHRISTIAN
                    Show me!

CYRANO
                         You wish
To read it?

CHRISTIAN
        Of course!
(He takes the letter; begins to read, looks up suddenly.)
                  What?—

CYRANO
                      What is it?

CHRISTIAN
                        Look—
This little circle—

CYRANO
(takes back the letter quickly, and looks innocent)
                Circle?—

CHRISTIAN
                  Yes—a tear!

CYRANO

So it is! ... Well—a poet while he writes
Is like a lover in his lady's arms,
Believing his imagination—all
Seems true—you understand? There's half the charm
Of writing— Now, this letter as you see
I have made so pathetic that I wept
While I was writing it!

CHRISTIAN

                You—wept?

CYRANO

                        Why, yes—

Because ... it is a little thing to die,
But—not to see her ... that is terrible!
And I shall never—
(CHRISTIAN looks at him.)
         We shall never—
(Quickly)
                        You
Will never—

CHRISTIAN
(snatches the letter)
        Give me that!

(Noise in the distance on the outskirts of the camp)

VOICE OF A SENTRY

                Halt—who goes there?

(Shots, shouting, jingle of harness)

CARBON

What is it?—

THE SENTRY ON THE PARAPET
      Why, a coach.
(They rush to look.)

CONFUSED VOICES

                What? In the Camp?
A coach? Coming this way— It must have driven
Through the Spanish lines—what the devil— Fire!—

No— Hark! The driver shouting—what does he say?
Wait— He said: "On the service of the King!"
(They are all on the parapet looking over. The jingling comes nearer.)

DE GUICHE

Of the King?
(They come down and fall into line.)

CARBON

          Hats off, all!

DE GUICHE

(speaks offstage)

               The King! Fall in,
Rascals!—

(The coach enters at full trot. It is covered with mud and dust. The curtains are drawn. Two FOOTMEN *are seated behind. It stops suddenly.)*

CARBON

(shouts)

     Beat the assembly—
(Roll of drums. All the CADETS *uncover.)*

DE GUICHE

               Two of you,
Lower the steps—open the door—
(Two men rush to the coach. The door opens.)

ROXANE

(comes out of the coach)

                Good morning!
(At the sound of a woman's voice, every head is raised. Sensation.)

DE GUICHE

On the King's service— You?

ROXANE

               Yes—my own king—
Love!

CYRANO

(aside)

    God is merciful . . .

CHRISTIAN
(hastens to her)
                        You! Why have you—
ROXANE
Your war lasted so long!
CHRISTIAN
                But why?—
ROXANE
                            Not now—
CYRANO
(aside)
I wonder if I dare to look at her . . .
DE GUICHE
You cannot remain here!
ROXANE
                    Why, certainly!
Roll that drum here, somebody . . .
(She sits on the drum which is brought to her.)
                            Thank you— There!
(She laughs.)
Would you believe—they fired upon us?
                            —My coach
Looks like the pumpkin in the fairy tale,
Does it not? And my footmen—
(She throws a kiss to CHRISTIAN.*)*
                    How do you do?
(She looks about.)
How serious you all are! Do you know,
It is a long drive here—from Arras?
(Sees CYRANO.*)*
                        Cousin,
I am glad to see you!
CYRANO
(advances)
                Oh—How did you come?
ROXANE
How did I find you? Very easily—
I followed where the country was laid waste
—Oh, but I saw such things! I had to see

To believe. Gentlemen, is that the service
Of your King? I prefer my own!
CYRANO
                    But how
Did you come through?
ROXANE
                    Why, through the Spanish lines,
Of course!
FIRST CADET
        They let you pass?—
DE GUICHE
                    What did you say?
How did you manage?
LE BRET
                    Yes, that must have been
Difficult!
ROXANE
        No— I simply drove along.
Now and then some hidalgo scowled at me
And I smiled back—my best smile; whereupon,
The Spaniards being (without prejudice
To the French) the most polished gentlemen
In the world—I passed!
CARBON
                    Certainly that smile
Should be a passport! Did they never ask
Your errand or your destination?
ROXANE
                    Oh,
Frequently! Then I dropped my eyes and said:
"I had a lover . . ." Whereupon, the Spaniard
With an air of ferocious dignity
Would close the carriage door—with such a gesture
As any king might envy, wave aside
The muskets that were levelled at my breast,
Fall back three paces, equally superb
In grace and gloom, draw himself up, thrust forth
A spur under his cloak, sweeping the air

With his long plumes, bow very low, and say:
"Pass, Señorita!"
CHRISTIAN
> But Roxane—

ROXANE
> I know—

I said "a lover"—but you understand—
Forgive me!—If I said "I am going to meet
My husband," no one would believe me!
CHRISTIAN
> Yes,

But—
ROXANE
What then?
DE GUICHE
> You must leave this place.

CYRANO
> At once.

ROXANE
I?
LE BRET
Yes—immediately.
ROXANE
> And why?

CHRISTIAN
(embarrassed)
> Because...

CYRANO
(same)
In half an hour...
DE GUICHE
(same)
> Or three quarters...

CARBON
(same)
> Perhaps

It might be better...
LE BRET
> If you...

ROXANE

       Oh— I see!
You are going to fight. I remain here.
ALL

       No—no!

ROXANE

He is my husband—
(Throws herself in CHRISTIAN'S *arms.)*
     I will die with you!

CHRISTIAN

Your eyes! . . . Why do you?—

ROXANE

       You know why . . .

DE GUICHE

(desperate)

          This post
Is dangerous—

ROXANE

(turns)
  How—dangerous?

CYRANO

       The proof
Is, we are ordered—

ROXANE

(to DE GUICHE*)*
      Oh—you wish to make
A widow of me?

DE GUICHE

     On my word of honor—

ROXANE

No matter. I am just a little mad—
I will stay. It may be amusing.

CYRANO

       What,
A heroine—our intellectual?

ROXANE

Monsieur de Bergerac, I am your cousin!

A CADET

We'll fight now! Hurrah!

ROXANE
(more and more excited)
                      I am safe with you—my friends!

ANOTHER
(carried away)
The whole camp breathes of lilies!—

ROXANE
                              And I think,
This hat would look well on the battlefield! . . .
But perhaps—
(Looks at DE GUICHE.*)*
                  The Count ought to leave us. Any moment
Now, there may be danger.

DE GUICHE
                           This is too much!
I must inspect my guns. I shall return—
You may change your mind— There will yet be
    time—

ROXANE
Never!
*(*DE GUICHE *goes out.)*

CHRISTIAN
(imploring)
          Roxane! . . .

ROXANE
                No!

FIRST CADET
(to the rest)
                    She stays here!

ALL
(rushing about, elbowing each other, brushing off their clothes)
                              A comb!—
Soap!—Here's a hole in my— A needle—Who
Has a ribbon?—Your mirror, quick!—My cuffs—
A razor—

ROXANE
(to CYRANO, *who is still urging her)*
No! I shall not stir one step!

CARBON
(having, like the others, tightened his belt, dusted himself, brushed off his hat, smoothed out his plume and put on his lace cuffs, advances to ROXANE *ceremoniously)*
In that case, may I now present to you
Some of these gentlemen who are to have
The honor of dying in your presence?
ROXANE
(bows)
                              Please!—
(She waits, standing, on the arm of CHRISTIAN, *while*
CARBON
—presents)
Baron de Peyrescous de Colignac!
THE CADET
(salutes)
Madame . . .
ROXANE
            Monsieur . . .
CARBON
(continues)
                  Baron de Casterac
De Cahuzac—Vidame de Malgouyre
Estressac Lésbas d'Escarabiot—
THE VIDAME
Madame . . .
CARBON
        Chevalier d'Antignac-Juzet—
Baron Hillot de Blagnac-Saléchan
De Castel-Crabioules—
THE BARON
                Madame . . .
ROXANE
                            How many
Names you all have!
THE BARON
              Hundreds!
CARBON
(to ROXANE*)*

                             Open the hand
That holds your handkerchief.
ROXANE
(opens her hand; the handkerchief falls)
                            Why?
(The whole company makes a movement toward it.)
CARBON
(picks it up quickly)
                                My company
Was in want of a banner. We have now
The fairest in the army!
ROXANE
(smiling)
                        Rather small—
CARBON
(fastens the handkerchief to his lance)
Lace—and embroidered!
A CADET
(to the others)
                          With her smiling on me,
I could die happy, if I only had
Something in my—
CARBON
(turns upon him)
                      Shame on you! Feast your eyes
And forget your—
ROXANE
(quickly)
                      It must be this fresh air—
I am starving! Let me see . . .
                          Cold partridges,
Pastry, a little white wine—that would do.
Will some one bring that to me?
A CADET
(aside)
                            Will some one!—
ANOTHER
Where the devil are we to find—

ROXANE
(overhears; sweetly)
       Why, there—
In my carriage.
ALL
    Wha-at?
ROXANE
       All you have to do
Is to unpack, and carve, and serve things.
           Oh,
Notice my coachman; you may recognize
An old friend.
THE CADETS
(rush to the coach)
    Ragueneau!
ROXANE
(follows them with her eyes)
      Poor fellows...
THE CADETS
(acclamations)
        Ah!
Ah!
CYRANO
(kisses her hand)
 Our good fairy!
RAGUENEAU
(standing on his box, like a mountebank before a crowd)
     Gentlemen!—
(Enthusiasm)
THE CADETS
      Bravo!
Bravo!
RAGUENEAU
  The Spaniard, basking in our smiles,
Smiled on our baskets!
(Applause)
CYRANO
(aside, to CHRISTIAN)
     Christian!

RAGUENEAU
>>They adored
The Fair, and missed—
(He takes from under the seat a dish, which he holds aloft.)
>>The Fowl!
(Applause. The dish is passed from hand to hand.)
CYRANO
(as before, to CHRISTIAN*)*
>>One moment—
RAGUENEAU
>>Venus
Charmed their eyes, while Adonis quietly
(Brandishing a ham)
Brought home the Boar!
(Applause; the ham is seized by a score of hands outstretched.)
CYRANO
(as before)
>>Pst— Let me speak to you—
ROXANE
(as the CADETS *return, their arms full of provisions)*
Spread them out on the ground.
(Calls.)
>>Christian! Come here;
Make yourself useful.

*(*CHRISTIAN *turns to her, at the moment when* CYRANO *was leading him aside. She arranges the food, with his aid and that of the two imperturbable* FOOTMEN.*)*

RAGUENEAU
>>Peacock, aux truffes!
FIRST CADET
(comes down, cutting a huge slice of ham)
>>Tonnerre!
We are not going to die without a gorge—
(Sees ROXANE; *corrects himself hastily.)*
Pardon—a banquet!

RAGUENEAU
(tossing out the cushions of the carriage)
                    Open these—they are full
Of ortolans!
(Tumult; laughter; the cushions are eviscerated.)
THIRD CADET
            Lucullus!
RAGUENEAU
(throws out bottles of red wine)
                        Flasks of ruby—
(And of white)
Flasks of topaz—
ROXANE
(throws a tablecloth at the head of CYRANO*)*
                    Come back out of your dreams!
Unfold this cloth—
RAGUENEAU
(takes off one of the lanterns of the carriage, and flourishes it)
                Our lamps are bonbonnières!
CYRANO
(to CHRISTIAN*)*
I must see you before you speak with her—
RAGUENEAU
(more and more lyrical)
My whip handle is one long sausage!
ROXANE
(pouring wine; passing the food.)
                            We
Being about to die, first let us dine!
Never mind the others—all for Gascoyne!
And if De Guiche comes, he is not invited!
(Going from one to another)
Plenty of time—you need not eat so fast—
Hold your cup—
(To another)
            What's the matter?

THE CADET
   (sobbing)
                              You are so good
   To us...
ROXANE
              There, there! Red or white wine?
                                      Some bread
   For Monsieur de Carbon!—Napkins—A knife—
   Pass you plate—some of the crust? A little more—
   Light or dark?—Burgundy?—
CYRANO
   (follows her with an armful of dishes, helping to serve)
                              Adorable!

ROXANE
   (goes to CHRISTIAN)
   What would you like?
CHRISTIAN
                  Nothing.
ROXANE
                          Oh, but you must!—
   A little wine? A biscuit?
CHRISTIAN
                      Tell me first
   Why you came—
ROXANE
                  By and by. I must take care
   Of these poor boys—
LE BRET
   (who has gone up stage to pass up food to the sentry on the parapet, on the end of a lance)
                          De Guiche!—
CYRANO
                                  Hide everything
   Quick!—Dishes, bottles, tablecloth—
                              Now look
   Hungry again—
   (To RAGUENEAU)
                  You there! Up on your box—
   —Everything out of sight?—

(In a twinkling, everything has been pushed inside the tents, hidden in their hats or under their cloaks. DE GUICHE *enters quickly, then stops, sniffing the air. Silence.)*

DE GUICHE

       It smells good here.

A CADET
(humming with an air of great unconcern)
Sing ha-ha-ha- and ho-ho-ho—

DE GUICHE
(stares at him; he grows embarrassed)
         You there—
What are you blushing for?

THE CADET
        Nothing—my blood
Stirs at the thought of battle.

ANOTHER
       Pom . . . pom . . . pom! . . .

DE GUICHE
(turns upon him)
What is that?

THE CADET
(slightly stimulated)
     Only song—only little song—

DE GUICHE
You appear happy!

THE CADET
      Oh yes—always happy
Before a fight—

DE GUICHE
(calls to CARBON, *for the purpose of giving him an order)*
     Captain! I—
(Stops and looks at him.)
       What the devil—
You are looking happy too!—

CARBON
(pulls a long face and hides a bottle behind his back)
        No!

DE GUICHE

                                         Here—I had
One gun remaining. I have had it placed
(He points offstage.)
There—in that corner—for your men.

A CADET
  (simpering)
                                         So kind!—

Charming attention!

ANOTHER
  (same business; burlesque)
                                  Sweet solicitude!—

DE GUICHE
  (contemptuous)
I believe you are both drunk—
(Coldly)
                                      Being unaccustomed
To guns—take care of the recoil!

FIRST CADET
  (gesture)
                                        Ah-h ... Pfft!

DE GUICHE
  (goes up to him, furious)
How dare you?

FIRST CADET
                     A Gascon's gun never recoils!

DE GUICHE
  (shakes him by the arm)
You *are* drunk—

FIRST CADET
  (superbly)
                         With the smell of powder!

DE GUICHE
  (turns away with a shrug)
                                           Bah!

(To ROXANE*)*
Madame, have you decided?

ROXANE
                                  I stay here.

DE GUICHE
You have time to escape—
ROXANE
                        No!
DE GUICHE
                        Very well—
Someone give me a musket!
CARBON
                      What?
DE GUICHE
                        I stay
Here also.
CYRANO
    (*formally*)
            Sir, you show courage!
FIRST CADET
                      A Gascon
In spite of all that lace!
ROXANE
                      Why—
DE GUICHE
                      Must I run
Away, and leave a woman?
SECOND CADET
    (*to* FIRST CADET)
                      We might give him
Something to eat—what do you say?
(*All the food reappears, as if by magic.*)
DE GUICHE
    (*his face lights up*)
                      A feast!
THIRD CADET
Here a little, there a little—
DE GUICHE
    (*recovers his self-control; haughtily*)
                      Do you think
I want your leavings?
CYRANO
    (*saluting*)
                    Colonel—You improve!

DE GUICHE
  I can fight as I am!
FIRST CADET
  (delighted)
                Listen to him—
He has an accent!
DE GUICHE
  (laughs)
                Have I so?
FIRST CADET
                      A Gascon!—
A Gascon, after all!
  (They all begin to dance.)
CARBON
  (who has disappeared for a moment behind the parapet, reappears on top of it)
                I have placed my pikemen
Here.
  (Indicates a row of pikes showing above the parapet.)
DE GUICHE
  (bows to ROXANE*)*
We'll review them; will you take my arm?
  (She takes his arm; they go up on the parapet. The rest uncover, and follow them upstage.)
CHRISTIAN
  (goes hurriedly to CYRANO*)*
Speak quickly!

(At the moment when ROXANE *appears on the parapet the pikes are lowered in salute, and a cheer is heard. She bows.)*

THE PIKEMEN
  (offstage)
                Hurrah!
CHRISTIAN
                What is it?
CYRANO
                    If Roxane . . .

CHRISTIAN
    Well?
CYRANO
        Speaks about your letters . . .
CHRISTIAN
                        Yes—I know!
CYRANO
    Do not make the mistake of showing . . .
CHRISTIAN
                        What?
CYRANO
    Showing surprise.
CHRISTIAN
                Surprise—why?
CYRANO
                      I must tell you! . . .
    It is quite simple—I had forgotten it
    Until just now. You have . . .
CHRISTIAN
                  Speak quickly!—
CYRANO
                          You
    Have written oftener than you think.
CHRISTIAN
                  Oh—have I!
CYRANO
    I took upon me to interpret you;
    And wrote—sometimes . . . without . . .
CHRISTIAN
                    My knowing. Well?
CYRANO
    Perfectly simple!
CHRISTIAN
             Oh, yes, perfectly!—
    For a month, we have been blockaded here!—
    How did you send all these letters?
CYRANO
                  Before
    Daylight, I managed—

CHRISTIAN
>> I see. That was also
Perfectly simple!
>> —So I wrote to her,
How many times a week? Twice? Three times?
Four?
CYRANO
Oftener.
CHRISTIAN
>> Every day?
CYRANO
>> Yes—every day . . .
Every single day . . .
CHRISTIAN
(violently)
>> And that wrought you up
Into such a flame that you faced death—
CYRANO
(sees ROXANE *returning)*
>> Hush—
Not before her!
(He goes quickly into the tent. ROXANE *comes up to* CHRISTIAN.*)*
ROXANE
>> Now—Christian!
CHRISTIAN
(takes her hands)
>> Tell me now
Why you came here—over these ruined roads—
Why you made your way among mosstroopers
And ruffians—you—to join me here?
ROXANE
>> Because—
Your letters . . .
CHRISTIAN
>> Meaning?
ROXANE
>> It was your own fault
If I ran into danger! I went mad—

Mad with you! Think what you have written me,
How many times, each one more wonderful
Than the last!
CHRISTIAN
                 All this for a few absurd
Love letters—
ROXANE
                  Hush—absurd! How can you know?
I thought I loved you, ever since one night
When a voice that I never would have known
Under my pillow breathed your soul to me . . .
But—all this time, your letters—every one
Was like hearing your voice there in the dark,
All around me, like your arms around me . . .
(More lightly)
                                    At last,
I came. Anyone would! Do you suppose
The prim Penelope had stayed at home
Embroidering,—if Ulysses wrote like you?
She would have fallen like another Helen—
Tucked up those linen petticoats of hers
And followed him to Troy!
CHRISTIAN
                     But you—
ROXANE
                             I read them
Over and over. I grew faint reading them.
I belong to you. Every page of them
Was like a petal fallen from your soul—
Like the light and the fire of a great love,
Sweet and strong and true—
CHRISTIAN
                     Sweet . . . and strong . . . and true . .
You felt that, Roxane?—
ROXANE
                  You know how I feel! . . .
CHRISTIAN
So—you came . . .

ROXANE

       Oh, my Christian, oh my king,—
Lift me up if I fall upon my knees—
It is the heart of me that kneels to you,
And will remain forever at your feet—
You cannot lift that!—
        I came here to say
"Forgive me"—(It is time to be forgiven
Now, when we may die presently)—forgive me
For being light and vain and loving you
Only because you were beautiful.

CHRISTIAN
(astonished)
         Roxane! . . . .

ROXANE

 Afterwards I knew better. Afterwards
(I had to learn to use my wings) I loved you
For yourself too—knowing you more, and loving
More of you. And now—

CHRISTIAN
     Now? . . .

ROXANE
         It is yourself
I love now: your own self.

CHRISTIAN
(taken aback)
       Roxane!

ROXANE
(gravely)
        Be happy!—
You must have suffered; for you must have seen
How frivolous I was; to be loved
For the mere costume, the poor casual body
You went about in—to a soul like yours,
That must have been torture! Therefore with words
You revealed your heart. Now that image of you
Which filled my eyes first—I see better now,
And I see it no more!

CHRISTIAN
     Oh!—

ROXANE
        You still doubt
Your victory?

CHRISTIAN
(miserably)
     Roxane!—

ROXANE
        I understand:
You cannot perfectly believe in me—
A love like this—

CHRISTIAN
      I want no love like this!
I want love only for—

ROXANE
      Only for what
Every woman sees in you? I can do
Better than that!

CHRISTIAN
     No—it was best before!

ROXANE
You do not altogether know me . . . Dear,
There is more of me than there was—with this,
I can love more of you—more of what makes
You your own self—Truly! . . . If you were less
Lovable—

CHRISTIAN
  No!

ROXANE
    —Less charming—ugly even—
I should love you still.

CHRISTIAN
     You mean that?

ROXANE
          I do
Mean that!

CHRISTIAN
                Ugly . . .

ROXANE
                        Yes. Even then!

CHRISTIAN
(agonized)
                                  Oh . . . God! . . .

ROXANE
Now are you happy?

CHRISTIAN
(choking)
                      Yes . . .

ROXANE
                            What is it?

CHRISTIAN
(pushes her away gently)
                                  Only . . .
Nothing . . . one moment . . .

ROXANE
                      But—

CHRISTIAN
(gestures toward the CADETS*)*
                              I am keeping you
From those poor fellows—Go and smile at them;
They are going to die!

ROXANE
(softly)
                      Dear Christian!

CHRISTIAN
                            Go—
(She goes up among the GASCONS, *who gather round her respectfully.)*
Cyrano!

CYRANO
(comes out of the tent, armed for the battle)
       What is wrong? You look—

CHRISTIAN
                          She does not
Love me any more.

CYRANO
(smiles)
                        You think not?

CHRISTIAN
                                She loves
You.

CYRANO
      No!—

CHRISTIAN
(bitterly)
            She loves only my soul.

CYRANO
                                    No!

CHRISTIAN
                                Yes—
That means you. And you love her.

CYRANO
                                    I?

CHRISTIAN
                                I see—
I know!

CYRANO
        That is true . . .

CHRISTIAN
                        More than—

CYRANO
(quietly)
                                More than that.

CHRISTIAN
  Tell her so!

CYRANO
            No.

CHRISTIAN
            Why not?

CYRANO
                    Why—look at me!

CHRISTIAN
  She would love me if I were ugly.

CYRANO
 (startled)
                              She—
Said that?
CHRISTIAN
            Yes. Now then!
CYRANO
 (half to himself)
                    It was good of her
To tell you that...
 (Change of tone)
                    Nonsense! Do you believe
Any such madness—
                  It was good of her
To tell you....
              Do not take her at her word!
Go on—you never will be ugly— Go!
She would never forgive me.
CHRISTIAN
                           That is what
We shall see.
CYRANO
          No, no—
CHRISTIAN
                 Let her choose between us!—
Tell her everything!
CYRANO
              No—you torture me—
CHRISTIAN
Shall I ruin your happiness, because
I have a cursed pretty face? That seems
Too unfair!
CYRANO
           And am I to ruin yours
Because I happen to be born with power
To say what you—perhaps—feel?
CHRISTIAN
                              Tell her!

CYRANO
                              Man—
  Do not try me too far!
CHRISTIAN
                    I am tired of being
  My own rival!
CYRANO
              Christian!—
CHRISTIAN
                         Our secret marriage—
  No witnesses—fraudulent—that can be
  Annulled—
CYRANO
          Do not try me—
CHRISTIAN
                         I want her love
  For the poor fool I am—or not at all!
  Oh, I am going through with this! I'll know,
  One way or the other. Now I shall walk down
  To the end of the post. Go tell her. Let her choose
  One of us.
CYRANO
        It will be you.
CHRISTIAN
                      God—I hope so!
  (He turns and calls.)
  Roxane!
CYRANO
        No—no—
ROXANE
  (hurries down to him)
                    Yes, Christian?
CHRISTIAN
                              Cyrano
  Has news for you—important.
  (She turns to CYRANO. CHRISTIAN *goes out.)*
ROXANE
  (lightly)
                              Oh—important?

CYRANO
    He is gone ...
    (To ROXANE*)*
                        Nothing—only Christian thinks
    You ought to know—
ROXANE
                        I do know. He still doubts
    What I told him just now. I saw that.
CYRANO
    (takes her hand)
                                Was it
    True—what you told him just now?
ROXANE
                                It was true!
    I said that I should love him even ...
CYRANO
    (smiling sadly)
                                The word
    Comes hard—before me?
ROXANE
                        Even if he were ...
CYRANO
                                Say it—
    I shall not be hurt!—Ugly?
ROXANE
                        Even then
    I should love him.
    (A few shots, offstage, in the direction in which CHRISTIAN *disappeared)*
                        Hark! The guns—
CYRANO
                                Hideous?
ROXANE
    Hideous.
CYRANO
            Disfigured?
ROXANE
                        Or disfigured.
CYRANO
                        Even

Grotesque?
ROXANE
How could he ever be grotesque—
Ever—to me!
CYRANO
But you could love him so,
As much as?—
ROXANE
Yes—and more!
CYRANO
(aside, excitedly)
It is true!—true!—
Perhaps—God! This is too much happiness . . .
(To ROXANE)
I—Roxane—listen—
LE BRET
(enters quickly; calls to CYRANO in a low tone)
Cyrano—
CYRANO
(turns)
Yes?
LE BRET
Hush! . . .
(whispers a few words to him)
CYRANO
(lets fall ROXANE's hand)
Ah!
ROXANE
What is it?
CYRANO
(half stunned, and aside)
All gone . . .
(More shots)
ROXANE
What is it? Oh,
They are fighting!—
(She goes up to look offstage.)
CYRANO
All gone. I cannot ever
Tell her, now . . . ever . . .

ROXANE
  (starts to rush away)
                    What has happened?
CYRANO
  (restrains her)
                                        Nothing.

(Several CADETS *enter. They conceal something which they are carrying, and form a group so as to prevent* ROXANE *from seeing their burden.)*

ROXANE
  These men—
CYRANO
            Come away . . .
  (He leads her away from the group.)
ROXANE
                          You were telling me
  Something—
CYRANO
              Oh, that? Nothing. . . . *(Gravely)*
                                        I swear to you
That the spirit of Christian—that his soul
Was—
(Corrects himself quickly.)
      That his soul is no less great—
ROXANE
  (catches at the word)
                          Was?

  (Crying out)
                                  Oh!—
  (She rushes among the men, and scatters them.)
CYRANO
  All gone . . .
ROXANE
  (sees CHRISTIAN *lying upon his cloak)*
            Christian!

LE BRET
(To CYRANO*)*
>   At the first volley.

*(*ROXANE *throws herself upon the body of* CHRISTIAN. *Shots; at first scattered, then increasing. Drums. Voices shouting)*

CARBON
(sword in hand)
>   Here

They come!—Ready!—

(Followed by the CADETS, *he climbs over the parapet and disappears.)*

ROXANE
>   Christian!

CARBON
(offstage)
>   Come on, there, You!

ROXANE
Christian!

CARBON
>   Fall in!

ROXANE
>   Christian!

CARBON
>   Measure your fuse!

*(*RAGUENEAU *hurries up, carrying a helmet full of water.)*

CHRISTIAN
(faintly)
Roxane! . . .

CYRANO
(low and quick, in CHRISTIAN'S *ear, while* ROXANE *is dipping into the water a strip of linen torn from her dress)*
>   I have told her; she loves you.

*(*CHRISTIAN *closes his eyes.)*

ROXANE
   (turns to CHRISTIAN*)*
                                    Yes,
   My darling?
CARBON
              Draw your ramrods!
ROXANE
   (to CYRANO*)*
                           He is not dead? . . .

CARBON
   Open your charges!
ROXANE
                 I can feel his cheek
   Growing cold against mine—
CARBON
                       Take aim!
ROXANE
                                 A letter—
   Over his heart— *(She opens it.)*
                     For me.
CYRANO
   (aside)
                      My letter . . .
CARBON
                                 Fire!

(Musketry, cries and groans. Din of battle.)

CYRANO
   (trying to withdraw his hand, which ROXANE, *still upon her knees, is holding)*
   But Roxane—they are fighting—
ROXANE
                           Wait a little . . .
   He is dead. No one else knew him but you . . .
   (She weeps quietly.)
   Was he not a great lover, a great man,
   A hero?

CYRANO
(standing, bareheaded)
    Yes, Roxane.
ROXANE
              A poet, unknown,
Adorable?
CYRANO
       Yes, Roxane.
ROXANE
              A fine mind?
CYRANO
Yes, Roxane.
ROXANE
          A heart deeper than we knew—
A soul magnificently tender?
CYRANO
(firmly)
                Yes,
Roxane!
ROXANE
(sinks down upon the breast of CHRISTIAN*)*
       He is dead now . . .
CYRANO
(aside; draws his sword)
                Why, so am I—
For I am dead, and my love mourns for me
And does not know.
(Trumpets in distance)
DE GUICHE
(appears on the parapet, disheveled, wounded on the forehead, shouting)
            The signal—hark—the trumpets!
The army has returned— Hold them now!—Hold them!
The army!—
ROXANE
       On his letter—blood . . . and tears.
A VOICE
(offstage)
Surrender!

THE CADETS
          No!
RAGUENEAU
                This place is dangerous!—
CYRANO
  (to DE GUICHE)
Take her away—I am going—
ROXANE
  (kisses the letter; faintly)
                          His blood . . . his tears . . .
RAGUENEAU
  (leaps down from the coach and runs to her)
She has fainted—
DE GUICHE
  (on the parapet; savagely, to the CADETS)
          Hold them!
VOICE OFFSTAGE
                    Lay down your arms!
VOICES
                                  No! No!
CYRANO
  (to DE GUICHE)
Sir, you have proved yourself— Take care of her.
DE GUICHE
  (hurries to ROXANE and takes her up in his arms)
As you will—we can win, if you hold on
A little longer—
CYRANO
          Good!
(Calls out to ROXANE, as she is carried away, fainting, by DE GUICHE and RAGUENEAU.)
          Adieu, Roxane!

(Tumult, outcries. Several CADETS come back wounded and fall on the stage. CYRANO, rushing to the fight, is stopped on the crest of the parapet by CARBON, covered with blood.)

CARBON
We are breaking—I am twice wounded—

CYRANO
(shouts to the GASCONS*)*
                              Hardi!
Reculez pas, Drollos!
(To CARBON, *holding him up)*
                  So—never fear!
I have two deaths to avenge now—Christian's
And my own!
(They come down. CYRANO *takes from him the lance with* ROXANE'S *handkerchief still fastened to it.)*
              Float, little banner, with her name!
(He plants it on the parapet; then shouts to the CADETS.*)*
Toumbé dessus! Escrasas lous!
(To the FIFER*)*
                        Your fife!
Music!

(Fife plays. The wounded drag themselves to their feet. Other CADETS *scramble over the parapet and group themselves around* CYRANO *and his tiny flag. The coach is filled and covered with men, bristling with muskets, transformed into a redoubt.)*

A CADET
(reels backward over the wall, still fighting. Shouts)
      They are climbing over!—
(And falls dead.)
CYRANO
                        Very good—
Let them come!— A salute now—
(The parapet is crowned for an instant with a rank of enemies. The imperial banner of Spain is raised aloft.)
                        Fire!
(General volley)
VOICE
(among the ranks of the enemy)
                        Fire!
(Murderous counter-fire; the CADETS *fall on every side.)*
A SPANISH OFFICER
(uncovers)
Who are these men who are so fond of death?

CYRANO
   (erect amid the hail of bullets, declaims)
   The Cadets of Gascoyne, the defenders
      Of Carbon de Castel-Jaloux—
   Free fighters, free lovers, free spenders—
   (He rushes forward, followed by a few survivors.)
   The Cadets of Gascoyne . . .
   (The rest is lost in the din of battle.)

                              (Curtain)

THE FIFTH ACT

   CYRANO'S GAZETTE

Fifteen years later, in 1655: THE PARK OF THE CONVENT *occupied by the Ladies of the Cross, at Paris.*

   Magnificent foliage. To the Left, the House upon a broad Terrace at the head of a flight of steps, with several Doors opening upon the Terrace. In the center of the scene an enormous Tree alone in the center of a little open space. Toward the Right, in the foreground, among Boxwood Bushes, a semi-circular Bench of stone.

   All the way across the Background of the scene, an Avenue overarched by the chestnut trees, leading to the door of a Chapel on the Right, just visible among the branches of the trees. Beyond the double curtain of the trees, we catch a glimpse of bright lawns and shaded walks, masses of shrubbery; the perspective of the Park; the sky.

   A little side door of the Chapel opens upon a Colonnade, garlanded with Autumnal vines, and disappearing on the Right behind the box-trees.

   It is late October. Above the still living green of the turf all the foliage is red and yellow and brown. The evergreen masses of Box and Yew stand out darkly against this Autumnal coloring. A heap of dead leaves under every tree. The leaves are falling everywhere. They rustle underfoot along the walks; the Terrace and the Bench are half covered with them.

Before the Bench on the Right, on the side toward the Tree, is placed a tall embroidery frame and beside it a little Chair. Baskets filled with skeins of many-colored silks and balls of wool. Tapestry unfinished on the Frame.

At the CURTAIN RISE *the nuns are coming and going across the Park; several of them are seated on the Bench around* MOTHER MARGUÉRITE DE JÉSUS. *The leaves are falling.*

SISTER MARTHE
(*to* MOTHER MARGUÉRITE)
Sister Claire has been looking in the glass
At her new cap; twice!

MOTHER MARGUÉRITE
(*to* SISTER CLAIRE)
                    It is very plain;
Very.

SISTER CLAIRE
       And Sister Marthe stole a plum
Out of the tart this morning!

MOTHER MARGUÉRITE
(*to* SISTER MARTHE)
                    That was wrong;
Very wrong.

SISTER CLAIRE
      Oh, but such a little look!

SISTER MARTHE
Such a little plum!

MOTHER MARGUÉRITE
(*severely*)
               I shall tell Monsieur
De Cyrano, this evening.

SISTER CLAIRE
                No! Oh, no!—
He will make fun of us.

SISTER MARTHE
               He will say nuns
Are so gay!

SISTER CLAIRE
        And so greedy!
MOTHER MARGUÉRITE
  (*smiling*)
                And so good ...
SISTER CLAIRE
  It must be ten years, Mother Marguérite,
  That he has come here every Saturday,
  Is it not?
MOTHER MARGUÉRITE
         More than ten years; ever since
  His cousin came to live among us here—
  Her worldly weeds among our linen veils,
  Her widowhood and our virginity—
  Like a black dove among white doves.
SISTER MARTHE
                    No one
  Else ever turns that happy sorrow of hers
  Into a smile.
ALL THE NUNS
          He is such fun!—He makes us
  Almost laugh!—And he teases everyone—
  And pleases everyone— And we all love him—
  And he likes our cake, too—
SISTER MARTHE
               I am afraid
  He is not a good Catholic.
SISTER CLAIRE
             Some day
  We shall convert him.
THE NUNS
         Yes—yes!
MOTHER MARGUÉRITE
               Let him be;
  I forbid you to worry him. Perhaps
  He might stop coming here.
SISTER MARTHE
            But ... God?

MOTHER MARGUÉRITE

                                        You need not
Be afraid. God knows all about him.

SISTER MARTHE

                                              Yes...
But every Saturday he says to me,
Just as if he were proud of it: "Well, Sister,
I ate meat yesterday!"

MOTHER MARGUÉRITE

                            He tells you so?
The last time he said that, he had not eaten
Anything, for two days.

SISTER MARTHE

                       Mother!—

MOTHER MARGUÉRITE

                                 He is poor;
Very poor.

SISTER MARTHE

          Who said so?

MOTHER MARGUÉRITE

                    Monsieur Le Bret.

SISTER MARTHE

Why does not someone help him?

MOTHER MARGUÉRITE

                              He would be
Angry; very angry...

(Between the trees up stage, ROXANE *appears, all in black, with a widow's cap and long veils.* DE GUICHE, *magnificently grown old, walks beside her. They move slowly.* MOTHER MARGUÉRITE *rises.)*

                    Let us go in—
Madame Madeleine has a visitor.

SISTER MARTHE

  (to SISTER CLAIRE*)*
The Duc de Grammont, is it not? The Marshal?

SISTER CLAIRE
(*looks toward* DE GUICHE)
I think so—yes.
SISTER MARTHE
              He has not been to see her
For months—
THE NUNS
              He is busy—the Court!—the Camp!—
SISTER CLAIRE
                            The world! . . .

(*They go out.* DE GUICHE *and* ROXANE *come down in silence, and stop near the embrodiery frame. Pause.*)

DE GUICHE
And you remain here, wasting all that gold—
For ever in mourning?
ROXANE
                For ever.
DE GUICHE
                      And still faithful?
ROXANE
And still faithful . . .
DE GUICHE
(*after a pause*)
                  Have you forgiven me?
ROXANE
(*simply, looking up at the cross of the Convent*)
I am here.
(*Another pause*)
DE GUICHE
          Was Christian . . . all that?
ROXANE
                      If you knew him.
DE GUICHE
Ah? We were not precisely . . . intimate . . .
And his last letter—always at your heart?
ROXANE
It hangs here, like a holy reliquary.

DE GUICHE
 Dead—and you love him still!
ROXANE
                    Sometimes I think
 He has not altogether died; our hearts
 Meet, and his love flows all around me, living.
DE GUICHE
 (after another pause)
 You see Cyrano often?
ROXANE
                    Every week.
 My old friend takes the place of my Gazette,
 Brings me all the news. Every Saturday,
 Under that tree where you are now, his chair
 Stands, if the day be fine. I wait for him,
 Embroidering; the hour strikes; then I hear,
 (I need not turn to look!) at the last stroke,
 His cane tapping the steps. He laughs at me
 For my eternal needlework. He tells
 The story of the past week—
 (LE BRET *appears on the steps.*)
                    There's Le Bret!—
 (LE BRET *approaches.*)
 How is it with our friend?
LE BRET
                    Badly.
DE GUICHE
                    Indeed?
ROXANE
 (to DE GUICHE*)*
 Oh, he exaggerates!
LE BRET
                    Just as I said—
 Loneliness, misery—I told him so!—
 His satires make a host of enemies—
 He attacks the false nobles, the false saints,
 The false heroes, the false artists—in short,
 Everyone!

ROXANE
                But they fear that sword of his—
No one dare touch him!

DE GUICHE
(with a shrug)
                            H'm—that may be so.

LE BRET
It is not violence I fear for him,
But solitude—poverty—old gray December,
Stealing on wolf's feet, with a wolf's green eyes,
Into his darkening room. Those bravoes yet
May strike our Swordsman down! Every day now,
He draws his belt up one hole; his poor nose
Looks like old ivory; he has one coat
Left—his old black serge.

DE GUICHE
                          That is nothing strange
In this world! No, you need not pity him
Overmuch.

LE BRET
(with a bitter smile)
            My lord Marshal! . . .

DE GUICHE
                                I say, do not
Pity him overmuch. He lives his life,
His own life, his own way—thought, word, and deed
Free!

LE BRET
(as before)
            My lord Duke! . . .

DE GUICHE
(haughtily)
                            Yes. I know—I have all;
He has nothing. Nevertheless, today
I should be proud to shake his hand . . .
(saluting ROXANE*)*
                            Adieu.

ROXANE
I will go with you.

(DE GUICHE *salutes* LE BRET, *and turns with* ROXANE *toward the steps.*)

DE GUICHE
(pauses on the steps, as she climbs)
                    Yes—I envy him
Now and then . . .
                    Do you know, when a man wins
Everything in this world, when he succeeds
Too much—he feels, having done nothing wrong
Especially, Heaven knows!—he feels somehow
A thousand small displeasures with himself,
Whose whole sum is not quite Remorse, but rather
A sort of vague disgust . . . The ducal robes
Mounting up, step by step, to pride and power,
Somewhere among their folds draw after them
A rustle of dry illusions, vain regrets,
As your veil, up the stairs here, draws along
The whisper of dead leaves.

ROXANE
(ironical)
                    The sentiment
Does you honor.

DE GUICHE
             Oh, yes . . .
(Pausing suddenly)
                  Monsieur Le Bret!—
(To ROXANE*)*
You pardon us?—
(He goes to LE BRET, *and speaks in a low tone.*)
              One moment— It is true
That no one dares attack your friend. Some people
Dislike him, none the less. The other day
At Court, such a one said to me: "This man
Cyrano may die—accidentally."

LE BRET
(coldly)
Thank you.

DE GUICHE
                You may thank me. Keep him at home
All you can. Tell him to be careful.
LE BRET
(shaking his hands to heaven)
                                Careful!—
He is coming here. I'll warn him—yes, but! ...
ROXANE
(still on the steps, to a NUN *who approaches her)*
                                       Here
I am—what is it?
THE NUN
                Madame, Ragueneau
Wishes to see you.
ROXANE
                Bring him here.
(To LE BRET *and* DE GUICHE*)*
                                He comes
For sympathy—having been first of all
A Poet, he became since then, in turn,
A Singer—
LE BRET
                Bathhouse keeper—
ROXANE
                            Sacristan—
LE BRET
Actor—
ROXANE
                Hairdresser—
LE BRET
                      Music master—
ROXANE
                              Now,
Today—
RAGUENEAU
(enters hurriedly)
            Madame!—
(He sees LE BRET.*)*
                      Monsieur!—

ROXANE

(smiling)
                              First tell your troubles
  To Le Bret for a moment.
RAGUENEAU
                    But Madame—
(She goes out, with DE GUICHE, *not hearing him.* RAGUENEAU *comes to* LE BRET.*)*
  After all, I had rather— You are here—
  She need not know so soon— I went to see him
  Just now— Our friend— As I came near his door,
  I saw him coming out. I hurried on
  To join him. At the corner of the street,
  As he passed— Could it be an accident?—
  I wonder!—At the window overhead,
  A lackey with a heavy log of wood
  Let it fall—
LE BRET
  Cyrano!
RAGUENEAU
              I ran to him—
LE BRET
  God! The cowards!
RAGUENEAU
                        I found him lying there—
  A great hole in his head—
LE BRET
                          Is he alive?
RAGUENEAU
  Alive—yes. But . . . I had to carry him
  Up to his room—Dieu! Have you seen his room?—
LE BRET
  Is he suffering?
RAGUENEAU
              No; unconscious.
LE BRET
                              Did you
  Call a doctor?

RAGUENEAU
     One came—for charity.
LE BRET
Poor Cyrano!—We must not tell Roxane
All at once . . . Did the doctor say?—
RAGUENEAU
          He said
Fever, and lesions of the— I forget
Those long names— Ah, if you had seen him there,
His head all white bandages!—Let us go
Quickly—there is no one to care for him—
All alone— If he tries to raise his head,
He may die!
LE BRET
(draws him away to the Right)
     This way— It is shorter—through
The Chapel—
ROXANE
(appears on the stairway, and calls to LE BRET *as he is going out by the colonnade which leads to the small door of the Chapel)*
    Monsieur Le Bret!—
*(*LE BRET *and* RAGUENEAU *rush off without hearing.)*
        Running away
When I call to him? Poor dear Ragueneau
Must have been very tragic!
(She comes slowly down the stair, toward the tree.)
       What a day! . . .
Something in these bright Autumn afternoons
Happy and yet regretful—an old sorrow
Smiling . . . as though poor little April dried
Her tears long ago—and remembered . . .
(She sits down at her work. Two NUNS *come out of the house carrying a great chair and set it under the tree.)*
       Ah—
The old chair, for my old friend!—
SISTER MARTHE
        The best one
In our best parlor!—

ROXANE

                Thank you, Sister—
(The NUNS withdraw.)
                              There—
(She begins embroidering. The clock strikes.)
The hour!—He will be coming now—my silks—
All done striking? He never was so late
Before! The sister at the door—my thimble . . .
Here it is—she must be exhorting him
To repent all his sins . . .
(A pause)
                He ought to be
Converted, by this time— Another leaf—
(A dead leaf falls on her work; she brushes it away.)
Certainly nothing could—my scissors—ever
Keep him away—

A NUN

(appears on the steps)
                Monsieur de Bergerac.

ROXANE

(without turning)
What was I saying? . . . Hard, sometimes, to match
These faded colors! . . .
(While she goes on working, CYRANO appears at the top of the steps very pale, his hat drawn over his eyes. The NUN who has brought him in goes away. He begins to descend the steps leaning on his cane, and holding himself on his feet only by an evident effort. ROXANE turns to him, with a tone of friendly banter.)
                After fourteen years,
Late—for the first time!

CYRANO

(reaches the chair, and sinks into it; his gay tone contrasting with his tortured face)
                Yes, yes—maddening!
I was detained by—

ROXANE

            Well?

CYRANO

                    A visitor,
Most unexpected.

ROXANE

(carelessly, still sewing)

                    Was your visitor
Tiresome?

CYRANO

        Why, hardly that—inopportune,
Let us say—an old friend of mine—at least
A very old acquaintance.

ROXANE

                    Did you tell him
To go away?

CYRANO

          For the time being, yes.
I said: "Excuse me—this is Saturday—
I have a previous engagement, one
I cannot miss, even for you— Come back
An hour from now."

ROXANE

                    Your friend will have to wait;
I shall not let you go till dark.

CYRANO

(very gently)

                    Perhaps
A little before dark, I must go . . .

(He leans back in the chair, and closes his eyes. SISTER MARTHE *crosses above the stairway.* ROXANE *sees her, motions her to wait, then turns to* CYRANO.*)*

ROXANE

                    Look—
Somebody waiting to be teased.

CYRANO

(quickly, opens his eyes)

                    Of course!

(In a big, comic voice)

Sister, approach!
(SISTER MARTHE *glides toward him.*)
     Beautiful downcast eyes!—
So shy—
SISTER MARTHE
(looks up, smiling)
    You—*(She sees his face.)*
     Oh!—
CYRANO
(indicates ROXANE*)*
     Sh!—Careful!
(Resumes his burlesque tone.)
      Yesterday,
I ate meat again!
SISTER MARTHE
    Yes, I know.
(Aside)
     That is why
He looks so pale . . .
(To him, low and quickly)
    In the refectory,
Before you go—come to me there—
      I'll make you
A great bowl of hot soup—will you come?
CYRANO
(boisterously)
      Ah—
Will I come!
SISTER MARTHE
    You are quite reasonable
Today!
ROXANE
   Has she converted you?
SISTER MARTHE
      Oh, no—
Not for the world!—
CYRANO
     Why, now I think of it,
That is so— You, bursting with holiness,

And yet you never preach! Astonishing
I call it...
(With burlesque ferocity)
    Ah—now I'll astonish you—
I am going to—
(With the air of seeking for a good joke and finding it)
    —let you pray for me
Tonight, at vespers!

ROXANE
      Aha!

CYRANO
      Look at her—
Absolutely struck dumb!

SISTER MARTHE
(gently)
      I did not wait
For you to say I might.
(She goes out.)

CYRANO
(returns to ROXANE, *who is bending over her work)*
     Now, may the devil
Admire me, if I ever hope to see
The end of that embroidery!

ROXANE
(smiling)
      I thought
It was time you said that.
(A breath of wind causes a few leaves to fall.)

CYRANO
     The leaves—

ROXANE
(raises her head and looks away through the trees)
      What color—
Perfect Venetian red! Look at them fall.

CYRANO
Yes—they know how to die. A little way
From the branch to the earth, a little fear
Of mingling with the common dust—and yet
They go down gracefully—a fall that seems
Like flying!

ROXANE
    Melancholy—you?

CYRANO
        Why, no,
Roxane!

ROXANE
   Then let the leaves fall. Tell me now
 The Court news—my gazette!

CYRANO
         Let me see—

ROXANE
           Ah!

CYRANO
(more and more pale, struggling against pain)
Saturday, the nineteenth; the King fell ill,
After eight helpings of grape marmalade.
His malady was brought before the court,
Found guilty of high treason; whereupon
His Majesty revived. The royal pulse
Is now normal. Sunday, the twentieth:
The Queen gave a grand ball, at which they burned
Seven hundred and sixty-three wax candles. Note:
They say our troops have been victorious
In Austria. Later: Three sorcerers
Have been hung. Special post: The little dog
Of Madame d'Athis was obliged to take
Four pills before—

ROXANE
     Monsieur de Bergerac,
Will you kindly be quiet!

CYRANO
       Monday . . . nothing.
Lygdamire has a new lover.

ROXANE
       Oh!

CYRANO
(his face more and more altered)
        Tuesday,
The Twenty-second: All the court has gone
To Fontainebleau. Wednesday: The Comte de Fiesque

Spoke to Madame de Montglat; she said No.
Thursday: Mancini was the Queen of France
Or—very nearly! Friday: La Montglat
Said Yes. Saturday, twenty-sixth....
(His eyes close; his head sinks back; silence.)

ROXANE

(surprised at not hearing any more, turns, looks at him, and rises, frightened)

                                      He has fainted—

(She runs to him, crying out.)
Cyrano!

CYRANO

(opens his eyes)
        What ... What is it? ...
(He sees ROXANE *leaning over him, and quickly pulls his hat down over his head and leans back away from her in the chair.)*
                            No—oh no—

It is nothing—truly!

ROXANE

                But—

CYRANO

                        My old wound—
At Arras—sometimes—you know....

ROXANE

                               My poor friend!

CYRANO

Oh it is nothing; it will soon be gone....
(Forcing a smile)
There! It is gone!

ROXANE

(standing close to him)
                We all have our old wounds—
I have mine—here ...
(Her hand at her breast)
                      under this faded scrap
Of writing.... It is hard to read now—all
But the blood—and the tears....
(Twilight begins to fall.)

CYRANO
His letter! ... Did you
Not promise me that some day ... that some day....
You would let me read it?
ROXANE
His letter?—You ...
You wish—
CYRANO
I do wish it—today.
ROXANE
(gives him the little silken bag from around her neck)
Here....
CYRANO
May I ... open it?
ROXANE
Open it, and read.
(She goes back to her work, folds it again, rearranges her silks.)
CYRANO
(unfolds the letter; reads)
"Farewell Roxane, because today I die—"
ROXANE
(looks up, surprised)
Aloud?
CYRANO
(reads)
"I know that it will be today,
My own dearly beloved—and my heart
Still so heavy with love I have not told,
And I die without telling you! No more
Shall my eyes drink the sight of you like wine,
Never more, with a look that is a kiss,
Follow the sweet grace of you—"
ROXANE
How you read it—
His letter!
CYRANO
(continues)
"I remember now the way
You have, of pushing back a lock of hair

With one hand, from your forehead—and my heart
Cries out—"
ROXANE
    His letter . . . and you read it so . . .
(The darkness increases imperceptibly.)
CYRANO
"Cries out and keeps crying: 'Farewell, my dear,
My dearest—' "
ROXANE
    In a voice. . . .
CYRANO
      "—My own heart's own,
My own treasure—"
ROXANE
(dreamily)
    In such a voice. . . .
CYRANO
      —"My love—"
ROXANE
—As I remember hearing . . .
(She trembles.)
    —long ago. . . .

(She comes near him, softly, without his seeing her; passes the chair, leans over silently, looking at the letter. The darkness increases.)

CYRANO
"—I am never away from you. Even now,
I shall not leave you. In another world,
I shall be still that one who loves you, loves you
Beyond measure, beyond—"
ROXANE
(lays her hand on his shoulder)
      How can you read
Now? It is dark. . . .

(He starts, turns, and sees her there close to him. A little movement of surprise, almost of fear; then he bows his head. A long

pause; then in the twilight now completely fallen, she says very softly, clasping her hands)

And all these fourteen years,
He has been the old friend, who came to me
To be amusing.

CYRANO
      Roxane!—

ROXANE
       It was you.

CYRANO
No, no, Roxane, no!

ROXANE
        And I might have known,
Every time that I heard you speak my name! . . .

CYRANO
No— It was not I—

ROXANE
      It was . . . you!

CYRANO
         I swear—

ROXANE
I understand everything now: The letters—
That was you . . .

CYRANO
    No!

ROXANE
       And the dear, foolish words—
That was you. . . .

CYRANO
    No!

ROXANE
       And the voice . . . in the dark. . . .
That was . . . you!

CYRANO
    On my honor—

ROXANE
        And . . . the Soul!—
That was all you.

CYRANO
                    I never loved you—
ROXANE
                              Yes,
You loved me.
CYRANO
  (desperately)
                    No— He loved you—
ROXANE
                              Even now,
You love me!
CYRANO
  (his voice weakens)
                    No!
ROXANE
  (smiling)
                    And why ... so great a "No"?
CYRANO
No, no, my own dear love, I love you not! ...
(Pause)
ROXANE
How many things have died ... and are newborn! ...
Why were you silent for so many years,
All the while, every night and every day,
He gave me nothing—you knew that— You knew
Here, in this letter lying on my breast,
Your tears— You knew they were your tears—
CYRANO
  (holds the letter out to her)
                              The blood
Was his.
ROXANE
        Why do you break that silence now,
Today?
CYRANO
        Why? Oh, because—

(LE BRET *and* RAGUENEAU *enter, running.*)

LE BRET

         What recklessness—
I knew it! He is here!

CYRANO

(smiling, and trying to rise)
        Well? Here I am!

RAGUENEAU

He has killed himself, Madame, coming here!

ROXANE

He— Oh, God. . . . And that faintness . . . was that?—

CYRANO

              No,
Nothing! I did not finish my Gazette—
Saturday, twenty-sixth: An hour or so
Before dinner, Monsieur de Bergerac
Died, foully murdered.

(He uncovers his head, and shows it swathed in bandages.)

ROXANE

        Oh, what does he mean?—
Cyrano!— What have they done to you?—

CYRANO

            "Struck down
By the sword of a hero, let me fall—
Steel in my heart, and laughter on my lips!"
Yes, I said that once. How Fate loves a jest!—
Behold me ambushed—taken in the rear—
My battlefield a gutter—my noble foe
A lackey, with a log of wood! . . .
          It seems
Too logical—I have missed everything,
Even my death!

RAGUENEAU

(breaks down)
     Ah, monsieur!—

CYRANO

       Ragueneau,
Stop blubbering! *(Takes his hand.)*
      What are you writing nowadays,
Old poet?

RAGUENEAU
(through his tears)
    I am not a poet now;
I snuff the—light the candles—for Molière!

CYRANO
 Oh—Molière!

RAGUENEAU
    Yes, but I am leaving him
Tomorrow. Yesterday they played "Scapin"—
He has stolen your scene—

LE BRET
       The whole scene—word for word!

RAGUENEAU
 Yes: "What the devil was he doing there"—
That one!

LE BRET
(furious)
    And Molière stole it all from you—
Bodily!—

CYRANO
  Bah— He showed good taste. . . .
(To RAGUENEAU*)*
        The Scene
Went well? . . .

RAGUENEAU
    Ah, monsieur, they laughed—and laughed—
How they did laugh!

CYRANO
      Yes—that has been my life. . . .
Do you remember that night Christian spoke
Under your window? It was always so!
While I stood in the darkness underneath,
Others climbed up to win the applause—the kiss!—

Well—that seems only justice— I still say,
Even now, on the threshold of my tomb—
"Molière has genius—Christian had good looks—"
*(The chapel bell is ringing. Along the avenue of trees above
the stairway, the* NUNS *pass in procession to their prayers.)*
They are going to pray now; there is the bell.
ROXANE
(raises herself and calls to them)
Sister!—Sister!—
CYRANO
(holding on to her hand)
     No,—do not go away—
I may not still be here when you return....
(The NUNS *have gone in the chapel. The organ begins to play.)*
A little harmony is all I need—
Listen....
ROXANE
    You shall not die! I love you!—
CYRANO
             No—
That is not in the story! You remember
When Beauty said "I love you" to the Beast
That was a fairy prince, his ugliness
Changed and dissolved, like magic.... But you see
I am still the same.
ROXANE
     And I—I have done
This to you! All my fault—mine!
CYRANO
          You? Why no,
On the contrary! I had never known
Womanhood and its sweetness but for you.
My mother did not love to look at me—
I never had a sister— Later on,
I feared the mistress with a mockery
Behind her smile. But you—because of you
I have had one friend not quite all a friend—
Across my life, one whispering silken gown!...

LE BRET
(points to the rising moon which begins to shine down between the trees)
Your other friend is looking at you.
CYRANO
(smiling at the moon)
                    I see. . . .
ROXANE
I never loved but one man in my life,
And I have lost him—twice. . . .
CYRANO
Le Bret—I shall be up there presently
In the moon—without having to invent
Any flying machines!
ROXANE
                What are you saying? . . .
CYRANO
The moon—yes, that would be the place for me—
My kind of paradise! I shall find there
Those other souls who should be friends of mine—
Socrates—Galileo—
LE BRET
(revolting)
                No! No! No!
It is too idiotic—too unfair—
Such a friend—such a poet—such a man
To die so—to die so!—
CYRANO
(affectionately)
                    There goes Le Bret,
Growling!
LE BRET
(breaks down)
            My friend!—
CYRANO
(half raises himself, his eye wanders)
                    The Cadets of Gascoyne,
The Defenders. . . . The elementary mass—
Ah—there's the point! Now, then . . .

LE BRET

                        Delirious—
And all that learning—
CYRANO
                  On the other hand,
We have Copernicus—
ROXANE
                Oh!
CYRANO
(more and more delirious)
                  "Very well,
But what the devil was he doing there?—
What the devil was he doing there, up there?" . . .
(He declaims.)
    Philosopher and scientist,
    Poet, musician, duellist—
      He flew high, and fell back again!
    A pretty wit—whose like we lack—
    A lover . . . not like other men. . . .
      Here lies Hercule-Savinien
    De Cyrano de Bergerac—
      Who was all things—and all in vain!
Well, I must go—pardon— I cannot stay!
My moonbeam comes to carry me away. . . .

(He falls back into the chair, half fainting. The sobbing of ROXANE *recalls him to reality. Gradually his mind comes back to him. He looks at her, stroking the veil that hides her hair.)*

I would not have you mourn any the less
That good, brave, noble Christian; but perhaps—
I ask you only this—when the great cold
Gathers around my bones, that you may give
A double meaning to your widow's weeds
And the tears you let fall for him may be
For a little—my tears. . . .
ROXANE
(sobbing)
                Oh, my love! . . .

CYRANO

(suddenly shaken as with a fever fit, he raises himself erect and pushes here away)

—Not here!—

Not lying down! . . .
(They spring forward to help him; he motions them back.)

Let no one help me—no one!—

Only the tree. . . .
(He sets his back against the trunk. Pause.)

It is coming . . . I feel
Already shod with marble . . . gloved with lead . . .
(Joyously)
Let the old fellow come now! He shall find me
On my feet—sword in hand—*(Draws his sword.)*

LE BRET

Cyrano!—

ROXANE
(half fainting)

Oh,
Cyrano!

CYRANO

I can see him there—he grins—
He is looking at my nose—that skeleton
—What's that you say? Hopeless?—Why, very well!—
But a man does not fight merely to win!
No—no—better to know one fights in vain! . . .
You there— Who are you? A hundred against one—
I know them now, my ancient enemies—
(He lunges at the empty air.)
Falsehood! . . . There! There! Prejudice— Compromise—
Cowardice—*(Thrusting)*

What's that? No! Surrender? No!
Never—never! . . .

Ah, you too, Vanity!
I knew you would overthrow me in the end—
No! I fight on! I fight on! I fight on!
(He swings the blade in great circles, then pauses, gasping. When he speaks again, it is in another tone.)
Yes, all my laurels you have riven away

And all my roses; yet in spite of you,
There is one crown I bear away with me,
And tonight, when I enter before God,
My salute shall sweep all the stars away
From the blue threshold! One thing without stain,
Unspotted from the world, in spite of doom
Mine own!—
(He springs forward, his sword aloft.)
            And that is . . .
(The sword escapes from his hand; he totters, and falls into the arms of LE BRET *and* RAGUENEAU.*)*

ROXANE
(bends over him and kisses him on the forehead)
                          —That is . . .

CYRANO
(opens his eyes and smiles up at her)
                                     My white plume. . . .

(Curtain)

for discussion

THE FIRST ACT

1. A good dramatist rarely thrusts his most important character upon an unprepared audience. What do you learn about Cyrano before he first appears? How does his dramatic entrance illustrate what has been said about him?
2. Cyrano gives two reasons for Montfleury's banishment. What are they, and what do they reveal about Cyrano?
3. What purpose is served by the scenes with the Meddler and the Vicomte de Valvert? What is meant by Cyrano's words to Valvert: "I carry my adornments on my soul. . . . I go caparisoned in gems unseen, trailing white plumes of freedom"?
4. Explain why Rostand included the brief episode with the Orange Girl.
5. Rostand shows his hero to be a man of sensitivity, intelligence, and eloquence. What evidence is there for this in the First Act? Referring to the last scene of this act, show that Cyrano also has

a flair for the dramatic and an instinct for placing himself center stage.
6. What kind of person is the Comte De Guiche? In your opinion, what will be his role in the play?
7. Note that Cyrano who, even while dueling with Valvert loses not a syllable, stammers badly in the scene with the Duenna. Why?
8. What types of people make up the theater audience of the Hôtel de Bourgogne? How do they react to Cyrano's banishment of Montfleury? To Cyrano's triumph in the Ballade scene? Through their behavior, what comment on human nature is Rostand making?
9. Rostand was known for the keenness of his satire. In the First Act whom does he satirize? How?

THE SECOND ACT

1. Why does Rostand begin the Second Act with Ragueneau, rather than with Cyrano? What is the relation between the character of Ragueneau and that of Cyrano?
2. Show how the playwright builds suspense from the Duenna scene in the First Act through the Cyrano-Roxane scene in the Second Act. What word shatters the suspense?
3. By what criteria does Roxane find Christian de Neuvillette an admirable person? What does this indicate about Roxane?
4. Why doesn't Cyrano respond to the plaudits of the crowd that invades Ragueneau's shop?
5. Step by step, Cyrano makes a bitter enemy of the Comte De Guiche. Trace these steps. In your opinion, how dangerous an enemy will De Guiche be? Why?
6. Le Bret charges that Cyrano's exaggerated striking of poses is ruining his career. In his reply to Le Bret, Cyrano reveals his credo and way of life. Describe this way of life. What things does Cyrano say he will not do? What things will he do?
7. What compels Christian to insult Cyrano? In what way is Christian's apparent success ironic?
8. What is the first thing that the older man finds to admire in the young cadet? How is this typical of Cyrano?
9. In the sixteenth and seventeenth centuries, French and English aristocrats adopted an excessively elaborate, artificial manner of speaking and acting. Point out examples of this in the first two acts of *Cyrano*. Why does the fact that Roxane is part of this fashion cause Christian to despair?
10. To win the beautiful Roxane, what pact do the two men make?

Do you think the success of such a plan could bring happiness to any of the three? Explain.
11. Show that Christian almost detects Cyrano's true feeling for Roxane. Why is he unable to achieve a complete understanding of what Cyrano feels?

THE THIRD ACT

1. As this act begins, the Duenna is waiting to accompany Roxane to a "psycho-colloquy." What is to be its subject? What does such a colloquy reveal about Roxane and the culture of the times?
2. Cyrano teases Roxane for her delight in Christian's poetry. What is his real reaction?
3. Roxane tricks the powerful Comte De Guiche when he comes to say farewell. What does she do? Why is there irony in his comment to her: "You, too, you play your little games, do you?" Of the four—De Guiche, Roxane, Christian, and Cyrano—who is not playing a "little game"? Explain your answer.
4. CHRISTIAN
   I know; I grow absurd.
   ROXANE
                        And that displeases me
   As much as if you had grown ugly.

   What is your reaction to Roxane when she is displeased with Christian's verbal awkwardness? What does it reveal about her character?
5. What does Cyrano mean when in the balcony scene he says:
   Must we keep on and on
   Sipping stale honey out of tiny cups
   Decorated with golden tracery
   Drop by drop, all day long?
   ... Love hates that game of words!
   It is a crime to fence with life. ...
   For whom is he *really* speaking?
6. How does Cyrano keep the Comte De Guiche away from the wedding ceremony for the necessary fifteen minutes? Which of Cyrano's qualities, demonstrated earlier in the play, makes his technique with the Comte believable?
7. What is De Guiche's immediate reaction to the news of the marriage? How does this reaction affect Cyrano? Roxane? What final request does she make of Cyrano?
8. One characteristic of a good play is the many-sidedness of its major characters. By the end of the Third Act, how is this quality

demonstrated by Cyrano and Roxane? What of Christian, De Guiche, Le Bret, Ragueneau, the Duenna?
9. Referring to the stage directions at the beginning of the Third Act, draw a ground plan of the set. How does the dialogue further "place" the action? Explain how both the dialogue and setting establish the mood of the Third Act.

THE FOURTH ACT

1. Describe the military situation at the beginning of the Fourth Act. What is the attitude of the Cadets toward the impending battle? How does Cyrano control them?
2. Recount the episode of the white scarf. How does it happen to be in Cyrano's pocket? What use does De Guiche make of it when the scarf is returned to him?
3. How was Roxane able to come through the Spanish lines? As she describes her adventure, does she seem different from the person you met earlier in the play? Explain your answer.
4. Point out various elements of humor in the banquet scene.
5. How does De Guiche react when confronted by Roxane's refusal to escape the scene of battle? How do Cyrano and the Cadets respond to this reaction?
6. When Roxane appears, Cyrano tries desperately to talk in secret with Christian. Why?
7. In her last moments together with Christian, Roxane shows she has changed. How has she changed? How does this change affect Christian? Cyrano?
8. Roxane has just affirmed her love by saying that even if Christian were "ugly . . . disfigured . . . grotesque" she would love him. Gunfire is heard, and Le Bret comes in to whisper to Cyrano. Cyrano exclaims, "Ah! . . . All gone!" What does he mean? Do you think he is correct?
9. How is Cyrano's behavior at the end of this act typical of him? How is the action at this point typical of the play?
10. The fourth act of a classical five-act play is usually a pivotal or crucial one. In it, the playwright introduces new elements into the plot and reveals changes that have occurred, or are beginning to occur, within the central characters. Show how these two characteristics apply to the Fourth Act of *Cyrano de Bergerac*.

THE FIFTH ACT

1. The Fourth Act ended on a note of high excitement. How does the Fifth Act begin? Note that the hour is dusk and the time of

year is autumn. How do these facts establish the mood of the last act?
2. Le Bret, De Guiche, Roxane, the nuns, all fill in the portrait of Cyrano de Bergerac. What contribution does each make?
3. How has De Guiche changed—if he has changed? How sympathetically does Roxane react to his expression of disillusionment and "vain regrets"? Why does he warn Le Bret of possible danger to Cyrano?
4. Just before Cyrano enters, a dead leaf falls on Roxane's embroidery frame. What does this detail symbolize?
5. When finally Cyrano appears, he says that he was "detained by a visitor—an old friend of mine—at least a very old acquaintance." Explain this, and translate the rest of the metaphor. Why does he shift from "an old friend" to "at least a very old acquaintance"?
6. After Sister Marthe leaves, Cyrano launches into the Gazette scene. Point out Rostand's masterful use here of contrasting elements to achieve an intense emotional effect.
7. When Cyrano reads the letter, how does he know who wrote it and what is in it? Show the steps by which Roxane discovers who wrote the letter.
8. In anguish Roxane cries out, "Why were you silent for so many years, all the while, every night and every day, he gave me nothing—you knew that." Why *was* Cyrano silent?
9. There is bitterness in Cyrano's comment about the Molière plagiarism. Is the bitterness justified? How? What reason does Cyrano give for his initial fear of the world's ridicule and his consequent self-isolation? In your opinion, was he right or wrong? Why?
10. Why does Cyrano insist on standing up at the end? Against what spectral figures does he fight? What is the one thing which they cannot take from him, the one crown which he will bear away with him to God? What does this one thing represent?

viewing the play as a whole

1. Perhaps the main reason for the popularity of *Cyrano de Bergerac* is the personality of its hero. Briefly describe Cyrano. What aspects of Cyrano's character account for his universal appeal? Explain your answer.
2. What do you consider to be the theme of *Cyrano de Bergerac?* Support your answer with specific lines from the play.
3. Look up the definition of *conflict* in the Glossary, page 545. Describe the main conflict in this play. What secondary conflicts

are there? In your opinion, do the secondary conflicts add to or detract from the play as a whole?
4. What, in your opinion, is the dramatic climax of the action for Cyrano—the letter-reading and love-revelation episode in the final scene, or the successful achievement of the Roxane-Christian wedding in the middle of the play? Or neither? Discuss this point.
5. Refer to the definition of *irony* in the Glossary, page 546. In what sense is the fate of each of the following characters ironic: Roxane, Cyrano, Christian, De Guiche, and Ragueneau.
6. *Cyrano de Bergerac* was written in France at the end of the nineteenth century. Through the play, Rostand is criticizing the conformity, the complacency, and the dullness of his own times. Referring to the characters in the play, its theme, and its setting, show how the playwright achieves his purpose.
7. What passages in the play did you find most effective?
8. Edmond Rostand's stage directions call for a colorful stage setting with a wealth of detail. Could the play be produced with equal effectiveness on a bare stage? Why or why not?
9. The playwright frequently alternates scenes of crowds with scenes of two or three people. Cite examples of this. What purpose is served by such alternation? Rostand also uses people in the background for the creating of a mood. Point out examples.
10. This play is written in the spirit of nineteenth century Romanticism (see Glossary, page 547). Show how its various characteristics are illustrated in *Cyrano de Bergerac*.
11. A good play should leave you with a vivid impression of its most dramatic scenes. Which scenes from *Cyrano* stand out in your memory? Why?

for composition

1. Write a composition in which you discuss your attitude toward Cyrano de Bergerac. Did you admire, pity, or dislike him? Explain your answer.
2. Discuss the role Cyrano played in the lives of Roxane and Christian. Explain why you think he was or was not wise to help Christian as he did?
3. It is interesting to imagine what would have happened had Christian not died. How might the Fifth Act have been different? Write a composition in which you describe the changes of plot or characterization you would make.

the cherry orchard

ANTON CHEKHOV
Translated by Stark Young

the cherry orchard

CHARACTERS

RANEVSKAYA, LYUBOFF ANDREEVNA, *landowner*
ANYA, *her daughter, seventeen years old*
VARYA, *her adopted daughter, twenty-four years old*
GAYEFF, LEONID ANDREEVICH, *brother of Ranevskaya*
LOPAHIN, YERMOLAY ALEXEEVICH, *a merchant*
TROFIMOFF, PYOTR SERGEEVICH, *a student*
SEMYONOFF-PISHTCHIK, BORIS BORISOVICH, *a landowner*
CHARLOTTA IVANOVNA, *a governess*
EPIHODOFF, SEMYON PANTELEEVICH, *a clerk*
DUNYASHA, *a maid*
FIERS, *a valet, an old man of eighty-seven*
YASHA, *a young valet*
A PASSERBY *or* STRANGER
THE STATIONMASTER
A POST-OFFICE CLERK
Visitors, Servants

The action takes place on the estate of L. A. Ranevskaya.

ACT 1

A room that is still called the nursery. One of the doors leads into ANYA'S *room. Dawn, the sun will soon be rising. It is May, the cherry trees are in blossom but in the orchard it is cold, with a morning frost. The windows in the room are closed. Enter* DUNYASHA *with a candle and* LOPAHIN *with a book in his hand.*

LOPAHIN

The train got in, thank God! What time is it?

DUNYASHA

It's nearly two. *(Blows out his candle.)* It's already daylight.

LOPAHIN

But how late was the train? Two hours at least. *(Yawning and stretching)* I'm a fine one, I am, look what a fool thing I did! I drove here on purpose just to meet them at the station, and then all of a sudden I'd overslept myself! Fell asleep in my chair. How provoking!—You could have waked me up.

DUNYASHA

I thought you had gone. *(Listening)* Listen, I think they are coming now.

LOPAHIN

(listening)

No—no, there's the luggage and one thing and another. *(A pause)* Lyuboff Andreevna has been living abroad five years. I don't know what she is like now—She is a good woman. An easy-going, simple woman. I remember when I was a boy about fifteen, my father, who is at rest—in those days he ran a shop here in the village—hit me in the face with his fist, my nose was bleeding—We'd come to the yard together for something or other, and he was a little drunk. Lyuboff Andreevna, I can see her now, still so young, so slim, led me to the washbasin here in this very room, in the nursery. "Don't cry," she says, "little peasant, it will be well in time for your wedding"—*(A pause)*

Yes, little peasant—My father was a peasant truly, and here I am in a white waistcoat and yellow shoes. Like a pig rooting in a pastry shop—I've got this rich, lots of money, but if you really stop and think of it, I'm just a peasant—*(Turning the pages of a book)* Here I was reading a book and didn't get a thing out of it. Reading and went to sleep. *(A pause)*

DUNYASHA

And all night long the dogs were not asleep, they know their masters are coming.

LOPAHIN

What is it, Dunyasha, you're so—

DUNYASHA

My hands are shaking. I'm going to faint.

LOPAHIN

You're just so delicate, Dunyasha. And all dressed up like a lady, and your hair all done up! Mustn't do that. Must know your place.

(Enter EPIHODOFF, *with a bouquet; he wears a jacket and highly polished boots with a loud squeak. As he enters he drops the bouquet.)*

EPIHODOFF

(picking up the bouquet)

Look, the gardener sent these, he says to put them in the dining room. *(Giving the bouquet to* DUNYASHA*)*

LOPAHIN

And bring me some kvass.

DUNYASHA

Yes, sir. *(Goes out.)*

EPIHODOFF

There is a morning frost now, three degrees of frost *(Sighing)* and the cherries all in bloom. I cannot approve of our climate—I cannot. Our climate can never quite rise to the occasion. Listen, Yermolay Alexeevich, allow me to subtend, I bought myself, day before yesterday, some boots and they, I venture to assure you, squeak so that it is impossible. What could I grease them with?

LOPAHIN
Go on. You annoy me.
EPIHODOFF
Every day some misfortune happens to me. But I don't complain, I am used to it and I even smile.

(DUNYASHA *enters, serves* LOPAHIN *the kvass.*)

EPIHODOFF
I'm going. *(Stumbling over a chair and upsetting it)* There *(As if triumphant)* there, you see, pardon the expression, a circumstance like that, among others—It is simply quite remarkable. *(Goes out.)*
DUNYASHA
And I must tell you, Yermolay Alexeevich, that Epihodoff has proposed to me.
LOPAHIN
Ah!
DUNYASHA
I don't know really what to—He is a quiet man but sometimes when he starts talking, you can't understand a thing he means. It's all very nice, and full of feeling, but just doesn't make any sense. I sort of like him. He loves me madly. He's a man that's unfortunate, every day there's something or other. They tease him around here, call him twenty-two misfortunes—
LOPAHIN
(cocking his ear)
Listen, I think they are coming—
DUNYASHA
They are coming! But what's the matter with me—I'm cold all over.
LOPAHIN
They're really coming. Let's go meet them. Will she recognize me? It's five years we haven't seen each other.
DUNYASHA
(excitedly)
I'm going to faint this very minute. Ah, I'm going to faint!

(Two carriages can be heard driving up to the house. LOPAHIN *and* DUNYASHA *hurry out. The stage is empty. In the adjoining rooms a noise begins.* FIERS *hurries across the stage, leaning on a stick; he has been to meet* LYUBOFF ANDREEVNA, *and wears an old-fashioned livery and a high hat; he mutters something to himself, but you cannot understand a word of it. The noise offstage gets louder and louder. A voice: "Look! Let's go through here—"* LYUBOFF ANDREEVNA, ANYA *and* CHARLOTTA IVANOVNA, *with a little dog on a chain, all of them dressed for traveling,* VARYA, *in a coat and kerchief,* GAYEFF, SEMYONOFF-PISHTCHIK, LOPAHIN, DUNYASHA, *with a bundle and an umbrella, servants with pieces of luggage—all pass through the room.)*

ANYA
Let's go through here. Mama, do you remember what room this is?

LYUBOFF ANDREEVNA
(happily, through her tears)
The nursery!

VARYA
How cold it is, my hands are stiff. *(To* LYUBOFF ANDREEVNA*)* Your rooms, the white one and the violet, are just the same as ever, Mama.

LYUBOFF ANDREEVNA
The nursery, my dear beautiful room—I slept here when I was little— *(Crying)* And now I am like a child— *(Kisses her brother and* VARYA, *then her brother again.)* And Varya is just the same as ever, looks like a nun. And I knew Dunyasha— *(Kisses* DUNYASHA.*)*

GAYEFF
The train was two hours late. How's that? How's that for good management?

CHARLOTTA
(to PISHTCHIK*)*
My dog eats nuts too.

PISHTCHIK
(astonished)
Think of that!
(Everybody goes out except ANYA *and* DUNYASHA.*)*

DUNYASHA

We waited so long— *(Taking off* ANYA's *coat and hat)*

ANYA

I didn't sleep all four nights on the way. And now I feel so chilly.

DUNYASHA

It was Lent when you left, there was some snow then, there was frost, and now? My darling *(Laughing and kissing her)*, I waited so long for you, my joy, my life—I'm telling you now, I can't keep from it another minute.

ANYA

(wearily)

There we go again—

DUNYASHA

The clerk Epihodoff, proposed to me after Holy Week.

ANYA

You're always talking about the same thing— *(Arranging her hair)* I've lost all my hairpins— *(She is tired to the point of staggering.)*

DUNYASHA

I just don't know what to think. He loves me, loves me so!

ANYA

(looks in through her door, tenderly)

My room, my windows, it's just as if I had never been away. I'm home! Tomorrow morning I'll get up, I'll run into the orchard— Oh, if I only could go to sleep! I haven't slept all the way, I was tormented by anxiety.

DUNYASHA

Day before yesterday, Pyotr Sergeevich arrived.

ANYA

(joyfully)

Petya!

DUNYASHA

He's asleep in the bathhouse, he lives there. I am afraid, he says, of being in the way. *(Taking her watch from her pocket and looking at it)* Somebody ought to wake him up. It's only that Varvara Mikhailovna told us not to. Don't you wake him up, she said.

VARYA

(enter VARYA with a bunch of keys at her belt)
Dunyasha, coffee, quick—Mama is asking for coffee.

DUNYASHA

This minute. *(Goes out.)*

VARYA

Well, thank goodness, you've come back. You are home again. *(Caressingly)* My darling is back! My precious is back!

ANYA

I've had such a time.

VARYA

I can imagine!

ANYA

I left during Holy Week, it was cold then. Charlotta talked all the way and did her tricks. Why did you fasten Charlotta on to me—?

VARYA

But you couldn't have traveled alone, darling; not at seventeen!

ANYA

We arrived in Paris, it was cold there and snowing. I speak terrible French. Mama lived on the fifth floor; I went to see her; there were some French people in her room, ladies, an old priest with his prayer book, and the place was full of tobacco smoke—very dreary. Suddenly I began to feel sorry for Mama, so sorry, I drew her to me, held her close and couldn't let her go. Then Mama kept hugging me, crying—yes—

VARYA

(tearfully)
Don't—oh, don't—

ANYA

Her villa near Mentone she had already sold, she had nothing left, nothing. And I didn't have a kopeck left. It was all we could do to get here. And Mama doesn't understand! We sit down to dinner at a station and she orders, insists on the most expensive things and gives the waiters rouble tips. Charlotta does the same, Yasha too demands his share; it's simply dreadful. Mama has her butler, Yasha, we've brought him here—

VARYA

I saw the wretch.

ANYA

Well, how are things? Has the interest on the mortgage been paid?

VARYA

How could we?

ANYA

Oh, my God, my God—!

VARYA

In August, the estate is to be sold—

ANYA

My God—!

LOPAHIN

(looking in through the door and mooing like a cow)
Moo-o-o— *(Goes away.)*

VARYA

(tearfully)
I'd land him one like that— *(Shaking her fist)*

ANYA

(embracing VARYA gently)
Varya, has he proposed? (VARYA *shakes her head.)* But he loves you—Why don't you have it out with him, what are you waiting for?

VARYA

I don't think anything will come of it for us. He is very busy, he hasn't any time for me—And doesn't notice me. God knows, it's painful for me to see him—Everybody talks about our marriage, everybody congratulates us, and the truth is, there's nothing to it—it's all like a dream— *(In a different tone)* You have a brooch looks like a bee.

ANYA

(sadly)
Mama bought it. *(Going toward her room, speaking gaily, like a child)* And in Paris I went up in a balloon!

VARYA

My darling is back! My precious is back! (DUNYASHA *has returned with the coffee pot and is making coffee.* VARYA *is standing by the door.)* Darling, I'm busy all day long with the house and I go around thinking things. If only you could be married to a rich man, I'd be more at peace too, I would go all by myself to a hermitage—then to Kiev—to Moscow, and I'd keep going like that from one holy place to another—I would go on and on. Heavenly!

ANYA

The birds are singing in the orchard. What time is it now?

VARYA

It must be after two. It's time you were asleep, darling. *(Going into* ANYA's *room)* Heavenly!

YASHA

(enters with a lap robe and a traveling bag. Crossing the stage airly)

May I go through here?

DUNYASHA

We'd hardly recognize you, Yasha; you've changed so abroad!

YASHA

Hm— And who are you?

DUNYASHA

When you left here, I was like that— *(Her hand so high from the floor)* I'm Dunyasha, Fyodor Kozoyedoff's daughter. You don't remember!

YASHA

Hm— You little peach!

(Looking around before he embraces her; she shrieks and drops a saucer; YASHA *hurries out.)*

VARYA

(at the door, in a vexed tone)
And what's going on here?

DUNYASHA

(tearfully)
I broke a saucer—

VARYA

That's good luck.

ANYA

(emerging from her room)
We ought to tell Mama beforehand: Petya is here—

VARYA

I told them not to wake him up.

ANYA

(pensively)

Six years ago our father died, a month later our brother Grisha was drowned in the river, such a pretty little boy, just seven. Mama couldn't bear it, she went away, went away without ever looking back— *(Shuddering)* How I understand her, if she only knew I did. *(A pause)* and Petya Trofimoff was Grisha's tutor, he might remind—

FIERS

(entering in a jacket and white waistcoat; going to the coffee urn, busy with it)

The mistress will have her breakfast here— *(Putting on white gloves)* Is the coffee ready? *(To* DUNYASHA, *sternly)* You! What about the cream?

DUNYASHA

Oh, my God— *(Hurrying out)*

FIERS

(busy at the coffee urn)

Oh, you good-for-nothing—! *(Muttering to himself)* Come back from Paris—And the master used to go to Paris by coach— *(Laughing)*

VARYA

Fiers, what are you—?

FIERS

At your service. *(Joyfully)* My mistress is back! It's what I've been waiting for! Now I'm ready to die— *(Crying for joy)*

(LYUBOFF ANDREEVNA, GAYEFF *and* SEMYONOFF-PISHTCHIK *enter;* SEMYONOFF-PISHTCHIK *is in a podyovka of fine cloth and sharovary.* GAYEFF *enters; he makes gestures with his hands and body as if he were playing billiards.)*

LYUBOFF ANDREEVNA

How is it? Let me remember—Yellow into the corner! Duplicate in the middle!

GAYEFF

I cut into the corner. Sister, you and I slept here in this very room once, and now I am fifty-one years old, strange as that may seem—

LOPAHIN
Yes, time passes.
GAYEFF
What?
LOPAHIN
Time, I say, passes.
GAYEFF
And it smells like patchouli here.
ANYA
I'm going to bed. Good night, Mama. *(Kissing her mother)*
LYUBOFF ANDREEVNA
My sweet little child. *(Kissing her hands)* You're glad you are home? I still can't get myself together.
ANYA
Goodbye, Uncle.
GAYEFF
(kissing her face and hands)
God be with you. How like your mother you are! *(To his sister)* Lyuba, at her age you were exactly like her.

(ANYA *shakes hands with* LOPAHIN *and* PISHTCHIK, *goes out and closes the door behind her.*)

LYUBOFF ANDREEVNA
She's very tired.
PISHTCHIK
It is a long trip, I imagine.
VARYA
(to LOPAHIN *and* PISHTCHIK*)*
Well, then, sirs? It's going on three o'clock, time for gentlemen to be going.
LYUBOFF ANDREEVNA
(laughing)
The same old Varya. *(Drawing her to her and kissing her)* There, I'll drink my coffee, then we'll all go. *(*FIERS *puts a small cushion under her feet.)* Thank you, my dear. I am used to coffee. Drink it day and night. Thank you, my dear old soul.

(Kissing FIERS*)*

VARYA

I'll go see if all the things have come. *(Goes out.)*

LYUBOFF ANDREEVNA

Is it really me sitting here? *(Laughing)* I'd like to jump around and wave my arms. *(Covering her face with her hands)* But I may be dreaming! God knows I love my country, love it deeply, I couldn't look out of the car window, I just kept crying. *(Tearfully)* However, I must drink my coffee. Thank you, Fiers, thank you, my dear old friend. I'm so glad you're still alive.

FIERS

Day before yesterday.

GAYEFF

He doesn't hear well.

LOPAHIN

And I must leave right now. It's nearly five o'clock in the morning, for Kharkov. What a nuisance! I wanted to look at you—talk— You are as beautiful as ever.

PISHTCHIK

(breathing heavily)

Even more beautiful— In your Paris clothes— It's a feast for the eyes—

LOPAHIN

Your brother, Leonid Andreevich here, says I'm a boor, a peasant money grubber, but that's all the same to me, absolutely. Let him say it. All I wish is you'd trust me as you used to, and your wonderful, touching eyes would look at me as they did. Merciful God! My father was a serf; belonged to your grandfather and your father; but you, your own self, you did so much for me once that I've forgotten all that and love you like my own kin—more than my kin.

LYUBOFF ANDREEVNA

I can't sit still—I can't. *(Jumping up and walking about in great excitement)* I'll never live through this happiness— Laugh at me, I'm silly— My own little bookcase—! *(Kissing the bookcase)* My little table!

GAYEFF

And in your absence the nurse here died.

LYUBOFF ANDREEVNA

(sitting down and drinking coffee)
Yes, may she rest in Heaven! They wrote me.

GAYEFF

And Anastasy died. Cross-eyed Petrushka left me and lives in town now at the police officer's. *(Taking out of his pocket a box of hard candy and sucking a piece)*

PISHTCHIK

My daughter, Dashenka—sends you her greetings—

LOPAHIN

I want to tell you something very pleasant, cheerful. *(Glancing at his watch)* I'm going right away. There's no time for talking. Well, I'll make it two or three words. As you know, your cherry orchard is to be sold for your debts; the auction is set for August 22nd, but don't you worry, my dear, you just sleep in peace, there's a way out of it. Here's my plan. Please listen to me. Your estate is only thirteen miles from town. They've run the railroad by it. Now if the cherry orchard and the land along the river were cut up into building lots and leased for summer cottages, you'd have at the very lowest twenty-five thousand roubles per year income.

GAYEFF

Excuse me, what rot!

LYUBOFF ANDREEVNA

I don't quite understand you, Yermolay Alexeevich.

LOPAHIN

At the very least you will get from the summer residents twenty-five roubles per year for a two-and-a-half acre lot and if you post a notice right off, I'll bet you anything that by autumn you won't have a single patch of land free, everything will be taken. In a word, my congratulations, you are saved. The location is wonderful, the river's so deep. Except, of course, it all needs to be tidied up, cleared— For instance, let's say, tear all the old buildings down and this house, which is no good any more, and cut down the old cherry orchard—

LYUBOFF ANDREEVNA

Cut down? My dear, forgive me, you don't understand at all. If there's one thing in the whole province that's interesting—not to say remarkable—it's our cherry orchard.

LOPAHIN

The only remarkable thing about this cherry orchard is that it's very big. There's a crop of cherries once every two years and even that's hard to get rid of. Nobody buys them.

GAYEFF

This orchard is even mentioned in the encyclopedia.

LOPAHIN

(glancing at his watch)

If we don't cook up something and don't get somewhere, the cherry orchard and the entire estate will be sold at auction on the twenty-second of August. Do get it settled then! I swear there is no other way out. Not a one!

FIERS

There was a time, forty-fifty years ago, when the cherries were dried, soaked, pickled, cooked into jam and it used to be—

GAYEFF

Keep quiet, Fiers.

FIERS

And it used to be that the dried cherries were shipped by the wagon-load to Moscow and to Kharkov. And the money there was! And the dried cherries were soft then, juicy, sweet, fragrant— They had a way of treating them then—

LYUBOFF ANDREEVNA

And where is that way now?

FIERS

They have forgotten it. Nobody remembers it.

PISHTCHIK

(to LYUBOFF ANDREEVNA)

What's happening in Paris? How is everything? Did you eat frogs?

LYUBOFF ANDREEVNA

I ate crocodiles.

PISHTCHIK

Think of it—!

LOPAHIN

Up to now in the country there have been only the gentry and the peasants, but now in summer the villa people too are coming in. All the towns, even the least big ones, are surrounded with cottages. In about twenty years very likely the summer resident will multiply enormously. He merely drinks tea on the porch now, but it might well happen that on this two-and-a-half acre lot of his, he'll go in for farming, and then your cherry orchard would be happy, rich, splendid—

GAYEFF

(getting hot)
What rot!

(Enter VARYA *and* YASHA.*)*

VARYA

Here, Mama. Two telegrams for you. *(Choosing a key and opening the old bookcase noisily)* Here they are.

LYUBOFF ANDREEVNA

From Paris *(Tearing up the telegrams without reading them)* Paris, that's all over—

GAYEFF

Do you know how old this bookcase is, Lyuba? A week ago I pulled out the bottom drawer and looked, and there the figures were burned on it. The bookcase was made exactly a hundred years ago. How's that? Eh? You might celebrate its jubilee. It's an inanimate object, but all the same, be that as it may, it's a bookcase.

PISHTCHIK

(in astonishment)
A hundred years—! Think of it—!

GAYEFF

Yes—quite something— *(Shaking the bookcase)* Dear, honored bookcase! I salute your existence, which for more than a hundred years has been directed toward the clear ideals of goodness and justice; your silent appeal to fruitful endeavor has not flagged in all the course of a hundred years, sustaining *(Tearfully)* through the generations of our family, our courage and our faith in a better future and nurturing in us ideals of goodness and of a social consciousness.

(A pause)

LOPAHIN
Yes.
LYUBOFF ANDREEVNA
You're the same as ever, Lenya.
GAYEFF
(slightly embarrassed)
Carom to the right into the corner pocket. I cut into the side pocket!
LOPAHIN
(glancing at his watch)
Well, it's time for me to go.
YASHA
(handing medicine to LYUBOFF ANDREEVNA*)*
Perhaps you'll take the pills now—
PISHTCHIK
You should never take medicaments, dear madam— They do neither harm nor good— Hand them here, dearest lady. *(He takes the pillbox, shakes the pills out into his palm, blows on them, puts them in his mouth and washes them down with kvass.)* There! Now!
LYUBOFF ANDREEVNA
(startled)
Why, you've lost your mind!
PISHTCHIK
I took all the pills.
LOPAHIN
Such a glutton!

(Everyone laughs.)

FIERS
The gentleman stayed with us during Holy Week, he ate half a bucket of pickles— *(Muttering)*
LYUBOFF ANDREEVNA
What is he muttering about?
VARYA
He's been muttering like that for three years. We're used to it.
YASHA
In his dotage.

(CHARLOTTA IVANOVNA *in a white dress—she is very thin, her corset laced very tight—with a lorgnette at her belt, crosses the stage.*)

LOPAHIN

Excuse me, Charlotta Ivanovna, I haven't had a chance yet to welcome you. (*Trying to kiss her hand*)

CHARLOTTA

(*drawing her hand away*)

If I let you kiss my hand, 'twould be my elbow next, then my shoulder—

LOPAHIN

No luck for me today. (*Everyone laughs.*) Charlotta Ivanovna, show us a trick!

CHARLOTTA

No. I want to go to bed. (*Exit*)

LOPAHIN

In three weeks we shall see each other. (*Kissing* LYUBOFF ANDREEVNA's *hand*) Till then, goodbye. It's time. (*To* GAYEFF) See you soon. (*Kissing* PISHTCHIK) See you soon. (*Shaking* VARYA's *hand, then* FIERS' *and* YASHA's) I don't feel like going. (*To* LYUBOFF ANDREEVNA) If you think it over and make up your mind about the summer cottages, let me know and I'll arrange a loan of something like fifty thousands roubles. Think it over seriously.

VARYA

(*angrily*)

Do go on, anyhow, will you!

LOPAHIN

I'm going, I'm going— (*Exit*)

GAYEFF

Boor. However, pardon—Varya is going to marry him, it's Varya's little fiancé.

VARYA

Don't talk too much, Uncle.

LYUBOFF ANDREEVNA

Well, Varya, I should be very glad. He's a good man.

PISHTCHIK

A man, one must say truthfully—A most worthy—And my Dashenka—says also that—she says all sorts of things— *(Snoring but immediately waking up)* Nevertheless, dearest lady, oblige me—With a loan of two hundred and forty roubles— Tomorrow the interest on my mortgage has got to be paid—

VARYA

(startled)

There's not any money, none at all.

LYUBOFF ANDREEVNA

Really, I haven't got anything.

PISHTCHIK

I'll find it, somehow. *(Laughing)* I never give up hope. There, I think to myself, all is lost, I am ruined and lo and behold—a railroad is put through my land and—they paid me. And then, just watch, something else will turn up—if not today, then tomorrow— Dashenka will win two hundred thousand— She has a ticket.

LYUBOFF ANDREEVNA

We've finished the coffee, now we can go to bed.

FIERS

(brushing GAYEEF's clothes, reprovingly)

You put on the wrong trousers again. What am I going to do with you!

VARYA

(softly)

Anya is asleep. *(Opening the window softly)* Already the sun's rising—it's not cold. Look, Mama! What beautiful trees! My Lord, what air! The starlings are singing!

GAYEFF

(opening another window)

The orchard is all white. You haven't forgotten, Lyuba? That long lane there runs straight—as a strap stretched out. It glistens on moonlight nights. Do you remember? You haven't forgotten it?

LYUBOFF ANDREEVNA

(looking out of the window on to the orchard)

Oh, my childhood, my innocence! I slept in this nursery and looked out on the orchard from here, every morning happiness awoke with me, it was just as it is now, then, nothing has changed. *(Laughing with joy)* All, all white! Oh, my orchard! After a dark, rainy autumn and cold winter, you are young again and full of happiness. The heavenly angels have not deserted you— If I only could lift the weight from my breast, from my shoulders, if I could only forget my past!

GAYEFF

Yes, and the orchard will be sold for debt, strange as that may seem.

LYUBOFF ANDREEVNA

Look, our dear mother is walking through the orchard—In a white dress! *(Laughing happily)* It's she.

GAYEFF

Where?

VARYA

God be with you, Mama!

LYUBOFF ANDREEVNA

There's not anybody, it only seemed so. To the right, as you turn to the summerhouse, a little white tree is leaning there, looks like a woman— *(Enter* TROFIMOFF, *in a student's uniform, well-worn, and glasses.)* What a wonderful orchard! The white masses of blossoms, the sky all blue.

TROFIMOFF

Lyuboff Andreevna! *(She looks around at him.)* I will just greet you and go immediately. *(Kissing her hand warmly)* I was told to wait until morning, but I hadn't the patience—

*(*LYUBOFF ANDREEVNA *looks at him puzzled.)*

VARYA

(tearfully)

This is Petya Trofimoff—

TROFIMOFF

Petya Trofimoff, the former tutor of your Grisha— Have I really changed so?

*(*LYUBOFF ANDREEVNA *embraces him, crying quietly.)*

GAYEFF

(embarrassed)

There, there, Lyuba.

VARYA

(crying)

I told you, Petya, to wait till tomorrow.

LYUBOFF ANDREEVNA

My Grisha—My boy—Grisha—Son—

VARYA

What can we do, Mama? It's God's will.

TROFIMOFF

(in a low voice tearfully)

There, there—

LYUBOFF ANDREEVNA

(weeping softly)

My boy was lost, drowned— Why? Why, my friend? *(More quietly)* Anya is asleep there, and I am talking so loud—Making much noise— But why, Petya? Why have you lost your looks? Why do you look so much older?

TROFIMOFF

A peasant woman on the train called me a mangy-looking gentleman.

LYUBOFF ANDREEVNA

You were a mere boy then, a charming young student, and now your hair's not very thick any more and you wear glasses. Are you really a student still? *(Going to the door)*

TROFIMOFF

Very likely I'll be a perennial student.

LYUBOFF ANDREEVNA

(Kissing her brother, then VARYA)

Well, go to bed— You've grown older too, Leonid.

PISHTCHIK

(following her)

So that's it, we are going to bed now. Oh, my gout! I'm staying here— I'd like, Lyuboff Andreevna, my soul, tomorrow morning— Two hundred and forty roubles—

GAYEFF

He's still at it.

PISHTCHIK

Two hundred and forty roubles— To pay interest on the mortgage.

LYUBOFF ANDREEVNA

I haven't any money, my dove.

PISHTCHIK

I'll pay it back, my dear— It's a trifling sum—

LYUBOFF ANDREEVNA

Oh, very well, Leonid will give— You give it to him, Leonid.

GAYEFF

Oh, certainly, I'll give it to him. Hold out your pockets.

LYUBOFF ANDREEVNA

What can we do, give it, he needs it— He'll pay it back.

(LYUBOFF ANDREEVNA, TROFIMOFF, PISHTCHIK *and* FIERS *go out.* GAYEFF, VARYA *and* YASHA *remain.*)

GAYEFF

My sister hasn't yet lost her habit of throwing money away. (*To* YASHA) Get away, my good fellow, you smell like hens.

YASHA

(*with a grin*)

And you are just the same as you used to be, Leonid Andreevich.

GAYEFF

What? (*To* VARYA) What did he say?

VARYA

(*to* YASHA)

Your mother has come from the village, she's been sitting in the servants' hall ever since yesterday, she wants to see you—

YASHA

The devil take her!

VARYA

Ach, shameless creature!

YASHA

A lot I need her! She might have come tomorrow.

(*Goes out.*)

VARYA

Mama is just the same as she was, she hasn't changed at all. If she could, she'd give away everything she has.

GAYEFF

Yes— If many remedies are prescribed for an illness, you may know the illness is incurable. I keep thinking, I wrack my brains, I have many remedies, a great many, and that means, really, I haven't any at all. It would be fine to inherit a fortune from somebody, it would be fine to marry off our Anya to a very rich man, it would be fine to go to Yaroslavl and try our luck with our old aunt, the Countess. Auntie is very, very rich.

VARYA

(crying)

If God would only help us!

GAYEFF

Don't bawl! Auntie is very rich but she doesn't like us. To begin with, Sister married a lawyer, not a nobleman— (ANYA *appears at the door*) Married not a nobleman and behaved herself, you could say, not very virtuously. She is good, kind, nice, I love her very much, but no matter how much you allow for the extenuating circumstances, you must admit she's a depraved woman. You feel it in her slightest movement.

VARYA

(whispering)

Anya is standing in the door there.

GAYEFF

What? *(A pause)* It's amazing, something got in my right eye. I am beginning to see poorly. And on Thursday, when I was in the District Court—

(ANYA *enters.*)

VARYA

But why aren't you asleep, Anya?

ANYA

I don't feel like sleeping. I can't.

GAYEFF

My little girl— *(Kissing* ANYA's *face and hands)* My child— *(Tearfully)* You are not my niece, you are my angel, you are everything to me. Believe me, believe—

ANYA

I believe you, Uncle. Everybody loves you, respects you— But dear Uncle, you must keep quiet, just keep quiet— What were you saying, just now, about my mother, about your own sister? What did you say that for?

GAYEFF

Yes, yes— *(Putting her hand up over his face)* Really, it's terrible! My God! Oh, God, save me! And today I made a speech to the bookcase— So silly! And it was only when I finished it that I could see it was silly.

VARYA

It's true, Uncle, you ought to keep quiet. Just keep quiet. That's all.

ANYA

If you keep quiet, you'd have more peace.

GAYEFF

I'll keep quiet. *(Kissing* ANYA's *and* VARYA's *hands)* I'll keep quiet. Only this, it's about business. On Thursday I was in the District Court; well, a few of us gathered around and a conversation began about this and that, about lots of things; apparently it will be possible to arrange a loan on a promissory note to pay the bank the interest due.

VARYA

If the Lord would only help us!

GAYEFF

Tuesday I shall go and talk it over again. *(To* VARYA*)* Don't bawl! *(To* ANYA*)* Your mother will talk to Lopahin; of course, he won't refuse her . . . And as soon as you rest up, you will go to Yaroslavl to your great-aunt, the Countess. There, that's how we will move from three directions, and the business is in the bag. We'll pay the interest. I am convinced of that— *(Putting a hard candy in his mouth)* On my honor I'll swear, by anything you like, that the estate shall not be sold! *(Excitedly)* By my happiness, I swear! Here's my hand, call me a worthless, dishonorable man, if I allow it to come up for auction! With all my soul I swear it!

ANYA

(a quieter mood returns to her; she is happy)
How good you are, Uncle, how clever! *(Embracing her uncle)* I feel easy now! I feel easy! I'm happy!

FIERS

(entering; reproachfully to GAYEFF*)*

Leonid Andreevich, have you no fear of God! When are you going to bed?

GAYEFF

Right away, right away. You may go, Fiers. For this once I'll undress myself. Well, children, beddy bye— More details tomorrow, and now, go to bed *(Kissing* ANYA *and* VARYA*)* I am a man of the eighties— It is a period that's not admired, but I can say, nevertheless, that I've suffered no little for my convictions in the course of my life. It is not for nothing that the peasant loves me. One must know the peasant! One must know from what—

ANYA

Again, Uncle!

VARYA

You, Uncle dear, keep quiet.

FIERS

(angrily)

Leonid Andreevich!

GAYEFF

I'm coming, I'm coming— Go to bed. A double bank into the side pocket! A clean shot—

(Goes out, FIERS *hobbling after him.)*

ANYA

I feel easy now. I don't feel like going to Yaroslavl; I don't like Great-aunt, but still I feel easy. Thanks to Uncle. *(Sits down.)*

VARYA

I must get to sleep. I'm going. And there was unpleasantness here during your absence. In the old servants' quarters, as you know, live only the old servants: Yephemushka, Polya, Yevstignay, well, and Karp. They began to let every sort of creature spend the night with them—I didn't say anything. But then I hear they've spread the rumor that I'd given orders to feed them nothing but beans. Out of stinginess, you see— And all that from Yevstignay— Very well, I think to myself. If that's the way it is, I think to myself, then you just wait. I call in

Yevstignay— *(Yawning)* He comes— How is it, I say, that you, Yevstignay— You're such a fool— *(Glancing at* ANYA*)* Anitchka!—*(A pause)* Asleep! *(Takes* ANYA *by her arm.)* Let's go to bed— Come on!— *(Leading her)* My little darling fell asleep! Come on— *(They go. Far away beyond the orchard a shepherd is playing on a pipe.* TROFIMOFF *walks across the stage and, seeing* VARYA *and* ANYA, *stops.)* Shh— She is asleep— asleep—Let's go, dear.

ANYA
(softly, half dreaming)
I'm so tired— All the bells!—Uncle—dear— And Mama and Uncle—Varya.

VARYA
Come on, my dear, come on. *(They go into* ANYA'S *room.)*

TROFIMOFF
(tenderly)
My little sun! My spring!

(Curtain)

ACT 2

A field. An old chapel, long abandoned, with crooked walls, near it a well, big stones that apparently were once tombstones, and an old bench. A road to the estate of GAYEFF *can be seen. On one side poplars rise, casting their shadows; the cherry orchard begins there. In the distance a row of telegraph poles; and far, far away, faintly traced on the horizon, is a large town, visible only in the clearest weather. The sun will soon be down.* CHARLOTTA, YASHA *and* DUNYASHA *are sitting on the bench;* EPIHODOFF *is standing near and playing the guitar; everyone sits lost in thought.* CHARLOTTA *wears an old peak cap; she has taken a rifle from off her shoulders and is adjusting the buckle on the strap.*

CHARLOTTA

(pensively)

I have no proper passport, I don't know how old I am—it always seems to me I'm very young. When I was a little girl, my father and mother traveled from fair to fair and gave performances, very good ones. And I did *salto mortale* and different tricks. And when Papa and Mama died, a German lady took me to live with her and began teaching me. Good. I grew up. And became a governess. But where I came from and who I am I don't know— Who my parents were, perhaps they weren't even married—I don't know. *(Taking a cucumber out of her pocket and beginning to eat it)* I don't know a thing. *(A pause)* I'd like so much to talk but there's not anybody. I haven't anybody.

EPIHODOFF

(playing the guitar and singing)

"What care I for the noisy world, what care I for friends and foes."—How pleasant it is to play the mandolin!

DUNYASHA

That's a guitar, not a mandolin. *(Looking into a little mirror and powdering her face)*

EPIHODOFF

For a madman who is in love, this is a mandolin— *(Singing)* "If only my heart were warm with the fire of requited love."

(YASHA sings with him.)

CHARLOTTA

How dreadfully these people sing— Phooey! Like jackals.

DUNYASHA

(to YASHA)

All the same, what happiness to have been abroad.

YASHA

Yes, of course. I cannot disagree with you.

(Yawning and then lighting a cigar)

EPIHODOFF

That's easily understood. Abroad everything long since attained its complete development.

YASHA

That's obvious.

EPIHODOFF

I am a cultured man. I read all kinds of remarkable books, but the trouble is I cannot discover my own inclinations, whether to live or to shoot myself, but nevertheless, I always carry a revolver on me. Here it is—*(Showing a revolver)*

CHARLOTTA

That's done. Now I am going. *(Slinging the rifle over her shoulder)* You are a very clever man, Epihodoff, and a very terrible one; the women must love you madly. Brrrr-r-r-r! *(Going)* These clever people are all so silly, I haven't anybody to talk with. I'm always alone, I have nobody and— Who I am, why I am, is unknown— *(Goes out without hurrying.)*

EPIHODOFF

Strictly speaking, not touching on other subjects, I must state about myself, in passing, that fate treats me mercilessly, as a storm does a small ship. If, let us suppose, I am mistaken, then why, to mention one instance, do I wake up this morning, look and there on my chest is a spider of terrific size— There, like that. *(Showing the size with both hands)* And also I take some kvass to drink and in it I find something in the highest degree indecent, such as a cockroach. *(A pause)* Have you read Buckle? *(A pause)* I desire to trouble you, Avdotya Feodorovna, with a couple of words.

DUNYASHA

Speak.

EPIHODOFF

I have a desire to speak with you alone— *(Sighing)*

DUNYASHA

(embarrassed)

Very well— But bring me my cape first—by the cupboard— It's rather damp here—

EPIHODOFF

Very well—I'll fetch it— Now I know what I should do with my revolver—*(Takes the guitar and goes out playing.)*

YASHA

Twenty-two misfortunes! Between us he's a stupid man, it must be said. *(Yawning)*

DUNYASHA

God forbid he should shoot himself. *(A pause)* I've grown so uneasy, I'm always fretting. I was only a girl when I was taken into the master's house, and now I've lost the habit of simple living—and here are my hands white, white as a lady's. I've become so delicate, fragile, ladylike, afraid of everything—Frightfully so. And, Yasha, if you deceive me, I don't know what will happen to my nerves.

YASHA

(kissing her)
You little cucumber! Of course every girl must behave properly. What I dislike above everything is for a girl to conduct herself badly.

DUNYASHA

I have come to love you passionately, you are educated, you can discuss anything. *(A pause.)*

YASHA

(yawning)
Yes, sir—To my mind it is like this: If a girl loves someone, it means she is immoral. *(A pause)* It is pleasant to smoke a cigar in the clear air—*(Listening)* They are coming here— It is the ladies and gentlemen—

(DUNYASHA *impulsively embraces him.*)

YASHA

Go to the house, as though you had been to bathe in the river, go by this path, otherwise, they might meet you and suspect me of making a rendezvous with you. That I cannot tolerate.

DUNYASHA

(with a little cough)
Your cigar has given me the headache. *(Goes out.)*

(YASHA *remains, sitting near the chapel.* LYUBOFF ANDREEVNA, GAYEFF *and* LOPAHIN *enter.*)

LOPAHIN

We must decide definitely, time doesn't wait. Why, the matter's quite simple. Are you willing to lease your land for summer cottages or are you not? Answer in one word, yes or no? Just one word!

LYUBOFF ANDREEVNA

Who is it smokes those disgusting cigars out here—? *(Sitting down)*

GAYEFF

The railroad running so near is a great convenience. *(Sitting down)* We made a trip to town and lunched there— Yellow in the side pocket! Perhaps I should go in the house first and play one game—

LYUBOFF ANDREEVNA

You'll have time.

LOPAHIN

Just one word! *(Imploringly)* Do give me your answer!

GAYEFF

(yawning)
What?

LYUBOFF ANDREEVNA

(looking in her purse)
Yesterday there was lots of money in it. Today there's very little. My poor Varya! For the sake of economy she feeds everybody milk soup, and in the kitchen the old people get nothing but beans, and here I spend money—senselessly— *(Dropping her purse and scattering gold coins)* There they go scattering! *(She is vexed.)*

YASHA

Allow me, I'll pick them up in a second. *(Picking up the coins)*

LYUBOFF ANDREEVNA

If you will, Yasha. And why did I go in town for lunch—? Your restaurant with its music is trashy, the tablecloths smell of soap— Why drink so much, Lyonya? Why eat so much? Why talk so much? Today in the restaurant you were talking a lot again, and all of it beside the point. About the seventies, about the decadents. And to whom? Talking to waiters about the decadents!

LOPAHIN

Yes.

GAYEFF

(waving his hand)
I am incorrigible, that's evident— *(To YASHA irritably)* What is it?—You are forever swirling around in front of us?

YASHA

(laughing)

I cannot hear your voice without laughing.

GAYEFF

(to his sister)

Either I or he—

LYUBOFF ANDREEVNA

Go away, Yasha. Go on—

YASHA

(giving LYUBOFF ANDREEVNA *her purse)*

I am going right away. *(Barely suppressing his laughter)* This minute. *(Goes out.)*

LOPAHIN

The rich Deriganoff intends to buy your estate. They say he is coming personally to the auction.

LYUBOFF ANDREEVNA

And where did you hear that?

LOPAHIN

In town they are saying it.

GAYEFF

Our Yaroslavl aunt promised to send us something, but when and how much she will send, nobody knows—

LOPAHIN

How much will she send? A hundred thousand? Two hundred?

LYUBOFF ANDREEVNA

Well—maybe ten, fifteen thousand—we'd be thankful for that.

LOPAHIN

Excuse me, but such light-minded people as you are, such odd, unbusinesslike people, I never saw. You are told in plain Russian that your estate is being sold up and you just don't seem to take it in.

LYUBOFF ANDREEVNA

But what are we to do? Tell us what?

LOPAHIN

I tell you every day. Every day I tell you the same thing. Both the cherry orchard and the land have got to be leased for summer cottages, it has to be done right now, quick— The auction is right under your noses. Do understand! Once you finally decide that there are to be summer cottages, you will get all the money you want, and then you'll be saved.

LYUBOFF ANDREEVNA

Summer cottages and summer residents—it is so trivial, excuse me.

GAYEFF

I absolutely agree with you.

LOPAHIN

I'll either burst out crying, or scream, or faint. I can't bear it! You are torturing me! *(To* GAYEFF*)* You're a perfect old woman!

GAYEFF

What?

LOPAHIN

A perfect old woman! *(About to go)*

LYUBOFF ANDREEVNA

(alarmed)

No, don't go, stay, my lamb, I beg you. Perhaps we will think of something!

LOPAHIN

What is there to think about?

LYUBOFF ANDREEVNA

Don't go, I beg you. With you here it is more cheerful anyhow— *(A pause)* I keep waiting for something, as if the house were about to tumble down on our heads.

GAYEFF

(deep in thought)

Double into the corner pocket— Bank into the side pocket—

LYUBOFF ANDREEVNA

We have sinned so much—

LOPAHIN

What sins have you—?

GAYEFF

(puts a hard candy into his mouth)

They say I've eaten my fortune up in hard candies— *(Laughing)*

LYUBOFF ANDREEVNA

Oh, my sins—I've always thrown money around like mad, recklessly, and I married a man who accumulated nothing but debts. My husband died from champagne—he drank fearfully—and to my misfortune I fell in love with another man. I lived with him, and just at that time—it was my first punishment—a blow over the head: right here in the river my boy was drowned and I went abroad—went away for good, never to return, never to see this river again—I shut my eyes, ran away, beside myself, and he after me—mercilessly, brutally. I bought a villa near Mentone, because he fell ill there, and for three years I knew no rest day or night, the sick man exhausted me, my soul dried up. And last year when the villa was sold for debts, I went to Paris and there he robbed me of everything, threw me over, took up with another woman; I tried to poison myself—so stupid, so shameful— And suddenly I was seized with longing for Russia, for my own country, for my little girl— *(Wiping away her tears)* Lord, Lord, have mercy, forgive me my sins! Don't punish me any more! *(Getting a telegram out of her pocket)* I got this today from Paris, he asks forgiveness, begs me to return— *(Tears up the telegram.)* That sounds like music somewhere.

(Listening)

GAYEFF

It is our famous Jewish orchestra. You remember, four violins, a flute and double bass.

LYUBOFF ANDREEVNA

Does it still exist? We ought to get hold of it sometime and give a party.

LOPAHIN

(listening)

Can't hear it— *(Singing softly)* "And for money the Germans will Frenchify a Russian." *(Laughing)* What a play I saw yesterday at the theater, very funny!

LYUBOFF ANDREEVNA

And most likely there was nothing funny about it. You shouldn't look at plays, but look oftener at yourselves. How gray all your lives are, what a lot of idle things you say!

LOPAHIN

That's true. It must be said frankly this life of ours is idiotic— *(A pause)* My father was a peasant, an idiot, he understood nothing, he taught me nothing, he just beat me in his drunken fits and always with a stick. At bottom I am just as big a dolt and idiot as he was. I wasn't taught anything, my handwriting is vile, I write like a pig—I am ashamed for people to see it.

LYUBOFF ANDREEVNA

You ought to get married, my friend.

LOPAHIN

Yes—That's true.

LYUBOFF ANDREEVNA

To our Varya, perhaps. She is a good girl.

LOPAHIN

Yes.

LYUBOFF ANDREEVNA

She comes from simple people, and she works all day long, but the main thing is she loves you. And you, too, have liked her a long time.

LOPAHIN

Why not? I am not against it— She's a good girl. *(A pause)*

GAYEFF

They are offering me a position in a bank. Six thousand a year— Have you heard that?

LYUBOFF ANDREEVNA

Not you! You stay where you are—

FIERS

(entering; bringing an overcoat to GAYEFF*)*

Pray, Sir, put this on, it's damp.

GAYEFF

(putting on the overcoat)

You're a pest, old man.

FIERS

That's all right— This morning you went off without letting me know. *(Looking him over)*

LYUBOFF ANDREEVNA

How old you've grown, Fiers!

FIERS

At your service.

LOPAHIN

She says you've grown very old!

FIERS

I've lived a long time. They were planning to marry me off before your papa was born. *(Laughing)* And at the time the serfs were freed I was already the head footman. I didn't want to be freed then, I stayed with the masters—*(A pause)* And I remember, everybody was happy, but what they were happy about they didn't know themselves.

LOPAHIN

In the old days it was fine. At least they flogged.

FIERS

(not hearing)

But of course. The peasants stuck to the masters, the masters stuck to the peasants, and now everything is all smashed up, you can't tell about anything.

GAYEFF

Keep still, Fiers. Tomorrow I must go to town. They have promised to introduce me to a certain general who might make us a loan.

LOPAHIN

Nothing will come of it. And you can rest assured you won't pay the interest.

LYUBOFF ANDREEVNA

He's just raving on. There aren't any such generals.

(TROFIMOFF, ANYA *and* VARYA *enter.*)

GAYEFF

Here they come.

ANYA

There is Mama sitting there.

LYUBOFF ANDREEVNA

(tenderly)

Come, come—My darlings—*(Embracing* ANYA *and* VARYA*)* If you only knew how I love you both! Come sit by me—there—like that.

(Everybody sits down.)

LOPAHIN

Our perennial student is always strolling with the young ladies.

TROFIMOFF

It's none of your business.

LOPAHIN

He will soon be fifty and he's still a student.

TROFIMOFF

Stop your stupid jokes.

LOPAHIN

But why are you so peevish, you queer duck?

TROFIMOFF

Don't you pester me.

LOPAHIN

(laughing)

Permit me to ask you, what do you make of me?

TROFIMOFF

Yermolay Alexeevich, I make this of you: you are a rich man, you'll soon be a millionaire. Just as it is in the metabolism of nature, a wild beast is needed to eat up everything that comes his way; so you, too, are needed.

(Everyone laughs.)

VARYA

Petya, you'd better tell us about the planets.

LYUBOFF ANDREEVNA

No, let's go on with yesterday's conversation.

TROFIMOFF

What was it about?

GAYEFF

About the proud man.

TROFIMOFF

We talked a long time yesterday, but didn't get anywhere. In a proud man, in your sense of the word, there is something mystical. Maybe you are right, from your standpoint, but if we are to discuss it in simple terms, without whimsy, then what pride can there be, is there any sense in it, if man physiologically is poorly constructed, if in the great majority he is crude, unintelligent, profoundly miserable. One must stop admiring oneself. One must only work.

GAYEFF

All the same, you will die.

TROFIMOFF

Who knows? And what does it mean—you will die? Man may have a hundred senses, and when he dies only the five that are known to us may perish, and the remaining ninety-five go on living.

LYUBOFF ANDREEVNA
 How clever you are, Petya!

LOPAHIN
 (ironically)
 Terribly!

TROFIMOFF
 Humanity goes forward, perfecting its powers. Everything that's unattainable now will some day become familiar, understandable; it is only that one must work and must help with all one's might those who seek the truth. With us in Russia so far only a very few work. The great majority of the intelligentsia that I know are looking for nothing, doing nothing, and as yet have no capacity for work. They call themselves intelligentsia, are free and easy with the servants, treat the peasants like animals, educate themselves poorly, read nothing seriously, do absolutely nothing; about science they just talk and about art they understand very little. Every one of them is serious, all have stern faces; they all talk of nothing but important things, philosophize, and all the time everybody can see that the workmen eat abominably, sleep without any pillows, thirty or forty to a room, and everywhere there are bedbugs, stench, dampness, moral uncleanliness— And apparently with us, all the fine talk is only to divert the attention of ourselves and of others. Show me where we have the day nurseries they are always talking so much about, where are the reading rooms? They only write of these in novels, for the truth is there are not any at all. There is only filth, vulgarity, orientalism— I am afraid of very serious faces and dislike them. I'm afraid of serious conversations. Rather than that, let's just keep still.

LOPAHIN
 You know I get up before five o'clock in the morning and work from morning till night. Well, I always have money, my own and other people's, on hand, and I see what the people around me are. One has only to start doing something to find out how few honest and decent people there are. At times when I can't go to sleep, I think: Lord, thou gavest us immense forests, unbounded fields and the widest horizons, and living in the midst of them we should indeed be giants—

LYUBOFF ANDREEVNA

You feel the need for giants— They are good only in fairy tales, anywhere else they only frighten us.

(At the back of the stage EPIHODOFF *passes by, playing the guitar.)*

LYUBOFF ANDREEVNA
(lost in thought)
Epihodoff is coming—

ANYA
(lost in thought)
Epihodoff is coming.

GAYEFF
The sun has set, ladies and gentlemen.

TROFIMOFF
Yes.

GAYEFF
(not loud and as if he were declaiming)
Oh, Nature, wonderful nature, you gleam with eternal radiance, beautiful and indifferent, you, whom we call Mother, combine in yourself both life and death, you give life and you take it away.

VARYA
(beseechingly)
Uncle!

ANYA
Uncle, you're doing it again!

TROFIMOFF
You'd better bank the yellow into the side pocket.

GAYEFF
I'll be quiet, quiet.

(All sit absorbed in their thoughts. There is only the silence. FIERS *is heard muttering to himself softly. Suddenly a distant sound is heard, as if from the sky, like the sound of a snapped string, dying away, mournful.)*

LYUBOFF ANDREEVNA
What's that?
LOPAHIN
I don't know. Somewhere far off in a mine shaft a bucket fell. But somewhere very far off.
GAYEFF
And it may be some bird—like a heron.
TROFIMOFF
Or an owl—
LYUBOFF ANDREEVNA
(shivering)
It's unpleasant, somehow. *(A pause)*
FIERS
Before the disaster it was like that. The owl hooted and the samovar hummed without stopping, both.
GAYEFF
Before what disaster?
FIERS
Before the emancipation.

(A pause)

LYUBOFF ANDREEVNA
You know, my friends, let's go. Twilight is falling. *(To* ANYA*)* You have tears in your eyes— What is it, my dear little girl? *(Embracing her)*
ANYA
It's just that, Mama. It's nothing.
TROFIMOFF
Somebody is coming.

(A STRANGER *appears in a shabby white cap, and an overcoat; he is a little drunk.)*

THE STRANGER
Allow me to ask you, can I go straight through here to the station?
GAYEFF
You can. Go by that road.

THE STRANGER
I am heartily grateful to you. *(Coughing)* The weather is splendid— *(Declaiming)* Brother of mine, suffering brother— Go out to the Volga, whose moans— *(To* VARYA*)* Mademoiselle, grant a hungry Russian man some thirty kopecks—

*(*VARYA *is frightened and gives a shriek.)*

LOPAHIN
(angrily)
There's a limit to everything.

LYUBOFF ANDREEVNA
(flustered)
Take this— Here's this for you— *(Searching in her purse)* No silver— It's all the same, here's a gold piece for you—

THE STRANGER
I am heartily grateful to you. *(Goes out. Laughter.)*

VARYA
(frightened)
I'm going—I'm going— Oh, Mama, you poor little Mama! There's nothing in the house for people to eat, and you gave him a gold piece.

LYUBOFF ANDREEVNA
What is to be done with me, so silly? I shall give you all I have in the house. Yermolay Alexeevich, you will lend me some this once more!—

LOPAHIN
Agreed.

LYUBOFF ANDREEVNA
Let's go, ladies and gentlemen, it's time. And here, Varya, we have definitely made a match for you, I congratulate you.

VARYA
(through her tears)
Mama, that's not something to joke about.

LOPAHIN
Achmelia, get thee to a nunnery.

GAYEFF
And my hands are trembling; it is a long time since I have played billiards.

LOPAHIN

Achmelia, Oh nymph, in thine orisons be all my sins remember'd—

LYUBOFF ANDREEVNA

Let's go, my dear friends, it will soon be suppertime.

VARYA

He frightened me. My heart is thumping so!

LOPAHIN

I remind you, ladies and gentlemen: August 22nd the cherry orchard will be auctioned off. Think about that!—Think!—

(All go out except TROFIMOFF *and* ANYA.*)*

ANYA

(laughing)

My thanks to the stranger, he frightened Varya, now we are alone.

TROFIMOFF

Varya is afraid we might begin to love each other and all day long she won't leave us to ourselves. With her narrow mind she cannot understand that we are above love. To sidestep the petty and illusory, which prevent our being free and happy, that is the aim and meaning of our life. Forward! We march on irresistibly toward the bright star that burns there in the distance. Forward! Do not fall behind, friends!

ANYA

(extending her arms upward)

How well you talk! *(A pause)* It's wonderful here today!

TROFIMOFF

Yes, the weather is marvelous.

ANYA

What have you done to me, Petya, why don't I love the cherry orchard any longer the way I used to? I loved it so tenderly, it seemed to me there was not a better place on earth than our orchard.

TROFIMOFF

All Russia is our orchard. The earth is immense and beautiful, and on it are many wonderful places. *(A pause)* Just think, Anya: your grandfather, great-grandfather and all your ancestors were slave owners, in possession of living souls, and can you doubt that from every cherry in the orchard, from every leaf, from every trunk, human beings are looking at you, can it be that you don't hear their voices? To possess living souls, well, that depraved all of you who lived before and who are living now, so that your mother and you, and your uncle no longer notice that you live by debt, at somebody else's expense, at the expense of those very people whom you wouldn't let past your front door— We are at least two hundred years behind the times, we have as yet absolutely nothing, we have no definite attitude toward the past, we only philosophize, complain of our sadness or drink vodka. Why, it is quite clear that to begin to live in the present we must first atone for our past, must be done with it; and we can atone for it only through suffering, only through uncommon, incessant labor. Understand that, Anya.

ANYA

The house we live in ceased to be ours long ago, and I'll go away, I give you my word.

TROFIMOFF

If you have the household keys, throw them in the well and go away. Be free as the wind.

ANYA

(transported)
How well you said that!

TROFIMOFF

Believe me, Anya, believe me! I am not thirty yet, I am young, I am still a student, but I have already borne so much! Every winter I am hungry, sick, anxious, poor as a beggar, and— where has destiny not chased me, where haven't I been! And yet, my soul has always, every minute, day and night, been full of inexplicable premonitions. I have a premonition of happiness, Anya, I see it already—

ANYA

(pensively)
The moon is rising.

(EPIHODOFF *is heard playing on the guitar, always the same sad song. The moon rises. Somewhere near the poplars* VARYA *is looking for* ANYA *and calling: "Anya! Where are you?")*

TROFIMOFF
  Yes, the moon is rising. *(A pause)* Here is happiness, here it comes always nearer and nearer, I hear its footsteps now. And if we shall not see it, shall not come to know it, what does that matter? Others will see it!

VARYA
  (off)
  Anya! Where are you?

TROFIMOFF
  Again, that Varya! *(Angrily)* It's scandalous!

ANYA
  Well, let's go to the river. It's lovely there.

TROFIMOFF
  Let's go. *(They go out.)*

VARYA
  (off)
  Anya! Anya!

(Curtain)

ACT 3

The drawing room, separated by an arch from the ballroom. A chandelier is lighted. A Jewish orchestra is playing—the same that was mentioned in Act 2. Evening. In the ballroom they are dancing grand rond. *The voice of* SEMYONOFF-PISHTCHIK: *"Promenade à une paire!" They enter the drawing room; in the first couple are* PISHTCHIK *and* CHARLOTTA IVANOVNA; *in the second,* TROFIMOFF *and* LYUBOFF ANDREEVNA; *in the third,* ANYA *with the* POST-OFFICE CLERK; *in the fourth,* VARYA *with the* STATION-MASTER, *et cetera—*VARYA *is crying softly and wipes away her tears while she is dancing.* DUNYASHA *is in the last couple through the drawing room,* PISHTCHIK *shouts: "Grand rond, balancez!" and "Les Cavaliers à genoux et remerciez vos dames!"*

FIERS *in a frock coat goes by with seltzer water on a tray.* PISHTCHIK *and* TROFIMOFF *come into the drawing room.*

PISHTCHIK

I am full-blooded, I have had two strokes already, and dancing is hard for me, but as they say, if you are in a pack of dogs, you may bark and bark, but you must still wag your tail. At that, I have the health of a horse. My dear father—he was a great joker—may he dwell in Heaven—used to talk as if our ancient line, the Semyonoff-Pishtchiks, were descended from the very horse that Caligula made a Senator—*(Sitting down)* But here's my trouble: I haven't any money. A hungry dog believes in nothing but meat—*(Snoring but waking at once)* And the same way with me—I can't talk about anything but money.

TROFIMOFF

Well, to tell you the truth, there is something of a horse about your figure.

PISHTCHIK

Well—a horse is a fine animal— You can sell a horse—

(The sound of playing billiards comes from the next room. VARYA *appears under the arch to the ballroom.)*

TROFIMOFF

(teasing)

Madam Lopahin! Madam Lopahin!

VARYA

(angrily)

A mangy-looking gentleman!

TROFIMOFF

Yes, I am a mangy-looking gentleman, and proud of it!

VARYA

(in bitter thought)

Here we have gone and hired musicians and what are we going to pay them with? *(Goes out.)*

TROFIMOFF

(to PISHTCHIK*)*

If the energy you have wasted in the course of your life trying to find money to pay the interest had gone into something else, you could very likely have turned the world upside down before you were done with it.

PISHTCHIK

Nietzsche—the philosopher—the greatest—the most celebrated—a man of tremendous mind—says in his works that one may make counterfeit money.

TROFIMOFF

And have you read Nietzsche?

PISHTCHIK

Well—Dashenka told me. And I'm in such a state now that I could make counterfeit money myself— Day after tomorrow three hundred and ten roubles must be paid—one hundred and thirty I've on hand— *(Feeling in his pockets, alarmed)* The money is gone! I have lost the money! *(Tearfully)* Where is the money? *(Joyfully)* Here it is, inside the lining— I was in quite a sweat—

(LYUBOFF ANDREEVNA *and* CHARLOTTA IVANOVNA *come in.*)

LYUBOFF ANDREEVNA

(humming "Lazginka," a Georgian dance)
Why does Leonid take so long? What's he doing in town? *(To* DUNYASHA*)* Dunyasha, offer the musicians some tea—

TROFIMOFF

In all probability the auction did not take place.

LYUBOFF ANDREEVNA

And the musicians came at an unfortunate moment and we planned the ball at an unfortunate moment— Well, it doesn't matter. *(Sitting down and singing softly)*

CHARLOTTA

(gives PISHTCHIK *a deck of cards)*
Here is a deck of cards for you, think of some one card.

PISHTCHIK

I have thought of one.

CHARLOTTA

Now, shuffle the deck. Very good. Hand it here; oh, my dear Monsieur Pishtchik. *Ein, zwei, drei!* Now look for it, it's in your coat pocket—

PISHTCHIK

(getting a card out of his coat pocket)
The eight of spades, that's absolutely right! *(Amazed)* Fancy that!

CHARLOTTA

(*holding a deck of cards in her palm; to* TROFIMOFF)
Tell me quick now, which card is on top?

TROFIMOFF

What is it? Well—the Queen of Spades.

CHARLOTTA

Right! (*To* PISHTCHIK) Well? Which card's on top?

PISHTCHIK

The Ace of Hearts.

CHARLOTTA

Right! (*Strikes the deck against her palm; the deck of cards disappears.*) And what beautiful weather we are having today!

(*A mysterious feminine voice answers her, as if from under the floor: "Oh, yes. The weather is splendid, madame." "You are so nice, you're my ideal—" The voice: "Madame, you too please me greatly."*)

THE STATIONMASTER

(*applauding*)
Madame Ventriloquist, bravo!

PISHTCHIK

(*amazed*)
Fancy that! Most charming Charlotta Ivanovna—I am simply in love with you.

CHARLOTTA

In love? (*Shrugging her shoulders*) Is it possible that you can love? *Guter Mensch aber schlechter Musikant.*

TROFIMOFF

(*slapping* PISHTCHIK *on the shoulder*)
You horse, you—

CHARLOTTA

I beg your attention, one more trick. (*Taking a lap robe from the chair*) Here is a very fine lap robe—I want to sell it— (*Shaking it out*) Wouldn't somebody like to buy it?

TROFIMOFF

(*amazed*)
Fancy that!

CHARLOTTA

Ein, zwei, drei!

(She quickly raises the lowered robe, behind it stands ANYA, *who curtseys, runs to her mother, embraces her and runs back into the ballroom amid the general delight.)*

LYUBOFF ANDREEVNA
(applauding)
Bravo, bravo—!

CHARLOTTA
Now again! *Ein, zwei, drei!*

(Lifting the robe: behind it stands VARYA, *she bows.)*

PISHTCHIK
(amazed)
Fancy that!

CHARLOTTA
That's all. *(Throwing the robe at* PISHTCHIK, *curtseying and running into the ballroom.)*

PISHTCHIK
(hurrying after her)
You little rascal—What a girl! What a girl! *(Goes out.)*

LYUBOFF ANDREEVNA
And Leonid is not here yet. What he's doing in town so long, I don't understand! Everything is finished there, either the estate is sold by now, or the auction didn't take place. Why keep it from us so long?

VARYA
(trying to comfort her)
Uncle has bought it, I am sure of that.

TROFIMOFF
(mockingly)
Yes.

VARYA
Great-aunt sent him power of attorney to buy it in her name and transfer the debt. She did this for Anya. And I feel certain, God willing, that Uncle will buy it.

LYUBOFF ANDREEVNA
Our Yaroslavl great-aunt has sent fifteen thousand to buy the estate in her name— She doesn't trust us, but that wouldn't be enough to pay the interest even. *(Covering her face with her hands)* Today my fate will be decided, my fate—

TROFIMOFF

(teasing VARYA*)*

Madam Lopahin!

VARYA

(angrily)

Perennial student! You have already been expelled from the University twice.

LYUBOFF ANDREEVNA

But why are you angry, Varya? He teases you about Lopahin, what of it? Marry Lopahin if you want to, he is a good man, interesting. If you don't want to, don't marry him; darling, nobody is making you do it.

VARYA

I look at this matter seriously, Mama, one must speak straight out. He's a good man, I like him.

LYUBOFF ANDREEVNA

Then marry him. What there is to wait for I don't understand!

VARYA

But I can't propose to him myself, Mama. It's two years now; everyone has been talking to me about him, everyone talks, and he either remains silent or jokes. I understand. He's getting rich, he's busy with his own affairs, and has no time for me. If there were money, ever so little, even a hundred roubles, I would drop everything, and go far away. I'd go to a nunnery.

TROFIMOFF

How saintly!

VARYA

(to TROFIMOFF*)*

A student should be intelligent! *(In a low voice, tearfully)* How homely you have grown, Petya, how old you've got. *(To* LYUBOFF ANDREEVNA, *no longer crying)* It is just that I can't live without working, Mama. I must be doing something every minute.

YASHA

(entering; barely restraining his laughter)

Epihodoff has broken a billiard cue!— *(Goes out.)*

VARYA

But why is Epihodoff here? Who allowed him to play billiards? I don't understand these people— *(Goes out.)*

LYUBOFF ANDREEVNA

Don't tease her, Petya; you can see she has trouble enough without that.

TROFIMOFF

She is just too zealous. Sticking her nose into things that are none of her business. All summer she gave us no peace, neither me nor Anya; she was afraid a romance would spring up between us. What business is that of hers? And besides, I haven't shown any signs of it. I am so remote from triviality. We are above love!

LYUBOFF ANDREEVNA

Well, then, I must be beneath love. *(Very anxiously)* Why isn't Leonid here? Just to tell us whether the estate is sold or not? Calamity seems to me so incredible that I don't know what to think, I'm lost—I could scream this minute—I could do something insane. Save me, Petya. Say something, do say....

TROFIMOFF

Whether the estate is sold today or is not sold—is it not the same? There is no turning back, the path is all grown over. Calm yourself, my dear, all that was over long ago. One mustn't deceive oneself, one must for once at least in one's life look truth straight in the eye.

LYUBOFF ANDREEVNA

What truth? You see where the truth is and where the untruth is, but as for me, it's as if I had lost my sight, I see nothing. You boldly decide all important questions, but tell me, my dear boy, isn't that because you are young and haven't had time yet to suffer through any one of your problems? You look boldly ahead, and isn't that because you don't see and don't expect anything terrible, since life is still hidden from your young eyes? You are braver, more honest, more profound than we are, but stop and think, be magnanimous, have a little mercy on me, just a little. Why, I was born here. My father and mother lived here and my grandfather. I love this house, I can't imagine my life without the cherry orchard and if it is very necessary to sell it, then sell me along with the orchard— *(Embracing* TROFIMOFF *and kissing him on the forehead)* Why, my son was drowned here—*(Crying)* Have mercy on me, good, kind man.

TROFIMOFF

You know I sympathize with you from the bottom of my heart.

LYUBOFF ANDREEVNA

But that should be said differently, differently—*(Taking out her handkerchief; a telegram falls on the floor.)* My heart is heavy today, you can't imagine how heavy. It is too noisy for me here, my soul trembles at every sound, I tremble all over and yet I can't go off to myself, when I am alone the silence frightens me. Don't blame me, Petya—I love you as one of my own. I should gladly have given you Anya's hand, I assure you, only, my dear, you must study and finish your course. You do nothing. Fate simply flings you about from place to place, and that's so strange— Isn't that so? Yes? And you must do something about your beard, to make it grow somehow— *(Laughing)* You look funny!

TROFIMOFF

(picking up the telegram)

I do not desire to be beautiful.

LYUBOFF ANDREEVNA

This telegram is from Paris. I get one every day. Yesterday and today too. That wild man has fallen ill again, something is wrong again with him— He asks forgiveness, begs me to come, and really I ought to make a trip to Paris and stay awhile near him. Your face looks stern, Petya, but what is there to do, my dear, what am I to do, he is ill, he is alone, unhappy, and who will look after him there, who will keep him from doing the wrong thing, who will give him his medicine on time? And what is there to hide or keep still about? I love him, love him— It's a stone about my neck, I'm sinking to the bottom with it, but I love that stone and live without it I cannot. *(Pressing* TROFIMOFF's *hand)* Don't think harshly of me, Petya, don't say anything to me, don't—

TROFIMOFF

(tearfully)

Forgive my frankness, for God's sake! Why, he picked your bones.

LYUBOFF ANDREEVNA

No, no, no, you must not talk like that. *(Stopping her ears)*

TROFIMOFF

But he is a scoundrel, only you, you are the only one that doesn't know it. He is a petty scoundrel, a nonentity—

LYUBOFF ANDREEVNA

(angry but controlling herself)

You are twenty-six years old or twenty-seven, but you are still a schoolboy in the second grade!

TROFIMOFF

Very well!

LYUBOFF ANDREEVNA

You should be a man—at your age you should understand people who love. And you yourself should love someone—you should fall in love! *(Angrily)* Yes, yes! And there is no purity in you; you are simply smug, a ridiculous crank, a freak—

TROFIMOFF

(horrified)

What is she saying!

LYUBOFF ANDREEVNA

"I am above love!" You are not above love, Petya, you are, as our Fiers would say, just a good-for-nothing. Imagine, at your age, not having a mistress—!

TROFIMOFF

(horrified)

This is terrible! What is she saying! *(Goes quickly into the ballroom, clutching his head.)* This is horrible—I can't bear it, I am going— *(Goes out but immediately returns.)* All is over between us. *(Goes out into the hall.)*

LYUBOFF ANDREEVNA

(shouting after him)

Petya, wait! You funny creature, I was joking! Petya! *(In the hall you hear someone running up the stairs and suddenly falling back down with a crash. You hear* ANYA *and* VARYA *scream but immediately you hear laughter)* What's that?

ANYA

(running in, laughing)

Petya fell down the stairs! *(Runs out.)*

LYUBOFF ANDREEVNA

What a funny boy that Petya is—! *(The* STATIONMASTER *stops in the center of the ballroom and begins to recite "The Sinner"* by A. Tolstoi. *They listen to him but he has recited only a few lines when the strains of a waltz are heard from the hall and the recitation is broken off. They all dance.* TROFIMOFF, ANYA, VARYA *and* LYUBOFF ANDREEVNA *come in from the hall.*) But, Petya—but, dear soul—I beg your forgiveness— Let's go dance.

(*She dances with* TROFIMOFF. ANYA *and* VARYA *dance.* FIERS *enters, leaving his stick by the side door.* YASHA *also comes into the drawing room and watches the dancers.*)

YASHA
What is it, Grandpa?

FIERS
I don't feel very well. In the old days there were generals, barons, admirals dancing at our parties, and now we send for the post-office clerk and the stationmaster, and even they are none too anxious to come. Somehow I've grown feeble. The old master, the grandfather, treated everybody with sealing wax for all sicknesses. I take sealing wax every day, have done so for twenty-odd years or more; it may be due to that that I'm alive.

YASHA
You are tiresome, Grandpa. (*Yawning*) Why don't you go off and die?

FIERS
Aw, you—good-for-nothing!— (*Muttering*)

(TROFIMOFF *and* LYUBOFF ANDREEVNA *dance in the ballroom and then in the drawing room.*)

LYUBOFF ANDREEVNA
Merci. I'll sit down awhile— (*Sitting down*) I'm tired.

ANYA
(*entering, agitated*)
And just now in the kitchen some man was saying that the cherry orchard had been sold today.

LYUBOFF ANDREEVNA
Sold to whom?

ANYA

He didn't say who to. He's gone.

(Dancing with TROFIMOFF, *they pass into the ballroom.)*

YASHA

It was some old man babbling there. A stranger.

FIERS

And Leonid Andreevich is still not here, he has not arrived. The overcoat he has on is light, mid-season—let's hope he won't catch cold. Ach, these young things!

LYUBOFF ANDREEVNA

I shall die this minute. Go, Yasha, find out who it was sold to.

YASHA

But he's been gone a long time, the old fellow. *(Laughing)*

LYUBOFF ANDREEVNA

(with some annoyance)

Well, what are you laughing at? What are you so amused at?

YASHA

Epihodoff is just too funny. An empty-headed man. Twenty-two misfortunes!

LYUBOFF ANDREEVNA

Fiers, if the estate is sold, where will you go?

FIERS

Wherever you say, there I'll go.

LYUBOFF ANDREEVNA

Why do you look like that? Aren't you well? You know you ought to go to bed—

FIERS

Yes—*(With a sneer)* I go to bed and without me who's going to serve, who'll take care of things? I'm the only one in the whole house.

YASHA

(to LYUBOFF ANDREEVNA*)*

Lyuboff Andreevna, let me ask a favor of you, do be so kind! If you ever go back to Paris, take me with you, please do! It's impossible for me to stay here. *(Looking around him, and speaking in a low voice)* Why talk about it? You can see for yourself it's an uncivilized country, an immoral people and not only that, there's the boredom of it. The food they give us in that kitchen is abominable and there's that Fiers, too, walking about and muttering all kinds of words that are out of place. Take me with you, be so kind!

PISHTCHIK

(entering)

Allow me to ask you—for a little waltz, most beautiful lady— (LYUBOFF ANDREEVNA *goes with him.*) Charming lady, I must borrow a hundred and eighty roubles from you—will borrow— *(Dancing)* a hundred and eighty roubles— *(They pass into the ballroom.)*

YASHA

(singing low)

"Wilt thou know the unrest in my soul!"

(In the ballroom a figure in a gray top hat and checked trousers waves both hands and jumps about; there are shouts of "Bravo, Charlotta Ivanovna!")

DUNYASHA

(stopping to powder her face)

The young lady orders me to dance—there are a lot of gentlemen and very few ladies—but dancing makes my head swim and my heart thump. Fiers Nikolaevich, the post-office clerk said something to me just now that took my breath away.

(The music plays more softly.)

FIERS

What did he say to you?

DUNYASHA

You are like a flower, he says.

YASHA

(yawning)

What ignorance—! *(Goes out.)*

DUNYASHA

Like a flower—I am such a sensitive girl, I love tender words awfully.

FIERS

You'll be getting your head turned.

(EPIHODOFF enters.)

EPIHODOFF

Avdotya Feodorovna, you don't want to see me— It's as if I were some sort of insect. *(Sighing)* Ach, life!

DUNYASHA

What do you want?

EPIHODOFF

Undoubtedly you may be right. *(Sighing)* But of course, if one considers it from a given point of view, then you, I will allow myself so to express it, forgive my frankness, absolutely led me into a state of mind. I know my fate, every day some misfortune happens to me, but I have long since become accustomed to that, and so I look on my misfortunes with a smile. You gave me your word and, although I—

DUNYASHA

I beg you, we'll talk later on, but leave me now in peace. I'm in a dream now. *(Playing with her fan)*

EPIHODOFF

I have a misfortune, something wrong happens every day—I will allow myself so to express it—I just smile, I even laugh.

VARYA

(entering from the ballroom)
You are not gone yet, Semyon? What a really disrespectful man you are! *(To DUNYASHA)* Get out of here, Dunyasha. *(To EPIHODOFF)* You either play billiards and break a cue or you walk about the drawing room like a guest.

EPIHODOFF

Allow me to tell you, you cannot make any demands on me.

VARYA

I'm not making any demands on you, I'm talking to you. All you know is to walk from place to place but not do any work. We keep a clerk, but what for, nobody knows.

EPIHODOFF

(offended)
Whether I work, whether I walk, whether I eat, or whether I play billiards are matters to be discussed only by people of understanding and my seniors.

VARYA

You dare to say that to me! *(Flying into a temper)* You dare? So I don't understand anything? Get out of here! This minute!

EPIHODOFF

(alarmed)

I beg you to express yourself in a delicate manner.

VARYA

(beside herself)

This very minute, get out of here! Get out! *(He goes to the door; she follows him.)* Twenty-two misfortunes! Don't you dare breathe in here! Don't let me set eyes on you! *(EPIHODOFF has gone out, but his voice comes from outside the door: "I shall complain about you.")* Ah, you are coming back? *(Grabbing the stick that FIERS put by the door)* Come on, come—come on, I'll show you— Ah, you are coming? You are coming? Take that then—!

(She swings the stick, at the very moment when LOPAHIN is coming in.)

LOPAHIN

Most humbly, I thank you.

VARYA

(angrily and ironically)

I beg your pardon!

LOPAHIN

It's nothing at all. I humbly thank you for the pleasant treat.

VARYA

It isn't worth your thanks. *(Moving away, then looking back and asking gently)* I haven't hurt you?

LOPAHIN

No, it's nothing. There's a great bump coming though.

(Voices in the ballroom: "Lopahin has come back." "Yermolay Alexeevich!")

PISHTCHIK

(enters)

See what we see, hear what we hear—! *(He and LOPAHIN kiss one another.)* You smell slightly of cognac, my dear, my good old chap. And we are amusing ourselves here too.

LYUBOFF ANDREEVNA
(entering)
Is that you, Yermolay Alexeevich? Why were you so long? Where is Leonid?

LOPAHIN
Leonid Andreevich got back when I did, he's coming.

LYUBOFF ANDREEVNA
(agitated)
Well, what? Was there an auction? Do speak!

LOPAHIN
(embarrassed, afraid of showing the joy he feels)
The auction was over by four o'clock— We were late for the train, had to wait till half-past nine. *(Sighing heavily)* Ugh, my head's swimming a bit!

(GAYEFF enters: with his right hand he carries his purchases, with his left he wipes away his tears.)

LYUBOFF ANDREEVNA
Lyona, what? Lyona, eh? *(Impatiently, with tears in her eyes)* Quick, for God's sake—

GAYEFF
(not answering her, merely waving his hand; to FIERS, *crying)*
Here, take it —There are anchovies, some Kertch herrings— I haven't eaten anything all day— What I have suffered! *(The door into the billiard room is open; you hear the balls clicking and* YASHA's *voice: "Seven and eighteen!"* GAYEFF's *expression changes, he is no longer crying)* I'm terribly tired. You help me change, Fiers. *(Goes to his room through the ballroom,* FIERS *behind him.)*

PISHTCHIK
What happened at the auction? Go on, tell us!

LYUBOFF ANDREEVNA
Is the cherry orchard sold?

LOPAHIN
It's sold.

LYUBOFF ANDREEVNA
Who bought it?

LOPAHIN

> I bought it. *(A pause.* LYUBOFF ANDREEVNA *is overcome. She would have fallen had she not been standing near the chair and table.* VARYA *takes the keys from her belt, throws them on the floor in the middle of the drawing room and goes out)* I bought it. Kindly wait a moment, ladies and gentlemen, everything is muddled up in my head, I can't speak—*(Laughing)* We arrived at the auction, Deriganoff was already there. Leonid Andreevich had only fifteen thousand and Deriganoff right off bids thirty over and above indebtedness. I see how things are, I match him with forty thousand. He forty-five. I fifty-five. That is to say he raises it by fives, I by tens.—So it ended. Over and above the indebtedness, I bid up to ninety thousand, it was knocked down to me. The cherry orchard is mine now. Mine! *(Guffawing)* My God, Lord, the cherry orchard is mine! Tell me I'm drunk, out of my head, that I'm imagining all this— *(Stamps his feet.)* Don't laugh at me! If only my father and grandfather could rise from their graves and see this whole business, see how their Yermolay, beaten, half-illiterate Yermolay, who used to run around barefoot in winter, how that very Yermolay has bought an estate that nothing in the world can beat. I bought the estate where grandfather and father were slaves, where you wouldn't even let me in the kitchen. I am asleep, it's only some dream of mine, it only seems so to me— That's nothing but the fruit of your imagination, covered with the darkness of the unknown— *(Picking up the keys, with a gentle smile)* She threw down the keys, wants to show she is not mistress any more—*(Jingling the keys)* Well, it's all the same. *(The orchestra is heard tuning up.)* Hey, musicians, play, I want to hear you! Come on, everybody, and see how Yermolay Lopahin will swing the ax in the cherry orchard, how the trees will fall to the ground! We are going to build villas and our grandsons and great-grandsons will see a new life here— Music, play! *(The music is playing.* LYUBOFF ANDREEVNA *has sunk into a chair, crying bitterly.* LOPAHIN *reproachfully)* Why, then, didn't you listen to me? My poor dear, it can't be undone now. *(With tears)* Oh, if this could all be over soon, if somehow our awkward, unhappy life would be changed!

PISHTCHIK

(taking him by the arm, in a low voice)
She is crying. Come on in the ballroom, let her be by herself— Come on— *(Taking him by the arm and leading him into the ballroom.)*

LOPAHIN

What's the matter? Music, there, play up! *(Sarcastically)* Everything is to be as I want it! Here comes the new squire, the owner of the cherry orchard. *(Quite accidentally, he bumps into the little table, and very nearly upsets the candelabra.)* I can pay for everything!

(Goes out with PISHTCHIK. *There is nobody left either in the ballroom or the drawing room but* LYUBOFF ANDREEVNA, *who sits huddled up and crying bitterly. The music plays softly.* ANYA *and* TROFIMOFF *enter hurriedly.* ANYA *comes up to her mother and kneels in front of her.* TROFIMOFF *remains at the ballroom door.)*

ANYA

Mama—! Mama, you are crying? My dear, kind, good Mama, my beautiful, I love you—I bless you. The cherry orchard is sold, it's not ours any more, that's true, true; but don't cry, Mama, you've your life still left you, you've your good, pure heart ahead of you— Come with me, come on, darling, away from here, come on— We will plant a new orchard, finer than this one, you'll see it, you'll understand; and joy, quiet, deep joy will sink into your heart, like the sun at evening, and you'll smile, Mama! Come, darling, come on!

(Curtain)

ACT 4

The same setting as in Act 1. There are neither curtains on the windows nor are there any pictures on the walls. Only a little furniture remains piled up in one corner as if for sale. A sense of emptiness is felt. Near the outer door, at the rear of the stage, is a pile of suitcases, traveling bags, and so on. The door on the left is open, and through it VARYA'S *and* ANYA'S *voices are heard.* LOPAHIN *is standing waiting.* YASHA *is holding a tray with glasses of champagne. In the hall* EPIHODOFF *is tying up a box, offstage at the rear there is a hum. It is the peasants who have come to say goodbye.* GAYEFF'S *voice: "Thanks, brothers, thank you."*

YASHA
The simple folk have come to say goodbye. I am of the opinion, Yermolay Alexeevich, that the people are kind enough but don't understand anything.

(The hum subsides. LYUBOFF ANDREEVNA *enters through the hall with* GAYEFF; *she is not crying, but is pale, her face quivers, she is not able to speak.)*

GAYEFF
You gave them your purse, Lyuba. Mustn't do that! Mustn't do that!

LYUBOFF ANDREEVNA
I couldn't help it! I couldn't help it! *(Both go out.)*

LOPAHIN
(calling through the door after them)
Please, I humbly beg you! A little glass at parting. I didn't think to bring some from town, and at the station I found just one bottle. Please! *(A pause)* Well, then, ladies and gentlemen! You don't want it? *(Moving away from the door)* If I'd known

that, I wouldn't have bought it. Well, then I won't drink any either. (YASHA *carefully sets the tray down on a chair.*) At least, you have some, Yasha.

YASHA

To those who are departing! Pleasant days to those who stay behind! *(Drinking)* This champagne is not the real stuff, I can assure you.

LOPAHIN

Eight roubles a bottle. *(A pause)* It's devilish cold in here.

YASHA

They didn't heat up today, we are leaving anyway. *(Laughing)*

LOPAHIN

What are you laughing about?

YASHA

For joy.

LOPAHIN

Outside it's October, but it's sunny and still, like summer. Good for building. *(Looking at his watch, then through the door)* Ladies and gentlemen, bear in mind we have forty-six minutes in all till train time! Which means you have to go to the station in twenty minutes. Hurry up a little.

TROFIMOFF

(in an overcoat, entering from outside)

Seems to me it is time to go. The carriages are ready. The devil knows where my rubbers are. They've disappeared. *(In the door)* Anya, my rubbers are not here! I can't find them.

LOPAHIN

And I have to go to Harkoff. I'm going on the same train with you. I'm going to live in Harkoff all winter. I've been dilly-dallying along with you, I'm tired of doing nothing. I can't be without work, look, I don't know what to do with my hands here, see, they are dangling somehow, as if they didn't belong to me.

TROFIMOFF

We are leaving right away, and you'll set about your useful labors again.

LOPAHIN

Here, drink a glass.

TROFIMOFF

I shan't.

LOPAHIN

It's to Moscow now?

TROFIMOFF

Yes. I'll see them off to town, and tomorrow to Moscow.

LOPAHIN

Yes— Maybe the professors are not giving their lectures. I imagine they are waiting till you arrive.

TROFIMOFF

That's none of your business.

LOPAHIN

How many years is it you've been studying at the University?

TROFIMOFF

Think of something newer. This is old and flat. *(Looking for his rubbers)* You know, perhaps, we shall not see each other again; therefore, permit me to give you one piece of advice at parting! Don't wave your arms! Cure yourself of that habit— of arm waving. And also of building summer cottages, figuring that the summer residents will in time become individual landowners; figuring like that is arm waving too— Just the same, however, I like you. You have delicate soft fingers like an artist, you have a delicate soft heart—

LOPAHIN

(embracing him)

Goodbye, my dear boy. Thanks for everything. If you need it, take some money from me for the trip.

TROFIMOFF

Why should I? There's no need for it.

LOPAHIN

But you haven't any!

TROFIMOFF

I have. Thank you. I got some for a translation. Here it is in my pocket. *(Anxiously)* But my rubbers are gone.

VARYA

(from another room)

Take your nasty things! *(Throws a pair of rubbers onto the stage.)*

TROFIMOFF

But what are you angry about, Varya? Hm— Why, these are not my rubbers.

LOPAHIN

In the spring I planted twenty-seven hundred acres of poppies and now I've made forty thousand clear. And when my poppies were in bloom, what a picture it was! So look, as I say, I've made forty thousand, which means I'm offering you a loan because I can afford to. Why turn up your nose? I'm a peasant —I speak straight out.

TROFIMOFF

Your father was a peasant, mine—an apothecary—and from that absolutely nothing follows. (LOPAHIN *takes out his wallet.*) Leave it alone, leave it alone— If you gave me two hundred thousand even, I wouldn't take it. I am a free man. And everything that you all value so highly and dearly, both rich men and beggars, has not the slightest power over me, it's like a mere feather floating in the air. I can get along without you, I can pass you by, I am strong and proud. Humanity is moving toward the loftiest truth, toward the loftiest happiness that is possible on earth and I am in the front ranks.

LOPAHIN

Will you get there?

TROFIMOFF

I'll get there. (*A pause*) I'll get there, or I'll show the others the way to get there.

(*In the distance is heard the sound of an ax on a tree.*)

LOPAHIN

Well, goodbye, my dear boy. It's time to go. We turn up our noses at one another, but life keeps on passing. When I work a long time without stopping, my thoughts are clearer, and it seems as if I, too, know what I exist for, and, brother, how many people are there in Russia who exist, nobody knows for what! Well, all the same, it's not that that keeps things circulating. Leonid Andreevich, they say, has accepted a position— he'll be in a bank, six thousand a year—the only thing is he won't stay there, he's very lazy—

ANYA

(*in the doorway*)

Mama begs of you until she's gone, not to cut down the orchard.

TROFIMOFF

Honestly, haven't you enough tact to— *(Goes out through the hall.)*

LOPAHIN

Right away, right away— What people, really! *(Goes out after him.)*

ANYA

Has Fiers been sent to the hospital?

YASHA

I told them to this morning. They must have sent him.

ANYA

(To EPIHODOFF, *who is passing through the room)*
Semyon Panteleevich, please inquire whether or not they have taken Fiers to the hospital.

YASHA

(huffily)
This morning, I told Igor. Why ask ten times over!

EPIHODOFF

The venerable Fiers, according to my conclusive opinion, is not worth mending, he ought to join his forefathers. And I can only envy him. *(Putting a suitcase on a hatbox and crushing it)* Well, there you are, of course. I knew it. *(Goes out.)*

YASHA

(mockingly)
Twenty-two misfortunes—

VARYA

(on the other side of the door)
Have they taken Fiers to the hospital?

ANYA

They have.

VARYA

Then why didn't they take the letter to the doctor?

ANYA

We must send it on after them— *(Goes out.)*

VARYA

(from the next room)
Where is Yasha? Tell him his mother has come, she wants to say goodbye to him.

YASHA

(waving his hand)
They merely try my patience.

(DUNYASHA *has been busying herself with the luggage; now when* YASHA *is left alone, she goes up to him.)*

DUNYASHA

If you'd only look at me once, Yasha. You are going away—leaving me— *(Crying and throwing herself on his neck)*

YASHA

Why are you crying? *(Drinking champagne)* In six days I'll be in Paris again. Tomorrow we will board the express train and dash off out of sight; somehow, I can't believe it. *Vive la France!* It doesn't suit me here—I can't live here— Can't help that. I've seen enough ignorance—enough for me. *(Drinking champagne)* Why do you cry? Behave yourself properly, then you won't be crying.

DUNYASHA

(powdering her face, looking into a small mirror)
Send me a letter from Paris. I loved you, Yasha, you know, loved you so! I am a tender creature, Yasha!

YASHA

They are coming here. *(Bustling about near the suitcases, humming low)*

(LYUBOFF ANDREEVNA, GAYEFF, *and* CHARLOTTA IVANOVNA *enter.)*

GAYEFF

We should be going. There is very little time left. *(Looking at* YASHA*)* Who is it smells like herring!

LYUBOFF ANDREEVNA

In about ten minutes let's be in the carriage— *(Glancing around the room)* Goodbye, dear house, old Grandfather. Winter will pass, spring will be here, but you won't be here any longer, they'll tear you down. How much these walls have seen! *(Kissing her daughter warmly)* My treasure, you are beaming, your eyes are dancing like two diamonds. Are you happy? Very?

ANYA

Very! It's the beginning of a new life, Mama!

GAYEFF

(gaily)

Yes, indeed, everything is fine now. Before the sale of the cherry orchard, we all were troubled, distressed, and then when the question was settled definitely, irrevocably, we all calmed down and were even cheerful— I'm a bank official. I am a financier now— Yellow ball into the side pocket, anyway, Lyuba, you look better, no doubt about that.

LYUBOFF ANDREEVNA

Yes. My nerves are better, that's true *(They hand her her hat and coat.)* I sleep well. Carry out my things, Yasha. It's time. *(To* ANYA*)* My little girl, we shall see each other again soon— I am going to Paris, I shall live there on the money your Yaroslavl great-aunt sent for the purchase of the estate—long live Great-aunt! But that money won't last long.

ANYA

Mama, you'll come back soon, soon— Isn't that so? I'll prepare myself, pass the examination at high school, and then I'll work, I will help you. We'll read all sorts of books together. Mama, isn't that so? *(Kissing her mother's hands)* We'll read in the autumn evenings, read lots of books, and a new, wonderful world will open up before us— *(Daydreaming)* Mama, do come—

LYUBOFF ANDREEVNA

I'll come, my precious. *(Embracing her daughter)*

*(*LOPAHIN *enters with* CHARLOTTA, *who is softly humming a song.)*

GAYEFF

Lucky Charlotta: she's singing!

CHARLOTTA

(taking a bundle that looks like a baby wrapped up)
My baby, bye, bye— *(A baby's cry is heard: Ooah, ooah—!)* Hush, my darling, my dear little boy. *(Ooah, ooah—!)* I am so sorry for you! *(Throwing the bundle back)* Will you please find me a position? I cannot go on like this.

LOPAHIN

We will find something, Charlotta Ivanovna, don't worry.

GAYEFF

Everybody is dropping us, Varya is going away. All of a sudden we are not needed.

CHARLOTTA

I have no place in town to live. I must go away. *(Humming)* It's all the same—

(PISHTCHIK *enters.*)

LOPAHIN

The freak of nature—!

PISHTCHIK

(out of breath)

Ugh, let me catch my breath—I'm exhausted— My honored friends— Give me some water—

GAYEFF

After money, I suppose? This humble servant will flee from sin! *(Goes out.)*

PISHTCHIK

It's a long time since I was here— Most beautiful lady— *(To* LOPAHIN*)* you here—? Glad to see you—a man of the greatest intellect— Here— Take it— *(Giving* LOPAHIN *some money)* Four hundred roubles— That leaves eight hundred and forty I still owe you—

LOPAHIN

(with astonishment, shrugging his shoulders)

I must be dreaming. But where did you get it?

PISHTCHIK

Wait—I'm hot— Most extraordinary event. Some Englishmen came and found on my land some kind of white clay— *(To* LYUBOFF ANDREEVNA*)* And four hundred for you—Beautiful lady—Wonderful lady— *(Handing over the money)* The rest later. *(Taking a drink of water)* Just now a young man was saying on the train that some great philosopher recommends jumping off roofs—"Jump!" he says, and "therein lies the whole problem." *(With astonishment)* You don't say! Water!

LOPAHIN
And what Englishmen were they?

PISHTCHIK
I leased them the parcel of land with the clay for twenty-four years— And now, excuse me, I haven't time—I must run along —I'm going to Znoykoff's—To Kardamonoff's— I owe everybody— *(Drinking)* I wish you well—I'll drop in on Thursday—

LYUBOFF ANDREEVNA
We are moving to town right away, and tomorrow I'm going abroad—

PISHTCHIK
What? *(Alarmed)* Why to town? That's why I see furniture— Suitcases— Well, no matter— *(Tearfully)* No matter— Men of the greatest minds—those Englishmen— No matter— Good luck! God will help you— No matter— Everything in this world comes to an end—*(Kissing* LYUBOFF ANDREEVNA's *hand)* And should the report reach you that my end has come, think of that well-known horse and say: "There was once on earth a so and so— Semyonoff Pishtchik— The kingdom of Heaven be his." Most remarkable weather—yes— *(Going out greatly disconcerted, but immediately returning and speaking from the door)* Dashenka sends her greetings! *(Goes out.)*

LYUBOFF ANDREEVNA
And now we can go. I am leaving with two worries. First, that Fiers is sick. *(Glancing at her watch)* We still have five minutes—

ANYA
Mama, Fiers has already been sent to the hospital. Yasha sent him off this morning.

LYUBOFF ANDREEVNA
My second worry—is Varya. She is used to getting up early and working, and now without any work she is like a fish out of water. She has grown thin, pale and cries all the time, poor thing— *(A pause)* You know this, Yermolay Alexeevich: I dreamed—of marrying her to you. And there was every sign of your getting married. *(Whispering to* ANYA, *who beckons to* CHARLOTTA; *both go out.)* She loves you, you are fond of her, and I don't know, don't know why it is you seem to avoid each other—I don't understand it!

LOPAHIN

I don't understand it either, I must confess. It's all strange somehow— If there's still time, I am ready right now even— Let's finish it up—and *basta*, but without you I feel I won't propose.

LYUBOFF ANDREEVNA

But that's excellent. Surely it takes only a minute. I'll call her at once.

LOPAHIN

And to fit the occasion there's the champagne. *(Looking at the glasses)* Empty, somebody has already drunk them. (YASHA *coughs.)* That's what's called lapping it up—

LYUBOFF ANDREEVNA

(vivaciously)

Splendid! We'll go out— Yasha, *allez!* I'll call her— *(Through the door)* Varya, drop everything and come here. Come on! *(Goes out with* YASHA.*)*

LOPAHIN

(looking at his watch)
Yes—

(A pause. Behind the door you hear smothered laughter, whispering, finally VARYA *enters.)*

VARYA

(looking at the luggage a long time)
That's strange, I just can't find it—

LOPAHIN

What are you looking for?

VARYA

I packed it myself and don't remember where. *(A pause.)*

LOPAHIN

Where do you expect to go now, Varvara Mikhailovna?

VARYA

I? To Regulin's. I agreed to go there to look after the house— As a sort of housekeeper.

LOPAHIN

That's in Yashnevo? It's nigh on to seventy miles. *(A pause)* And here ends life in this house—

VARYA

(examining the luggage)
But where is it? Either I put it in the trunk, perhaps— Yes, life in this house is ended—it won't be any more—

LOPAHIN

And I am going to Harkoff now—By the next train. I've a lot to do. And I am leaving Epihodoff—on the ground here—I've hired him.

VARYA

Well!

LOPAHIN

Last year at this time it had already been snowing, if you remember, and now it's quiet, it's sunny. It's only that it's cold, about three degrees of frost.

VARYA

I haven't noticed. *(A pause)* And besides our thermometer is broken— *(A pause; a voice from the yard through the door calls:* Yermolay Alexeevich.*)*

LOPAHIN

(as if he had been expecting this call for a long time)
This minute! *(Goes out quickly.)*

(VARYA, *sitting on the floor, putting her head on a bundle of clothes, sobs quietly. The door opens,* LYUBOFF ANDREEVNA *enters cautiously.)*

VARYA

(she is not crying any longer, and has wiped her eyes)
Yes, it's time, Mama. I can get to Regulin's today, if we are just not too late for the train— *(Through the door)* Anya, put your things on! (ANYA, *then* GAYEFF *and* CHARLOTTA IVANOVNA *enter.* GAYEFF *has on a warm overcoat, with a hood. The servants gather, also the drivers.* EPIHODOFF *busies himself with the luggage)* Now we can be on our way.

ANYA

(joyfully)
On our way!

GAYEFF

My friends, my dear, kind friends! Leaving this house forever, can I remain silent, can I restrain myself from expressing, as we say farewell, those feelings that fill now my whole being—

ANYA

(beseechingly)
Uncle!

VARYA

Dear Uncle, don't!

GAYEFF

(dejectedly)
Bank the yellow into the side pocket— I am silent—

(TROFIMOFF *and then* LOPAHIN *enter.*)

TROFIMOFF

Well, ladies and gentlemen, it's time to go!

LOPAHIN

Epihodoff, my coat!

LYUBOFF ANDREEVNA

I'll sit here just a minute more. It's as if I had never seen before what the walls in this house are like, what kind of ceilings, and now I look at them greedily, with such tender love—

GAYEFF

I remember when I was six years old, on Trinity Day, I sat in this window and watched my father going to Church—

LYUBOFF ANDREEVNA

Are all the things taken out?

LOPAHIN

Everything, I think. *(Putting on his overcoat; to* EPIHODOFF*)* Epihodoff, you see that everything is in order.

EPIHODOFF

(talking in a hoarse voice)
Don't worry, Yermolay Alexeevich!

LOPAHIN

Why is your voice like that?

EPIHODOFF

Just drank some water, swallowed something.

YASHA

(with contempt)

The ignorance—

LYUBOFF ANDREEVNA

We are going and there won't be a soul left here—

LOPAHIN

Till spring.

VARYA

(She pulls an umbrella out from a bundle. It looks as if she were going to hit someone; LOPAHIN pretends to be frightened) What do you, what do you— I never thought of it.

TROFIMOFF

Ladies and gentlemen, let's get in the carriages— It's time! The train is coming any minute.

VARYA

Petya, here they are, your rubbers, by the suitcase. *(Tearfully)* And how dirty yours are, how old—!

TROFIMOFF

(putting on the rubbers)

Let's go, ladies and gentlemen!

GAYEFF

(greatly embarrassed, afraid he will cry)

The train— The station— Cross into the side, combination off the white into the corner—

LYUBOFF ANDREEVNA

Let's go!

LOPAHIN

Everybody here? Nobody there? *(Locking the side door on the left)* Things are stored here, it must be locked up, let's go!

ANYA

Good-by, house! Good-by, the old life!

TROFIMOFF

Long live the new life!

(Goes out with ANYA. VARYA casts a glance around the room and, without hurrying, goes out. YASHA and CHARLOTTA, with her dog, go out.)

LOPAHIN
> And so, till spring. Out, ladies and gentlemen— Till we meet. *(Goes out.)*

(LYUBOFF ANDREEVNA *and* GAYEFF *are left alone. As if they had been waiting for this, they throw themselves on one another's necks sobbing, but smothering their sobs as if afraid of being heard.)*

GAYEFF
> *(in despair)*
> Oh, Sister, Sister—

LYUBOFF ANDREEVNA
> Oh, my dear, my lovely, beautiful orchard! My life, my youth, my happiness, good-by!

ANYA
> *(her voice gay, appealing)*
> Mama—!

TROFIMOFF
> *(his voice, gay, excited)*
> Aaooch!

LYUBOFF ANDREEVNA
> For the last time, just to look at the walls, at the window— My dear mother used to love to walk around in this room—

GAYEFF
> Oh, Sister, Sister—!

ANYA
> *(from outside)*
> Mama—!

TROFIMOFF
> *(from outside)*
> Aaooch—!

LYUBOFF ANDREEVNA
> We are coming! *(They go out.)*

(The stage is empty. You hear the keys locking all the doors, then the carriages drive off. It grows quiet. In the silence you hear the dull thud of an ax on a tree, a lonely, mournful sound. Footsteps are heard. From the door on the right FIERS *appears.*

He is dressed as usual, in a jacket and a white waistcoat, slippers on his feet. He is sick.)

FIERS
(going to the door and trying the knob)
Locked. They've gone. *(Sitting down on the sofa)* They forgot about me— No matter— I'll sit here awhile— And Leonid Andreevich, for sure, didn't put on his fur coat, he went off with his topcoat— *(Sighing anxiously)* And I didn't see to it— The young saplings! *(He mutters something that cannot be understood.)* Life has gone by, as if I hadn't lived at all— *(Lying down)* I'll lie down awhile— You haven't got any strength, nothing is left, nothing— Ach, you—good-for-nothing — *(He lies still.)*

(There is a far-off sound as if out of the sky, the sound of a snapped string, dying away, sad. A stillness falls, and there is only the thud of an ax on a tree, far away in the orchard.)

(Curtain)

for discussion

ACT 1

1. In his first monologue, what background information does Lopahin give about himself and about Lyuboff Andreevna? Explain what Lopahin means when he compares himself to "a pig rooting in a pastry shop."
2. At the beginning of the play, Lyuboff Andreevna is returning home, after having spent five years in Paris with her daughter and servants. Describe her experience in Paris. Why did she leave home to go there?
3. What is the problem Lyuboff Andreevna faces upon returning home? What solution does Lopahin suggest? How do Lyuboff Andreevna and her brother respond to Lopahin's suggestion?
4. Describe Gayeff. What does his salute to the hundred-year-old bookcase reveal about his character and personality?

5. After Lopahin has left, Gayeff calls him a "boor," but Lyuboff Andreevna characterizes him as "a good man." In light of Lopahin's actions, whom do you think is right? Why?
6. Cite specific lines which reveal Lyuboff Andreevna's attitude toward the cherry orchard. What significance is there in the fact that she sees a vision of her mother in it?
7. Describe the three servants: Fiers, Yasha, and Dunyasha. What kind of relationship does each have with his master?
8. At the end of the act, Gayeff assures Anya and Varya that the cherry orchard will not be sold. What plans does he have to raise the money to pay the mortgage? At this point, do you think he and his sister will be able to keep the orchard? Defend your answer.
9. The characters in Chekhov's plays often do not listen to one another, nor do they appear to care if the other characters are listening to them. Frequently, therefore, there is little connection between one statement and the next, and the dialogue seems disjointed and aimless. Point out examples of this type of conversation in the first act of *The Cherry Orchard*. Do you think such conversations are common in day-to-day life? Explain your answer.

ACT 2

1. Reread the opening stage directions of this act. Explain why Chekhov set Act 2 outside an old abandoned chapel. What other details of the setting help to establish the predominant mood of the act?
2. The first scene of this act is devoted to the minor characters in the play. Why does Chekhov do this?
3. Lyuboff Andreevna drops her purse, and the coins spill out. What significance is there in this detail? What else happens in this act which makes the same point?
4. Speaking to Lopahin and Gayeff, Lyuboff Andreevna refers to her "sins." What are they? How does she feel she has been punished for them? Do you agree with Gayeff who, in the first act, referred to his sister as a "depraved woman"? Defend your answer.
5. Contrast Lopahin and Trofimoff. What does each, perhaps, envy in the other?
6. Explain Trofimoff's criticism of the Russian intelligentsia and upper classes. How applicable do you think it is to the characters in this play? Explain your answer.

7. What effect does the far-off sound, "like the sound of a snapped string, dying away, mournful" have upon the group? Why do you think Chekhov included this detail? Of what might the sound be symbolic?
8. Discuss Trofimoff's attitude toward the cherry orchard, as it is reflected in his conversation with Anya on pages 410-411. Contrast this attitude with Lyuboff Andreevna's attitude toward the orchard; with Lopahin's. Explain how the attitudes of these characters toward the cherry orchard reflect their attitudes toward the past and/or the future.
9. As the second act ends, the moon is rising, Epihodoff is heard in the distance singing a song, and Varya is looking for Anya. What mood is established by these details. Is this mood consistent with the mood of the rest of the act? Why or why not?

ACT 3

1. For whom are the main characters waiting at the beginning of the act? Why?
2. Describe the relationship between Varya and Trofimoff. Why is Varya opposed to the "romance" which is developing between him and Anya? What does Trofimoff say which further annoys Varya?
3. Cite the lines in which Lyuboff Andreevna sums up to Trofimoff her feelings about the cherry orchard. Does Trofimoff sympathize with these feelings? Explain.
4. When Trofimoff asserts that he is "above love," Lyuboff Andreev answers, "Well, then, I must be beneath love." What does she mean? In Russian, the word *lyuboff* means "love." Explain why Chekhov gave his main character this name.
5. The minor characters weave in and out of the act. Have any of them changed since the beginning of the play? Refer to specific lines or incidents to support your answer.
6. Chekhov provides many light and humorous details throughout most of this act. Point out some of these. What piece of slapstick does he include upon Lopahin's entrance? Explain how these humorous touches, as well as the gay party atmosphere, heighten the impact of Lopahin's announcement.
7. Pointing to specific lines, identify the climax of this act. How has the playwright foreshadowed the climax? Why does he have Lopahin, not Gayeff, break the news to Lyuboff Andreevna? What other techniques does he use to make the climax an especially dramatic one?

8. In his moment of jubilation, Lopahin expresses his feelings about the cherry orchard. Describe them. When he accidentally collides into a table and almost upsets the candelabra, he says, "I can pay for everything!" What insight into Lopahin's character does Chekhov give through this detail?
9. Describe the note on which the act ends. Do you find it a moving ending to the act or not? Explain your answer.

ACT 4

1. Contrast the opening of Act 4 with the opening of Act 1. How does the change in setting reflect what has taken place during the intervening months?
2. Lopahin says to Yasha, "It's devilish cold in here. . . . Outside it's October, but it's sunny and still, like summer." Explain the symbolism of this description.
3. Although Yasha drinks the champagne Lopahin brought for the occasion, Trofimoff does not. Why not?
4. What advice does Trofimoff give to Lopahin upon leaving? Do you think it is good advice? Why or why not? In what spirit does Lopahin take this advice?
5. What provision has been made for old Fiers? When do you first suspect that the plan has not been carried out? Whose fault is it?
6. Cite the lines in which Anya envisions a bright future together with her mother. Where else has Anya spoken in this manner? Knowing Lyuboff Andreevna, do you think such a life would appeal to her? Explain your answer.
7. Just before the final leave-taking, Pishtchik rushes into the house to repay part of his debts to Lopahin and Lyuboff Andreevna. What has happened which enables him to do this? What prediction would you make as to Pishtchik's future?
8. On several occasions Lopahin has said to Lyuboff Andreevna that he plans to propose to Varya, but he never does. Why? Explain why he remains silent in Act 4, even though given a perfect opportunity to propose.
9. Describe the way each of the following characters feels about leaving the cherry orchard: Lyuboff Andreevna, Yasha, Anya, Trofimoff, Varya, and Gayeff. What are the plans each has for the future?
10. Alone in the house, Fiers realizes he has been forgotten. What does the playwright indicate will happen to him? Explain why this fact suggests the theme of the play. How do the sounds

heard just before the curtain falls also suggest the theme of the play?

viewing the play as a whole

1. In Act 2, Fiers says to Lopahin that, in the old days, ". . . the peasants stuck to the masters, the masters stuck to the peasants, and now everything is all smashed up, you can't tell about anything." How does this statement apply to the action of *The Cherry Orchard*. Is this the theme of the play? Explain your answer.
2. Human loneliness is a pervasive theme in much of contemporary literature. In what way is this theme illustrated in *The Cherry Orchard?* Cite specific examples to support your answer.
3. Explain why Lyuboff Andreevna and Gayeff were unable to prevent the sale of the cherry orchard. Discuss the author's attitude toward each of these characters. Is it primarily critical? satirical? sympathetic?
4. Explain why Chekhov included so many minor characters in *The Cherry Orchard*. Do their actions provide "comic relief" to the sadness of the central incident? How does their presence further the themes of the play and help to establish its mood?
5. Look up the definition of *symbolism* in the Glossary (page 548). What aspects of *The Cherry Orchard* are symbolic? Explain how Chekhov's use of these symbols reinforces the theme of his play.
6. Chekhov's plays are written in a low key; they avoid the melodramatic, the theatrical equivalents of italics. Show how this is true of *The Cherry Orchard*. Be sure to refer to the climax of the play.
7. Describe the predominant mood of *The Cherry Orchard*. Show how the characterizations, the dialogue, and the setting all serve to establish the mood.
8. Some years ago, *The Cherry Orchard* was the basis of a Broadway play, *The Wisteria Trees*, which was set in the American South. What similiarities do you find between the situation Chekhov describes in his play, and the situation the South faced after the Civil War.
9. In what respects is *The Cherry Orchard* different from other plays you have seen or read? In what respects is it similar? Why, despite an unexciting and minimal amount of plot, do you think it is regarded as a classic of the modern theater?

for composition

1. Write an essay which describes either Lopahin, Lyuboff Andreevna, or Yasha five years after the events described in this play. Your predictions should follow logically from the character's personality, as it has been developed throughout *The Cherry Orchard*.
2. Explain why Lyuboff Andreevna and Gayeff are unable to prevent the cherry orchard from being sold. Be sure to make clear why they reject Lopahin's suggestion to convert the orchard into a summer resort.
3. *The Cherry Orchard* reflects the disintegration of a way of life, the breakup of the feudal order in Russia at the end of the nineteenth century. Write an essay which shows specifically how Chekhov's play does this. Refer to the characterizations, the central action, and the symbols the playwright uses.
4. In all his plays, Chekhov attempted to "de-theatricalize" the theater, to make what happens on stage correspond more closely with what happens in real life. Write a well-organized essay which shows how he accomplished this aim in *The Cherry Orchard*.
5. Many critics have maintained that *The Cherry Orchard* is, first and foremost, a comedy. Paying special attention to its characterizations, discuss the comic aspects of the play.

thieves' carnival

JEAN ANOUILH
Translated by Lucienne Hill

thieves' carnival

CHARACTERS

PETERBONO
HECTOR } *thieves*
GUSTAVE
LORD EDGARD
LADY HURF
JULIETTE } *her nieces*
EVA
DUPONT-DUFORT SENIOR
DUPONT-DUFORT JUNIOR
THE TOWN CRIER
THE POLICEMAN
THE NURSEMAID
THE LITTLE GIRL
THE MUSICIAN

ACT 1

The public gardens of a watering place which saw its heyday in the 1880's. In the middle, a bandstand. The orchestra is represented by a single MUSICIAN, *who at the rise of the Curtain is executing a solo of superlative virtuosity on the clarinet. A woman deckchair* ATTENDANT *goes to and fro. Summer visitors stroll up and down to the rhythm of the music. In the foreground* EVA *and* HECTOR *are locked in a dramatic screen embrace. The music stops. So does the kiss, from which* HECTOR *emerges, reeling a little. Applause for the* MUSICIAN.

HECTOR

(covered in confusion)
I say, steady. They're applauding us!

EVA

(bursts out laughing)
Of course not, it's the orchestra. I must say you appeal to me enormously.

HECTOR

(instinctively fingering his hair and mustache)
What do you like about me, specially?

EVA

Everything. *(She blows him a kiss.)* We mustn't stay here, it's too risky. I'll see you tonight at eight in the Phoenix bar. And if you should meet me with my aunt, whatever you do, pretend you don't know me.

HECTOR

(yearningly)
Your little hand, once more.

EVA

Careful. My aunt's old friend Edgard is over there by the bandstand reading his paper. He'll see us. *(She holds out her hand, but turns away to watch* LORD EDGARD.*)*

HECTOR
(passionately)
I want to inhale the perfume of your hand!

(He bends over her hand, and surreptitiously draws a jeweler's eyeglass from his pocket to take a closer look at EVA's *rings.* EVA *withdraws her hand, unaware of the maneuver.)*

EVA
Till tonight. *(She goes.)*

HECTOR
(weak at the knees)
My beloved—*(He follows her out of sight, then comes down stage again, putting away his eyeglass, and mutters with icy self-possession.)* A good two hundred thousand. And not a flaw in the lot.

(At this point the TOWN CRIER *enters with his drum and the crowd gathers round to listen.)*

TOWN CRIER
Townsmen of Vichy! The Municipality, anxious to preserve the well-being and security of the invalids and bathers, issues a warning for their information and protection! Numerous complaints from visitors have been lodged at the Town Hall and at the main police station, Market Street. A dangerous pack of picklepockets—*(He has a little trouble with this word, at which the* CLARINET *plays a little accompaniment. The* TOWN CRIER *swings round on him, furious.)*—a dangerous pack of pockpickets—*(Again the* CLARINET *renders the word in music.)*—is at this very hour within our gates. The local police is on the watch. Members of the Force, in plain clothes and in uniform, are ready to protect our visitors—*(Indeed, even as he speaks* POLICEMEN *are threading their several ways gracefully through the* CROWD.*)* Visitors are nevertheless requested to exercise the greatest possible caution, particularly on the highway, in public parks and in all other places of public resort. A reward in kind is offered by the Tourist Association to anyone supplying in-

formation leading to the apprehension of the felons! Tell your friends!

(A roll of drums. During the proclamation HECTOR *has relieved the* TOWN CRIER *of his enormous copper watch and bulging purse. The crowd scatters, and the drum and the harangue are heard again further off.* HECTOR *takes a seat, and the* CHAIRWOMAN *approaches.)*

CHAIRWOMAN
Will you take a ticket, sir, please?
HECTOR
(largely)
Since it's customary—
CHAIRWOMAN
That'll be five francs, please.

(While HECTOR *feels for the money, the* WOMAN *steals his wallet, then the huge watch and the purse he has just taken from the* TOWN CRIER.*)*

HECTOR
(seizing the hand on its next trip into his pocket)
Hey! What do you think you're up to? *(The* WOMAN *struggles to free herself, and loses her wig.)* Have you gone crazy? *(He lifts his own wig and mustache a trifle.)* It's me!

(The CHAIR ATTENDANT *readjusts her wig. It is* PETERBONO.*)*

PETERBONO
Sorry, old chap. It's me too. Had a good day?
HECTOR
The purse and a watch, and a cigarette lighter.
PETERBONO
(examining them)
I know that watch. It's the Town Crier's and it's made of copper. I put it back into his pocket, the poor devil, that and the purse, which you'll find if you check up contains just fifteen

cents and the receipt for a registered parcel. As for the lighter, we've already got nine hundred and three, out of which only a couple work. I've known you to do better, my lad!

HECTOR

I've a date tonight with a girl who'll be mine before you can say mischief, and who wears over two hundred thousand francs worth of diamonds on her middle finger.

PETERBONO

We'll look into it. Have you noticed that little thing over there? The necklace?

HECTOR

(examining the girl through the fieldglasses he wears round his neck)
Phew! The stones are enormous!

PETERBONO

No wishful thinking. They're smaller to the naked eye. Still, off we go. Small change maneuver. I get offensive and you interfere. *(They cross to the* GIRL *with a terrible affectation of indifference.)* Ticket? Ticket? *(The* GIRL *gives him a coin.* PETERBONO *begins to yell.)* I've got no change! I tell you I've got no change! No change, do you hear? No change at all, I keep on telling you!

HECTOR

What's this? No change, eh? Excuse me, Mademoiselle, allow me to put this insolent baggage in her place!

(There follows a tussle under cover of which HECTOR *investigates the clasp of the girl's necklace.)*

THE GIRL

(violently freeing herself)
No, you don't!

HECTOR

(taken aback)
What do you mean, no you don't!

PETERBONO

No you don't what?

THE GIRL

(lifting her wig. It is GUSTAVE.*)*
It's me.

HECTOR

(falling into a chair)
Charming!

PETERBONO

(exploding)
That's what comes of not working to plan! I can't rely on anybody! Running errands, that's all you're fit for! Errand boys! If it weren't for your poor old mother who put you in my charge to learn the business, you'd be out on your ear, the pair of you. Do you hear me? Out on your ear! And without your week's pay in lieu of notice, make no mistake! And complain to the union if you dare! I'll tell them a thing or two, the dance you've led me, both of you! *(To* GUSTAVE*)* You! You haven't done a stroke today, naturally!

GUSTAVE

Yes I have. I've done two. First, there's this magnificent wallet.

PETERBONO

Let's have a look. *(He examines it, then searches himself anxiously.)* Where did you get this? Who from?

GUSTAVE

I got it in the Boulevard Ravachol off an old gentleman with a long white beard—

PETERBONO

(terrible in his anger)
—check trousers, olive-green jacket and deer-stalker cap, am I right, pigeon-brain?

GUSTAVE

(quaking)
Yes, sir. Did you see me?

PETERBONO

(sinks into a chair, flattened by this latest blow)
That was me, idiot, that was me! At this rate we'll be lucky if we cover our expenses!

GUSTAVE

But I've got something else, Mr. Peterbono, sir.

PETERBONO

(profoundly discouraged)
If it's something else you stole from me, you can imagine my curiosity.

GUSTAVE

It isn't a thing, it's a girl. And she looks rich.

HECTOR

(jumping up)

Good God! Don't say it's the same girl. A redhead? About twenty-five? Name of Eva?

GUSTAVE

No. Dark hair, about twenty. Name of Juliet.

HECTOR

Oh, that's all right.

PETERBONO

What did you get?

GUSTAVE

Nothing yet. But I helped her fish a kid out of the Thermes Fountain. We sat in the sun to dry and we got talking. She told me she liked me.

PETERBONO

Any jewels?

GUSTAVE

One very fine pearl.

PETERBONO

Good. We must look into that. Hector, can you spare a moment this afternoon, other engagements permitting?

GUSTAVE

No! I'd like to handle this myself.

PETERBONO

What's this? What's this? Handle it yourself, would you? Well, whatever next?

GUSTAVE

It was me she took a fancy to.

PETERBONO

All the more reason. Hector will swallow her in one.

GUSTAVE

No, I tell you! Not this one!

PETERBONO

(severely)

Gustave, listen to me. Your mother put you in my care, and I took you into the firm as assistant decoy. You're young and you're ambitious. That's fine. I was ambitious myself when I was your age. But just a minute! In our profession, as in all professions, you have to work your way up from the bottom. Hector here is the finest professional seducer I know this side of Monte Carlo. There's a chap who hits the bull's eye three times out of four, and take it from me, that's a pretty handsome average. You don't mean to tell me that you, a mere apprentice, expect to turn out better work than that?

GUSTAVE

To hell with it! I'll get her for myself.

PETERBONO

(tight-lipped)

If you wish to do a job on the side in your spare time there's nothing to stop you. You'll owe me just the sixty-five per cent on what you make, that's all.

HECTOR

(who has been watching a NURSEMAID *during this altercation)*
Peter?

PETERBONO

Hector?

HECTOR

That nursemaid over there. See the gold chain?

PETERBONO

(contemptuously)
Pooh! It's probably gilded fuse wire.

HECTOR

Listen, it's ten to seven. We've ten minutes in hand before supper.

PETERBONO

Very well, if you're set on it. We'll give her the Three Musketeers maneuver.

HECTOR

Three Musketeers maneuver?

PETERBONO

It's the classic routine for nursemaids. Number one gets off with her, number two plays ten little pigs with the baby, and number three starts whistling bugle calls without a break to make her senses reel.

(They go. Enter LADY HURF *and* JULIETTE.*)*

JULIETTE

The little boy was barely five years old. He was only in up to his waist, but he was frightened and he kept falling over. He would have drowned, I'm sure.

LADY HURF

How dreadful! Have you noticed all these little chimney-pot hats everywhere? How absurd they look!

JULIETTE

Fortunately this young man came to the rescue. He was wonderful, and very sweet.

LADY HURF

All children are sweet at five. But at twelve they begin to get silly. That's why I never wanted any.

JULIETTE

I was talking about the young man, Aunt.

LADY HURF

Oh, yes, of course. There's another of those grotesque little hats. The young man was very sweet—yes, go on.

JULIETTE

That's all.

LADY HURF

We must invite him to dinner.

JULIETTE

He's gone. I'd never seen him before.

LADY HURF

Good. One always knows far too many people. Besides, I can't stand stories about drowning. Your poor uncle swam like a lump of lead. He drowned himself seven times, I could have hit him. Ah, there's Edgard. Edgard, have you seen Eva?

LORD EDGARD

(appearing from behind his paper)
How are you, my dear?

LADY HURF

I asked if you'd seen Eva.

LORD EDGARD

Eva? No, I haven't. That's very odd. Now what can I have done with her? Perhaps she's at the Baths.

LADY HURF

At seven o'clock at night? Don't be silly.

JULIETTE
  Shall we try the Phoenix bar? She often goes there.
LADY HURF
  Edgard, don't stir from this spot for any reason whatsoever.
LORD EDGARD
  Very good, my dear.
LADY HURF
  (going)
  But of course if you see her, run after her.
LORD EDGARD
  Very good, my dear.
LADY HURF
  Or better still, don't; you'd only lose her—just come and tell us which way she went.
LORD EDGARD
  Very good, my dear.
LADY HURF
  On second thoughts, no. You'd never manage to find us. Send one attendant after her, another attendant to let us know, and put a third in your place to tell us where you've gone so we can pick you up on the way home if we should happen to be passing.
LORD EDGARD
  Very good, my dear.

(He retires, stunned, behind his paper. Exit LADY HURF *with* JULIETTE. *Enter the* DUPONT-DUFORTS, *father and son, accompanied by the little jig on the clarinet, which is their signature tune.)*

D. D. SENIOR
  Let's follow. We'll meet them casually on the promenade, and try to tempt them to a cocktail. Didier, I don't know what's come over you. You, a hard-working, conscientious lad, brimful of initiative, and look at you. You're not paying an atom of attention to young Juliette.
D. D. JUNIOR
  She snubs me.

D. D. SENIOR

What does that matter? To begin with, you aren't just anybody. You are Dupont-Dufort junior. Her aunt thinks a great deal of you. She's prepared to make any investment on your recommendation.

D. D. JUNIOR

That ought to be enough for us.

D. D. SENIOR

Son, in matters of money there's no such thing as enough. I'd far and away prefer you to pull off this marriage. Nothing short of that will put our bank fairly and squarely on its feet again. So let me see a bit of charm, a little fascination.

D. D. JUNIOR

Yes, Dad.

D. D. SENIOR

We couldn't wish for more propitious circumstances. They're bored to tears, and there's nobody here in the least presentable. So let's make ourselves agreeable, superlatively agreeable.

D. D. JUNIOR

Yes, Dad.

(Exeunt the DUPONT-DUFORTS. LORD EDGAR, *who has heard every word, looks over his* Times *to watch them go.* PETERBONO, HECTOR, *and* GUSTAVE *come in dressed as soldiers as the* MUSICIAN *begins his second number. The* POLICEMEN *enter at the same time from the other side. They all perform a flirtatious little ballet round the* NURSEMAID, *the maneuvers of the* POLICEMEN *seriously impeding those of the* THREE THIEVES. *The* NURSEMAID *finally goes; the* POLICEMEN, *twirling their white batons behind their backs, make gallant attempts to hinder her departure. During the ballet* LADY HURF *returns alone and goes to sit beside* LORD EDGAR. *The music stops at the exit of the* POLICEMEN *and the* NURSEMAID.)

PETERBONO

(thwarted)

Lads, that's the first time I've ever known the Three Musketeers maneuver to miscarry.

LADY HURF

(to LORD EDGARD)

Well, Edgard my dear, and what have you done with yourself today?

LORD EDGARD

(surprise and embarrassed as always at LADY HURF'S customary abruptness)

I—er—I read the *Times*.

LADY HURF

(sternly)

The same as yesterday?

LORD EDGARD

(ingenuously)

Not the same copy as yesterday.

HECTOR

(who has been watching the scene, gives a whistle of admiration)

See those pearls?

PETERBONO

Four millions!

HECTOR

How about it? What's it to be? Russian princes?

PETERBONO

No. She knows her onions by the look of her. Ruined Spanish noblemen.

GUSTAVE

That's bright of you. Whenever you masquerade as Spaniards you're rigged out like a couple of rats.

PETERBONO

Quiet, shaver! You're speaking of a trade you know nothing about.

GUSTAVE

Well, anyway, if you think I'm dressing up as your ecclesiastical secretary like the last time, it's no go. I'm not wearing a cassock in this heat.

PETERBONO

Gustave, you're trying my patience! Come along, home! Hector and I will be Spanish Grandees, and you'll put on that cassock, heat or no heat.

(The unwilling GUSTAVE *is borne away, to the accompaniment of a little jig on the clarinet.)*

LADY HURF
(who has been deep in thought)
Edgard, the situation is grave—

LORD EDGARD
I know. According to the *Times*, the Empire—

LADY HURF
No, no, here.

LORD EDGARD
(looking round him anxiously)
Here?

LADY HURF
Listen to me. We have two tender creatures in our care. Intrigues are fermenting—marriages are brewing. Personally I can't keep track of them—it gives me the vertigo. Who is to uncover them, Edgard, who is to supervise them?

LORD EDGARD
Who?

LADY HURF
Juliette is a scatterbrain. Eva is a scatterbrain. As for me, I haven't a notion what's going on and the mere idea of it bores me to extinction. Besides, I've no more common sense than those two senseless girls. That leaves you in the midst of these three scatterbrains.

LORD EDGARD
That leaves me.

LADY HURF
Which is another way of saying nobody. I am perplexed, excessively perplexed. Anything may happen in this watering place. Intrigues spring up under one's very feet like so much jungle vegetation. Should we do better to leave Vichy, I wonder? Ought we perhaps to bury ourselves in some rustic backwater? Edgard, for heaven's sake say something! You are the guardian of these two young things, aren't you?

LORD EDGARD
We might ask Dupont-Dufort his advice. He seems to be a man of character.

LADY HURF

A deal too much character. What a ninny you are. He's the last man from whom we want advice. The Dupont-Duforts are after our money.

LORD EDGARD

But they're rich.

LADY HURF

Exactly. That's what worries me. They're after a lot of money. An investment or a marriage settlement. Our two little ones with their millions are exceptionally tempting morsels.

LORD EDGARD

Could we not telegraph to England?

LADY HURF

What for?

LORD EDGARD

Scotland Yard might send us a detective.

LADY HURF

That would be a great help, I must say! They're crooked as corkscrews, the lot of them!

LORD EDGARD

The problem, then, is in effect insoluble.

LADY HURF

Edgard, you simply must bestir yourself. Our fate, the girls' and mine, is in your hands.

LORD EDGARD

(looks at his hands, very worried)

I don't know that I am very well equipped.

LADY HURF

(sternly)

Edgard, do you call yourself a man? And a gentleman?

LORD EDGARD

Yes.

LADY HURF

Then make a decision!

LORD EDGARD

(firmly)

Very well! I shall nevertheless summon a detective from Scotland Yard, with a special proviso that I want him honest.

LADY HURF
 Over my dead body! If he's honest, he'll philander with the kitchen maids and he won't wash. It will be insufferable. And yet I don't know why I should be telling you all this. What do I want with absolute security? I'm as bored as a piece of old carpet!
LORD EDGARD
 Oh, my dear—!
LADY HURF
 That's all I am, a piece of old carpet.
LORD EDGARD
 You, who were once so beautiful.
LADY HURF
 Yes, in the nineteen-hundreds. Oh, I could scream with rage! I want to enjoy my last few years—I want to laugh a little. Sixty years I've spent deluded into thinking life a serious business. That's sixty years too long. I am in the mood, Edgard, for a gigantic piece of folly.
LORD EDGARD
 Nothing dangerous, I hope?
LADY HURF
 I don't know. I'll see what occurs to me. *(She leans towards him.)* I think I should like to massacre the Dupont-Duforts.

(In they come, accompanied by their particular little tune, with EVA *and* JULETTE.*)*

D. D. SENIOR
 How are you today, milady?
D. D. JUNIOR
 Milady.
D. D. SENIOR
 Ah, dear Lord Edgard.
LORD EDGARD
 (drawing him aside)
 Take the greatest possible care.
D. D. SENIOR
 But why, milord?

LORD EDGARD
   Hush! I can't tell you. But take care. Leave Vichy.

D. D. JUNIOR
   We ran into these ladies on the promenade.

EVA
   Vichy's an impossible place. Nothing to do, nowhere to go, and all the men are hideous.

D. D. JUNIOR
   Oh, how true! Quite, quite hideous, all of them!

D. D. SENIOR
   All of them! *(Aside to his son)* Excellent thing for us.

EVA
   I have an engagement tonight, Aunt. I shall be late for dinner—if I'm back at all.

D. D. SENIOR
   (aside to his son)
   With you?

D. D. JUNIOR
   No.

JULIETTE
   Eva, I haven't told you. I rescued a little boy who fell into the Thermes Fountain, and I met an enchanting young man, who helped me to save him.

LADY HURF
   Juliette talks of nothing else.

(The DUPONT-DUFORTS *look at each other anxiously.)*

D. D. SENIOR
   Wasn't that you?

D. D. JUNIOR
   No.

JULIETTE
   We sat in the sun till we were dry, and chatted. You've no idea how pleasant he was! He's slight, with dark hair and—he's not the same as yours by any chance?

EVA
   No. Mine's tall, with red hair.

JULIETTE
   Thank goodness!

D. D. SENIOR
(whispers)
Sonny, you have absolutely *got* to sparkle. *(Raising his voice)* Didier, dear boy, have you been to the swimming pool with these ladies yet? You must give them a demonstration of your impeccable crawl. You could have rescued the toddler with the greatest of ease.

JULIETTE
Oh, the crawl would have been quite useless. The Thermes Fountain is only eighteen inches deep.

(Towards the end of this scene, PETERBONO, as a very noble—all too noble—old Spanish gentleman, HECTOR as a Grandee, an equally spectacular achievement, and GUSTAVE, their ecclesiastical secretary, come in and slowly approach the others.)

PETERBONO
Careful. This is big game. Stay close, and take no risks.

HECTOR
Your monocle.

PETERBONO
The big act, "Noblesse oblige." Wait for the word go. Gustave, two paces behind.

(The CLARINET strikes up a march, heroic and ultra-Spanish. Suddenly, LADY HURF, who has been watching this curious trio, runs to them and throws her arms around PETERBONO's neck.)

LADY HURF
Why, if it isn't that dear dear Duke of Miraflores!

(Music stops.)

PETERBONO
(surprised and uneasy)
Uh?

LADY HURF
Don't say you've forgotten! Biarritz 1902. The luncheon parties at Pampeluna! The bullfights! Lady Hurf.

PETERBONO

Ah—! Lady Hurf. Bullfights. Lunch. Dear friend. *(To the other two)* I must have made up like one of her acquaintances.

LADY HURF

I am so, so happy! I was disintegrating with boredom. But where is the Duchess?

PETERBONO

Dead.

(Tremolo from the ORCHESTRA)

LADY HURF

Oh, heavens! And your cousin the Count?

PETERBONO

Dead.

(Tremolo from the ORCHESTRA)

LADY HURF

Oh, heavens! And your friend, the Admiral?

PETERBONO

Also dead. *(The ORCHESTRA begins a funeral march. PETERBONO turns to his friends.)* Saved!

LADY HURF

My poor friend. So many funerals.

PETERBONO

Alas! However, may I present my son, Don Hector? And my ecclesiastical secretary, Dom Petrus?

LADY HURF

Lord Edgard, whom you knew years ago. It was he whom you beat each morning at golf, and who was always losing his golf balls.

PETERBONO

Ha, golf—yes. Dear friend.

LORD EDGARD

(panic-stricken, to LADY HURF)
But, my dear—

LADY HURF
(sternly)
What's the matter? Do you mean to say you don't remember the Duke?
LORD EDGARD
This is insane. Come now, think back—
LADY HURF
Your memory is abominable. Don't say another word or I shall lose my temper. My nieces, Eva and Juliette, who worry me so dreadfully because they're both very marriageable, and their dowries are exceptionally tempting to fortune hunters.

(The DUPONT-DUFORTS *look at each other.)*

D. D. SENIOR
Dignity, lad, dignity.
D. D. JUNIOR
She can't mean us.

*(*PETERBONO *and* HECTOR *indulge in violent nudging.)*

LADY HURF
I am so delighted to have met you again. Vichy is such a dull hole. Tell me, do you remember the Ridottos on the Riviera?
PETERBONO
I should think I do!
D. D. JUNIOR
(to his father)
We're forgotten.
D. D. SENIOR
Let's introduce ourselves. Dupont-Dufort, senior.
D. D. JUNIOR
Junior.

(During the introductions, EVA *stares hard at* HECTOR, *who simulates an enormous interest in the conversation.* GUSTAVE *has all but disappeared into his briefcase, and rummages feverishly among his papers to avoid* JULIETTE'S *gaze, which is fixed on him in puzzled interest.)*

LADY HURF

You must be as bored as I am. It's an undreamed of stroke of fortune, our meeting, don't you think?

PETERBONO

(*nudging* HECTOR)
Undreamed of.

HECTOR

(*nudging* PETERBONO)
Yes. Undreamed of—absolutely undreamed of.

(*In their glee, they go much too far, but no one seems to notice.*)

LADY HURF

Your son is most charming. Don't you think so, Eva?

EVA

Yes.

PETERBONO

He was the most dashing officer in the entire Spanish army—before the revolution.

LADY HURF

Alas! You suffered a great deal?

PETERBONO

A great deal.

LADY HURF

Where are you staying? Not at a hotel?

PETERBONO

(*vaguely*)
Yes.

LADY HURF

It's out of the question, Edgard! The Duke is staying at a hotel!

LORD EDGARD

But, my dearest, I assure you—

LADY HURF

Be quiet! Dear Duke, you cannot, you simply cannot stay at an hotel. Will you do us the honor of accepting our humble hospitality? Our villa is enormous, and we shall put the west wing entirely at your disposal.

PETERBONO
Certainly, certainly, certainly, certainly—

(Stupendous nudging between PETERBONO *and* HECTOR. *The* DUPONT-DUFORTS *exchange crestfallen glances.)*

LADY HURF
You may, needless to say, bring your entourage. *(She looks enquiringly at* GUSTAVE.) Is he looking for something?

PETERBONO
A document, yes. Dom Petrus!

GUSTAVE
(emerging from the brief case)
Your Grace? *(He has put on some dark glasses.)*

LADY HURF
Has he got bad eyes?

PETERBONO
Oh, very bad. His condition requires a certain amount of care. I couldn't burden you with his presence. Dom Petrus, we shall accept Lady Hurf's generous offer of hospitality. Call at the hotel, will you, and have our luggage sent on. And stay there until further notice. You will collect the mail and come to us each morning for instructions.

GUSTAVE
(furious)
But, your Grace—

PETERBONO
Enough!

GUSTAVE
Your Grace—

PETERBONO
Off with you!

*(*HECTOR *gives* GUSTAVE *a push, and he wanders reluctantly away.)*

LADY HURF
(moved)
Just as he used to be! That same commanding tone—the vocal magic of the Miraflores! Your cousin had it too.

PETERBONO
  Alas!
LADY HURF
  How did he die?
PETERBONO
  Er, how he died?
LADY HURF
  Yes—I was so fond of him.
PETERBONO
  You want me to relate the circumstances of his passing?
LADY HURF
  Yes.
PETERBONO
  (*turns to* HECTOR *in his panic*)
  Well, he died—

(HECTOR *mimes a motor accident, but this* PETERBONO *cannot grasp.*)

PETERBONO
  He died insane.
LADY HURF
  Ah, poor fellow! He always was eccentric. But your wife, the dear Duchess?
PETERBONO
  Dead.
LADY HURF
  Yes, I know. But how?

(HECTOR *touches his heart several times.* PETERBONO *is slow to take the suggestion, but as he has no imagination whatever himself, he gives way.*)

PETERBONO
  Of love.
LADY HURF
  (*in confusion*)
  Oh, I beg your pardon! And your friend the Admiral?

PETERBONO
Ah, now the Admiral—

(He looks at HECTOR, *who indicates that he has run out of ideas. He again misinterprets the pantomime.)*

Drowned. But please excuse me, you are re-opening wounds which time has not yet healed.

LADY HURF
Oh, forgive me, dear friend, forgive me! *(To the* OTHERS*)* What breeding! What grandeur in adversity! Don't you think so, Edgard?

LORD EDGARD
My dear, I still insist that—

LADY HURF
Do stop insisting. Can't you see the Duke is suffering?

D. D. SENIOR
(to his son)
Let us join in the conversation.

D. D. JUNIOR
What an appalling avalanche of misfortunes!

D. D. SENIOR
Falling on such venerable heads!

(No one listens.)

LADY HURF
(in a peal of laughter)
How beautiful Biarritz was in those days. Do you remember the balls?

PETERBONO
Ah, the balls—

LADY HURF
And Lina Veri?

PETERBONO
Lina Veri. I can't quite recall—

LADY HURF

Come, come. Why, you were intimate! *(To the* OTHERS*)* He's aged so much.

PETERBONO

Oh, Lina Veri. Of course. The darling of Italian society.

LADY HURF

No, no, no. She was a dancer.

PETERBONO

Oh yes, but her mother was the darling of Italian society.

LADY HURF

(to the OTHERS*)*

He's wandering a little. He's very tired. My dear Duke, I would like to show you your apartments right away. The villa is close by, at the end of the avenue.

PETERBONO

With pleasure.

(GUSTAVE *comes running in, this time as his own charming self, but magnificently dressed.*)

GUSTAVE

Good morning, Father!

PETERBONO

(off his balance)

Little basket! Allow me to present my second son, Don Pedro, whom I'd forgotten to mention.

LADY HURF

Gracious, you have another son? By whom?

PETERBONO

(panicking again)

Ah, that's a long story—*(He looks at* HECTOR, *who signs to him to go carefully.)* But that one also opens wounds as yet unhealed by time.

LADY HURF

Come along, Edgard.

LORD EDGARD

But, my dear—

LADY HURF
And keep quiet!

(They go, HECTOR *paying elaborate attentions to* EVA, *who has continued to stare at him.)*

JULIETTE
(to GUSTAVE*)*
Now will you kindly tell me what is going on?

GUSTAVE
Ssh! I'll explain later.

(They go too. The DUPONT-DUFORTS *are left alone.)*

D. D. JUNIOR
Father, they've forgotten us—!

D. D. SENIOR
All the same, we'll follow. And, Didier, twice the affability. Let's hope these young men are already attached or better still that they aren't interested in women!

(They go.)

(Curtain)

ACT 2

A drawing room in LADY HURF'S *house. It is evening, after dinner, and* JULIETTE *and* GUSTAVE *are sitting side by side; a little romantic air is heard in the distance.*

JULIETTE
It's nice here. No one is disturbing us tonight.
GUSTAVE
Yes, it is nice.
JULIETTE
For three days now you've been sad. Are you homesick for Spain?
GUSTAVE
Oh no.
JULIETTE
I'm sorry now I wouldn't work at my Spanish at school. We might have spoken it together. It would have been fun.
GUSTAVE
I only speak a few words myself.
JULIETTE
Do you? That's funny.
GUSTAVE
Yes, it is rather.

(A silence)

JULIETTE
It must be amusing to be a prince.
GUSTAVE
Oh, one gets used to it, you know.

(A silence)

JULIETTE

Don Pedro, what's the matter? We were much friendlier three days ago.

GUSTAVE

Nothing's the matter.

(A pause. LORD EDGARD *crosses the room laden with papers.)*

LORD EDGARD

(muttering)

Though I should die in the endeavor, I'll set my mind at rest. *(He drops his papers. They jump up to help him but he bars their path.)* Don't touch them! Don't touch them! *(He picks up the papers himself and goes out muttering.)* This momentous discovery, if discovery there must be, must be surrounded with the greatest possible precautions.

GUSTAVE

What is he looking for? He's done nothing but ferret about among those old papers since we came here.

JULIETTE

I don't know. He's a little mad. Only he's painstaking as well, you see, so sometimes the results are quite prodigious.

(A LITTLE GIRL *comes in.)*

Oh, here's my little friend.

CHILD

Mademoiselle Juliette, I've picked some daisies for you.

JULIETTE

Thank you, darling.

CHILD

They haven't many petals. Daddy says they aren't the ones that lovers use.

JULIETTE

Never mind.

CHILD

Shall I get some others?

JULIETTE

No. Yes. You're very sweet. *(She kisses her.)* Run away now. *(The* CHILD *goes.* JULIETTE *turns to* GUSTAVE, *shamefaced.)* Do you think it's silly of me?

GUSTAVE

No.

JULIETTE

You said you loved me, Don Pedro, yet for three days now you haven't even looked at me.

GUSTAVE

I do love you, Juliette.

JULIETTE

Then why—?

GUSTAVE

I can't tell you.

JULIETTE

My father wasn't titled, I know, but my aunt is a Lady, and my grandfather was an Honorable.

GUSTAVE

How funny you are. It isn't that.

JULIETTE

Do you think the Duke of Miraflores would consent to my marrying you?

GUSTAVE

(smiling)

I'm sure he would.

JULIETTE

Why do you look so sad then, if you love me and everyone approves?

GUSTAVE

I can't tell you.

JULIETTE

But you do feel, don't you, that our lives might meet and join one day?

GUSTAVE

I would be lying if I told you I felt that.

JULIETTE

(turning away)

That's unkind of you.

GUSTAVE
Careful. Here's your cousin.
JULIETTE
Come into the garden. It's getting dark. I want you to tell me everything.

(*The music fades as they go.* EVA *comes in, followed by* HECTOR, *in a totally different make-up from the one he wore in Act 1.*)

HECTOR
There, you see, they've left us the place to ourselves.
EVA
But I don't in the least need a place to myself—that's the pity of it—I could adapt myself quite easily to a great crowd around us.
HECTOR
How cruel you are!
EVA
I don't like you. I'm cruel to those I dislike. It's in my nature. But on the other hand, when someone appeals to me, there's hardly anything I wouldn't do for him.
HECTOR
(*in despair*)
Why, why can I not manage to appeal to you a second time?
EVA
You know perfectly well why. You're not the same now.
HECTOR
What abominable absent-mindedness! This disguise, I tell you, is the fancy of an aristocrat wearied to death of his own personality, a pastime which affords him an escape from his oppressive self. And for this accursed fancy, must I lose my love?
EVA
I remember with delight a young man who spoke to me in the park. Find him for me. I might still think him lovable.
HECTOR
This is ridiculous! Won't you even tell me if I'm getting warm? At least tell me, did I have a beard when I first appealed to you?

EVA

But it wouldn't amuse me if I were to tell you.

HECTOR

(who has turned away to change his make-up, turns back again wearing a completely new face)

It wasn't like this, I suppose?

EVA

(in a burst of laughter)

No, oh no!

HECTOR

Yet you remember my voice, my eyes?

EVA

Yes, but it isn't enough.

HECTOR

I'm the same height as I was. I'm tall, well built—I assure you I am, very well built.

EVA

I only judge by faces.

HECTOR

This is horrible! Horrible! I'll never find the face that pleased you, ever! It wasn't as a woman, by any chance?

EVA

What do you take me for?

HECTOR

Or as a Chinaman?

EVA

You're evidently out of your mind. I'll wait till you're in it again. *(She goes to sit further off; he starts to follow her and she turns on him.)* No, no, no! For heaven's sake, will you stop following me about and changing your beard every five minutes! You're making my head spin.

HECTOR

(stricken)

And to think that idiot Peterbono keeps on swearing it was as a test pilot!

(LORD EDGARD *crosses the room laden with papers.*)

LORD EDGARD

This is unthinkable! I must find this letter, from which the truth will spring in such a curious fashion. *(He sees HECTOR in his latest make-up, drops his papers and leaps on him.)* At last! The detective from Scotland Yard.

HECTOR

No sir. *(He makes to go.)*

LORD EDGARD

Excellent! The perfect answer. I specially stipulated secrecy. But don't be afraid, I am Lord Edgard in person. You may disclose your identity.

HECTOR

I tell you I'm not the man you're expecting. *(He goes.)*

LORD EDGARD

(following him)
I see! I see! Perfect! You're keeping word for word to my instructions! I stressed the need for caution!

(LADY HURF *enters, holding a magazine.*)

LADY HURF

My little Eva is bored, isn't she?

(EVA *smiles and says nothing. Unseen by* LADY HURF, HECTOR *comes back in another make-up, which he silently shows* EVA. *She shakes her head and he retires, heavy-hearted.* LADY HURF *puts down her magazine with a sigh.*)

LADY HURF

My little Eva is as bored as she can be.

EVA

(with a smile)
Yes, Aunt.

LADY HURF

So am I, darling, very bored.

EVA

Only I'm twenty-five, so you see, it's rather sad.

LADY HURF
You'll see how much sadder it can be when you are sixty.
For you there's always love. As you may guess, it's several years now since I officially renounced it.

EVA
Oh, love!

LADY HURF
What a deep sigh! Since you've been a widow, surely you've had lovers?

EVA
I never had a single one who loved me.

LADY HURF
You want the moon. If your lovers bore you, marry one of them. That will give the others an added fascination.

EVA
Marry? Whom?

LADY HURF
Needless to say these Dupont-Duforts exasperate us both. What about the Spaniards?

EVA
Prince Hector chases after me changing his mustache in the hope of rediscovering the one that first appealed to me.

LADY HURF
Truly appealed to you?

EVA
(smiling)
I don't remember.

LADY HURF
They're curious individuals.

EVA
Why?

LADY HURF
Oh, I don't know. I tell you, I'm an old carcass who doesn't know what to do with herself. I've had everything a woman could reasonably, or even unreasonably, wish for. Money, power, lovers. Now that I'm old, I feel as alone inside my skin as I did as a little girl and they made me face the wall when I'd been naughty. And here's the rub; I know that between that little girl and this old woman, there has been, under the charivari and the noise, nothing but an even greater loneliness.

EVA

I've always thought of you as happy.

LADY HURF

You don't see much, do you? I am playing a part. Only, like everything else I do, I play it well, that's all. Yours now, you play badly, little girl. *(She strokes her hair.)* Child, child, you will always find yourself pursued by desires with changing beards and never have the courage to tell one of them: stay as you are—I love you. Don't think yourself a martyr now. All women are the same. My little Juliette, though, will come through because she is romantic. Her simplicity will save her. It's a favor only granted to few.

EVA

There are some who can love.

LADY HURF

Yes. There are some who love a man. Who kill him with loving, who kill themselves for him, but they are seldom heiresses to millions. *(She strokes her hair again, with a rueful smile.)* Ah, you'll finish up like me, an old woman covered in diamonds who plays at intrigues in an effort to forget that she has never lived. And yet, I'd like to laugh a little. Here am I, playing with fire, and the fire won't even burn my fingers.

EVA

What do you mean, Aunt?

LADY HURF

Shush—here come our marionettes.

(PETERBONO *and* HECTOR *appear in the doorway, preceded by the* MUSICIAN, *and followed almost at once by the* DUPONT-DUFORTS. *They all rush towards the* LADIES, *but it is the* THIEVES *who get there first to kiss their hands.* LADY HURF *jumps to her feet and utters a sudden cry.)*

Ah! I have an idea!

PETERBONO

(frightened, to HECTOR)

She scares the life out of me. Every time she screams like that, I think my beard's loose.

LADY HURF
  Where is Juliette?
EVA
  In the garden, with Prince Pedro. They're inseparable.
PETERBONO
  Ah, the dear children!
LADY HURF
  (calling)
  Juliette!
JULIETTE
  (coming in with GUSTAVE*)*
  Did you want me, Aunt Emily?
LADY HURF
  (drawing her aside)
  Your eyes are red, child. Now mind, you mustn't be unhappy, or I cut the strings and the puppets will fall down.
JULIETTE
  What do you mean, Aunt?
LADY HURF
  If I appear to be talking through my hat, it's precisely so you won't understand me. Come along, both of you. *(She takes them by the waist and leads them into the garden.)* I have an idea to brighten up this evening; I want you to tell me what you think of it.

(They go. The DUPONT-DUFORTS *look at each other.)*

D. D. SENIOR
  After them, sonny. And a hundred times more charm. Remember, it's our future that's at stake.
D. D. JUNIOR
  Yes, Pa.

(Left alone, the three THIEVES *can unbend.)*

HECTOR
  (offering PETERBONO *a box of cigars)*
  Would you care for a cigar?

PETERBONO
(helping himself)
I'm savoring them. They're remarkably good.
HECTOR
(pouring out)
A little brandy?
PETERBONO
Thank you.

(They drink.)

HECTOR
Another cigar, perhaps?
PETERBONO
(grabbing a fistful without more ado)
You're too kind. No, no really, you embarrass me. *(He feels a slight remorse, and takes the box.)* But may I in return press you to a cigar?
HECTOR
(pulling them out of his pockets in handfuls)
Thank you so much. I'm all right just now.

(There is a moment of beatitude and exquisite refinement. They spread themselves blissfully on the sofa. Suddenly, HECTOR *indicates* GUSTAVE, *sitting sad and somber in his corner.)*

PETERBONO
(rises and goes to him)
What's wrong, laddie? Why so sad? Here you are with a wonderful room, lovely food, and a pretty little thing to flirt with, you're playing at princes, and for all that you can manage to be gloomy?
GUSTAVE
I don't want to stay here.

(The other two give a start.)

PETERBONO
Uh? You want to leave?

GUSTAVE
  Yes.
PETERBONO
  Leave here?
GUSTAVE
  Yes—leave here.
PETERBONO
  Hector, the boy's lost his reason.
HECTOR
  What do you want to leave for?
GUSTAVE
  I'm in love with Juliette.
HECTOR
  Well then?
GUSTAVE
  Really in love.
HECTOR
  Well then?
PETERBONO
  Why not? You've never been better off. She takes you for a prince, and rich at that. Go in and win, lad, she's as good as yours.
GUSTAVE
  I don't want to take her, for a day, and then be forced to leave her.
PETERBONO
  You'll have to leave her one day.
GUSTAVE
  And—I'm ashamed of this game I have to play with her. I'd rather go away, now, and never see her again.
HECTOR
  He's out of his mind.
PETERBONO
  Completely.
GUSTAVE
  Look, what are we here for?
PETERBONO
  What are we here for? We're working, lad. It's the height of our season.

GUSTAVE
We're here to do a job. Let's do it then and go.
PETERBONO
And the preliminaries? Have you spared a single thought for the preliminaries?
GUSTAVE
They've gone on long enough, your damn preliminaries.
PETERBONO
I ask you, Hector, isn't it painful? Having to listen to an apprentice teaching us our trade!
HECTOR
Of course we'll do a job; that's what we came for, but have you even the first idea what that job's going to be?
GUSTAVE
Strip the drawing room?
PETERBONO
With carpet bags, eh? Like raggle-taggle gypsies! The lowness, Hector, the abysmal lowness of this youngster's mind! Understand, boy, that we haven't yet decided on the job we're going to do. And if our behavior strikes you, a novice, as peculiar, tell yourself it's because we're in the process of investigating the possibilities of this—establishment.
GUSTAVE
You're lingering on here for the brandy and cigars, and because Hector still hopes he'll get Eva to remember him. But in actual fact you haven't the smallest inkling what you want to do. I may be an apprentice, but I'll tell you something—that's no way to work.
PETERBONO
(*running to* HECTOR)
Hector, hold me back!
HECTOR
(*still blissfully smoking*)
Gustave, don't be difficult. Try to understand.
PETERBONO
Hector, hold me back!
HECTOR
You see, we're wavering—

PETERBONO
  Hold me back, Hector! Hold me back!
HECTOR
  (takes his arm to please him)
  All right, I've got you.
PETERBONO
  (deflated)
  Just as well.
HECTOR
  (to GUSTAVE)
  We're wavering between several possible courses of action—
GUSTAVE
  Which?
HECTOR
  Shall we confide in him, Pete? Is it safe to risk the indiscretion of a youth?
PETERBONO
  (shrugs)
  Oh, confide in him, do. Since we're answerable to him now.
HECTOR
  Right. Tell him your idea first, Pete.
PETERBONO
  After you, Hector, after you.
HECTOR
  (embarrassed)
  Aaaaaaah—well—
GUSTAVE
  You haven't thought of a thing!
HECTOR
  (in righteous rage)
  We haven't thought of a thing?!!! We're wavering between the trick of the dud cheque given in exchange for real jewels on a Saturday, which gives the weekend to make our getaway, or the trick of the good cheque received in exchange for dud jewels under the same conditions. We've also considered giving Lady Hurf some orchids sprayed with ether (taking good care not to smell them ourselves) so as to relieve her of the pearls as soon as she nods off.

PETERBONO
(equally incensed)
Or we might provoke the Dupont-Duforts to a duel! We wound them and then in the commotion we make off with the silver!

GUSTAVE
What if you're the ones to get wounded?

PETERBONO
Impossible!

GUSTAVE
Why?

PETERBONO
(yelling)
I don't know. But it's impossible!

HECTOR
Or again we could make out we'd been robbed and demand a colossal sum for hush-money!

PETERBONO
Pretend we found a pearl in the oysters at dinner, for instance, and swap it for a pearl of Lady Hurf's, or something.

GUSTAVE
There's no "r" in the month.

PETERBONO
I said for instance!

GUSTAVE
In other words you just don't know. Well, I'm going to do the job tonight, and then I'm off.

PETERBONO
Tonight? And why not right away?

GUSTAVE
Yes, why not right away? I want to go away. I want to leave here as soon as possible.

PETERBONO
He'll be the ruin of us! Gustave, think of your poor old mother, who put you in my care!

GUSTAVE
No!

PETERBONO
   I'll put my curse on you! Naturally you don't care a rap if I put my curse on you?
GUSTAVE
   No.
PETERBONO
   (bellowing)
   Hector! Hold me back! *(He seizes* GUSTAVE.*)* Just another fortnight. We'll do the job all right, but it's nice here, and it isn't so often we're in a nice place—
GUSTAVE
   No. I'm too unhappy. *(He goes.)*
HECTOR
   (leaps after him)
   After him! We've got to stop him before he starts a scandal.
PETERBONO
   (calling after him)
   I've got an idea! Suppose we pretended not to know him?

(HECTOR shrugs his shoulders and goes out, refusing even to consider such a solution. Enter LORD EDGARD, *preceded by the* MUSICIAN *playing a succession of tremolos as if he had intimations of a sudden blow of destiny. He is rummaging in his ever-present pile of papers. All of a sudden he utters a loud cry and falls in a dead faint among his scattered letters. The* MUSICIAN *runs for help, emitting isolated notes from his instrument.)*

JULIETTE
   (comes in)
   Uncle, Uncle, what's the matter? *(She props him up on a sofa and feels his hands.)* Ice-cold! What's this? *(She picks up a letter; reads it, and hurriedly thrusts it into her pocket. Running out)* Aunt Emily! Aunt Emily! Come quickly!

(The MUSICIAN *in great confusion multiplies his tragic tremolos.* EVERYONE *comes rushing in, shouting at once:)*

Stroke!
At his age!

No, he's only fainted.
Stand back—give him air.
Get a doctor!
He's coming round.
He's all right now.
A sudden shock.
Perhaps he found what he was looking for.

(The music stops. An enormous silence)

PETERBONO
(breathes to HECTOR *in the silence)*
The chance of a lifetime.
HECTOR
Yes. But what do we do about it?
PETERBONO
Well, nothing, obviously, but it's still the chance of a lifetime.
LORD EDGARD
(sitting up slowly, says in a toneless voice)
My friends, I have a ghastly piece of news for you. The Duke of Miraflores died in Biarritz in 1904.

(EVERYONE *looks at* PETERBONO, *who is very ill at ease. An impish little jig on the clarinet.)*

PETERBONO
Nonsense!
HECTOR
(aside)
Talk about the chance of a lifetime!
PETERBONO
This is a fine time to be funny! Ease over to the window.
LADY HURF
Edgard, are you out of your mind?
LORD EDGARD
No, I tell you. I've found the notification. I knew I'd find it eventually. Ever since the day—*(He searches himself.)* Where is it? This is too much! Where is it! I had it a moment ago! Oh, my goodness! It's gone again.

D. D. SENIOR

Everything is coming to light!

D. D. JUNIOR

We are saved. *(To* PETERBONO, *who is imperceptibly edging towards the window)* Aren't you staying to make sure your host is all right?

PETERBONO

Yes, oh yes!

LADY HURF

Edgard, that's a ridiculous joke to play on the dear Duke.

LORD EDGARD

But, my dear, I guarantee—

LADY HURF

Come along, dear Duke, and show him you aren't dead.

PETERBONO

(uneasy)

No, no. I'm not dead.

LORD EDGARD

Yet I found the notification—

LADY HURF

(pinching him)

Edgard, you're making a mistake, I'm sure. You must apologize.

LORD EDGARD

(rubbing his arm)

Ouch! Why yes, now that you mention it, I think I must have been confusing him with the Duke of Orleans.

LADY HURF

Of course. Shall we call the incident closed?

PETERBONO

(in great relief)

Completely closed.

LADY HURF

Let's go outside, shall we? I've ordered coffee on the terrace. I want to tell you about my idea.

D. D. SENIOR

(in step with her)

I think it's a wonderful idea.

LADY HURF
(exasperated)
Wait a minute, my dear man, I haven't told you yet. Listen. They're holding a Thieves' Carnival tonight at the Casino. We're all going to dress up as thieves and go to it.
D. D. SENIOR *and* JUNIOR
(immediately burst out laughing)
He! He! He! How terribly, terribly amusing!
D. D. SENIOR
(to his son as they go out)
Play up to her, Son. *(Exits.)*
PETERBONO
(furious, as he goes out with HECTOR*)*
I call that in very poor taste, don't you?

*(*JULIETTE *is alone. She stands motionless a moment. The* MUSICIAN *is heard some way away, playing a romantic theme.* JULIETTE *takes out the fatal letter and reads it.)*

JULIETTE
"We regret to announce the sad death of His Serene Highness the Duke of Miraflores y Grandes, Marquis of Priola, Count of Zcstc and Galba. The funeral will take place—" *(She stands in thought a moment.)* If his father isn't the Duke of Miraflores—then who can he be? Why has he taken the car out of the garage? Why is he hiding from me?
CHILD
(entering)
Mademoiselle Juliette, I found some. Look, daisies with lots of petals.
JULIETTE
Haven't you gone to bed yet?
CHILD
I was picking daisies for you.
JULIETTE
Thank you, you're an angel. *(She kisses her.)* His father may be an adventurer, but you see, he loves me. He does love me, doesn't he?

CHILD
  Yes, of course he does.

JULIETTE
  We don't care, do we, if he's an adventurer, or worse? If you were me, you'd love him, wouldn't you, just the same? Only why does that hard look come into his eyes whenever I ask him about himself? If he has designs on me, and he'd be wise to have, because I'm very rich, he should be very pleasant to me all the time—whereas—do you think he prefers Eva? That would be terrible—

CHILD
  I don't know.

JULIETTE
  No, of course you don't. Come along, I'll take you home. Are you afraid of the dark?

CHILD
  No.

JULIETTE
  That's a good girl. Nor am I. There's nothing to be afraid of, you know. Thieves won't hurt you.

(They go.)

(Curtain)

ACT 3

The same set. The room is dark; a FIGURE *is seen moving about with a torch. It is* GUSTAVE, *dressed in dark clothes and wearing a cap. He is silently examining the objects in the drawing room. Suddenly he hears a noise and switches off the torch; a low whistle; two dark* FIGURES *spring up, two torches flash, and focus on* GUSTAVE.

GUSTAVE
Who's that?
FIGURE
Tonight's the night.
GUSTAVE
Peterbono?
FIGURE
No. We're the new ones.
2ND FIGURE
The new bandits.
GUSTAVE
For God's sake, what's going on? *(He draws a revolver.)* Hands up!
D. D. SENIOR
(it is no other)
Ha ha ha! That's good! Where did you get the gun? It's magnificent!
GUSTAVE
Stay where you are or I fire!
D. D. SENIOR
Come quietly! The game's up.
GUSTAVE
Stay where you are, damn you! *(He fires.)*
D. D. SENIOR
(blissfully unaware of his danger)
Oh, well done! Bravo!

GUSTAVE
   What do you mean, bravo? *(He fires again.)*
D. D. JUNIOR
   It's a wonderful imitation! Where on earth did you buy those caps?
GUSTAVE
   For the last time, stay where you are! *(He fires again and shatters a vase, which falls with a terrible clatter.)*
D. D. SENIOR
   Didier, why do you have to be so clumsy!
D. D. JUNIOR
   (protesting in the dark)
   But, Dad, I didn't do it!
D. D. SENIOR
   Well, it can't have been I, can it? I'm in the middle of the room.
D. D. JUNIOR
   But, Dad, so am I!
D. D. SENIOR
   (suddenly anxious)
   Well, then, who broke the vase?
LORD EDGARD
   (enters and switches on the light. He is dressed up as a policeman.)
   Now, now, what is all this noise? How do you like my helmet?
D. D. SENIOR
   (who has got himself up, along with his son, in a terrifying apache disguise)
   Superb, my lord, superb! *(Exit* LORD EDGARD. D. D. SENIOR *goes to* GUSTAVE.*)* My word, I don't think much of your costume. It doesn't come off—it's much too simple. It's the little touches that mean so much. For instance, look, this little scar here.
D. D. JUNIOR
   And the black eye patch.
GUSTAVE
   What are you doing dressed up like that?
D. D. SENIOR
   We're going to the Casino.
D. D. JUNIOR
   To the Thieves' Carnival. And so are you.

GUSTAVE

Oh? Oh yes, of course. So am I.

D. D. SENIOR

Only if I were you, I'd touch up your make-up, my boy. It's a shade too simple. You don't look a bit like a thief.

GUSTAVE

You're quite right. I'll see to it at once. *(He turns at the door.)* Tell me, is everybody going to the Thieves' Carnival?

D. D. SENIOR

Of course; everybody.

GUSTAVE

That's fine. See you later. *(He goes.)*

D. D. SENIOR

Not an ounce of imagination in him, that boy.

D. D. JUNIOR

If the other two have rigged themselves up as absurdly as that, which they probably have, we're well on the way. The girls will have eyes for nobody but us!

D. D. SENIOR

Have you seen the latest batch of telegrams?

D. D. JUNIOR

Yes.

D. D. SENIOR

If we don't leave this house with a fat settlement, it's the colonies for us, I can tell you. Make yourself irresistible, there's a good boy.

D. D. JUNIOR

I'm doing my best, Dad.

D. D. SENIOR

I know you are. You're an honest, conscientious lad, but you mustn't slacken for one moment. The success of this evening's entertainment means a great deal to us. What's more, there's something shady about our rivals which is bound to give rise to a scandal one of these days. It was quite obviously Lady Hurf who made the old duffer keep quiet this afternoon, when he insisted the Duke of Miraflores died in 1904. Keep your eyes open, and be ready for any emergency.

D. D. JUNIOR

We have got to get rid of these gallivanters. It's a matter of life and death.

D. D. SENIOR
   We'll let them dig their own graves, while we'll be more and more agreeable. Ssh! Here comes Lady Hurf.

(*Enter* LADY HURF *and* EVA *as thieves in petticoats. The* DUPONT-DUFORTS *cough desperately to attract attention.*)

LADY HURF
   (*seeing them*)
   Oh, breathtaking! Aren't they, Eva? Breathtaking! Who would have thought they had it in them! What do you think of our guests, Eva?
EVA
   What a spectacular effect! How in the world did you manage it?
D. D. SENIOR
   (*simpering*)
   We're delighted.
D. D. JUNIOR
   That we delight you.
LADY HURF
   They always look as though they're waiting for a tip.
EVA
   Which, in a way, they are.
LADY HURF
   The Duke and his sons are being very slow.
EVA
   I called out to them as I went. They can't manage to dress up as thieves, they said.
LADY HURF
   (*as she goes*)
   Go up and fetch them, gentlemen, if you would be so good, and give them a few wrinkles.
D. D. SENIOR
   Certainly! Certainly! (*Aside to his son*) Let us be pleasant.
D. D. JUNIOR
   Very, very pleasant.

(*They bow themselves out.* JULIETTE *crosses furtively.*)

EVA
Why, you're not dressed!
JULIETTE
I'm going up now.
EVA
You'll make us late.
JULIETTE
Go on ahead. I'll take the two-seater.
EVA
(unexpectedly)
Are you in love with this boy?
JULIETTE
Why do you ask me?
EVA
Yes indeed, why does one ask people if they're in love, when one can tell at a glance, always.
JULIETTE
Can you tell?
EVA
Yes.
JULIETTE
Well, you're wrong. I'm not in love with anyone.

(She turns to go, then EVA calls her back.)

EVA
Juliette! Why do you look upon me as your enemy?
JULIETTE
You are my enemy.
EVA
No, I love you very much. Sit down.
JULIETTE
(turning on her)
You're in love with him too, that's it, isn't it? You're going to take him away from me, and you want to warn me first so that I won't be hurt too much? Why, you've even agreed on that between you, probably. You have, haven't you? Haven't you? For heaven's sake, say something! Why do you smile like that?
EVA
How lucky you are to be in love as much as that.

JULIETTE

You're prettier than I am; you can get any man you want.

EVA

Oh, if I could only bring myself to want one.

JULIETTE

Don't you want him then?

EVA

No, little silly.

JULIETTE

Have you never spoken to him when I wasn't looking?

EVA

Had I ever wanted to I should have found it very difficult. He only has to come near me by accident and you can't take your eyes off us.

JULIETTE

I'm wary. I love him, you see.

EVA

Little gambler!

JULIETTE

You swear you've never set out to attract him?

EVA

I swear.

JULIETTE

Even the day you danced with him twice running?

EVA

The orchestra had struck up a second tango.

JULIETTE

Even the day you went out on the river while the Dupont-Duforts tried to teach me roulette?

EVA

Even then. He looked so sad that I suggested he should row straight back, but we couldn't find you anywhere.

JULIETTE

That day I'm not so sure. He had a strange look in his eyes that evening.

EVA

Because he'd asked me if I thought you cared for him, and I said you were an unpredictable little girl and there was no knowing what went on inside your heart.

JULIETTE

Was that truly why? *(A little pause)* All the same, I do think you might have told him something else.

EVA

Are you satisfied now?

JULIETTE

Did you never try to attract him, not even at the beginning, not even the very first day?

EVA

Not even the first day.

JULIETTE

Yes, then, I'm satisfied.

EVA

Why will you never trust me? I feel like an old woman beside you sometimes.

JULIETTE

You're so much better-looking than I am, so much more poised, more feminine.

EVA

Do you think so?

JULIETTE

It surprises me, you know, in spite of what you say. You must admit that he's a good deal more attractive than Hector, and you don't mind *his* attentions.

EVA

Do you think I couldn't have denied myself a mere flirtation, when I could see you were so much in love?

JULIETTE

That's grand of you.

EVA

Oh no. I wish I could have wanted him so much that I'd have sacrificed you without giving you a moment's thought.

JULIETTE

When you chew your pearls, I know there's something wrong.

EVA

Yes, there's something wrong.

JULIETTE

Yet you look so lovely tonight. You'll have all the men around you at the Ball.

EVA
 All of them.
JULIETTE
 I'm not joking.
EVA
 Nor am I. I'll have them all. And yet it's very sad.
JULIETTE
 Aren't you happy?
EVA
 No.
JULIETTE
 Yet it's so easy. You only need to let yourself go. Why, hardly a moment goes by that one isn't unhappy, yet I think that must be what it means, to be happy.
EVA
 You've always thought me cleverer, stronger, more beautiful than you because the men flocked around me. And yet, you see, there's only you who is alive, in his house—you're the only one perhaps in Vichy, perhaps in the whole world.
JULIETTE
 (smiling, lost in her dream)
 Yes, I am alive.
EVA
 And untouched, and eager to believe—
JULIETTE
 To believe everything.
EVA
 You haven't even a jewel at your throat, not a ring on your finger. You're wearing nothing but this simple linen dress, and you're twenty years old, and you are in love. *(JULIETTE sits motionless, yielding to the unseen with a faint smile. Eva suddenly looks sharply at her.)* Juliette, why are you not in thieves' dress like the rest of us?
JULIETTE
 (bursting with sudden joy)
 Oh, I'm too happy! I haven't the courage to stay beside you who are sad. When I'm a little less happy, I'll think of you, I swear I will! *(She kisses her and runs off.)* Ssh!

EVA
All this mystery! What are you trying to say?

(*Enter* LADY HURF *with the* DUPONT-DUFORTS.)

LADY HURF
We will make a truly magnificent entrance.
D. D. SENIOR
The Spanish gentlemen are ready.
LADY HURF
Do they look all right?
D. D. SENIOR
That's a matter of taste.
D. D. JUNIOR
Anyway, here they come.

(*Enter* PETERBONO *and* HECTOR. *They have contrived to disguise themselves as absolutely ludicrous comic opera bandits. They are greeted with shrieks of laughter.*)

HECTOR
What are they laughing at?
PETERBONO
What do they *think* thieves look like? Don't they ever go to the theater?
LADY HURF
But, my dear Duke, what are you supposed to be?
PETERBONO
A thief.
HECTOR
(*to* EVA)
It wasn't like this, I suppose?
EVA
Heavens, no!
PETERBONO
(*to* LADY HURF)
Don't you like us?
LADY HURF
Enormously!

PETERBONO
   Admit there's something wrong.
LADY HURF
   My dear friend, one really can't expect a Spanish grandee to make much of a showing as a common thief.
PETERBONO
   Well said, eh, Hector? (*Enormous nudgings*)
LADY HURF
   Come along, all of you. The car's waiting. Where is Lord Edgard? Still glued to the mirror, I suppose. Edgard!

(*He appears, still in his own suit, and wearing his police helmet, but he has shaved off his mustache.*)

LORD EDGARD
   Do you think I did well to shave off my mustache?
LADY HURF
   (*without looking at him*)
   I don't know! Come along! To the Carnival!

(*The* MUSICIAN *immediately strikes up a lively quadrille, which the* THIEVES *dance to with the* LADIES, *without the* DUPONT-DUFORTS *getting a look-in. Then follows a piece of extremely vulgar jive, and the* DUPONT-DUFORTS, *making the best of a bad job, finish up by dancing together with tremendous spirit. All dance their way out.*)

D. D. SENIOR
   (*bringing up the rear with his son*)
   Things are getting better and better and better.
D. D. JUNIOR
   Let's be as witty as the very devil!
D. D. SENIOR
   And remember, Didier, twice as nice.

(*The room remains empty for an instant. A* SERVANT *comes in to close the windows and turn out the lights. Another moment of silence, and* GUSTAVE *appears, and listens. The car is heard driving off. He goes right round the room, examining its contents one by one. All of a sudden he flattens himself against the wall.*)

JULIETTE
(enters, dressed for a journey)
Here I am.

GUSTAVE
What are you doing here? Why didn't you go with the others?

JULIETTE
I've come to find you.

GUSTAVE
Get out of here, will you?

JULIETTE
Why are you so harsh with me?

GUSTAVE
Go on, get out!

JULIETTE
I'll go, of course, if you don't want me, only I thought you would want me. What's the matter?

GUSTAVE
I've got a headache. I want to stay here.

JULIETTE
Why this yarn, to me?

GUSTAVE
It isn't a yarn. Get out, will you. Go on, quick march!

JULIETTE
But—you've never spoken to me like this!

GUSTAVE
There's a first time for everything.

JULIETTE
What have I done?

GUSTAVE
Nothing in particular. It's too difficult to explain, and anyway you wouldn't understand.

JULIETTE
But, Señor Pedro—

GUSTAVE
There isn't any Señor Pedro, for a start. My name is Gustave. And secondly, will you please go away?

JULIETTE
And there was I thinking that you loved me—

GUSTAVE
We all make mistakes, don't we?

JULIETTE

But you used to tell me so.

GUSTAVE

I was lying.

JULIETTE

Oh, no! I don't believe it!

GUSTAVE

(going to her purposefully)

Listen, my little pet, I'm telling you to get out of here, double quick.

JULIETTE

Why?

GUSTAVE

You'll see why later on. In the meantime go up to your room and weep over your lost illusions. *(He takes her arm to lead her to the door.)* What are you dressed up in this coat for? What kind of a costume is that meant to be?

JULIETTE

Traveling costume.

GUSTAVE

Traveling costume? You're mad.

JULIETTE

Please don't be angry. I came to find you so we could go away. You told me once we'd go away together.

GUSTAVE

I was joking. Anyway, how do you know I mean to go away?

JULIETTE

I know.

GUSTAVE

You look as though you know a lot of things. Come along with me.

JULIETTE

We might meet one of the servants in the passage. *(He looks at her.)* We'd better not move from here. We'll be quite safe in this room.

GUSTAVE

The Dupont-Duforts must be waiting for you. Go and dress up as a pickpocket like the rest of them.

JULIETTE

Don't pickpockets ever wear traveling clothes?

GUSTAVE
You're not going to travel. You're going to a carnival.
JULIETTE
Once they've stolen, thieves go away as a rule. Why won't you let me come with you, since you're going away?
GUSTAVE
(seizes her)
You know too much, my girl!
JULIETTE
Oh, please, don't hurt me!
GUSTAVE
Don't be afraid. Just a precaution. *(He ties her to a chair, and searches in her handbag.)*
JULIETTE
Oh, don't rob my bag. There's nothing in it. Anyway, I give it to you.
GUSTAVE
Thank you. All I want is a handkerchief.
JULIETTE
What for?
GUSTAVE
To gag you with. *(He finds her handkerchief, which is microscopic.)* I ask you, what's the point of a handkerchief that size? Never mind, mine's clean.
JULIETTE
I'm not going to scream—I swear I won't scream—Señor Pedro! Gustave—Gusta—
GUSTAVE
(he gags her)
There. If you think this a Thieves' Carnival, my lass, you'll have to think again. I'm a real thief, I am. So is Hector, and so is the Duke of Miraflores. Except that those two, they're imbeciles as well. You've built yourself a castle in the air, that's all, and your aunt, who's got bats in her belfry, has built herself a dozen. But let me tell you *I* came to do a job, and I intend to do it.

(She struggles.)

All right. All right. It's no good trying to soften me. I'm used to girls. *(He begins to fill his sacks with the most unlikely objects in the room. After a while he looks at her with misgiving.)* It's not too tight, is it? *(She shakes her head.)* That's a good girl. You see, old girl, I did a bit of billing and cooing, I know, but to be frank I didn't mean a word of it. I had to do it for the job.

(She struggles again.)

Does that upset you? Yes, I know, it isn't very pretty. But then in every trade there's always a little bit like that which isn't very pretty. Apart from that, I'm an honest sort of chap in my own way. I follow my trade, simply, without frills and fancies. Not like Hector and Peterbono. Peterbono has to be the Duke of Miraflores. One must be honest in one's own particular line. Life's not worth living otherwise. *(He takes a furtive look at her.)* You sure it's not too tight? *(He gives her a smile.)* It worries me a bit, playing a trick like that on you, because you know, I lied just now. I am fond of you really. *(He goes back to his work.)* After all, when God invented thieves he had to deprive them of a thing or two, so he took away from them the esteem of honest folk. When you come to think of it, it's not so terrible. It could have been much worse. *(He shrugs, and laughs, without daring to meet her eyes.)* In a little while, you'll see, we'll have forgotten all about it.

(He goes on collecting objects. She struggles again, and he looks at her.)

If there's anything you care for specially, you must tell me. I'll leave it for you, as a souvenir. I mean, I'd *like* to give you a little present. *(She looks at him and he stops in embarrassment.)* Please, don't look at me like that! You're breaking my heart! Can't you see I've got to do this? So just let me get quietly on with my job.

(She moves.)

Are you uncomfortable? You're not choking, are you? Look,

Juliette, if you swear not to call out, I'll take the gag off. Do you swear? *(She nods.)* All right then, I trust you. *(He removes the handkerchief.)* What are you going to say to me, now that you know I'm a real thief? *(He sits down, resigned.)*

JULIETTE

(the moment she is ungagged)
This is absurd! Absolutely absurd. Untie me at once!

GUSTAVE

Oh, no! I'm a good sort, but business is business.

JULIETTE

At least listen to me!

GUSTAVE

What do you want to say?

JULIETTE

You don't imagine I came to find you, wearing my travelling coat, merely in order to sit here like a nincompoop bound and gagged in a chair? Of course I know you're a thief. If you weren't a real thief, I wouldn't have thought you were planning to leave in the middle of the night, would I, seeing you're a guest of my aunt's?

GUSTAVE

What are you talking about?

JULIETTE

I've been telling you over and over again for the last hour. I love you. I saw you take a car out of the garage, I guessed you really were a thief, and that tonight was the night. As I supposed you'd go the moment the job was done, I dressed and got ready to go with you. You don't intend to stay, do you?

GUSTAVE

That's no question to ask a thief.

JULIETTE

Well then, take me with you.

GUSTAVE

But I'm a thief.

JULIETTE

(crying out in exasperation)
I tell you I know you're a thief! There's no need to go on and on about it. I wonder you don't draw attention to yourself. Come along, untie my hands.

GUSTAVE

But, Juliette—

JULIETTE

Untie my hands. They're terribly painful.

GUSTAVE

Do you swear not to run away and raise the alarm?

JULIETTE

Yes, yes, I swear. Oh, how stupid you are!

GUSTAVE

I trust you, of course, but I just don't understand.

(He unties her. She immediately powders her face, and then gets up with determination.)

JULIETTE

We've wasted at least a quarter of an hour. Make haste. It would not do to get caught now. Have you enough with this lot? *(She indicates the sacks with her foot.)*

GUSTAVE

What are you doing?

JULIETTE

Really, I shall begin to wonder if you're all there soon. Yes, or no, do I appeal to you?

GUSTAVE

Oh·yes, but—

JULIETTE

Good. That's the main thing. Now, listen to me. Gustave, if you like me, I love you and I want to be your wife—oh, don't worry, if you're afraid of awkward questions at the Registry Office, we won't get properly married. There. Now then— *(She picks up one of the sacks.)* Is this all we're taking with us?

GUSTAVE

(snatching the sack from her)

Juliette, no! You don't know what you're doing! You mustn't come with me. What would become of you?

JULIETTE

I'd help you. I'd keep a look-out, and I'd whistle when I saw someone coming. I can whistle beautifully. Listen—*(She gives an earsplitting whistle.)*

GUSTAVE

(terrified)

Ssssh! For heaven's sake!

(They listen for a moment.)

JULIETTE

(humbly)

I'm sorry. What a fool I am. Take me away. I'll whistle very quietly, I promise you, and then only when it's absolutely necessary.

GUSTAVE

Juliette, this is only a whim. You're playing with me. It's unkind of you.

JULIETTE

Oh no, you mustn't think that! Never think that! I love you.

GUSTAVE

But do you know the dangers of this kind of life?

JULIETTE

Yes. Kiss me.

GUSTAVE

Juliette, it's goodbye to your tranquillity.

JULIETTE

It was on the way to killing me, my tranquillity. Kiss me.

GUSTAVE

But you're happy here, Juliette. You don't know what it means to be on the run, to be afraid. You're used to luxury.

JULIETTE

Why, we're rich! Look at this! If it worries you, we won't steal so long as the police are out looking for me.

GUSTAVE

Thieves aren't wealthy folk. You get precious little for what you sell.

JULIETTE

Well, we'll be poor then. Kiss me. *(They join in a long kiss. Radiantly)* I am so happy. Now, hurry. *(She stops.)* Why, you haven't taken the little Fragonards. You're mad, my darling, they're the most valuable things in the house. *(She runs to take them down.)* And the little enamels. *(She rummages in the sack.)* Leave the candlesticks. They're imitation bronze. You see how useful I am to you. I shall be such a help, you'll see. Kiss me.

GUSTAVE

(taking her in his arms again)
My little robber girl.

(They go.)

(Curtain)

ACT 4

In the conservatory, an hour later. The CLARINET, *which has begun by playing the Carnival theme, takes it up again in a nostalgic manner. The* CHARACTERS *wander in single file, heads hanging, and sit down, vexed and dejected.*

LADY HURF

It's positively absurd.

HECTOR

I do think they might have let us in.

LADY HURF

Too absurd. Fancy writing the title of the Carnival in microscopic lettering. Economy is an absolute obsession with the French.

LORD EDGARD

We were turned away in the most humiliating fashion.

EVA
> What do you expect, Uncle? I can quite see that our attire alarmed them.

LADY HURF
> A Carnival of Leaves! The idiocy of it!! A Carnival of Leaves!

D. D. SENIOR
> What puzzles me is how you could confuse a Carnival of Leaves with a Carnival of Thieves.

LADY HURF
> You should have consulted the notices yourself then, my good friend, if your eyesight is so sharp.

D. D. SENIOR
> But dammit—

D. D. JUNIOR
> Don't be rash, Dad.

LADY HURF
> To begin with, it's thanks to your disguises that our party was shown the door.

PETERBONO
> I should definitely have got in, for one. It's a funny thing. They quite thought I was going as a palm tree.

LADY HURF
> Of course, but for them we should all have been admitted. What abominable taste! Look at them, will you? They might be a couple of pantomine buccaneers.

D. D. SENIOR
> I should have thought for a Carnival of Thieves—

LADY HURF
> Leaves! Leaves! Leaves! Are you going to spend the rest of the evening calling it a Carnival of Thieves?

D. D. JUNIOR
> Keep calm, Father. *(To* LADY HURF*)* We are dreadfully sorry.

D. D. SENIOR
> *(abjectly)*
> We'll never do it again.

LADY HURF
> A fine time to say so!

LORD EDGARD
> Could we not perhaps spend the evening as we are, among ourselves, so as not to waste our efforts altogether?

LADY HURF

Edgard, what an insane idea. Let us go up and change. We'll play yet one more stupefying game of bridge.

(She sighs and the GUESTS *sigh with her.)*

LORD EDGARD

If I'd known we were going to play bridge, I would have preferred to keep my mustache.

LADY HURF

(distractedly)

So would I! *(To* PETERBONO, *on her way out)* My dear Duke, can you forgive me for this wasted evening?

PETERBONO

(nudging HECTOR*)*

No evening is ever really wasted.

LADY HURF

Another time I'll be more careful when I read the posters, and more discriminating in my choice of company.

(She goes with EVA *and* LORD EDGARD.*)*

PETERBONO

Ring. Pearls.

HECTOR

Pocketbook.

PETERBONO

Perfect.

(The DUPONT-DUFORTS *find themselves alone.)*

D. D. SENIOR

Things are going badly.

D. D. JUNIOR

Very badly.

D. D. SENIOR

These gay dogs are here on the same errand as we are, that's quite obvious, but everything is going their way and nothing is coming ours.

D. D. JUNIOR
(looking in a mirror)
Yet we achieved a really lovely make-up.
D. D. SENIOR
Not for a Carnival of Leaves.
D. D. JUNIOR
Fancy organizing a Carnival of Leaves!
D. D. SENIOR
Fancy, what's more, reading "Carnival of Thieves" when it's down in black and white on all the posters "Carnival of Leaves." The old goose!
D. D. JUNIOR
(catching sight of the drawing room through the open window)
Daddy!
D. D. SENIOR
What is it?
D. D. JUNIOR
Look at the wall!
D. D. SENIOR
What about the wall?
D. D. JUNIOR
The Fragonards!
D. D. SENIOR
If you think at a time like this I feel like going into ecstasies over a lot of paintings!
D. D. JUNIOR
Daddy, the Fragonards aren't on the wall. *(He rushes into the room.)*
D. D. SENIOR
Well?
D. D. JUNIOR
(from the room)
Nor are the enamels! The bronze candlesticks are missing! And the snuff boxes. All the drawers are open! *(Rushing out again)* Daddy, there's been a burglary!
D. D. SENIOR
Let's go. They'll think we did it.

D. D. JUNIOR

Don't be ridiculous! We were at the carnival with everybody else! Daddy! There's been a robbery here!

D. D. SENIOR

(who has been to make sure)

You're absolutely right. There's been a robbery. But what are you so pleased about? That won't set our affairs to rights.

D. D. JUNIOR

Don't you understand? There's been a robbery while we were at the Casino. Don't you see suspicion can only fall on the one person who made himself conspicuous by his absence? Now then, who, I ask you, made himself conspicuous by his absence?

D. D. SENIOR

Young Pedro?

D. D. JUNIOR

Of course! Young Pedro.

D. D. SENIOR

In that case, surely the others would be his accomplices.

D. D. JUNIOR

They are his accomplices. They came with us to allay suspicion, that's quite clear. But now you may be sure they're gone, or will have before very long.

D. D. SENIOR

Didier, you're magnificent! You do my old heart good. Kiss me, son! At last they are unmasked. They're done for, laddie, and our affairs have never looked so promising.

D. D. JUNIOR

We must clinch matters. There's to be no escape and no denial. We must telephone the police at once. *(He picks up the receiver.)* Give me the police, please. And hurry!

D. D. SENIOR

(trundling round the drawing room and bellowing)

The Fragonards! The enamels! The candlesticks! The snuff boxes! Two drawers burst open! Magnificent!

D. D. JUNIOR

Hallo? Is that the police station? This is the Villa des Boyards. A serious robbery has just taken place. Yes, the thieves are still on the premises. You'll catch them red-handed if you hurry. Hurry!

D. D. SENIOR
(coming back radiant)
Come to your father, laddie!

(They embrace.)

D. D. JUNIOR
Let's call the company and confront the rascals! Hey there! Come quickly, everybody!

D. D. SENIOR
Hey there! Hey!

LORD EDGARD
(entering; he, and likewise the others when they come down, have all changed back into their usual clothes)
What's the matter?

D. D. JUNIOR
There's been a burglary!

LORD EDGARD
That's no surprise to anybody in these troubled times. Where?

D. D. JUNIOR
Here!

LORD EDGARD
Here!

D. D. SENIOR
(breathless with excitement)
Here! Here in this very room!

LORD EDGARD
In the drawing-room? What did they take?

D. D. SENIOR
(like a street hawker)
Fragonards! Enamels! Snuff boxes! Candlesticks! Drawers! Come in and see! Come and see!

(LORD EDGARD *goes into the room, comes back and staggers into an armchair.*)

LORD EDGARD
Terrible! Terrible! I had an idea this would happen.

D. D. SENIOR
D. D. JUNIOR } So had we!

LORD EDGARD
  Do you know who did it?
D. D. SENIOR
  We have an idea!
LORD EDGARD
  So have I! *(Enter* EVA*)* My child, we've just been burgled!
EVA
  What?
D. D. SENIOR
  (off again)
  The Fragonards! The enamels! The candlesticks! The snuff boxes!
EVA
  I'm glad about the candlesticks, they were appalling. But it's a shame about the Fragonards.
HECTOR
  (enters triumphantly in a new make-up)
  Eva, this time I've got it!
EVA
  No.
LORD EDGARD
  (leaping on him)
  At last! The detective! My dear fellow, you're in the nick of time. A serious robbery has just been committed. We suspect some impostors whom we are entertaining at the moment, owing to a curious fancy of my cousin's. Kindly arrest them at once, my dear fellow.
EVA
  What's come over you, Uncle? That's Prince Hector. Hector, do take off that beard.
HECTOR
  (modestly, as he reveals himself)
  Yes sir, it's me.
LORD EDGARD
  (in a sudden rage)
  How much longer do you intend to make a fool of me, young man?
HECTOR
  (backing imperceptibly towards the door)
  But your lordship, I'm not making a fool of you, really.

LORD EDGARD
I can take a joke, in doubtful taste though it is with a man of my years, but don't repeat it a dozen times a day!

HECTOR
(nearing the door)
But I'm not making a fool—

(He bumps into the DUPONT-DUFORTS, *who have cut off his retreat.)*

D. D. JUNIOR
Oh no.

D. D. SENIOR
Of course you're not making a fool of him. Don't go. Everything will be all right.

HECTOR
Look here, what's going on? Am I under suspicion?

EVA
Gentlemen, will you please leave His Highness alone?

HECTOR
I should think so. Why, it's absurd, isn't it, Eva?

LADY HURF
(entering with PETERBONO)
What is all this shouting? I've never heard such a commotion!

PETERBONO
We simply can't hear ourselves speak!

LORD EDGARD
It's terrible! There's been a dreadful robbery! I had my suspicions all along. I told you he died in 1904! I told you they were all impostors!

D. D. SENIOR
(at the same time)
The Fragonards! The enamels! The snuff boxes! The candlesticks! The drawers!

LADY HURF
One at a time, please! I don't know what you're talking about. First of all I must sit down. I'm worn out.

(During the ejaculations of the OTHERS, *and the silence which follows,* HECTOR *is desperately indicating to* PETERBONO *that they must be off.* PETERBONO *thinks his cuff links are undone, his tie crooked or that something is hanging down. He brushes himself, looks in the mirror, still fails to understand, and finally shrugs his shoulders and gives up.)*

LADY HURF
Now. Tell me all about it.

PETERBONO
(engagingly)
Splendid idea. Tell us all about it.

LORD EDGAR
(before they stop him)
Didn't I tell you he died in—

D. D. SENIOR
(at the same time)
Everything! Everything! The Fragonards! The—*(They look at each other and stop dead.)*

EVA
There's been a burglary.

LADY HURF
A burglary?

EVA
Yes. While we were out the enamels were stolen, and the Fragonards and believe it or not, the candlesticks.

LADY HURF
Oh good. They were imitation.

LORD EDGAR
I told you so! I told you so!

LADY HURF
One of the servants, I expect. Are they all here?

EVA
I don't know.

D. D. SENIOR
We must inform the police.

LADY HURF
No.

D. D. SENIOR
What do you mean, no?

LADY HURF
No, I tell you. I will not have policemen in my house.
D. D. JUNIOR
But we've already telephoned, your ladyship.
LADY HURF
My good sirs, have you completely forgotten your manners? I beg you to remember that this is my house. You appear to have abandoned every vestige of constraint these last few days.
D. D. JUNIOR
But we—
D. D. SENIOR
You see, we—
LADY HURF
Eva, ring through at once and tell them not to come.
D. D. SENIOR
Too late. They're bound to be on the way.

(All this time PETERBONO *and* HECTOR *have been quietly edging towards the door. When* LADY HURF *tells* EVA *to call off the police, they stop, still hopeful. At these last words, they make a frenzied dash for it.)*

Look! They're getting away!
D. D. JUNIOR
This is too much! We'll save you, whether you like it or not! Hands up!
D. D. SENIOR
Hands up!

(They cover the THIEVES *with their revolvers.)*

LADY HURF
Gentlemen, I am mistress in this house! I order you to put away those firearms!
D. D. JUNIOR
No!
D. D. SENIOR
No. You'll thank us for it later on.

LADY HURF
> Eva, I'm going to have hysterics! Call the servants! Emile! Here, quickly! Joseph! Help!

(Enter POLICE, *during her cries.)*

POLICEMAN
> Here we are! Horace, you take the fat one! *(They have seen these two horrible bandits pointing their guns at the gentry. Without a moment's indecision, they hurl themselves on the* DUPONT-DUFORTS.) Aha, me beauties! We've got you!

D. D. SENIOR and JUNIOR
> *(backing away)*
> But—but— We didn't do anything! No, no, not us! Not us! Quite the reverse! We're the ones who telephoned! This is preposterous! It's they!

(They collide as they retreat, try to escape the other way and collide again, in the course of a droll little ballet which culminates in their capture.)

POLICEMEN
> *(hoisting them on their shoulders with the showmanship of circus acrobats)*
> Upsadaisy! *(To* HECTOR*)* If you'd like to give us a hand, sir, by taking the trouble to open the door, sir, it'd be much appreciated.

HECTOR
> No trouble. Absolutely no trouble at all.

(The POLICEMEN *carry off the* DUPONT-DUFORTS *despite their agonizing protestations.)*

LORD EDGARD
> *(wildly)*
> But, my dear—

LADY HURF
> *(sternly)*
> Edgard! Be quiet.

D. D. SENIOR
(yelling in vain as he is borne away)
For God's sake, say something! Tell them! Tell them!

D. D. JUNIOR
(as he whirls past her)
Mademoiselle Eva!

(They have gone, played out by their own little melody.)

LADY HURF
(calmly)
There! That's a relief. Three whole weeks those folk have been here, and I hadn't a notion how to get rid of them.

LORD EDGARD
(overcome by so many emotions, falls semi-conscious into an armchair)
When I think I came here to cure my liver trouble!

LADY HURF
Eva dear, run up and get your uncle his smelling salts. (EVA *goes.* LADY HURF *looks at* PETERBONO, *who ever since the arrest of the* DUPONT-DUFORTS *has been choking in the grip of irrepressible hysteria.)* My dear man, save your laughter. I know perfectly well you are the real thief. *(He stops dead. She feels in his pocket.)* Give me back my pearls. You haven't been very clever.

PETERBONO
What do you mean?

LADY HURF
Have you a lot of luggage? How long will it take you to pack?

PETERBONO
(piteously)
Not long.

LADY HURF
Then I advise you to make the greatest possible haste upstairs.

PETERBONO
Yes.

HECTOR
(enters; superbly)
There. The rascals are in good hands, your Ladyship. (PETERBONO *coughs.*) Father dear, are you not feeling well?

LADY HURF
No, he's not feeling at all well. I think you had better both go up to your rooms.

HECTOR
Really, Father? Where's the trouble exactly?

LORD EDGARD
(*himself once more*)
I told you the Duke of Miraflores died in 1904!

LADY HURF
I knew it long ago, my dear.

HECTOR
(*still not understanding* PETERBONO's *desperate dumbshow, says waggishly*)
Ha! ha! ha! Still the same old joke, eh?

LADY HURF
The Duke died in my arms, or near enough. So that I knew quite well whom we were dealing with. Only you see, my poor old Edgard, I was so very, very bored.

HECTOR
(*finally going to* PETERBONO)
What's the matter, for heaven's sake?

PETERBONO
Idiot! I've been trying to tell you for the last half-hour. The game's up, but she's letting us go free.

HECTOR
Uh? Don't be silly, they've arrested the others.

LADY HURF
(*going to them with a smile*)
You don't, I'm sure, want to await the visit of the inspector of police, gentlemen.

HECTOR
This is unthinkable! What are we accused of? We were with you the whole evening!

PETERBONO
Don't be canny. Come on.

HECTOR
My dear father, I don't know what you're talking about. Madam, we are here as your guests, and this robbery is no reason to treat us, the Miraflores y Grandes, in this cavalier fashion.

PETERBONO

(unable to suppress a giggle, despite the tragic situation)
Miraflores y Grandes! Oh, my Lord! You're off your head, old chap. Come on.

LADY HURF

Go along, sir, do as everyone advises you.

HECTOR

I will not tolerate this attitude. *(To* PETERBONO*)* Play up, will you?

EVA

(coming back)
Here are the salts.

HECTOR

I will not tolerate this attitude. Because if you consider our presence undesirable, I laugh to scorn—do you hear, to scorn, your utterly unfounded and insulting allegations. There's someone here, I know, who will think my presence far from undesirable. Eva, Eva my darling, I've found my face at last! *(He turns away and rapidly recreates the appearance he had in the first scene.)*

PETERBONO

Hector, stop playing about. The police are on their way.

HECTOR

(making up)
Let me alone. We're saved, I tell you!

LADY HURF

(sits down, dispirited)
Edgard, if this headstrong child falls in love with him again, the situation is absolutely hopeless.

LORD EDGARD

I have not the faintest idea of what is going on. What is he doing? Is this another piece of comicality? He goes very much too far, that boy.

HECTOR

(turning round triumphantly)
Eva beloved! It *was* like this, wasn't it?

(A silence. EVA *looks at him. The* OTHERS *hold their breath.)*

EVA
(calmly breaking the tension)
Yes, that's how you were. Only I must have looked at you too hastily, I think, because now you don't appeal to me at all.
LADY HURF
(leaping up)
Heaven be praised! Now, off with you! Quickly, off with you!
HECTOR
But, Eva, listen! Eva, I can't believe—
PETERBONO
(in a whisper)
Hurry, idiot, hurry! She's taken back the necklace, but I've still got the ring.

(They go with great dignity. A gay little tune signals their departure.)

LADY HURF
(watching them go with a tender little smile)
Poor old fellow. I let him keep the ring. They stayed here a full fortnight after all, because of me. We haven't any right to make them waste their time. I imagine it's a trade which can't bring in all that much.
LORD EDGARD
What I don't fathom is where the boy comes in. *(The TWO WOMEN look at him in sudden anguish.)* The boy, the young one, who was so pleasant, you remember?
EVA
Juliette! Where's Juliette?
LADY HURF
Juliette! She didn't come to the Carnival. Isn't she upstairs? Perhaps in the morning room? Or in the garden?
EVA
I'll run and see. Oh, it's inconceivable.
LORD EDGARD
What is inconceivable? I don't understand, quite. (LADY HURF *drops onto the sofa, and plays nervously with her pearls.*) Why do you look so tragic? It's all over now, isn't it?

LADY HURF

No, stupid, it is not all over. This boy has carried off Juliette along with the pictures in the drawing room. How many times did I tell you to bestir yourself and take precautions if we didn't want disaster?

EVA

(coming back)
She's not upstairs. The servants are combing the grounds.

LADY HURF

It's horrible!

LORD EDGARD

Juliette, our little Juliette. Is it possible? Can she have been stolen?

EVA

Yes.

LORD EDGARD

But she's a big girl now. She could have defended herself. Or called for help. The house is overrun with staff.

LADY HURF

Can't you understand? She's in his power! He's bewitched her. He'll make her steal for him, or walk the streets!

LORD EDGARD

The streets. *(It dawns on him.)* The streets!

(He staggers under the blow. The CLARINET *plays an air heavy with tragedy. The three of them lapse into pensive and painful silence. The* CLARINET *resumes its tragic theme with an overtone of mockery, and then leads into the romance which is indeed altogether fitting at this moment, for* GUSTAVE *enters on tiptoe, laden with so many things that he cannot see where he is going. He is carrying* JULIETTE, *who is asleep, and his various sacks. He crosses the drawing room, unseen by anybody; suddenly he bumps into an armchair. He drops his sacks with a clatter, and startles the others, who see him and cry out: "He's killed her!"* GUSTAVE, *terrified, makes to put* JULIETTE *down on the sofa, but at the cries she awakens and clings to him.)*

JULIETTE

No, no, no! Why did you bring me back? No, he's not to go! If he goes I'm going with him!

LADY HURF

Juliette!

LORD EDGARD

My child.

JULIETTE

(screaming through a flood of tears)

Yes, you despise him, I know, but I love him. Don't try to tell me anything—I want to go with him because I love him. Don't say a word, I'd only hate you for it. Gustave, Gustave, why did you bring me back? *(He struggles and tries to run away but she clutches him.)* No. Stay here, or let me come with you. Why did you bring me back? Was I too stupid for you? Too naive? Is it because I fell asleep beside you in the car that you don't want me? It's true one doesn't as a rule doze off the night of one's elopement, but I was tired, my darling. I'm not used to staying up so late. *(She hides her head in his arms.)*

LORD EDGARD

What is she saying?

LADY HURF

(moved)

Do be quiet! It's very lovely what she is saying.

JULIETTE

(turning to them like a little fury, without letting go of GUSTAVE*)*

No, no, I'm not ashamed! I'm not ashamed! You can say anything you like, I'll never be ashamed! I love him. I want him for my lover, since you will never let him be my husband. Look. I'm going to kiss him now in front of you.

(She throws her arms around his neck. He holds back for a second, then as he sees her tousled hair and her radiant tear-stained face, he too forgets the OTHERS.*)*

GUSTAVE

I love you, Juliette.

JULIETTE

You see, we're kissing here, in front of them. *(They kiss.)*

LORD EDGARD

(adjusting his pince-nez)
Why, they're kissing.

LADY HURF

That's right. They're kissing. What about it? Did you never do as much? *(She contemplates them, entranced.)* How enchanting they are!

LORD EDGARD

Aren't they? Do you remember, Emily?

LADY HURF

They make a delightful couple, don't they?

LORD EDGARD

(lost in his memories)
Delightful. Do you remember? The Crystal Palace?

LADY HURF

She's nearly as tall as he is. He is adorable. Look at the breeding in that profile. The exquisite shyness and yet the strength of it. He will make a fairy-tale husband for our terrible, gentle little Juliette. *(She stops.)* Edgard, what are you talking me into? He's a thief!

LORD EDGARD

(smiling)
Ah yes, a thief.

LADY HURF

Well then, it's out of the question. He must go at once.

(The CLARINET stops from shock.)

LORD EDGARD

(crestfallen)
But—but they love each other.

LADY HURF

I know they love each other. But it's the only thing to do. Absolutely the only thing. She simply cannot marry a boy who has neither a father nor a mother.

LORD EDGARD

Ah! *(He thinks furiously for a moment, then cries suddenly.)* Wait a minute! Wait a minute!

(GUSTAVE and JULIETTE, startled by his cry, come out of their embrace. LORD EDGARD runs out like one demented.)

LADY HURF
  Where do you suppose he's going?
JULIETTE
  I'll never leave him, never, never, never.
GUSTAVE
  (holding her to him, says by way of explanation)
  We love each other.

  (The CLARINET *plays a little supplication.)*

LADY HURF
  I gather so. But there it is. You're nothing but a nobody, if not worse. I'm afraid you'll have to go.

  (Another entreaty from the CLARINET*)*

JULIETTE
  If he goes I go with him.
LADY HURF
  This time we will be here to stop you. *(The* CLARINET *screams in heart-rending imploration.* LADY HURF *turns furiously on the* MUSICIAN.*)* As for you, my good sir, you're beginning to get on my nerves! Go away! *(The* CLARINET *attempts a musical protest.)* Get out of here this instant!

  (She drives him out. Pathetically the MUSICIAN *goes, expressing his despair on his instrument.* LORD EDGARD *returns like a meteor carrying ribbons, medals and a photograph. He marches threateningly over to* GUSTAVE.*)*

LORD EDGARD
  You are twenty years old, are you not?
GUSTAVE
  Yes.
LORD EDGARD
  Right. *(He looks at the photograph, looks at it a second time, backs, screwing up his eyes in the manner of a painter scrutinizing a picture.)* Hold your head up. Fine. Open your shirt. Fine. Now for the mark behind the ear. *(He turns back his ear.)* Fine. *(He shows him the medal.)* Do you recognize this medal?

GUSTAVE

No.

LORD EDGARD

(throwing it away)

Never mind. You are my son! My son who was stolen from me at a tender age. *(He falls into his arms.)*

LADY HURF

Edgard, have you taken leave of your senses?

GUSTAVE

(furiously)

Let me go, sir. I don't know what you're talking about. *(To* JULIETTE*)* What's the matter with him?

LORD EDGARD

(to LADY HURF*)*

Do you deny that a son was stolen from me at a tender age? *(To* GUSTAVE.*)* Do you deny that you are uncertain of your paternal origins? Yes, yes, you are my son, my own son, my beloved son! *(He falls on his neck again.)*

JULIETTE

Isn't that lucky! Gustave, isn't that lucky!

GUSTAVE

(freeing himself roughly)

No, it won't work.

LORD EDGARD

What won't work?

GUSTAVE

I'm quite sure I'm not your son.

LORD EDGARD

So I shall have waited twenty years for Heaven to give me back my child, and now when Heaven at last sees fit to give him back to me, it is this very child who refuses to acknowledge his own father!

GUSTAVE

No. It's all a scheme because you can see your little girl is in love with me, but I'm sorry, I can't accept.

LADY HURF

That's very honorable of him.

LORD EDGARD

This is horrible! Horrible! My son denies me! *(He prances with rage.)*

GUSTAVE

No, I can't accept. It's nice of you to do it, very nice of you. But I can't. I'm not one of your sort.

LADY HURF

It is really unfortunate that this boy should be the only one among us to suffer from class-consciousness.

LORD EDGARD

I am abominably humiliated. Such contempt from my own son! I shall crumple up with sorrow. *(He does in fact crumple up with sorrow on the nearest sofa.)* Here I am, crumpled up. How much longer do I have to stay crumpled?

LADY HURF

Couldn't you see your way to accepting? You're making your father very unhappy.

GUSTAVE

How can I! I haven't any reason—

JULIETTE

Oh, but you have! Come into the garden as you did before. I'm going to explain all your reasons to you. Do come, please. Come anyway. You haven't anything to lose after all, by coming into the garden. *(She drags him out.)*

LADY HURF

(as soon as they're gone)

Edgard, it's not true! You never had a son stolen from you at a tender age!

LORD EDGARD

No, it isn't true. It's a picture I cut out of a magazine.

LADY HURF

So you've acted like an imbecile for over fifty years and yet you had it in you to think of that all by yourself.

EVA

How happy they are going to be.

LADY HURF

(dreamily)

Yes.

EVA

And I shall continue to play the young and charming widow who is always such a great success.

LADY HURF
My poor Eva, faith is a gift, alas, and there's no learning it. It's over, our fine escapade. Here we are alone again, like bobbing corks. It's only for those who have played it with all the zest of youth that the comedy is a success, and only then because they were playing their youth, a thing which succeeds always. They were not even conscious of the comedy.

(Enter a BEARDED GENTLEMAN.)

BEARDED GENTLEMAN
I am from Scotland Yard.

LORD EDGARD
(lets out a roar, leaps onto him and pulls his beard)
Oh no, it won't work this time!

DETECTIVE
Stop it! You're hurting me!

LORD EDGARD
(greatly astonished)
What! Do you mean it's your own?

DETECTIVE
Of course it's my own!

LORD EDGARD
Then you really are the detective I sent for?

DETECTIVE
I've just said so, haven't I?

LORD EDGARD
Well, we don't need you any more. The entertainment is over.

DETECTIVE
(blithely)
In that case—

(He pulls his clarinet out of his pocket—for it is none other than the MUSICIAN—and strikes up a quick-step which does duty as a finale. The CHARACTERS come in through all the doors, dancing and exchanging beards.)

(Curtain)

for discussion

ACT 1

1. Reread the opening stage directions and the first scene between Hector and Eva. Explain how the playwright succeeds in engaging your attention at the very outset of his play.
2. How successful are Hector, Peterbono, and Gustave as thieves? Explain your answer.
3. What impression do you get of Lady Hurf from her first conversations with Juliette and with Lord Edgard?
4. Describe the Dupont-Duforts. Note that D. D. Senior often begins a sentence which D. D. Junior finishes. Why does the playwright have them speak in this manner?
5. Compare the behavior of the Dupont-Duforts with the behavior of the three thieves. What comment on conventional morality is the playwright making through this contrast?
6. When Lady Hurf greets the "Duke of Miraflores," Lord Edgard protests, "But my dear—This is insane. Come now, think back—." But Lady Hurf pays no attention to him and invites the Duke to stay at her villa. Explain why she acts as she does. Cite specific lines to support your answer.
7. Lady Hurf asks the Duke several questions about "common acquaintances." Describe how Peterbono arrives at his answers. Do you think Lady Hurf is fooled by them?
8. Several times during the act, Gustave disagrees with Peterbono. Point out these times. Explain how Gustave succeeds in beating Peterbono at his own game at the end of the act.
9. What is the function of the lone musician on the stage? Cite the occasions on which he plays his clarinet. In each instance, explain why his music is dramatically appropriate.
10. In the first scene between Hector and Eva, the playwright leads you to expect one thing and then gives you the opposite of what you expected. Where else does he do this? Explain why this technique is effective.

ACT 2

1. Explain why the playwright introduces a little girl into the opening scene. Of what significance is the fact that she speaks to Juliette only?
2. Contrast the scene between Eva and Hector with the one between Juliette and Gustave. Why is Eva no longer interested in Hector? Explain how Hector seeks to win her back.
3. How does the playwright prepare you, during the opening scenes, for Lord Edgard's revelation later in the act?
4. Explain what Lady Hurf means when she says to Eva, "I am playing a part. Only, like everything else I do, I play it well, that's all." Who else in this play is "playing a part"? Who is not? Defend your answer.
5. According to Lady Hurf, what is the difference between Eva and Juliette? What fate does she predict for each of them?
6. Cite specific lines which show that Lady Hurf knows that the "Spanish nobles" are impostors.
7. Why does Gustave plan to leave the villa as soon as possible? What reasons do Hector and Peterbono give to persuade him to stay? Basing your answer on this scene, explain what you think is the essential difference between Gustave and his two companions.
8. Why does Juliette hide the letter which Lord Edgard has discovered? What does she learn from this letter? What else leads her to conclude that Gustave is not whom he claims to be?
9. Why does the playwright have the child come in again at the end of the act? Explain the irony of Juliette's last lines, "There's nothing to be afraid of, you know. Thieves won't hurt you."

ACT 3

1. The opening of Act 3 describes a highly ironic situation. What is it? What does D. D. Senior say to Gustave which is especially ironic? Explain.
2. Explain what Lady Hurf means when she says that D.D. Senior and D. D. Junior "always look as though they're waiting for a tip." Note the stage directions on p. 504. How does the playwright make the Dupont-Duforts appear ridiculous?
3. In the scene between Juliette and Eva, the differences between the two sisters is made further apparent. What are they? In light of these differences, explain why each of them is appropriately named.

4. Eva says to Juliette, ". . . there's only you who is alive, in this house—you're the only one perhaps in Vichy, perhaps in the whole word." What does she mean? Cite the lines in Act 2 in which Lady Hurf expressed a similar idea about Juliette.
5. Afraid that Juliette will call for help, Gustave ties her to a chair and gags her. What does he say and do afterwards which reveals his tender feelings toward her?
6. What does Gustave mean when he says to Juliette, "One must be honest in one's own particular line. Life's not worth living otherwise." To which of Lady Hurf's ideas is this one similar? Which characters in this play are "honest"? Which are not?
7. What does Juliette do upon being untied? How is this action characteristic of her? How is it in keeping with the tone of the whole scene?
8. Gustave says that, as a robber's wife, Juliette will have to give up her "tranquillity." What is Juliette's answer? Explain.

ACT 4

1. When the Dupont-Duforts discover the robbery, they are jubilant. Explain why.
2. Describe the reaction of Lord Edgard to the news of the robbery. How do Eva and Lady Hurf react? In what ways are these reactions consistent with their characters?
3. Explain why Hector constantly appears before Eva in different costumes. Which character is most baffled by these disguises?
4. Why do the police mistake the Dupont-Duforts for the bandits? Do you think Lady Hurf was right not to expose the true thieves? Defend your answer.
5. After the Dupont-Duforts are carried off, Lady Hurf tells Peterbono that she knows he and his friends are the real thieves, and she orders them to leave. Why does she choose this moment to "cut the strings" so that the "puppets fall down"?
6. Having found the right face, Hector turns to Eva, confident he will win her back. What is Eva's reaction? Is it consistent with her character as it has been developed throughout the play? Explain.
7. What is the initial reaction of Lady Hurf and Lord Edgard to Juliette's plans. What consideration leads Lady Hurf to change her mind? Why is this amusing?
8. What melodramatic cliché does the playwright use to resolve the conflict? Is his use of this cliché in keeping with the spirit of the play as a whole? Defend your answer.

viewing the play as a whole

1. There are two important themes in *Thieves' Carnival*. The first is that a person must be honest with himself; that he must *be* something, not merely play at being something. The second is that things are not always what they seem; and that often it is difficult to distinguish between reality and illusion. Referring to the characters, plot, and dialogue, show how each of these themes is developed in *Thieves' Carnival*.
2. In Act 1, Lady Hurf describes Eva, Juliette, and herself as three "scatterbrains." Do you think this description is a valid one? Why or why not?
3. Who are the heroes in this play? Who are the villains? Explain your answers.
4. How many climaxes are there in *Thieves' Carnival*? Identify them. Which of them do you think is the more effective? Why?
5. Reread the ending of Act 2 and the opening of Act 3. Explain how the playwright "hooks" the two acts together. What transitional device does he use to "hook" Act 3 with Act 4?
6. Dramatic irony occurs when the audience knows something which the characters in the play don't know and which they should know. For example, at the beginning of Act 3 D. D. Senior and Junior are unaware that they have caught Gustave in the act of a real robbery, and that he has been shooting real bullets at them. Cite other examples of dramatic irony in the play.
7. *Thieves' Carnival* is a fantasy; that is, it involves much that is highly imaginative, fanciful, and fantastic. Select several scenes in which the fantasy aspects of the play are most obvious. Do you find these scenes dramatically effective or not? Explain.
8. Although *Thieves' Carnival* is a comedy, it contains several highly serious scenes and some characters who seem more tragic than comic. Point out the scenes you think are serious, the characters who are tragic. Do you think Anouilh strengthened, or weakened, his play by mingling the comic and the serious? Defend your answer.

for composition

1. Lady Hurf maintains that most people play a role in life and that only a few are completely sincere and genuine. Do you agree with her? Support your answer with specific examples from your own experience.

2. Write an essay which contrasts Eva with Juliette, or Hector and Peterbono with Gustave. Be sure to indicate your attitude toward each of them.
3. The villains of *Thieves' Carnival* are undoubtedly the Dupont-Duforts, whom the playwright satirizes mercilessly. Explain why they are the villains, and mention the ways in which Anouilh pokes fun at them.
4. In many of his plays, Jean Anouilh suggests that life is not as simple as many people believe it to be. What a person thinks is real is often illusory; what he thinks is genuine may be an imitation. Write an essay which illustrates how Anouilh succeeds in dramatizing this idea in *Thieves' Carnival*.

about the playwrights

Jean Anouilh (1910-   ) was born in Bordeaux, France. As a boy, he watched with fascination the operettas performed in the casino, where his mother played the violin. He wrote his first play at the age of 10, a poetic romance in the tradition of Edmond Rostand.

At law school in Paris, Anouilh continued to write both short stories and his first full-length play. His first published work, *Humulus*, was a one-act farce about a man who was permitted to speak only one word a day, and who wisely saved up the words in order to propose to the woman he loved. Highly fanciful and sophisticated, *Humulus* prefigured many of Anouilh's later plays, which he was to call *pièces roses*—comedies or fantasies with serious underlying ideas—in contrast to his *pièces noire*, or tragedies. Upon graduation, Anouilh practiced law for a year and a half. He also wrote advertising copy, which he claimed taught him the value of "precision, conciseness, and agility of expression," three qualities which have distinguished all his writing.

In 1932, *L'Hermine* was produced and Anouilh's career as a playwright was successfully launched. In the plays that followed, Anouilh often adapted old stories for the modern stage, treating them in a fresh and individual manner. *Jezabel* was based on the biblical story; *Eurydice, Antigone*, and *Médeé* on Greek dramas; and *Roméo et Jeannette* on the Shakespearean tragedy. *Antigone*, written in 1942 best illustrates how Anouilh made these classics pertinent in the modern age. In his handling of this ancient tragedy by Sophocles, Anouilh made the conflict between the central characters clearly reflect the conflict that was occurring between the French resistance fighters and the collaborationists in France during World War II.

Since the 1950's, Anouilh's plays have become increasingly popular in America. Among the best known are *The Lark, Becket, Time Remembered*, and *The Waltz of the Toreadors.*

About the Playwrights

Anton Chekhov (1860-1904) was born in Taganrog, in the south of Russia. His father was a stern disciplinarian and, as Chekhov ironically remarked in later life, he learned "to believe in progress in my early childhood, because of the tremendous difference between the time when I was still whipped and the time I was not." When his father went bankrupt and moved his family to Moscow, he left Anton behind to finish his education. Chekhov's childhood was far from a happy one, but it taught him to be independent.

In 1879, Chekhov went to Moscow where he entered medical school. Here, he supported himself and most of his family by writing humorous sketches for periodicals. After he received his M.D. in 1884, he rarely practiced medicine but instead devoted his energies to writing. Being a compassionate, and highly responsible person, however, Chekhov interrupted his literary career on several occasions to offer his medical services —during a cholera epidemic in the town where he was living, and another time to make a study of penal conditions in Sakhalin for the government.

His stories and humorous sketches were well-received, and by 1890 he had established himself as one of the world's outstanding short story writers. About this time, he first began writing plays. His first full-length play, *Ivanov*, (1889), was a great success, as were his two one-act farces, *The Boor* (1888) and *The Marriage Proposal* (1889). His next two full-length plays, however, *The Wood Demon* (1889) and *The Sea Gull* (1895) failed miserably. When a poor performance of *The Sea Gull* was booed off the stage, Chekhov vowed never to write for the theater again. Fortunately, he did not keep this vow.

In 1897, Chekhov began his association with the newly formed Moscow Art Theater. Under the brilliant direction of Stanislavsky, *The Wood Demon* (revised and given a new title, *Uncle Vanya*) and *The Sea Gull* were successfully revived. Chekhov wrote his last two plays, *The Three Sisters* (1901) and *The Cherry Orchard* (1904) for the Moscow Art Theater. The latter was finished six months before his untimely death at the age of 43.

About the Playwrights

Henrik Ibsen (1828-1906) was born in Skien, a small coastal town in Norway. After a childhood of great poverty, he left home and moved to Grimstad, where he served as a druggist's apprentice for five years. The job gave him no satisfaction, and he relieved his misery by writing poetry and sharp satirical sketches of local personages.

In 1850, Ibsen went to Christiania (now Oslo) to study medicine, but he quickly gravitated towards journalism and the theater. His first two plays, *Cataline* and *The Viking's Barrow*, were published during this year and, on the strength of them, he was appointed "theater poet" of the newly created Norwegian Theater in Bergen in 1851. In 1857, he became the "artistic director" of the Norwegian Theater of Christiania, a position which he held until 1862 when the theater went bankrupt. During these ten years, Ibsen wrote six plays which he produced himself, directed the production of scores of other plays, and gained experience which was to prove invaluable to him in the years ahead.

In 1864, Ibsen left Norway for southern Europe and did not return until twenty-seven years later. The reasons for his self-imposed exile have never been fully understood. Perhaps he was embittered by the difficulty he had experienced procuring a government pension to which he felt he was entitled. Perhaps he was disillusioned with Norway's neutrality during the war between Prussia and Denmark (Ibsen felt that Norway should have come to the aid of Denmark). Whatever the reasons, Ibsen wrote his greatest plays in the major cities of Italy and Germany, and only returned to Christiania in 1891, after he was a world celebrity. He suffered a series of strokes in 1899 which rendered him almost helpless until his death seven years later.

Ibsen's works fall into three distinct periods which exemplify the three types of drama which have dominated the theater for the past hundred years: the romance, the realistic play, and the symbolic drama. In his early period, Ibsen wrote traditional romances in the fashion of the nineteenth century. Of the twelve plays written in this vein, *Brand* (1866) and *Peer Gynt* (1867)—the inspiration for Edvard Grieg's suite—remain the most highly praised. The plays written during Ibsen's middle period are his greatest and have earned him the title of "father of the modern drama." These plays have themes which were pertinent to the age in which he lived, and were written in a realistic manner that had a permanent effect on later playwrights. These plays include: *A Doll's House* (1879), *Ghosts* (1881), *An Enemy of the People* (1882), *The Wild Duck* (1884), *Rosmersholm* (1886), and *Hedda Gabler* (1890). The plays of Ibsen's last period are highly symbolic. The best known are *The Master Builder* (1892) and *When We Dead Awaken* (1899).

Edmond Rostand (1868-1918) was born in Marseilles, France. His first published work, *Les Musardies* (1890), was a collection of delicate verse which he presented to his wife, the poet Rosemonde Gerard, as a wedding gift. During the next seven years, he wrote three plays—*The Romancers* (1894), *The Princess Faraway* (1895), and *The Women of Samaria* (1896)—and succeeded in gaining a modest reputation as a playwright.

It was *Cyrano de Bergerac* which firmly established Rostand's place in French literature. Written for the great French actor, Benoît Constant Coquelin, whose expansive gestures and rich voice did full justice to the title role, *Cyrano* was given a tumultuous ovation at its première in Paris on December 28, 1897. Since then, it has been performed in theaters all over the world, and been made into successful motion pictures in France and in America.

None of the plays that Rostand wrote after *Cyrano de Bergerac* achieved its extraordinary popularity. Nevertheless, *L'Aiglon* (1900) and *Chantecler* (1910) have become standard works of the French repertoire. In 1902, Rostand was elected to the French Academy, the youngest man ever to be thus honored. When ill health forced him to leave Paris, he retired to his estate in the Basque country of France. He died of influenza at the age of fifty.

glossary of terms

act: one of the main divisions of the action of a play, generally separated from other acts by an intermission.
action: the psychological, emotional, and physical happenings that convey the meaning and story of the play. See *rising action* and *falling action*.
allegory: a literary work in which objects, persons, or events are equated with meanings outside the work itself.
antagonist: the force that opposes the central character or protagonist. The antagonist may be some weakness, desire, or belief within the protagonist himself. Or it may be some outside force, such as another character, circumstances, nature, environment, or Fate.
anticlimax: an outcome that is disappointing because it falls short of what the preceding action led the reader or viewer to expect.
aside: a remark made by one character in the presence of others but assumed not to be heard by them.
atmosphere: the over-all feeling of a play; for example, the brooding atmosphere in a Eugene O'Neill play.

character: a person in a play. A *dynamic character* undergoes some change or development during the course of the play. A *static character* undergoes little if any change during the course of the play.
characterization: the development of a character through what he says and does and through what other characters say about him.
classicism: adherence to the aesthetic principles and methods of ancient Greece and Rome. The classical writers valued formal elegance, simplicity, restraint, order, proportion, and dignity. They followed strict rules to achieve these ends, which, in the drama, included maintaining unity of time and place, avoiding all elements that do not further the central action and theme, and refraining from depicting any violent action on stage.
climax: the moment of greatest dramatic intensity; the turning point in the action, usually followed by a decrease in suspense.

comedy: a form of drama that is light and amusing and typically has a happy ending. Many comedies poke fun at manners, customs, social or political institutions, or types of people.

conflict: the struggle between two opposing forces, ideas, or beliefs, which is the basis of the plot. In most plays the conflict is resolved when one force—usually the protagonist—succeeds or fails in overcoming the opposing force. Sometimes, the protagonist gives up the struggle as too difficult or not worthwhile. The term *inner conflict* refers to a struggle within the heart and mind of the protagonist. The term *external conflict* refers to a struggle between the protagonist and an outside force.

denouement: the "working out" of the plot, following the climax. In this final part of the play—usually brief but sometimes a full act—the playwright brings the conflict to an end and explains how and why everything turned out as it did.

dialogue: the conversation between two or more characters in a play.

dramatic irony: a mode of expression in which the words or actions of a character have a meaning unperceived by himself but understood by the audience. For example, a character—unaware that he has a poisoned drink—might say, "Ah! This will refresh me!"

dramatic purpose: the purpose which a character, incident, or particular line, or lines, serves in furthering the action of a play, creating suspense, changing or intensifying the mood, increasing the emotional effect, contributing to the humor, or helping to reveal character.

epigram: a short witty saying, sometimes having a satirical or ironical meaning.

episode: an event, or set of events, that helps to make up the main plot or, at times, is incidental to it.

exposition: the background information that reveals "how it all began"; namely, what happened prior to the time covered in a play, what the main characters are like (sometimes before they appear), and what situation has arisen that will lead to a problem that must be solved.

fantasy: a type of play characterized by highly imaginative and improbable situations and a general tone of unreality. The mood is usually light, the playwright intentionally avoiding the more unpleasant aspects of reality, in order to create a make-believe world. Though some fantasies are intended merely to entertain, others have a serious purpose as well; namely, to poke fun at outmoded customs or at the stupidity of certain people or groups of people.

falling action: the action following the climax; also referred to as *resolution* or *denouement*.

farce: a form of drama in which the humorous effect is achieved largely through the creation of exaggerated or far-fetched situations or characters.

flashback: a dramatic device by which the playwright interrupts the main action of the play to present a situation or incident which occurred at an earlier time.

foreshadowing: the technique of dropping hints or suggestions that lead the reader or theater audience to anticipate subsequent events or situations.

irony: a mode of expression in which the intended meaning of the words used is the direct opposite of the literal or usual meaning; also, an outcome of events contrary to what would naturally be hoped for or expected. See *dramatic irony*.

melodrama: a drama with sensational and often violent action, and usually with a happy ending.

monologue: a long speech of one character in a play.

mood: the frame of mind or state of feeling created by the setting, the lines spoken by the characters, or a particular situation or sequence of events.

moral: the lesson or "teaching" that is brought out through the action of the play or is explicity stated or implied by one of the characers.

naturalism: a theory that literature should depict life with scientific objectivity and that the writer should include every realistic detail of the subject about which he is writing. Naturalism emphasized the crucial role played by heredity and environment in human life and character development.

plot: the series of events or episodes that make up the action of a play.

poetic justice: an outcome of events that rewards the virtuous and punishes the vicious; an ending in which each character gets exactly what he deserves.

protagonist: the opposing force in the conflict most responsible for bringing the conflict to an end; usually the central or leading character.

realism: a manner of writing in which people, scenes, and events are presented as they are in real life, without romantic or idealistic coloring.

resolution: the events following the climax of a play; sometimes called *falling action*.

rising action: the series of events, preceding the climax, which intensify the conflict and, thereby, create a feeling of suspense about the outcome.

romance: a type of play in which the setting and incidents are very remote from those of everyday life. In a romance, the heroic, the adventurous, and the mysterious are often emphasized.

romanticism: a literary movement of the eighteenth and nineteenth centuries which was a reaction against Neo-classicism with its emphasis on reason and the strict adherence to formal laws of composition. The romantic playwright stressed the importance of individuality, and found new forms whereby he could express himself. He emphasized emotion, and a love of nature, personal liberty, and the common man.

satire: the use of irony, sarcasm, or ridicule to poke fun at customs, manners, individuals, or social or political institutions.

scene: a short episode in which the time, and possibly the place, are different from that of a previous episode; also, an incident or happening in the play that develops naturally out of the preceding action and flows into the action that follows.

scenery: the backdrop, walls, furniture, etc., used onstage to represent the place in which the action of a scene occurs.

setting: the time and place in which the events in a play occur.

soliloquy: lines spoken by a character to himself rather than to another character; a kind of "thinking out loud" for the purpose of revealing information about the character or about events which the reader or theater audience needs to know.

stage directions: the words, phrases, sentences, and even paragraphs, printed in italics and enclosed in parentheses, through which the playwright indicates what is taking place on the stage and how he wants the characters to speak, feel, or act. Occasionally, he uses the stage directions to comment on a character or situation or to suggest the particular mood to be created at that point in the play.

stock character: a character who has been used in so many plays that the audience immediately recognizes him and knows how he will think and act.

style: the distinctive manner in which the playwright uses language: his choice and arrangement of words.

subplot: a secondary series of events or episodes that is subordinate to the main plot but, in most cases, contributes to it.

suspense: a feeling of excitement, curiosity, or expectation about the outcome of the play.

symbolism: a technique whereby ideas and emotions are represented by indirect suggestion rather than by direct statement. When used symbolically, a character, situation, or object in a play "stands for," or points to, a meaning greater than itself, which illuminates the playwright's theme or subject. For example, the selling of the orchard in *The Cherry Orchard* symbolizes the end of a way of life. Cyrano's plume symbolizes his honor.

theme: the idea, view of life, or commentary on human behavior that is dramatized through the words and deeds of the characters.

tone: the feeling conveyed by a playwright through style and choice of words, which reveals his attitude toward his subject; for example, a satirical tone.

tragedy: a form of drama in which the protagonist undergoes a morally significant struggle and is defeated, often because of a flaw in his own character. For example, Macbeth's excessive ambition is the cause of his downfall.

unity: the quality in a play that gives it the effect of being a harmonious whole.